Eric Treacy

Eric Treacy

John S. Peart-Binns

LONDON

IAN ALLAN LTD

9 2
T 71

8202123

First published 1980

ISBN 0 7110 1039 0

Published by Ian Allan Ltd, Shepperton, Surrey;
and printed by Ian Allan Printing Ltd at their works
at Coombelands in Runnymede, England

Cover photograph courtesy of Sild of Wakefield

Contents

Preface

In the midst of death we are in life! Such is the purpose of a biography written shortly after the subject's death. The historical dimension may be partial but there are compensating advantages. The recollections of the living recreate the pulsating throb of the dead.

This is not the biography of a gargoyle but of a man — *Eric Treacy*. It discloses a 'character' — a very human being with a curiously complex personality. The inner uncertainties and gnawing sense of inferiority were concealed from an admiring public by an outward certitude and engaging directness. The enigma was carefully wrapped before display.

This writer is committed to his subject. Enthusiastic yet objective commitment is more likely to unravel mystery and perceive truth than unadorned and unassuming neutrality. This is not the record of a pious and holy life unstained by sin and unsullied by worldliness. Eric Treacy's halo, like his life, was off centre. In various degrees many of the saints of the Christian Church have been like that — 'characters', the inspired fools of the world. Their convictions have been disclosed by their exuberances and extravagances, their prejudices and their falterings. Eric Treacy began as an unbridled enthusiast in a Church which liked and admired equilibrium. He ended as a stabilising force in the same Church which was subject to every gust of secular and temporising wind.

Eric Treacy had planned an impossible range of literary activity for his retirement. He was hoping to write a number of works including his autobiography; books on the Church of England; pastoralia; a history of the 59th (4th West Lancs) Medium Regiment; an Open Letter to a newly instituted priest. There were to be more books on railways and at least one volume of his remarkable landscape photographs.

His autobiography had been promised to Ian Allan so it seems appropriate that he should be the publisher of this biography. I think Eric Treacy will be chuckling at the amount of religion shunted on to Ian Allan's editorial desks and saying 'Do them good'.

Eric Treacy had had many stabs at writing his autobiography — the first as early as 1948 whilst Rector of Keighley. He kept full diaries at various, though very short, periods of his life. These have been a useful source of material, but what I have used has been chosen with discrimination. In his 'War Diary' he notes '*6 June 1944*. I find as I write my day to day journal that I cannot free myself from the feeling that what I write will be read by an outside eye — and in consequence, try as I will, I cannot help writing to interest the imaginary reader'. Some of his diaries are obviously, even blatantly, written for the public eye. The surviving autobiographical manuscript is a fairly full document taking his life to the end of the Keighley period. There is only a small account of Halifax and only odd notes relating to Pontefract and Wakefield. Many of his sermons and addresses have survived, together with some miscellaneous papers.

A complete list of acknowledgements and thank you's would extend this biography by another chapter. I have been overwhelmed by the number of contributions. Only extracts from a fraction of them appear in print but all have been vitally helpful in enabling me to arrive at what I hope is a perspective which is balanced, an estimate which is just and a portrait which is worthy. To all these people who wrote or spoke to me I utter a heart felt Thank You.

It is necessary to add a few words of special gratitude. Above all and most obviously to Mrs May Treacy. From the moment when we first talked about her beloved Eric she has been a whole and full hearted supporter of the project. Their marriage was one of total mutual dependence, one on the other. She kindly and charmingly placed both herself and Eric's papers at my disposal. My many questions were answered patiently and fully. When she had read the manuscript I was both relieved and pleased that she not only recognised the subject of the biography but also was able to say that it was her Eric — warts and all!

A special word of gratitude goes to Bishop Roger Wilson who read the manuscript, offered constructive criticism and perhaps saved me from some obvious mistakes and wrong emphases. Needless to say he can be in no wise to blame for any errors or omissions that remain.

Archdeacon Ted Henderson of Pontefract and Mr C. B. Beverley — Bev—Wakefield Diocesan Secretary · — have been a constant source of assistance to me as has Mr David Ward, Passenger Marketing Manager of British Rail, London Midland Region. To them - thank you.

Finally, if Eric Treacy had his May so John Peart-Binns has his Annis without which there would be no book. She is the enabling foundation on which the structure is built. To her — my love as always.

JSP-B
August 1979

1
Genial Oaf

'Baiting Yorkshiremen' is a hobby that only a lunatic or a lover would proclaim, let alone pursue. Not even the thickest or flattest Yorkshire pudding would be that daft. To advertise it as a recreation in *Who's Who* suggests a person with an inordinate desire to commit hara-kiri. Yet this is what a six feet, fourteen and a half stone, blue-eyed, fair haired man of above average intelligence with few claims to intellect did!

The man was Eric Treacy, eighth Bishop of Wakefield, member of the House of Lords, proud possessor of an Honorary Doctorate of Laws from Leeds University, Member of the Order of the British Empire, Freeman of Halifax, Patron Saint of Steam and much else besides.

With unerring self-knowledge and devastating directness he could write of himself at the age of 68:

'To his surprise, he finds that he can hold his own wherever he finds himself. This is due to a quick wit, a good memory, and more than a fair share of curiosity. This discovery, which has gradually unfolded itself in the army, in the House of Lords, amongst his brother Bishops, has given him a confidence that has come late but is none the less welcome for that.

'For most of his life he has been haunted by the fear that he would be found out: that his abysmal lack of education would stand revealed, but he has learned to take avoiding action whenever a confrontation is likely.

'He is a quick reader and a voracious gatherer of other people's ideas so that he can often give the impression of knowing more than he does. His enemies would say that Eric Treacy is an ecclesiastical "con-man"; and his friends would say that he has overcome his educational disadvantages by his ability to grasp the essentials of important issues.

'What he lacked in scholarship, he made up for in a capacity for human understanding, and this was largely because he knew what was in himself.'

Eric Treacy was a member of an old Irish family from County Tipperary. An ancestor was William de Traci, or Tracy, who was one of the knights who slew Thomas à Becket. On that account Treacy was not the first of his line to spend time in Yorkshire, for the four knights who murdered Becket took refuge for a period in Knaresborough Castle. Though safe from the vengeance of man, the curse of the Church followed them continuously. It is recorded that for ever afterwards William de Traci and his descendants felt a miraculous wind blowing against their faces; from which was evolved the couplet:

Oh, Woe to the Tracies
With ever the wind and the rain in their faces.

The Anglicised branch of the family dropped the 'de' and incorporated the 'e' in the new name Treacy.

In his autobiographical notes his parents and childhood are dismissed in one hundred words. That will not do, for they have an interest of their own as well as providing a few clues to the 'character' that Eric Treacy became. He always discounted the influence of heredity. Not 'like father like son' but 'every man's the son of his own deeds' was his unwavering view. It was a strongly if strangely held opinion. As he is now beyond the pulpit's 'six feet above contradiction', I hope he will smile benevolently on the following paragraphs relating to his background and perhaps allow that certain characteristics were transmitted, if transmuted, from forbears to offspring.

A great-grandparent had been an Admiral of the Fleet. One grandparent was a bit of a rake, given to riotous living and persistent debt. His paternal grandfather, John Treacy, became a District Commissioner in Burma. John Treacy was an Irishman and married a Scottish lady, Flora Johnstone, in Rangoon in 1861 but by 1872 both were dead. John Treacy died on board the ss *Killarney* en route to England and he was buried in the Red Sea.

There was a son of that marriage, George, who was born in Mandalay, the then capital of Burma, in 1866. Orphaned at six years of age he was sent to England for his education and eventually entered Christ's Hospital, London, where he became a Grecian. As a first rate classical scholar the path to university should have been easy and assured. But he was an orphan without money or patron so he had to forfeit a university education and make his own way in life. He became a furniture salesman at Maples. As Eric Treacy reflected, 'If ever a man was wasted he was, but never did he show a trace of bitterness.'

George Treacy married twice. His first marriage was a very unhappy experience for him. His second wife, Annie Kate, was the daughter of Alfred Jopp from Aberdeen who had married a Stratford-on-Avon girl, Annie Wilson.

Twins were born of this marriage on 2 June 1907 but one of them died within a few days of birth. The survivor was Eric who was joined by a sister, Mary, three years later. He was born in Harlesden in North London. The contrast between his two parents could not have been greater. His father was a gentleman with a quiet dignity and courtesy and a total unconsciousness of social differences so that he had friends in many walks of life. His passions — if such they can be called — were freemasonry, fishing and bowls. This calm landscape was frequently disfigured by the lightning and electric storms of his mother.

Sister Mary (van der Kaay) writes of her brother Eric's inheritance from his parents:

'Father was a quiet and gentle man, not forceful or dominating, saddened by a lonely childhood; artistic, methodical and loving. Mother was the dominating influence with a personality that could engender admiration, annoyance and frustration. Her maternal instincts were noble in themselves, but so embracing that they became abrasive. Filled with energy and determination she gave of her all to nurture her children in the ways of goodness and morality, but loath to release the reigns of authority when the time called for it. She had strength and forcefulness, and a potential that was never realised, causing her to be embittered. Eric inherited some of these qualities and by the grace of God was able to channel them into the right direction. So from his father gentleness and from his mother drive and determination.'

This combination did not make for a happy childhood. The frustrated and tyrannical mother ensured that father had little peace. One-sided rows were constant. In addition her youngest brother, Arthur Jopp, who disliked Eric and Mary, lived with them from time to time. He was a rake and a rogue, the opposite to their mother's unmarried sister, Christine, who was all tranquility and light. She was awarded the OBE after World War I for her Government service and, as Mary recalls, 'she was loving towards us which we returned, much to the chagrin of our mother who always referred to her as "Miss Jopp". Many were the times when we met Aunt Chris without our mother's knowledge.'

After attending a small private school in Willesden Green Eric Treacy went to the Haberdashers' Aske's School, Hampstead, in 1918. The family were then living in Cricklewood in a house that overlooked the Midland Railway lines.

Eric Treacy thought 'the standard of teaching was pretty low. I distinguished myself not at all in the field of learning: partly because of a woeful inability to concentrate, and partly because those who taught me thought that I was an oaf, and didn't try very hard.' He places himself in the ranks of middle-class ordinariness. On the whole he was liked by both masters and boys because he was genial, uncomplicated, but by no means mild and obedient. He was often beaten but bore no ill will to those who administered the punishment.

What this 'genial oaf', as he described himself, lacked in academic concentration and ability was amply counterbalanced by his enthusiasm for and skill at sport. He played in the first XV, was Russell's House Cricket Captain and won the Heavyweight Boxing Championship two years running, as also the Shot. He was a sergeant in the OTC, Head of his House, and a close friend of the groundsman, who was an endearing rogue of an Irishman. Ever sensitive to atmosphere, Eric Treacy could always conjure up places by recapturing the smells and sounds as well as sights. Fifty years later he observed 'I can still smell the groundsman's cubby hole — a mixture of cut grass, linseed oil and creosote.' It was to be the same much later with steam engines. Railway noises took on the quality of music — the clank of shunting, the shriek of an LMS siren, the faint tinkle of a signal bell. Or the unique smells — of sulphur and oil which is the body odour of the steam engine, and the fishy smell of a guard's van.

In an issue of the school magazine, *The Skylark* (Summer 1924) Eric Treacy contributed a short article on *Cricket Games* in which he contrasted the different conditions under which cricket is played, from test matches to gutter cricket. For whatever reason men take bat and ball to become 'flannelled fools' as Kipling called cricketers, Eric Treacy contended that the game 'has a finer, more noble influence in life, namely to teach its devotees the way to learn the epitaph of a good sportsman, "He played the game".' 'Playing the game', 'Doing your duty' and such sentiments were going to be more than schoolboy phrases or pious expressions in Eric Treacy's life.

Contemporaries remember him variously as 'a rather burly genial lad', 'always cheerful', 'not academic'. His school nickname is accounted for by George Martin: 'On one occasion we went to Lyons Cadbury House on a school outing to see the machinery of this great concern, and on leaving we were all given miniature tins of treacle. Eric Treacy somehow managed to obtain a spoon and on the coach back to school consumed his treacle out of the tin, and for many years after was known as "Treacle Treacy".'

There were no great influences or influencers at Haberdashers'. The Headmaster, F. J. Kemp, was ordained, joyless and dull. He manifested little Christian experience in his conduct of morning worship. Along with 55 other boys, Eric Treacy was confirmed on 6 July 1922 at All Saints, Cricklewood, by the Bishop Suffragan of Willesden, W. W. Perrin, who communicated the importance of the occasion. Alas, the preparation classes were uninspiring, and if knowledge was imparted disciples were not made.

Up to this time Eric and his sister were sent, rather than taken, to Sunday School, but under Eric's leadership they grew pretty adept at avoiding it. He confesses:

'We would play truant, pass our time in damming up some local stream, spend even longer removing all traces of mud from ourselves, and return home hoping that we should not be questioned too closely as to the subject of the lesson. Our one dread was that our parents would check up with the Vicar, but as they were not, at the time, churchgoers themselves, we were not found out.'

Summer holidays at Mundesley in Norfolk were rather different. Here the Children's Special Service Mission (CSSM) held house-parties and missions on the sands. CSSM could be syrupy and superficial in presenting the Gospel but it brought many children to a firm commitment to Christ. Although the Treacy children were not members of the house parties they were allowed to join in some of the games on the shore, morning services and evening squashes. Looking back Eric Treacy said: 'I see that the beginning of my Christian life dates from those holidays. It was then that I began to pray rather than say my prayers.' There is probably a greater degree of romantic hindsight in such words than the expression of a recaptured fact.

It was soon after the confirmation service that the whole Treacy family began to attend the Church of St Jude-on-the-Hill in Hampstead Garden Suburb. Besides bringing a partial sense of unity in the family this also brought them in touch with the Vicar of St Jude's, Basil Graham Bourchier, brother of the actor Arthur Bourchier. This colourful cleric was to have a real influence on Eric Treacy. In an age of the vanishing 'character' it is interesting to read his pen portrait of Bourchier:

'A bachelor, with a liking for rich living, Basil Bourchier had about him a magic such as I have never encountered since. He was a large man, with a superb presence and a personality which drew enormous crowds to the huge Lutyens Church. A High Churchman, he loved ritual and processions, and took a naive delight in the ceremonies of the Church. In the pulpit, he was magnificent: his sermons were topical and often passionate. He could move himself to tears when preaching: he was often theatrical, but so genuine did his performances appear, that few of his flock were critical.

'He certainly spent more time out of the parish than in it. He enjoyed the life of the London clubs: lesser men that he would not have got away with it, but in a remarkable way he succeeded in persuading the people that he was needed elsewhere. There were from time to time rumours about him: perhaps he was going to become a bishop: perhaps he was going to become engaged to some lady of title: perhaps someone had seen him coming home late at night a bit the worse for wear. But he survived them all and the devotion of his large band of followers never wavered. Indeed, I think that he encouraged some of these rumours in the hope that they increased the mystery surrounding him.

'He was a man with many faults, but they were obvious ones, and I think it is true to say that he was held in affection because of them, and not in spite of them.

'He was always very kind to me, but I never felt at ease with him. He was so sophisticated that he made me feel clumsy and tongue tied. In the great band of servers which he gathered around him, of which I was one, he had certain favourites, of which I was not one. His snobbery was blatant and magnificent. He could not resist a title. Many a noble gentleman he produced to grace the parish occasions. One let the side down by coming to open a sale of work in such a state of alcoholic un-focus that we were treated to a long harangue on the virtues of the Tory Party.

'Bourchier was a good example of the man who could exploit his undoubted gifts of personal magnetism as a substitute for hard work. For one thing I shall always be grateful to him. He was the means of bringing my father back to the comforts of the Christian faith. My father was a man of the greatest integrity and personal goodness, but the Church had not played much part in his life. He found in Bourchier a man he could admire, whose preaching spoke to his condition, and whose friendship, strengthened, doubtless, by their both being Freemasons, brought him to regular worship (he became a sidesman) so that when he died, he was firmly grounded in the Faith.'

These reflections are interesting for they were written by Eric Treacy when he had himself become a 'character' and 'personality' and both loved and needed the role which he had in part created and which had in part been thrust upon him, although with him there was never any substitute for hard work.

It was Mrs Treacy who decided that son Eric should become a server, an idea which at first appalled him. He was shy and dreaded making a fool of himself in public. But, worse, as a masculine male regarding himself as something of a 'tough' the thought of wearing a lace cotta and red sanctuary slippers made him cringe. Swinging the censer he did not mind. He had to learn the intricacies of the art of serving. There was so much to think about in the performance of the ritual and he was usually in a state of watchful dither. The drill mattered more than the worship. He remembered 'how critical we young prigs were if a visiting celebrant got it wrong. Occasionally we had a bishop as celebrant, and if he perchance went wrong, how we chattered about it afterwards.'

Neither his attendance at St Jude's not his home life widened his narrow horizons. These were the years of unemployed street bands, of trams and pirate buses taunting danger in their efforts to steal passengers from the London General Omnibus Company, of crystal sets with a cat's whisker and miles of wire wound about a cardboard tube. All of this and the hardships that were being endured by the vast proportion of the working population by-passed Eric Treacy. Haberdashers' insulated the boys from the harsh realities with which many would be faced.

Although the Treacys were far from affluent the children managed to enjoy themselves on an allowance of pocket money that rarely exceeded sixpence a week. Eric's pleasures were simple, his tastes unsophisticated — sport outdoors and reading, mostly adventure stories, indoors.

Eric Treacy's schooling was coming to an end. It had not been quite a disaster for his school reports on 'Character' referred to 'powers of leadership'. His matriculation achievements however were below average. He had no thirst for knowledge and no clear conviction of what he wanted to do with his life. There were two reasons why University was out of the question. He had not the brains to make it and his father could not afford it.

As for the opposite sex Treacy was like many boys of that age and time, an innocent, as he relates:

'Girls had no part in my life. At the age of 19 I had never taken a girl out: had never kissed or been kissed. What used to surprise me was the facility with which certain unprepossessing and, to me, unpleasant boys managed so many conquests in this field. This still surprises me in the adult world.

'I remember one coy young woman who used to haunt the school gates in the afternoon. She was in great demand and was the subject of a good deal of adolescent boasting and suggestiveness, but she terrified me. I used to climb over a wall to avoid her, although I don't know what she would have done to me. I was healthy and well developed by the age of 19, and I do not recall that I was at all bothered with sex as a problem.

'I had no secret hoard of dirty pictures: I very rarely heard any dirty stories, although it is possible that some of the stories I heard were dirty without my realising it.

'We had a revolting art master who used to cuddle any boy who got near enough to be grabbed: and there was a sportsmaster who used to take obvious pleasure in using the cane. The schoolboy of the 1960s and 1970s would obviously know what was wrong with both of them. We didn't.

'I claim no virtue in this innocence. Life in the 1920s was singularly free from the stimuli that abound today. Neither was there so much talk about it. Sex was not constantly being dealt with by experts in "personal relationships", who, in these days, lash into VIth forms and below with talks about contraception, petting and "how far you can go without getting caught". But I am bound to say that I grew up in an age when sex was thought of as something that was taboo to a clean living young man. Sex and physical fitness did not go together. It may surprise some moderns when I confess that until I was 20, I thought that if you kissed a girl, the only decent thing was to marry her, to make an honest woman of her.

'I must admit to one or two love affairs, but as the objects of my affections were unaware of my feelings for them, no harm came of them. Very rarely did I go to the theatre. As a family we could not afford such luxuries, but whenever we did I fell in love with the leading lady. Faith Celli, who played Peter Pan in the 1920s; Gladys Cooper and the Dolly Sisters all had their places in my heart. It is all very laughable now, but it was most serious at the time. I couldn't bear to think of their going home to their husbands, and I often imagined myself taking them out to tea, in the course of which they would tell me all their troubles.'

Schooling was over. Eric Treacy left at Christmas 1925 with little of an academic nature to show for his years at Haberdashers'. Let the school magazine *The Skylark* (Summer 1926) have the last word under the heading of 'Football Characters': 'Treacy E. — A big forward, who shoved well in the scrum, but clumsy in the loose. Good in defence. Slow off the mark; but difficult to stop when he got moving.'

2
Frustrated Vocation

With a nearly blank academic record, no sense of vocation or inclination to any sphere of work and little drive to do anything in particular, Treacy drifted into the first opportunity that materialised. His sister Mary writes:

'His first venture into the business world was his employment in the mail room of the Anglo-Saxon Petroleum Company at St Helen's Court, off Leadenhall Street in the City of London. Coming from a sheltered home he found this a completely new environment — an order given that was embellished with a cuss word, exchanges of smutty jokes — had he stayed on in this job he most certainly would have progressed and taken it in his stride, but his ever-protective mother decided that he should leave, and leave he did.'

This led to a formative period of employment with the Clerical, Medical & General Life Assurance Society. Treacy referred to his advent into employment thus:

'An insurance company, which rather prided itself on the presentability and social graces of those whom it employed, decided to lower its standards somewhat and take me on its strength. So I found myself tied to a desk in a gloomy backroom in St James Square.
'I was put in the Actuarial Department, not that I ever had the slightest hope of becoming an actuary, but because there happened to be a vacant chair there. I started on a salary of 25s per week, on which I had to clothe myself, pay my fares, pay for my holidays and contribute something at home.'

Office life has changed surprisingly little over the years. 'Organisation and Methods' and 'Time and Motion' are merely the latest techniques for worshipping the same god — efficiency. Efficiency requires a common obedience and neither likes nor trusts imagination. Deviation from the required rule is watched. The chasm between management and desk slaves was as wide as ever it could be in a factory. Management was mainly concerned with profit and pocket, their domains having lots of 'No Trespassing' signs posted outside to repel intruders. The clerks were there, like draughts on a board, to be manipulated seemingly at whim or will. It gave Treacy great pleasure to visit his old firm when he was Bishop of Wakefield. He called at the Office and asked to be admitted to the manager's lair, whereupon he sat back in the chair, put his feet on the manager's desk and said: 'I've been longing to do this all my life. Once I worked here.' The result of the encounter was belly laughter and lunch at Treacy's club.

Treacy hated office life and he never lost sympathy for and an understanding of clerical workers in a big city. The daily fight for a place in train or bus, the monotony of an office, the irritating habits of fellow employees, the awful little snacks that form the daily diet, the petty system of status which dominates the relationships of an office — all combine to create conditions of frustration. He refers to this when recalling the yawn-inducing and balked years in St James Square:

'Although much is said about the monotonous conditions of work which obtain in industry, I doubt if they are nearly as soul deadening as those which are to be found in an office. There is a warmth and unity of relationship between factory workers that are altogether missing in the large office. You sit for hours gazing at a column of figures, or copying endless entries into a register, the atmosphere of the office dependent upon the chief clerk or departmental manager. The hours tick slowly by, and you long for a diversion: even a row between two frustrated members of the department is a welcome diversion. I must confess that a shilling placed on a horse with the connivance of one of the commissionaires, gave certain afternoons a tang of excitement which made the long day passable. And the passage of a comely typist through the room was like a ray of sunshine. We were a well assorted lot. There was T who was a church organist, and who had a never ending fund of dirty stories: there was old Mr B, a quiet and charming old pensioner earning a few extra shillings clerking, who had a pretty rough time from "jacks in office" who were irritated by his obvious breeding: there was W, loud and foul mouthed, aiming to live up to his own image of a sergeant in the Territorials. There was P, a gentle soul whose spare time was dedicated to amateur theatricals and who lived in a world of make-believe, muttering his latest "part" to himself as he moved about the corridors of the office.'

Relief from the office desk came on Saturday afternoons which Treacy devoted to Rugby. He played for the XV of the old Haberdashers' boys club and occasionally received honourable mention in the match reports which appeared in the press of Monday mornings. What a sport! Men shoving and pushing each other, cursing and grunting, twisting each other, whipping their legs from under them, united in the one intention of placing a mud caked and sodden ball over a thin white line. Here is Treacy's description of the scrum:

'I found my home in the second row of the scrum which, on reflection, I think to be about the lowest position offered by any sport known to man. In front of you three muddy bottoms, so close that it seemed nothing could separate them — linked to your partner you charged this muddy wall hitting it with a sickening thud: if you were lucky your head forced its way into the narrow space between the buttocks of the front row: no sooner this done than a thump from behind indicating that the back row had joined the party. If this mass of human beef did not fall flat on its face in the mud, the referee usually decided that it wasn't straight and ordered it to wheel a few degrees right or left. The pivot of this movement was the necks of the second row which were then screwed beyond anything nature had intended. The next agony was when the hooker brought back his heel with a sickening hack on your shins.'

Another old boy, Douglas Baker, remembers:

'One very wet Saturday we found we had to cross one or two very muddy fields to reach our opponents' ground. It was decided by a number of players that the best thing to do was to change into our rugger gear before crossing these fields and so we proceeded to change under a hedge quite out of view of the road or any dwellings. My memory is of Eric standing under the hedge in his birthday suit wearing only his bowler hat.'

After the game the players immersed themselves in a vicious mixture of mud and hot water euphemistically called a bath. Treacy usually parted company from his companions after that stage. They repaired to the pub to lower several pints of beer and then spent the next week sweating it out of their systems in paroxysms of training. Treacy went his own way as, on his wage, he could not afford to pay his whack amongst his team mates on their spree. He was probably grateful for the excuse for he did not want to embrace all the after-match activities in this brainless, cheerful and noisy world.

Treacy rose no further than a county trial where he failed to catch the eye of the selectors. This was nothing of which to be ashamed for after his last game of Rugger in 1929 at the age of 22 the Rugby Correspondent of *The Morning Post* wrote, 'Treacy was the best forward on the field'. His 'retirement' from the field of play or battle, depending on whether you are spectator or participant, was compulsory for he had a misplaced cartilage, which played him up for the rest of his life.

Whilst it lasted Rugby was important to Treacy. 'As an office worker, these Saturday afternoon exertions were the highlight of the week. From Monday to Wednesday I relived the match of the previous Saturday, cursing myself for missed opportunities and dropped passes and from Thursday onwards thinking of next Saturday's match.'

One office colleague was an enthusiastic member of the Artists' Rifles, into whose ranks he persuaded Treacy. It was a short lived affair where not even one stripe was achieved, for, as he recalls, 'I was a not very good territorial soldier. I fell down on the number of drills I put in, and I evaded the camps. I never quite fitted in to this world of peace time amateur soldiers, many of whom were clerks like myself, and who found in their soldiering a compensation for the drabness of office life. They were noisy, immature and socially pretentious.' No 6791799 Treacy Eric, Rank Private, was discharged at his own request on 26 May 1927.

Treacy still attended St Jude's and in October 1927 he volunteered to take charge of a Sunday School class of boys between the ages of 8 and 14. He was expected to teach them in Sunday School and lead them socially. He excelled at the latter rather than the former.

Life proceeded in a tranquil rut until the Clerical & Medical elevated Treacy to the giddy heights of Inspector. He had as much pre-training for that position as he did later for a parish priest. No one told him what to do. He had not sought the position even though the desk job was driving him to distraction. He was not sure what he had to 'inspect' unless it were the Company's agents. It was not a case of 'Here am I, send me' but 'Seek and ye will find'. So he went into South West London. Brixton, Balham and Tooting were relieved by Wimbledon, Croydon and Westerham. The only guidance came from the senior Inspector who gave the Inspectors a talk on the importance of leaving the office empty handed at 9.30 and returning at 5.30 pockets bulging with proposal forms from potential customers.

The agents Treacy visited by tube or bus or on foot were an assortment of bank managers, solicitors and insurance brokers. They were united by a common affliction — they did not produce business. Accordingly he ate in the cafes provided by that edible trinity of ABC, Joseph Lyons and Express Dairy, and returned to base each day without the precious forms. He learned to stall by giving the impression that he was just about to land a big fish. His misery is reflected in his later recollections:

'Often, I would bump into the representative of another company coming out, as I went it, to see an agent. He would greet me cheerfully, obviously having beaten me by a few minutes in obtaining a proposal.

'On very wet days I would steal away into some quiet cinema to rest my aching and damp limbs, and I would detect in the gloom other representatives of the insurance world similarly taking shelter. Perhaps some of us, with a desire to convince our superiors of our devotion to duty, would persuade the cinema manager to accept appointment as an agent.

'It was a miserable life. If I had any tendency to strong drink, I think that I might well have succumbed to long sessions in the pubs which abounded in that part of London. Mercifully, my only addiction was hot, strong tea — and still is.'

Although Treacy was what might be termed 'sporty' he was not a natural extrovert. He may have had few or no angularities of character but he was still shy and unsure of himself. The insurance world was responsible for some important friendships and in particular a special friendship with Alan Gardner (later an Actuary) 'for he set me on a path which eventually led me to Holy Orders, to my marriage, and to the long and happy years in the North.' Alan Gardner remembers nightly cups of tea and toast at the Express Dairy, Charing Cross Road, before they went home. He writes, 'Here we discussed together every subject under the sun. It was of course his charm and good looks which led to him, and not me, being invited by the waitress who tended to our needs as a guest to her wedding.'

The Clerical & Medical friendships gave Treacy a bottom layer of self-confidence and opportunities to develop the gift of the gab. His circle of acquaintances began to widen and he spent more time with them away from the suffocating and stormy atmosphere of his home. His sister remembers the change:

'He was so enamoured with the life style of his companions that he ran an overdraft at the Bank. I remember the horror and fear that this engendered — shades of Uncle Arthur! I fear that his small income did not adequately cover his efforts to be "one of the boys". The error was righted very quickly and is the only episode that I remember which caused the family any anxiety.'

At the time of the General Strike in 1926 Treacy had his first practical experience with the railways — though not yet with steam. It was nearly his last encounter too, as Alan Gardner recalls: 'Eric volunteered to drive an electric train on the Metropolitan Railway. He nearly met an untimely end as, wanting to go into liquidation, he modestly went behind a train to be hailed by shouts in all directions to stop from electrifying himself by relieving himself on the live rail.'

Treacy began to spend much of his time in the free and happy atmosphere of the Gardner home. There were holidays too and Alan Gardner has a recollection of one at Minehead. 'After a long walk on a lovely Sunday we called at the Luttrell Arms, Dunster, and slaked our thirst with draught cider which very quickly went to Eric's head. Walking back to Minehead we ran into the evening church parade and he graciously doffed his hat to all and sundry asking them if they had enjoyed the sermon.' There was an additional attraction in the female form of Helen Gardner (now Dame Helen Gardner, Professor of Poetry in the University of Oxford). Treacy writes of her:

'Of her charity she was very kind to me, although she must have found me a pretty dull companion. This was my first venture in the tender realms of female companionship — at the age of 20! How slow by modern standards. The extent of my activities was an occasional play in London and an infrequent dance, at which I was incredibly bad. However, dear Helen was patient and kind, and our ways soon parted, but not without my being deeply grateful to her for bringing me out of my shell.'

It was at this time that he started attending St Anne's Church, Highgate, with the Gardner family. The Vicar of this High Church parish was the Rev the Hon James Adderley. Jimmy Adderley, as he was always known, was a fervent Christian Socialist. 'His sermons were short and pithy', Treacy writes, 'and contained some choice epigrams that I still remember'. Sermon tasting was not the limit of the Adderley influence. Treacy was still comfortably complacent about the world around him and he was not particularly religious in his habits. Politically he was unaware. The mind may have been open but it was inclined to be so at both ends. But here was a priest who made his congregation feel uncomfortable. Adderley regarded the prevailing economic system as immoral and un-Christian; its appeal as nakedly to self interest; its technique as economic competition leading to exploitation of the weak by the strong and promoting mass-selfishness, class-division and international war. He prised open the eyes of his congregation to the 'deceitfulness of riches' and to a system which made money their god, its possession their chief privilege and its acquisition their prime test of success. His simplistic socialist solutions irritated when they did not amuse, but when he spoke of the squalor of the London slums and the rampant profiteering of some companies there was no mistaking the intensity of his knowledge and conviction. People were moved, for he spoke from his experience of working as Head of Oxford House, Bethnal Green in London's East End.

Adderley was an extraordinary man. Arthur Shearley Cripps, the priest poet, regarded him as 'a comrade in tramping, dossing and preaching the Gospel'. In a Memoir *(Father Adderley*, by T. P. Stevens. T. W. Laurie 1943) the following words appear:

'His sermons came from his experience and were not mere words culled undigested from the books of others. When he was impulsive and over hasty he was quick to repent and had a grand humility. Those who knew him and loved him best were conscious that he had consecrated a unique personality comprising the qualities of the actor and orator, the journalist and writer, the humorist, philanthropist and saint, to God and His service.'

It was at this time that Treacy began to think about Ordination, or rather that the idea of being a clergyman began to nag him. Father Adderley was an influence and an example. Treacy had also become a member of Toc H. One of the obligations of membership was to give up some spare time to social or community work. Here he met Alex Churcher who was at that time the Honorary Secretary of the Aldenham Boys Club in Kentish Town. Alex Churcher needed a boxing instructor for his junior boys, Treacy had an obligation to meet and Alan Gardner provided the coupling. It is well to record the impressions of Treacy and Alex Churcher. First Treacy's:

'Alex was an enthusiast and like most enthusiasts, pretty ruthless with his friends. So I found myself two or three evenings every week making my way to Kentish Town to help with a company of the Lads Brigade which contained as nice a bunch of young cockneys as you could wish to know. The "powers of leadership" referred to in my school character were not particularly evident, but I came on under the tutelage of Alex Churcher.'

And *his* recollections:

'Eric Treacy's approach to the job was not at first one of which the rest of us approved, being condescending and almost contemptuous but he was undoubtedly good at boxing and he soon came to be popular with the boys and gradually became involved in other activities of the club.

'During this period we spent a number of holidays together on the Norfolk Broads and I still have vivid recollections of him asleep on his feet, propped against the mast usually at inappropriate moments. He was incredibly strong physically and threw himself into every physical activity with enthusiasm to the point of exhaustion.

'In his young days he had been very unhappy at home and some of us, especially Alan Gardner, did our best to provide proxy homes for him. It was a real sorrow to us that after his departure to Liverpool he seemed content to forget us. An attempted reunion a good many years later at a lunch at the RAC, during one of his infrequent visits to London for some ecclesiastical purpose was not a success for he showed little or no interest in what had happened to any of his old friends and talked continuously about himself. As with so many people he was nicer before he was successful, I think. I feel it right to mention this as biographies should present a full picture of their subjects. But his rise from humble and unfavourable beginnings to a position of high leadership in the Church was due to a personality which had both great charm and great determination. I am glad I knew him.'

Treacy may have been pretty beefy physically but he was spiritually and mentally frail. He remembers having to give short addresses at the Club Bible Class:

'How I dreaded those sessions. Many were the times when I dried up after a couple of minutes, my mind empty of thought, my tongue dry and my lips feeling as if they were glued together. I don't think the lads minded those two minute flashes before my light went out. They were very dull flashes, based largely on Paterson Smyth's *Life of Christ*. The trouble, I suppose, was that I spoke not from experience but from memory — memory of passages which I thought would suit the occasion. Memory is a less stable foundation than experience when talking to a group of fidgeting youngsters.'

The Vicar of Kentish Town, Ernest Duval, was a frequent visitor to the Club. First appearances were deceptive. Always clad in sober black with a flat crowned shovel hat, he smiled little and seemed to be fairly disapproving. As Treacy came to know him, so he learned to respect him as a devoted parish priest who cared for the people committed to his charge with a selfless love united with that genuine paternal authority and love which was a commendable characteristic of many clergy of those days. Too many clergy today act as bewildered men without authority because they will not recognise that they are under authority.

The recurrent idea that he ought to be ordained continued to pester Treacy and it both troubled and puzzled him, as he noted:

'I wasn't particularly religious in my habits. My prayers were intermittent, my reading of theology non-existent. At first I dismissed the idea as preposterous. But I could not get rid of it: it kept nagging at me, until I had to share it with someone.'

The opportunity came quite soon. Through Toc H friends Treacy was persuaded to attend Evensong at All Hallows, Barking-by-the-Tower where the Rev P. B. 'Tubby' Clayton was Vicar, whom Treacy remembers as 'a person of remarkable personal magnetism with a genius for gathering young men around him. He could turn a piquant phrase as no other man I have ever heard. He had an extraordinary power to create imitators, most of whom were quite unaware that they were imitating him. He had an extraordinarily deep voice with a kind of hesitation — which was a prolonged epiglotal a-a-a-h, with his mouth slightly open like a benevolent frog. Throughout Toc H there were clergymen whose manner of speech revealed close association with Tubby.'

On his first Sunday at All Hallows an appeal was made for volunteers to sing in the choir. Almost as musically dim as a Toc H lamp, Treacy offered himself. He could scarcely sing a note. Apart from knowing that he was not a Treble he had no idea what he was. He need not have feared. They would take anyone and there was no voice test. Bellowing to the glory of God in cassock and surplice was all that was required. And ordination?

'I remember an evening with Tubby Clayton when we drove round Epping Forest in a car which wasn't his, but into which he jumped outside All Hallows, without the owner's knowledge or permission. Mercifully, he was well known for this kind of absent-mindedness, so the police were not informed that a car had been stolen. He listened to my tale, and spent the best part of an hour giving me good reasons why I should not be ordained. I have often wondered, since, whether he was testing my determination, or whether he really thought that I should be a disaster in the ministry.

'Whatever his intentions, it had the effect on me of making me more determined than ever. And, by jove, I needed to be, for there followed a succession of disappointments and frustrations. As a class of men I did not like clergymen — with individual exceptions. Those that I had met struck me as emasculated creatures who laid down the law, liked their own way, and seemed to be more sure of what I ought not to do, than what I should do, to achieve salvation. Why on earth should I want to join that lot?'

Not easily deterred, Treacy took some tentative steps to prepare himself for ordination. He entered King's College, London as an evening student. It was a step foredoomed to falter and then halt. At the end of a day attempting to sell insurance he was supposed to start preparing to offer people assurance. After a quick snack he took his place in the class at King's to listen to a series of turgid lectures on the Old Testament, Christian Doctrine and Church History. He was too tired for concentration and assimilation. Sometimes he would drop off to sleep and awaken to see his fellow students disappearing. His attitude was that even if he was not achieving anything it could not be said that he was not trying. But a fourteen-hour day supported only by two semi-digestible snacks was not taking him one step nearer to his goal.

He still worshipped at St Jude's intermittently, and Basil Bourchier regarded the Associate of King's College (AKC) certificate with disdain. 'Entry by the back door' he said. He insisted on Cambridge. Meanwhile Treacy had met an influential clergyman, Frank Woolnough, who combined the chaplaincy of Christ's College, Cambridge, with the Secretaryship of a body that looked after ordination candidates. He operated from a room in Church House, Westminster.

'It was a happy day for me when I met Frank. He was wonderfully kind and encouraging, and I needed it after some of the knocks that I had experienced. He not only made me feel that my vocation was genuine, but he tackled the problem of grants for me, and put me in touch with a sponsor. He insisted that I went to Christ's College, Cambridge — but there remained the hurdle of "Little-go" (How on earth did that name originate?). My school certificate results were so lamentable that I needed to pass in five subjects.'

Working extremely hard, Treacy succeeded in passing four subjects but he was ditched on the all-important Latin paper. He left King's College in order to slog away at Tacitus and Ovid, putting five shillings an hour four times a week into the pocket of the Principal of the local education institute. In addition there were unpaid efforts. Alan Gardner notes 'My mother tried unsuccessfully to teach him Latin', and Alex Churcher adds 'At this time he was trying hard to pass exams and I was able to be of help to him in this as a coach, although I don't think he ever passed! He was not academically gifted or inclined and his subsequent "success" was always due to his personality rather than his brain power.'

Treacy failed Latin a second time and a third time. Far from deterring him he had the cheek to approach a bishop! Arthur Foley Winnington-Ingram, Bishop of London, was his first target. Winnington-Ingram was past his peak and was ill-cast for a diocese the size and complexity of London. But in his heyday he was one of the most influential figures in the Church. He had been an effervescent man whose flair for simplicity and whose sense of the dramatic had made him an extremely effective and compelling crusader. His personality was magnetic. What a different man Treacy encountered:

'I was interviewed at a Church Lads' Brigade Camp somewhere on the East Coast. The old man was on a visit to the camp, and it was suggested that, as a possible ordinand, he might see me. This he did sitting in a deck chair in a field. At the time there was a plague of flies, and I was equipped with a fly whisk and bidden to deal with flies that buzzed around the episcopal head. The interview, which lasted for about ten minutes, was interspersed with a succession of lunges with my whisk. The old man could not have been kinder. He called me "my dear boy" repeatedly. I told him my somewhat undistinguished life story, and, greatly encouraged, knelt to receive his blessing, and left the presence. But I never heard another word. Perhaps I should have written to remind him but in those days ordinands were a good deal shyer than they are today.'

Treacy's second choice was Cyril Forster Garbett, Bishop of Southwark and later a great Archbishop of York. What did Treacy encounter at Kennington in South London where Garbett had his habitation?

'Garbett was then in his episcopal prime. Cold, efficient, and not to be deceived by any youthful aspirations to the ordained life which were not genuine. For me it was not an interview that I remember with pleasure. I thought him a cold fish, arrogant, and without the ability to draw out of a man his deepest hopes or to encourage confidences. However, in 30 minutes precisely, I was dismissed, and without much confidence that I had made any impression on him. In the event, how right I was, for once again, I heard no more.'

Nevertheless by the end of 1928 Treacy had informed the Clerical & Medical of his plans and given them provisional notice. In January 1929 he was almost ready to attempt the Latin paper for the fourth time. Then, something happened which changed everything. On Monday morning 28 January 1929 his father was found dead in his bed. Mary (van der Kaay) writes of the end:

'The day before his death I had gone with him to St Jude's for the morning service. The weather was cold and grim, but strangely he also went alone to Evensong. On returning he found Eric and my mother having a fierce argument over a new suit which Eric had bought but which my mother had taken and hidden, for some inexplicable reason. My father left the sitting-room and his last words were: "Can't you leave me in peace". Then he went to bed.'

Treacy writes:

'On that morning I found myself with a bereaved mother and a sister at school. Obviously Cambridge was out, and for good. Mercifully the insurance company were kind to me and allowed me to stay on. My father's death was a tremendous blow to me, for between him and me existed a very deep bond of affection and understanding. I cannot ever remember a cross word passing between us. I don't think he quite understood my desire to be ordained, but, although he could not produce any money for my training, he gave me every encouragement. The word "gentleman" is much overworked, and difficult in definition, but if I had to produce a perfect specimen, I would produce my father.'

It looked as if insurance would have to be Treacy's policy for life. Latin was dropped like a hot potato and ordination receded as a practical proposition even though the inner desire remained. Nearly all Treacy's time away from his work was spent doing voluntary work in boys' clubs. Someone suggested that he should apply for a full-time club leader's post. There was a vacancy as Missioner at the Shrewsbury School Mission which was situated in the Scotland Road area of Liverpool. On the basis that there was little hope but, equally, nothing to lose he applied for the post. The work consisted of organising and managing a large boys' club, superintending a boys' home which formed part of Shrewsbury House, visiting Shrewsbury School, and keeping past and present Salopians in touch with the Mission. There was an important annual camp attended by members of the school. The emolument was £150 per annum with full board and residence for the Missioner — and his wife! As to the kind of person the school was seeking, only one clue was given on the official form: 'The Missioner may be either a Clergyman or a Layman, but on the whole a Layman would be preferred, especially if reading for Holy Orders. He need not be a Salopian, though a Salopian would naturally be welcomed.'

To Treacy's surprise he was invited to Shrewsbury, there to be interviewed by the Headmaster, Canon H. A. P. Sawyer (Bob) — 'This rotund, cherubic, little man, who behind a front of benevolence was a shrewd operator.' Shrewsbury in the 1920s still looked back on the magic days of C. A. Alington, who had gone to Eton from the 'Schools' as they are known. There were members of staff who had been appointed by Alington, and who had never forgotten it. Treacy remembered:

'From all accounts Alington had glamour, and made the most of it. Whether he was, or was not, a great Headmaster, I have no means of knowing, but he appeared to have the power to make people think he was.

'Sawyer had none of the glamour. He was just a thoroughly nice man — more like a country parson than a headmaster. So far as I could judge, he was a good headmaster. He appointed good and able men to his staff and left them to get on with the job. He had a reputation for absent-mindedness, but anyone who thought this was genuine was in for a shock. When need arose, he was as sharp as a needle, and when toughness was needed, he could be tough.

'As one grew to know him, one realised that behind this gentle benevolence there was something of steel — one also realised that you didn't get much closer to him. There was an inner man whom few really knew. I suspect that even his reputation for absent-mindedness was something he encouraged. I find that many of the old type schoolmasters cast a roll for themselves, and may even have originated the mythical stories that grew up around them.

'It was a curious interview. Shrewsbury was playing Repton that afternoon, so Bob and I walked up and down the touch line, and there were frequent moments of non-concentration on the work of the School Mission. I must confess to feeling that I hadn't made much impact, and when I was dismissed with the promise that I would be hearing from him, I had little doubt that I should receive a polite "No".'

Two days later Treacy received a letter from Canon Sawyer, addressed in spidery writing, appointing him to teach maths at Shrewsbury. Another gentleman interviewed on the same day for the maths teaching post was no doubt surprised to find that he had been consigned to Liverpool as School Missioner. Canon Sawyer had inadvertently transposed the names! This was duly corrected and Treacy was asked to commence duties as Missioner as quickly as possible.

There was a Mission Committee whose Chairman was J. Russell Hope-Simpson and he remembers 'that it was thought a bit of a gamble as Eric was clearly an inexperienced and callow young man. In fact no suitable applicants for the post turned up and Eric was something of a leap in the dark. We did not realise that we had picked a winner.'

One day in April 1929 Treacy booked a single ticket from London Euston to Liverpool Lime Street. The 21-year old man on the train was not the sporty but diffident duffer who had left Haberdashers'. Granted, academically he had still much to be modest about, but his character was being shaped by his circumstances, his lessons learned in the gritty school of life. Of course he was a mass of conflicting qualities at this stage of his life. Yet there were some ingredients in his personality that had surfaced in London, were going to be in full flight at Liverpool and remain with him to the end of his life even if in a less strident form. The constants were earnestness and impulsiveness. He had the intuition of the enthusiast cutting short logical thinking. He was a young man of initiative, an innovator, a natural leader. He was an individualist who liked his own way and could deal summarily with anyone who hindered him. He was as quick to apologise and was capable of deep understanding and affection.

Another thing is certain. He had no idea of what lay ahead.

3
Shrewsbury's Two Faces

The initial excitement of the new opportunity receded as the train approached its destination. 'All the bounce had gone out of me,' Treacy recalled 'I felt very lonely and not a little frightened. I knew no one in this great city of Liverpool and I was cold and hungry. Funds didn't run to a meal on the train. The train drew in under the great arch of Lime Street station. As I emerged from the station on to the St George's Plateau it was raining, the sky was leaden, the wind was biting. St George's Hall loomed like a great black monster in the gloom.'

Treacy had no idea how to find Shrewsbury House and there was no one to meet him. He asked two people how to find it but they did not know. Or did they? It was his first encounter with the Liverpool dialect — a mixture of guttural noises, shortened vowels and words uttered at such speed that they ran into each other.

Eventually he found a policeman on point duty who told him to take a 3 car to Mile End and walk down Dryden Street. Treacy recalls the new experience:

'The "car" was a tram on four wheels, which rocked like a ship on a rough sea, en route from Dingle to Dalton. I shall never forget the smell of that tram. A mixture of dockers' twist, wet shawls and human bodies. It was all very friendly, everyone was talking to one another, but I had never heard such an accent.

'After a short journey through shabby streets thronged with women in those large black shawls which they hugged to themselves and which did duty as top coats; with men and boys, ill clad, and thumping about in clogs, I was decanted from the "car" at Mile End. This was in Scotland Road, in those days one of the roughest streets in England. It was the boundary line between the Protestant heights of Everton and the Roman Catholic area around the Docks. Down Dryden Street, across Great Homer Street, up Roscommon Street, into Portland Place, and so to Shrewsbury House.'

Shrewsbury House was founded in 1903 and the first Missioner was the Rev Digby Kittermaster, an old Salopian, who ventured into this poverty stricken area at a time when policemen would only go in pairs though three was the preferred and safer number. The Mission, or Club, consisted of four converted houses over 130 years old in 1932. There was a 60ft by 30ft indoor gymnasium, well equipped with apparatus and a boxing ring; an open-air playground completely enclosed by netting; a library of over 700 volumes; and a chapel with seating accommodation for 110 bottoms. In addition to the Missioner's accommodation there was a dormitory for 12 boys who were residents. These were boys who had reached the age limit of local orphanages, or whose houses were undesirable and who were in need of care and attention — and affection. There were a few itinerants who had never had homes, and sometimes probation officers asked the Missioner to accept

25

boys who had transgressed the law. The ordinary club membership numbered about 150 but there was invariably a waiting list.

Massive unemployment, deplorable housing and appalling poverty made the area in which Shrewsbury House was situated one of the most deprived in Britain. Even so there was little bitterness in the victims of those conditions, just a forlorn acceptance of the inevitability of their lot in life. The majority of the men wanted to work, but there was no work for them. The longer they were unemployed the more unemployable they became. They were physically flabby from lack of activity and mentally indolent through daily tedium. Small wonder that these second class citizens found some passing excitement in a pitch and toss school, and some anaesthetic in the ale house. As for the women and children, Treacy writes:

'The wives of these men were, for the most part, magnificent. They had large families — not for them the benefits of family planning — they were short of money, their houses were totally inadequate for their families, their sanitary arrangements appalling, and yet, they cared for their families with wonderful devotion, dealing with drunken husbands, unruly children, and constant shortages of money and food with uncomplaining courage. Such triumphs are no justification for the conditions that produced them but it must be said that these women shone like bright lights in a very sombre world.

'The children were, miraculously, abounding in energy, sharp as needles, and full of guts. That they were undernourished was revealed by various physical defects. Many of them had chest complaints and there were cases of serious heart deterioration in children under 12 years of age.'

Shrewsbury House was in a religious no man's land. Towards the river the population was predominantly Roman Catholic and towards the Everton heights mostly Protestant. Virulent and villainous religious bigotry was exacerbated by men like Pastor Longbottom of Everton who led a sect called the Protestant Reformers, though reform was what they did not want! The unbending and popular Roman Catholic Archbishop of Liverpool was well named Downey! The strength and fire of the Protestant zealots was rooted and stocked in the many Orange Lodges. The colourful drum and fife bands paraded in provocative strength, and on the Anniversary of the Battle of the Boyne, each 12 July, they joined battle with the stalwart legions of the Pope. There was nothing remotely Christian about the activities of these warriors of the Lord. 12 July was imprinted on Treacy's mind:

'For several nights, the scrapping went on, although it must be said, the fighting, if violent, was clean. There was no shooting, there were no petrol bombs, property was, more or less, respected. Certainly bricks were thrown, people were beaten up and the casualty departments of the hospitals were kept busy. It mattered not to the protagonists that their leaders were at peace with each other — it was the battle that mattered. I remember once drinking cocoa in the local Presbytery with the local Roman Catholic fathers, whilst our respective flocks were knocking hell out of each other in the street below. We might have received the same treatment had the crowd known that we were thus fraternising!'

Shrewsbury House was in the Parish of St Peter, Everton, whose Vicar was a craggy Irishman called Henry Frazer. There was a toughness and tirelessness about him which meant that he was a force to be reckoned with, but he did not make Christianity attractive. Treacy remembers him as:

'A real North of Ireland Protestant, utterly humourless, but entirely devoted to his flock. He had the courage of a lion, and didn't mind what he said and to whom he said it. He would walk into a pub, and pull out some massive docker who was spending his money on beer and not his family. This happened more than once to my certain knowledge. Occasionally, he suffered physical violence, but he always came up for more. He was a holy lesson in his attitude to the "Demon Drink" being a rabid teetotaller himself. And well he might be, as his parish abounded in examples of the evil effect of strong drink.'

Treacy's predecessor was an old Salopian. David Temple, a schoolmaster, had left his mark on Shrewsbury House although he had only been there for two and a half years. He was something of a character, incurably untidy and doubtfully clean. Rumour had it that he had once been caught shaving, attired in hat and overcoat before dashing off to catch a train. He managed to maintain a seemly discipline and counter mutinous manoeuvrings whilst at the same time arousing affection from the boys, who mimicked him endlessly. Someone describes him as a 'rugged, studious, pedagogic type'. On one score Treacy had good reason to be critical of him. When he left the Mission he did not go. His constant return to old haunts made Treacy's early months rather difficult. However, Temple had gathered together a number of old Salopians who lived in Merseyside as helpers in the Club. They included Fred Pritchard, later a High Court Judge — but then a promising young barrister on the North Western Circuit who visited the Club every Sunday to play the wheezing harmonium, miscalled an organ. Treacy describes some of the other helpers:

'The Gibbons Brothers, Willie and Reggie, had been faithful to the club from the days of Digby Kittermaster. They were an odd couple, incredibly generous and kind-hearted. Willie managed one of Liverpool's stores — Hendersons — and Reggie was unemployed but involved in a number of good works in the city. Willie was somewhat astringent in his approach and very sparing with his praise. He always made me feel that I was an abysmal failure. Reggie rather bumbled — slow in his reactions, stubborn and reserved. They were bachelors living in a huge Victorian mansion presided over by a formidable mother. It took me some time to realise what kind hearts beat behind those frosty exteriors.

'Then there was Barr Adams, about as unlike a product of a public school as could be imagined. Highly strung, rather shrill, with few friends in his own social setting and finding a deep satisfaction in his relationships with club boys. Like many bachelors in this kind of social work he was possessive and jealous of his friendships and cultivated a number of favourites. A master of the sharp and wounding phrase he knew how to hurt, and often did. To his credit it must be said that he was totally dedicated to his work in the club, and did a tremendous job in starting up the Old Boys Association for the boys over 18 who would, otherwise, have left the club.

'I can't pretend that, at first, I was happy with this lot. I may have been wrong, but I felt that as a non-Salopian I was not entirely accepted. Fortunately I got on well with the lads. They were friendly and cheerful and, I think, took to me. Of course I was feeling my way, and was not an expert.'

Despite, or perhaps resulting from, these initial hesitations Treacy entered into his work with vocational gusto. The Boys Club met every evening of the week, and was organised for competitive purposes into Houses, bearing the unimaginative names of Blue, Green, Red and White. Each evening ended with prayers in the chapel at 10 o'clock, and on Sunday evenings there was a service at which attendance at least twice a month was obligatory. The boys paid a weekly subscription, and exercised a good deal of responsibility in running the Club themselves. Although they were a mixed bunch they shared a common background of dire deprivation. They were the unwanted, the lepers of a rotting society. Occasionally, one or two of them would disappear without trace only to reappear after several weeks with a guilty look, and more money in their pockets than they could ever have acquired legitimately. At that time it was the only Boys Club in Liverpool whose boys regularly attended a night school for educational classes. Once a week all club members between the ages of 14 and 18 went for instruction in English composition, literature, drawing and handicrafts.

The work of a club leader is a work of love before it is a work of competence. The meagre rewards come not in cups and medals, neither by way of filling the pocket, but in friendships made, trust given and ideals shared. Treacy quickly earned the respect and trust of the boys by his dynamism and then their affection by his obvious caring. H. H. Hardy, who succeeded 'Bob' Sawyer as Headmaster of Shrewsbury, speaks for other helpers and friends when referring to the manifold activities of the Mission and Club — 'all receive their motive power from the enthusiasm and inspiration of our Missioner.'

The specification for the post of Missioner listed 'An important feature of the Mission is the Annual Camp, held in the first week in August, in the School grounds, and attended by past and present members of the School, as well as boys of the Club.' The Camp had always been held in the Craig Field at Shrewsbury School to which up to 100 boys would entrain from Lime Street station. That is where the holidays started:

'These journeys had their moments: for instance at Crewe, where our train stopped to be joined with a portion from Manchester, there was always a raid on the refreshment room and it took some pretty violent measures to get the little monkeys back on the train. Whenever a count was made there were always two or three missing, allegedly in the lavatory. On one occasion one was found on the engine, the driver being his uncle. This cheerful band of pilgrims would leap out of the train at Shrewsbury, pour down the steps, under the subway and out of the station yard where they would be met by the reception committee of Salopians.

'The shops were an irresistible magnet to the boys, but somehow we got them up to the Craig Field. Then started a week under canvas, which was good fun but there were embarrassing moments. None more so than when the ladies of Kingsland (Shrewsbury School) visited the Reservation, some with painfully obvious condescension, which was quickly spotted by the boys, who had their own unmistakable ways of taking the mickey out of them.'

Sometimes trouble started before the departure from Lime Street, as once when one boy was fooling about on the station and put his head into a milk churn. Greatly attracted to the cavity his head stuck in it! Treacy had to take the boy and milk churn to the Infirmary so that the two could be parted. There were other incidents too. The Rev Leslie Mitchell, who helped at the club recalls one. 'Eric Treacy was full of anger at the display outside one shop of indecent postcards. He told us that he had been so shocked that he had bought the lot and destroyed them. He was a bit surprised when it was suggested that this was good for trade!'

After a few years of camping at Shrewsbury Treacy decided that there should be a change of venue. He felt there were too many 'experts' on camping on the staff at Shrewsbury. There was opposition but he was determined to have his way. He did not brook any interference when it came to the question of who was in charge of the camp and of the boys! Neither did he take kindly to receiving advice from the 'nobs of Shrewsbury School' as he called them. He felt the boys needed the benefit of sea air so future camps were held at Penmaenmawr and Aber in North Wales where staff and boys of the School came as 'visitors'.

Prior to the camps Treacy had to cycle the length and breadth of Liverpool requesting, begging or cajoling employers to give the boys leave for the week's camp. 'Some were marvellous, and not only gave the boy his holiday with pay, but also gave me a donation for the camp. Others were monstrous in their attitude. "Yes, he could have a week off but he can have his cards when he gets back," some would say.'

Camps were exciting for the boys and exacting for the Missioner and his helpers. There was a bit of shoplifting in order to get a present to take home to mum. There was a certain amount of gambling in the tents after 'lights out'. Sometimes the local residents complained that their hens were not keeping up their productivity agreements and some of the local maidens were 'dated', to their parents' horror, by these young savages from Liverpool. Most of it however was good honest fun by Liverpool standards.

It was a condition of Treacy's Missionership that he should visit Shrewsbury School once a fortnight, spending a night and a day in one of the Houses. Having attended a day school this was a new and alien world to him. He later admitted that he trod extremely warily at first lest he show any unfamiliarity with the way of life in a Public boarding school. The wariness was not as evident to the people at Shrewsbury. Perhaps because Treacy had an inferiority complex about his social and academic background there was an endeavour to 'make his mark'. One young master at Shrewsbury, R. St J. Pitts-Tucker (later Headmaster of Pocklington School) writes 'Eric was regarded with some awe as a wild man who could say outrageous, shocking things and get away with it. He was physically very energetic and combined a passionate devotion to his boys in the club with a disturbing understanding of their peculiar Liverpudlian outlook — they could not shock him.'

Treacy's initial visits to Shrewsbury were considerably helped by his acquaintance with another master, Roger Wilson, who became Treacy's closest friend and will appear later in this biography as Bishop successively of Wakefield and Chichester. If Treacy was a wild man it was an attraction of opposites as he recalls:

'It was within a few days of my arriving at Shrewsbury House that a friendship started which has been one of the most precious relationships in my life. Roger Wilson, a master at Shrewsbury, was visiting the Club and our first encounter was across a billiards table. It is strange that it ever happened because Roger's background and temperament are utterly different from mine. He was at Winchester and Keble, Oxford, followed by a spell at Westcott House, Cambridge. He was, and is, a steady man with a disciplined spiritual life. He is gentle, cultured and a reserved person.

'In fact we had nothing in common with each other. He was everything that I should like to be. With a First in Mods, and a Second in Greats, he belonged to a different intellectual world from me. Indeed, I belonged to no intellectual world at all. I was far from a "steady" man — I know myself to be impetuous and uncertain of myself. My spiritual life, so far as I had one, was far from disciplined — it was a daily struggle against indolence and a lack of concentration. Yet, at the moment of our meeting, a friendship started which now, 40 years later, still remains cherished by us both [and until Treacy's death]. I have often wondered how it came about? Did Roger detect my loneliness? I cannot think what he saw to draw him to me.'

Bishop Roger Wilson's recollections of Treacy at this time are important:

'A young man in the early twenties, still boyish in his enthusiasms, impulsive by nature and intellectually footloose. His predecessor, David Temple, was a loyal follower of the Salopian tradition. Eric, without Salopian links, came to Shrewsbury House as an adventure in the service of the young in a great city, for which Shrewsbury School was but an external ally and support. Hitherto, my impression was that the Mission tended to be regarded as an extension of the School into social service. Eric gave this a new alignment . . . . In fact during his time the links between School and Mission matured into a more fruitful partnership and neither end suffered. This was very largely due to Eric's own make-up; he combined a great loyalty to friends and associates in Shrewsbury with an independence of spirit which insisted on working things out in his own way.'

Shrewsbury School contrasted sharply with Haberdashers'. The one in a magnificent setting high on a hill above the Severn, the other surrounded by suburban streets. The Shrewsbury buildings were set round a magnificent playing field with views to the Long Wynd and the hills around Church Stretton. Not that the buildings themselves were beautiful. The main building was a converted workhouse, the chapel was Victorian Gothic most notable for its creaking pews — not a place in which to preach — and the various Houses a mixture of late 19th or early 20th century building. It was the total effect of space and dignity that gave it its beauty.

For Treacy there was more to do than grow languid in the sun. He brought more than greetings from the slum, soot-laden atmosphere of Liverpool. It was his task to report on his activities and solicit help for them. What a contrast! Slumping in a leather arm chair in a Housemaster's study surrounded by a litter of sports gear, sports trophies and college groups was a far cry from Everton. At Shrewsbury he found cosy masculine sanctuaries with an incense of pipe tobacco. Many of the Housemasters became his friends. 'They were good men with a highly developed sense of right and wrong, men who inculcated their boys with a way of life that was honourable — and shared responsibility with them.'

The new Headmaster (from 1932), H. H. Hardy, was a product of the parsonage, a no-nonsense sort of person of inflexible principles who lived in a world of blacks and whites and who thought that most sins could be sweated out of the system by a run before breakfast and a cold bath. As an old Rugbeian, Hardy was a typical product of the late Victorian Public School system having a very highly developed sense of duty, although he sometimes saw things in terms of duty when they were not. He was an old-fashioned Evangelical and named by some as a 'Protestant Incurable'. Treacy's sessions with him were more in the nature of interviews than consultations.

There were other members of staff who at once irritated and fascinated Treacy. They had an assurance which eluded him. They assumed a casualness in dress which seemed to be totally unconscious but which was really a carefully cultivated fashion. There were eccentrics in plenty who flourished in the tolerant and cultural atmosphere of the place. *Au fond* they were probably snobs but it was unassertive snobbery. Yet pleasant as they were, and beguiling as the Shrewsbury visits became, Treacy found himself growing increasingly impatient of the cosy smugness of the Shrewsbury end. He could not reconcile the contrast between the appalling conditions in Everton and the comforts of Shrewsbury. In reality, of course, Shrewsbury was indeed an alien world to him. Reflecting on this later when his thoughts were clearer he wrote:

'I did not feel that Salopians, as a whole, questioned a system that produced extremes of poverty and wealth. Rather did they feel that conditions such as existed in Liverpool, and other great cities, were unfortunate, and that it was a plain duty of those whose lives were set in more prosperous conditions to do something about those who suffered the cruelties of poverty, unemployment and bad housing.

'The School Mission was a way of discharging this responsibility for the underprivileged. Parcels of old clothes and books, bank holiday trips and summer camps, occasional visits to the Mission were the expressions of this responsibility. Never once do I recall, in all my contacts with the Schools did I ever encounter, anyone who asked "why should these things be?" or who questioned a system that acquiesced in such gross inequalities. When I expressed these feelings in a Foreword to the Annual Report of the Mission, they were expunged by the Headmaster.'

Treacy admits that he did not think politically about all this as his impatience was too incoherent to find ideological expression. 'It just made me bloody minded. I found it increasingly difficult to beg money and old clothes off the rich. I loathed writing letters of thanks to people who had sent me that which cost them little for my kids at the Mission although there were one or two Housemasters' wives who needed playing up to. Basically the whole thing stood for that which I never had, and I suppose that there was an element of personal jealousy in my attitudes.'

Treacy gained far more from Shrewsbury than he was prepared to admit. Bishop Roger Wilson recalls how:

'Shrewsbury helped to develop one side of his personality. Having missed a university course of study, he felt the loss of a cultural element in his life, which books, talk, a society engaged in the pursuit of knowledge even at the school level, represented. Certainly he was making up for this over the years; books became a perennial source of interest (and no doubt expense) as he read and collected them widely. How much he liked to discuss them! His shelves were as orderly as a platoon of Guards. Even so, it was always people rather than subjects that attracted him. Biographies, personal reminiscences, travel, yes, and fiction, abounded on those shelves — everything that was connected with the contemporary world and reinforced his own conviction that "the proper study of mankind is man".'

The junior inmates of Shrewsbury School benefited more from the Mission and from Treacy than he realised at the time. Every weekend in term-time, six boys from one of the Houses spent a weekend at the Mission. Their programme was to spend Saturday evening in the club getting to know the boys, at which some were better than others. Many of them were shy which could not be said of the club boys. After a violent football match in the gym, at which the Salopians were usually beaten, to bed. Treacy adds:

'On the Sunday morning I took them to morning service at the Cathedral, which was a variable occasion. In the days of Dean F. W. Dwelly, the services lacked nothing in dignity, but the pulpit performances were pretty dreary. The one exception was Charles Raven, whose sermons were often well above the heads of most of us, but delivered with such fire and magnetism that he captured the attention of the dullest boy. Raven had an extraordinary power as a preacher — he literally burned in the pulpit and gave the impression of a flame. His appearance was a great help — tall, ascetic looking with piercing eyes, he dominated the largest audience. His English was superb and his command of language dazzling. His fellow canons may have been good men, but they were "also rans" in the preaching stakes.

'So, after florid Matins we would return to the Mission for dinner — cut off the roast, two veg, followed by tinned fruit and custard. Then the young explorers from Salop would set out on an afternoon's tour of Liverpool dockland, which, I suspect not infrequently, ended up at the Adelphi with a good "tuck-in".

'The evening was spent in chapel at the club service, then a rollicking game of basketball in the gym, in which the superior physique of the Salopians was no match for the cunning of the club boys. By this time the barriers were down, and the young men were meeting each other unselfconsciously and friendships were beginning to blossom.

'Monday morning, early breakfast, train back to Shrewsbury, and a group of Salopians returned to the Schools having discovered how the other three-quarters of the world lived. Some soon forgot! Others did not, and there were a number who ultimately were ordained, and whose vocations, I like to think, could be traced to their visits to the Mission.'

Some ten known vocations to the ordained ministry sprang from Treacy's Missionership. Often it was a question of removing a question mark. Prebendary Richard Hill is one of many Salopians who stayed at the Mission for a period of months, in his case:

'While I was trying to decide whether I ought to offer myself for ordination. Over the years, many young men were helped to sort out their aims in life by staying at, or by visits to, the Club; and Eric's example and influence, and his interest in each individual, were, I have no doubt, decisive factors in the lives of many. It was during my conversation with him on the platform at Lime Street station, when he saw me off at the end of my stay, that I found myself telling him, in reply to his question, that I had made up my mind.'

Of the Missioner who provided the atmosphere Prebendary Hill comments:

'Eric was always cheerful, vigorous, down to earth and practical, exasperated often by evils that could not be put right, but never irritable and with an urgent "hunger and thirst after righteousness". He was no academic, but he thought deeply and was always stimulating in discussion, informal, unconventional.'

Prebendary Hill's brother, James, another Salopian who stayed at the Mission (and was later himself Missioner from 1943-53) was another 'whose vocation to the Ministry was directly the result of contact with Eric.'

In the 1930 *Annual Report* Treacy concluded by stating: 'I cannot help feeling that these boys for whom Shrewsbury House exists have far more to give us then we have to give them; and I do pray that those who come to Shrewsbury House to help, may be humble minded enough to realise this and to benefit by the lessons that these youngsters are constantly teaching us.' Treacy, the energetic romantic yet with his feet firmly on the ground could end his 1932 *Annual Report* thus: 'In theological text books there are five arguments for the existence of God. I would add one more — it would be quite short — in fact, more of an invitation than an argument. I should write, "Come to the slums, for there you will find more real evidences for the existence of a loving God than anywhere else in the world".'

Treacy regarded Shrewsbury House as much more than a Boys' Club. 'It endeavours to its very utmost to be a source of joy and help to the neighbourhood: so often the surest way to capture the boy is by helping his family.' Not that helping the parents was an easy task. Tom France, a Salopian who later helped in the Club, remembers one incident:

'One night after the Club was closed and they (Eric and May) were going to bed they were knocked up by one of the boys who had come back for Eric's help as the boy's father and mother were having a terrific row. Eric went out and, as he told us, by about 12.30am had calmed the parents down; so he said to the wife, "Now kiss your husband to show that you really have forgiven him." Her reply was "What me kiss 'im wot 'as never called me anything else but 'er for the last ten years, not bloody likely." Thereupon the row started again and it took Eric until 2am to calm things down again.'

Treacy was still a layman but he felt that the most important work of all was that which was done in the Club Chapel. It was the greatest cohesive force in the Club. He invited a number of local clergy and lay people to give addresses at the services. On Sunday evenings an attendance of 100 was usual. Treacy commented: 'These services are remarkable for their warmth and spontaneity, and whoever may be privileged to be preaching is sure of the boys' unwavering attention on the one condition that he is sincere.'

Writing in the 1933 *Annual Report* on *The Religious Life of the Club* Treacy revealed his feelings born of experience as Missioner:

'It would surprise many of you to discover how, to most of our younger members, religion and the goodness of life are two quite separate things. Religion to them means Church, hymn singing, sometimes long and wearying sermons — in short, a Sunday hobby for those who have clothes nice enough in which to go to church. They never think of connecting the goodness they admire so much in men when they see it, with Religion; to them Jesus Christ is the exclusive possession of churchgoers. Sad to relate, they do not identify the fine qualities of character they never fail to admire, with Christ.

'Our task then is to help our boys to recognise that Christ is the source of all goodness, is certainly not the exclusive property of those who go to churches, and, if one may say so, regards work well and conscientiously done as a prayer; *laborare est orare* I believe to be a great truth, and one which we must preach to boys whose only hope of regular prayer is in action rather than meditation. They must learn that Religion is not something added on to life, but a quality of life; not so much doing anything different day by day, but doing everything differently — their Utmost for the Highest.'

4
Twice Collared

Ordination had not glided to the back of Treacy's mind. He felt the pull of the Cloth as keenly as ever even though he had suffered major setbacks. Moreover, he was still conscious of his lack of qualifications to travel to the starting line let alone to traverse it. He was excessively occupied with his work at the Mission and had little or no time or inclination for careful and sustained study.

Shortly after his arrival at the Mission the Archdeacon of Liverpool, C. F. Twitchett, had come to take a service. Twitchett had accumulated a good deal of power in the Liverpool Diocese and despite a certain archdiaconal ponderousness, he was a kind and helpful man. He asked Treacy about his background and was told of the forlorn attempts at ordination. Treacy said he could only see his future in youth work. Twitchett retorted 'It seems a pity to drop your idea of ordination' and went his way.

Some time after, Treacy was summoned by Albert Augustus David, Bishop of Liverpool. These were days when bishops could and did summon people into their presence. Treacy did not connect this with Twitchett's interrogations but thought that he might have done something to earn episcopal disapproval. Accordingly he obeyed the summons with a mixture of curiosity and anxiety.

A. A. David was essentially a scholar bishop with a reforming instinct. Having been successively Headmaster of Clifton and Rugby the headmasterly air was always thick about him. In manner he was forbidding but that was due in part to a natural reserve. He was not possessed of much small talk which often resulted in embarrassingly long silences in conversation with him. There was about David an air of authority, a dignity which was entirely unselfconscious. He was a very considerable figure and not only in the Church of England. He made no effort to be popular, so did not ingratiate himself with the clergy as does many a modern bishop. David was a friend of William Temple and each possessed a defect, if such it be, that is characteristic of many men who are innocent and fundamentally decent. They cannot conceive that anyone could be less decent and direct than themselves. They are therefore apt to accept a person's own estimate of himself and credit him with being better than he is.

Treacy recalls the interview: 'I entered the rather forbidding presence of the Bishop. Then he smiled. Bishop David's smile was something you didn't forget; it revealed a sweetness and gentleness which made him particularly vulnerable to some of the monsters that then inhabited the Liverpool Diocese. He told me that ordination was possible.'

After meeting Bishop David's ordination candidates' committee Treacy was offered a chance of combining his work at Shrewsbury House with attendance at St Aidan's College, Birkenhead, to prepare for ordination. He accepted, perhaps unwisely, for the kind of haphazard training he received was a grossly inadequate and inept preparation for the priesthood. The mausoleum of St Aidan's was presided over by one F. B. Heiser who, though a good man, was grim, inarticulate and cold. Treacy could never feel affection for the College even though he later spoke well of it and supported it publicly. But privately he wrote, 'It suffered from being situated in the suburbs of an industrial town. The buildings had no atmosphere whatever. The students, like myself, were all non-graduates, with the result that the intellectual activity of the place was almost non-existent. The staff of nine tutors were nice men but lacked the ability to arouse intellectual curiosity, or to give that personal attention which I so badly needed.'

Treacy was not popular at St Aidan's, partly because he tended to 'bulldoze' and partly because he refused to take part in the initiation ceremony!! If he had thought that the evening classes of King's College, London, following a day's work were a hectic time, they were nothing compared with the Shrewsbury

House-Birkenhead shuttle service. It was the most exhausting period of a too hectic life. This is how he remembers it:

'I would cycle through the Mersey Tunnel from Liverpool to St Aidan's for lectures at 9am; after lunch I would cycle back to Liverpool to do my work at the Club in the afternoon; then back again for a lecture after tea, returning to the Club for the evening. Shall I ever forget that grind through the fumes of the Mersey Tunnel pushing that bicycle up the hill?

'My memory of those months is that they were hell. They certainly tested my vocation. More than once, I nearly threw in the towel, but my native stubbornness prevailed, and I struggled with my General Ordination Examination (GOE).

'Was the Church right to allow such preparation for the Ministry? I am quite sure that it would never be tolerated today. I am equally sure that if the Bishop of Liverpool had not given his approval to this kind of training, I should never have been ordained. I owe Bishop David an enormous debt for his kindness and encouragement.

'My academic achievements may have been of a low order but I gained in other ways from the labours of those days. It toughened me and gave me a sense of intellectual inferiority which remains with me to this day, which has been a constant stimulus to compensate by wide reading for what I lacked during my time as a student. I think I can say that I have overcome any jealousy I may have had for those who passed smoothly from school to university to theological college.'

The disfiguring scars of St Aidan's always showed on Treacy. The training underscored rather than erased his lack of academic qualifications. It was a nonsense of a training. James Hill remembers Treacy rushing off to St Aidan's from the Mission 'though as often something prevented him from going. Most of his reading, such as it was, was done late at night after the Club had closed and there were frequent occasions when he would wake up in his chair at about 4am with his book open, but unread on his lap.' Bishop Roger Wilson recalls an occasion of exhaustion at Shrewsbury School: 'He had had a packed evening in the School and thereafter had stayed up with his host until long after midnight; when he staggered up to his bedroom he was dog tired — and woke up two hours later still on his knees by his bedside after an abortive attempt to say his prayers.'

Tiredness was a constant companion throughout his life for he always carried on *con spirito*. All was *vivace: andante* was an unknown pace to him.

In 1932 Bishop David, of his mercy, decided that Treacy should be made deacon. He had failed one of the two sets of junior examinations at Trinity 1931 and was excused the other set of Michaelmas 1931. He was 'let through' rather than 'got through'. It was agreed that he should serve his title at the Parish Church of Liverpool, Our Lady and St Nicholas, combining the assistant curacy with his work at Shrewsbury House. At first sight this appeared to be a good arrangement. St Nicholas was only a mile and a quarter from the Mission and there were two other curates and a lady worker on the staff which meant that Treacy would not be needed for parochial duty. There would be the opportunity of preaching occasionally to a congregation other than club boys, and it would give him the companionship of other clergy.

Treacy was made deacon in Liverpool Parish Church on 21 February 1932 by Herbert Gresford Jones, Bishop Suffragan of Warrington. Gresford Jones became a friend to Treacy, who remembers him as:

'An old-fashioned evangelical, a man of great simplicity and considerable spiritual depth. He was something of a snob but in such a nice way that no one minded. (His critics dubbed him "Gushford"). He was a warm person who responded naturally to people and situations.

'Mrs Gresford Jones (Lily) remains our most fragrant memory of the Liverpool Diocese. She was to us the dearest friend. Wherever she went she took peace and grace with her. She had a lovely sense of humour and could bring sunshine into the darkest corners. Somehow, troubles and worries seemed to dissolve in her presence, not because she minimised them, but because she lived so close to God that she helped one to feel that all things *must* work together for good. It was a joy to hear her twitting her husband. Dear Herbert was occasionally given to pomposity, but he was quickly shaken out of it if Lily was about.

'I remember one afternoon when I (with May) was driving to a Speech Day at Darley Dale School. It was a hot day, and as we passed a Walls Ice Cream tricycle I suggested that she should "stop and buy some". The idea clearly did not appeal to his lordship, but it did to Mrs Bishop. So we stopped and bought three ice creams which we consumed with hilarious pleasure, what time the Bishop passed from disapproval to envy. We arrived at the destination, three of us sticky and the Bishop with his dignity intact.'

Bishop Gresford Jones belonged to the epoch of the 'gentleman-in-holy-orders' — 'gentleman' in the social sense. Most of these men came from prosperous mercantile families whose wealth derived from the Industrial Revolution. They had been to public school and graduated at Oxford or Cambridge. They took their place naturally amongst the gentry and the wealthy. Their hobbies and interests were those of the cultured. Many of them had private means, therefore they were not concerned over much with stipends or expense allowances. They could be charming and sometimes intolerably aloof. Treacy had mixed feelings about them, a kind of critical admiration for them, as he reflects: 'Frankly, they were snobs, with ears acutely tuned to accents, and eyes that missed little in the way of manners. To the poor, they were kindly, sympathetic, but they did not see the gulf between the rich and poor as something contrary to the will of God. The gulf was unfortunate, inevitable and needed bridging rather than eliminating.'

It is easy to criticise this generation of churchmen now. Even if they accepted the world of poverty and hardship as part of the fixed order of things, they did at least tackle the work that had to be done in the more squalid areas of big cities. The critics may call it 'slumming' but they made their homes amongst the poor, they brought up their families in the surroundings of poverty and even if they were not troubled by thoughts of identification, they shared the lives of those to whom they ministered. Today when a new breed of clergymen is full of talk and emphasis on service and identification there is a parallel unwillingness to serve humbly and gladly in the worst of the inner city areas.

Running concurrently with Treacy's emergence in a dog collar was Cupid's dance. He was rising 24 in 1931 and had not had much time for the opposite sex.

He was sensitive to their charms and was himself a charmer with more than a pinch of the Irish variety too. He recalls the period:

'I put the idea of marriage out of my mind, because I had nothing to offer a wife. £3 a week, two rooms in a Liverpool slum, and, as far as I could see, no future. I certainly wasn't particularly eligible, and clearly this view was shared by the few people I knew in Liverpool, judging by the lack of invitations to meet any suitable candidates for my hand.

'The squash pro at the Adelphi Hotel was a comely young woman, but in spite of considerable efforts on my part, and playing an awful lot of squash, I failed to make any impression at all. Perhaps my squash was too bad.

'What was a young man to do in his spare time? Rugby football and cricket were "out" because I had to spend my Saturday afternoon cheering on the Club sides or running weekend camps. Shortage of money ruled out theatres and concerts, as did lack of time. Pubs I abominated. I didn't dance.'

One Sunday in 1931 Treacy was lunching with Arthur Snell, a member of the Liverpool branch of the Toc H. The sequence of events is best related by Treacy himself:

'Lunch over, Arthur said that we had been invited to the Shone's in Hoylake and he hoped I would go for he wanted me to meet one of the daughters called May.

'Now, I had heard tell of Miss May Shone, and what I had heard interested me. She was much involved in voluntary social work in Liverpool, and had quite a supporters club amongst the young lawyers who assisted with the Poor Man's Lawyer panel run by the Personal Service Society. So when Arthur made this suggestion I thought "Why not?" We went to Hoylake and my fate was sealed, although I little knew how crucial this meeting was going to be.

'I remember how fascinated I was with this young woman. She had style. She had grace. She was gay, and had a marvellous gift, which has never left her, of making people feel they are important to her. For once the reports I had heard of her only told half of it. More than once I had heard "rave" notices of some young woman, only to be sadly disappointed when introductions had taken place.

'Well, there I sat gazing at her. Yes, the bell had rung, the penny had dropped. This was it. At least it was for me; the important question was, had I made any sort of impression? I suppose other people's love sagas are pretty tedious to those who are not themselves involved. Enough of this but to say that a succession of meeting in Liverpool cafes, walks in the streets of the north end of Liverpool, telephone calls, led to a moment on Sunday 15 February 1931 at 5.30pm when I proposed marriage and was, to my amazement, accepted.'

Treacy was shocked as well as amazed for, as he recorded in his war journal: 'Thurs Feb 15 1945. The anniversary of my engagement. A wholly unpremeditated act which was most surprisingly accepted on the spot!'

The proposal to May took place in a bed sitting room in the house of a Mrs O'Hagan in Great Mersey Street, in which May was lodging in order to live in the area in which she was doing her social work.

The Shone family was a large one. May had three brothers, two sisters and a host of aunts and cousins scattered on Merseyside. Treacy notes:

'Papa Shone [James Arthur Shone] was a flour miller, and a very good one. He was a magistrate and a member of the Mersey Docks & Harbour Board. He was a devoted, but not bigoted, Methodist. He died rich in years in 1949 at the age of 84. He was a simple man, in the best sense, enjoying above everything, the pleasures of his home and a vast gramophone. To the end of his days he taught in the Sunday School. I found him reserved and, at first, difficult to know but with the passing of time I came, first to respect him as a man of profound integrity and deep Christian faith. Then I came to have a deep affection for him as a wise counsellor and a man who had discovered the secret of living. He was a happy man because he "counted his blessings day by day" and found joy in the simple things of life. It was true of him that the pure in heart shall see God.

'This inter-family relationship was pretty one-sided. May (christened Mary Leyland) had, what seemed to me an enormous family, whereas all I had to show was a sister, an aunt and a widowed mother.

'I had Thursday night off from the Club and on successive Thursdays I did the grand tour from uncles to aunts, cousin to cousin. I did my best to be a credit to May but I fancy that they were rather disappointed that she hadn't done better for herself. However, she, bless her, didn't think that she could — and that was all that mattered. Before I came on the scene she had held at bay a Member of Parliament and a wealthy solicitor, both of whom could have offered her much more in the way of creature comforts than I could.'

Whatever the Shone family thought of Treacy there was the formidable prospect for May of meeting Mrs Treacy. Fortunately Treacy had loosened if not severed the strangling cord when he left London for Liverpool so Mrs Treacy had only to be faced, not overcome. If Treacy expected his mother to be vituperative and vindictive he was not disappointed. May, for her part, was marvellously graceful and understanding when confronted by the adversarial prospective mother-in-law. Treacy's sister reflects:

'Eric's sense of duty was highly developed — never did he waver — though his patience was sorely tried. He tried, how he tried, to show his filial affection for my mother, but he was everlastingly rebuffed. Nothing pleased her. No son ever tried harder — no daughter-in-law ever stood beside her husband as May did, who received insults and hurts which she bore nobly because of her love for her husband.'

Life at Shrewsbury House continued to be hectic and now Treacy was engaged and a curate at the Parish Church. The Rector of Liverpool was John C. H. How, later to become Bishop of Glasgow and Galloway and Primus of the Scottish Episcopal Church. He had a great reputation as a speaker, a retreat conductor and trainer of curates. Unfortunately Treacy missed the 'training' for John How was often away as he was in great demand outside the parish. Further, although Treacy was on his staff he was not of it. Whenever How wanted him he seemed to be at Shrewsbury or involved at the Mission. It was a part-time curacy on a nominal stipend. Once again Treacy was not receiving adequate training. Nevertheless there were three things he learned at Liverpool Parish Church which were of value to him throughout his ministry.

Treacy learned from John How the importance of a tidy altar when celebrating the Holy Communion. Very sound foundations were laid in the strict observance of the Daily Offices. Every morning at 7am the staff were on parade in Church for Matins, followed by the Eucharist and every evening at 5.30 for Evensong.

The importance of the use of a Church school was stressed. Treacy had to take his share of opening worship and then spend half an hour teaching in the school. He did not find this easy, as he recalls:

'There was never a morning that I did not exhaust my material within 20 minutes, which meant that I had to fill in the last 10 minutes with some sort of entertainment, which often got so badly out of hand that the Headmaster had to come to the rescue. This experience gave me an understanding of, and admiration for, the work of the teacher. There were mornings that I thought the bell would never ring, and sometimes the noise in my class was so overpowering that I shouldn't have heard it when it did. I owe Croxford, the Headmaster, a great deal for his patience, and for the help he gave me in tackling this weekly incursion into the world of education. How much I taught those kids I don't know, but I soon began to know, and be known by, these youngsters as I walked through the streets of the parish, and this was all gain. Through them, I gained easy and natural entry to their homes.'

Treacy's time at the Parish Church was not trouble free. Within the first few months there were two crises each concerning the Methodist Church. One made him angry, the other hurt him.

There was a thriving Methodist Church in Great Homer Street where the Minister was Douglas Griffiths who became a close friend of Treacy's. Their work overlapped in that the parents of a number of boys at the club worshipped in his church. Treacy was asked to preach at one of the services and John How, though not enthusiastic, gave his permission. Treacy records the ensuing developments:

'Methodists have the unfortunate habit of plastering the front of their chapels with the names of their preachers. My name appeared in large six-inch capitals outside the chapel followed — in brackets — with the description of "Liverpool Parish Church". Then the fat was in the fire. News soon reached St Nicholas and I was summoned by John How and told that I must withdraw. Apparently it was all right if no one knew about it, but all wrong if they did. I felt that, in conscience, I could not break my promise to preach to the Methodists. I was in a difficult position. I was a deacon and under authority, but I could not think how I could explain my withdrawal to the Methodists without presenting my own Church in a very bad light. After all, they knew that I had obtained permission. How could I explain to them that it was only all right provided that it was kept dark.

'I took the course which then seemed right to me, and still does, of telling the Rector that I could not do as he asked, and that, in view of my defiance I must accept the consequences.

'I really thought that this was the end, so I took myself off to see Charles Raven who was in charge of the newly ordained. His advice was to stand my ground and see what happened. "I don't think you will hear any more about it," said Charles Raven. "John How is a kind old thing, and now that you have had the thunder, he'll soon forget it".

'Raven was right in his judgement of How, but not in saying that he would forget. I don't think that he ever did. I can see his point of view. He was the leader of the Anglo Catholic "club" in Liverpool, and it could not have been easy for him having one of his curates preaching in a nonconformist chapel.

'Before long I did something that made matters worse. I married May in St Luke's Methodist Church, Hoylake, on 16 June 1932. This really was a bombshell for the faithful at Liverpool Parish Church. It was made abundantly clear to me that this wasn't a valid marriage. I was even invited to bring May to St Nicholas' for a service of blessing to make it "proper". This was a great sadness to me. The wedding was boycotted by those from St Nicholas' whom we invited. After all, what was more natural? This was May's family church: she and her family had worshipped there all their lives. It was usual for the wedding to take place in the girl's church. This made me very sad. I felt that my own church had been particularly un-loving.'

I should add that May was Confirmed along with some boys of Shrewsbury House by the Bishop Suffragan of Warrington, Herbert Gresford Jones.

The congregation at the Parish Church was an eclectic one. Treacy was rather cynical about people who went to churches other than their own parish church because they liked the form of worship or the preaching. Little did he realise that he would be Vicar of such a parish in Halifax. Of Liverpool Parish Church he commented:

'I suspect that there were many who came because they could avoid being committed. I got this feeling that many of them didn't want to be known, but just to slip away after the services without being grabbed by the clergy. This meant that congregational fellowship was almost non-existent. As a young curate I did not feel, nor did May, that we were taking our place in a closely-knit fellowship. In fact, my memory is that we were almost totally ignored, a fact not unconnected I think with our marriage in a Methodist Church.'

Despite a boyhood background of High Church parishes in London he felt a little out of place at Liverpool Parish Church where the curates rejoiced in the appellation 'Father'. Treacy was frequently disconcerted when hailed as 'Father' in the precincts of Exchange Station by a dozen little urchins.

His troubles were not over yet. He had committed the serious crime of getting married whilst he was yet a deacon. He was under 25 years of age and he had paid for his own training so he did not think that it was anyone's business but his. However, others thought differently and he was left in no doubt that he was in disgrace. He was punished by having a period added to his diaconate so instead of being ordained priest in Lent 1933 it was deferred until Trinity, 11 June 1933 when he was priested by Bishop David in Liverpool Cathedral. But as he said, 'I thought it to be a small price to pay for the happiness of my marriage.'

The marriage at Hoylake may have been boycotted by the Parish Church but it was celebrated by the Shrewsbury School Mission. A party of boys from the Mission attended. Treacy's best man was David Bevan, a Master at Shrewsbury School and then Chairman of the Mission and Boys' Club Committee. The marital oneness of Eric and May — partnership seems too detached a word to use in their special case — was the most crucial factor in his life. Bishop Roger Wilson has some important observations to make on the marriage and Treacy's ordination:

'When in the summer of 1930 Eric came up to London to see me off for work in South Africa (a typically generous gesture) he was an unmarried layman. Two and a half years later I returned to find him ordained and with his wife May installed in the confined quarters of the Missioner's flat. Ordination was the step to which the pastoral care of his boys, rightly, inevitably led. He had given them the faith of a layman, simple, straightforward and ethically directed; but there came a time when, as he confessed to me, he felt the need to "take them all the way". It was a mark of his own spiritual growth over the years as well as a recognition of their need, that he saw this within the communion and fellowship of the church. I have always felt that this desire to take people all the way, and with them "to go unto the altar of God", to be spiritually a comrade in arms rather than to pontificate from on high, was at the heart of his own pastoral ministry. From the fledgling priest in Shrewsbury House to the Bishop in his diocese it was the same.

'In all this, it would be difficult to overestimate what marriage meant to him, not only for the wonderful companionship which May provided, but because she brought with her also another facet of religious life and experience. Liverpool Parish Church, in so far as he was able to share in its life as a part-time curate, was an admirable foundation, a varied, outward-going congregation in the heart of the city, with a strong sensible Catholic tradition. But there was also some conflict inside Eric between order and freedom, discipline and spontaneity. Left to himself he might have found that the urge to be free from formality, following his own exuberant hunches and even his whims, tended to overwhelm any disciplined pattern of life. May, however, was a dedicated Methodist, tender in conscience, well schooled in evangelical piety and altogether, at this stage in their marriage, the stabilising, if not restraining influence. Spiritually as well as temperamentally, they complemented each other. There were some growing pains, even tensions, but the closeness of their companionship, in some way heightened by the sad absence of children, helped to make these creative, and produced a singularly rich partnership of a lifetime.'

Eric and May spent a few days' honeymoon in North Wales, finishing at Shrewsbury but calling at Crewe station en route. Then it was back to the robust and unpredictable life of the School Mission. It was a life without privacy, as their living room was also the Common Room for anyone who was living at, or visiting the Mission. Even their bedroom was open to all and sundry, due to his pre-marriage habit of keeping sports tackle under the bed. One incident was not forgotten by Treacy:

'One night May was preparing to take to her bed when the door burst open, and a club boy, with a muttered "Excuse me, Miss" dived under the bed and emerged with two cricket bats and three sets of pads.

'These were immensely happy days for both of us. One or two of the old Salopian bachelor helpers were not, at first, able to reconcile themselves to having a Mrs Missioner about the place, but with a genius for evoking affection, May soon had them at her feet. She brought a graciousness which was needed to our male establishment. Perhaps her greatest victory was with my housekeeper, Elizabeth MacAlpine, who had mothered me for a couple of years, and who did not take at all kindly to having another woman about the place. After one or two skirmishes she gave up the struggle, with the result that I had to cope with two mothering females with the single intention of keeping me in order.'

There was another incident at the Parish Church more humorous in hindsight than it was annoying at the time. A rumour developed that Treacy was addicted to the bottle and so persistent did it become that he was taxed about it by John How, as Treacy recalls.

' "Of course my dear Treacy" said John How, "I don't believe there is anything in it, but, for your sake, this must be cleared up."

'I was flabbergasted because I had been a teetotaller for at least two years and my strongest tipple was hot sweet tea.

'The explanation was that one of the choristers who came in every Sunday from Wigan, spent the time between morning and evening service in a local hostelry. By the evening, he was well loaded. It so happened that he was the last to file in the choir, and, as the junior member of staff, my place in the procession was immediately behind the choir.

'On our perambulation round the church singing the processional hymn, my chorister friend exhaled a good deal of tainted breath. The congregation, noticing the distinctive aroma, looking for the source, observed this large curate with a shining red face, and jumped to the obvious, but wrong conclusion. They could scarcely be blamed because the chorister was a pale-faced, ascetic looking type who looked as if he existed on a diet of milk. I was less bothered than others to lay this rumour. Perhaps it is, with me, a form of pride, but I have a rooted objection to explaining myself to the sort of people to be found in every congregation who feed on rumours. My own conscience was clear, and that for me was enough. I left it to my rector to say what he thought was necessary.

'I became a teetotaller in 1930, not that I had been a heavy drinker. Actually, I thought beer was a revolting drink. So many people seemed to like it, that I had done my best to appreciate its better charms, but without success. My tastes were more expensive in that I enjoyed good wine.

'When I started youth work it seemed to me that it would be wiser to set an example of total abstinence. So I decided to renounce alcohol. I can't pretend that it was difficult. It is a decision that I have never regretted, and it has saved me a vast amount of money.'

In *Punch* of 22 January 1936 a prohibitionist stated 'Total drunkenness is passing out.' Treacy commented, 'Could he have put it better?'

Gambling was another matter. He regarded it as a social evil. Groups of boys would often establish gambling schools on doorway steps or on the pavement and sometimes when Treacy was writing at his desk in the sitting room, he would hear the clink of coins and voices from the street below. He would then dash from the room, hurtle downstairs and charge out through the front door, causing sudden panic among the boys who would fly off as fast as their legs would carry them.

In Treacy's diary for 2 February 1936 there is an ominous entry:

'Desperately worried today. I found quite by accident last night that practically the whole senior section of the club had been gambling — not only playing cards, but playing for pools at billiards. I blame myself partly for not discovering it earlier. It's an awfully difficult thing to know what to do — punishment scarcely meets the case. As I told them — the real blow lies in the fact that they have betrayed a trust — and that is a thing that can never be assessed by mere punishment. In the end I told them that by far the easiest thing would be to punish them severely — but by far the most difficult thing to do would be not to punish them but to go on trusting them in spite of their behaviour and it was this second course that I was going to take. I put them on their honour never to gamble again. I expect some of them were smiling to themselves and saying that they have got away with it — but let 'em — they haven't; they are merely being slowly reclaimed by Christ's methods — at least I hope that is what it amounts to. One thing is certain, it all started with one boy whom I was lucky enough to spot and expel from the club: but wickedness spreads — and how people hate to stand up for their principles in public!'

As if there were not already an abundance of different activities at the Mission yet more were started after the marriage. May initiated a Mothers' Club and 'The Midgets' for young children. These were highly successful and not without their amusement. May recalls an occasion when Eric was coming back from a football match with the Midgets. It was pouring with rain. He spotted an empty hearse presumably having deposited its contents! Little short of a 'hijack' took place with the result that the hearse drew up at Shrewsbury House with the Midgets in the back.

In many ways the 1930s was the golden age of Clubs and club leaders. Treacy was an outstanding leader with a reputation travelling far outside Liverpool. James Hill puts it well:

'Club membership was very much prized, and to lose it meant losing everything. One result was that a very strong corporate spirit was created in the Club. — The great difference between the modern approach to youth work now and half a century ago, is that today youth centres are places which young people can use, whereas in those days they were places to which boys *belonged*, and which fostered their loyalty and which became the focus and centre of their lives.'

James Hill also refers to the centrality of the Club Chapel to the life of Shrewsbury House:

'One of the most impressive and astonishing things to a visitor would be the change from the noisy and chaotic activity of the Club to the quiet which prevailed in the packed chapel for the two or three minutes of Prayers each evening.
    'In Eric's day the Church Universal was co-terminus with the Club chapel. But if the vision was narrow, it certainly ran deep, and the loyalty engendered then, meant that present day grandfathers still look back at the Club as an anchor and a continuing and enduring influence on their lives.

'Eric always appeared to be the extrovert, slightly larger than life, often rushing in where angels would hesitate to tread, and nearly always the dominant figure in any group. There were therefore occasional inevitable clashes of personalities; but beneath the sometimes rather bombastic "hit or miss" approach, there was deep sensitivity and sympathy, and a humility which outward appearances might obscure.'

Treacy may not have been an easy person for the boys to mimic, but he was certainly hero worshipped by many of them. One boy of the time, John D'Arcy remembers him:

'I was a boy of 13 years of age when I first met Eric Treacy. As a young man he was a crusading evangelist. He had a strong sense of discipline and a hatred of all the social vices. He dealt out punishments to the wrongdoers with a firmness that in these days of laxity would be described as severe. His judgements were fair and his retribution swift.
    'He believed in treating us in an adult manner and always appealed to our sense of responsibility and fair play. I am sure his example had a very big influence on my development. I abhor injustice in any shape or form.
    'I remember that Eric Treacy was concerned about the health of members because in the days before the Health Service and the Welfare State he organised a health survey. I don't know who he recruited to do the check, probably Old Salopian doctors, but all the boys in the club at the time were very thoroughly examined and those who were found wanting were advised on steps to take.'

Treacy's vital and burning spirit inspired his work at Shrewsbury House, and fellow helpers and boys alike recognised in him a true leader. He was continually assessing himself. He had met the challenge of Shrewsbury House 'head on' and if the results of his exhausting work are considered in the light of those searching words of Christ: 'Freely ye have received, freely give,' he had truly served.

5
Impulsive Incumbent

Treacy was beginning to think what should be the next stage of his ministry. He had ceased being attached to the Parish Church in 1934 and thereafter had a general licence to officiate in the Liverpool Diocese. May was engrossed in the Club and in various forms of social work centred on the Mission. She was also a voluntary probation officer and still did some visiting for the Personal Service Society. Treacy was getting restless: 'We were young people and we could stick the pace but I began to long for a place of our own in which we could live a normal married life. We scarcely ever seemed to be alone' — to which might be rather tartly added 'And whose fault was that?'

Ever active but not ever sure, Treacy was reading as much as time would allow but most of his constructive thinking was done on his feet. He continued to be concerned about the appalling conditions in which people lived out their existences.

In 1936 Treacy was 29. His parochial experience was almost nil, limited to what he had overheard rather than experienced at Liverpool Parish Church. Similarly he was but an onlooker of the work of a parish priest. Parochial Church Councils were yet but fiction to him. He needed a second, real and effective curacy under a strong and experienced incumbent. Instead he received a telephone call from the Rector of West Derby asking if he would accept the parish of St Mary, Edge Hill, Liverpool, of which he was patron.

This predominantly working class parish had a population of eleven thousand souls with far too many of them secularly as well as spiritually unemployed. The Church, built in 1813, had a commanding position on a cross roads known as the Edge Hill Lamp. It was the end of the penny fare stage from the centre of Liverpool and looked down the hill known as Paddington, to the University. It was one of Liverpool's best known churches, more for its position than for its performance.

The interior of the Church could not be called beautiful. It was a preaching box with galleries, and a sanctuary stuck on to the east wall.

The two churchwardens, Willie Holmes and Willie Shaw, were, like Zacchaeus, of small stature, but with big hearts. At first they were suspicious of Treacy for he had been at Liverpool Parish Church and he might have a desire to introduce High Church practices at St Mary's. Treacy writes:

'It did not take me long to convince them that I had no intention of changing what I found. I think that they were rather uneasy about my youth, but they weren't half as uneasy as I was. The situation was solved by the fact that they decided to "father" me, and I let them. Together they showed me the ropes and I learned fast. I did not allow them to run me, but when I was not sure of myself I asked them their advice, and never once did they fail me. They were a wonderful couple and I owe them a great deal.'

The Vicarage was the end house of a terrace on a corner round which the trams rattled and squeaked at all hours of the day.

Treacy was Instituted by the Bishop of Liverpool and Inducted by the Archdeacon of Warrington (J. P. Baker) on Friday 10 July 1936. And then?

'The morning after the Institution, I realised that I was on my own and that a start had to be made. Well where did one start? I went into church and said my Matins — then I decided to beat the bounds of the parish on my bicycle, and being Liverpool I did not lack for greetings from postmen, policemen, shopkeepers, women out shopping, the unemployed hanging around the street corners, and railwaymen going to work. There was I in charge of a parish, with minimal preparation for the parochial ministry, feeling my way in an altogether strange world.'

Treacy's first Sunday was not uneventful:

'In the morning I had disposed of the 39 Articles, as by law required, and in the evening I was to deliver my first sermon. Knowing how much can depend upon a vicar's first sermon in a new parish, I had determined that it should be short. In the event, it turned out even shorter than I had intended. After less than ten minutes in the pulpit, I gave out the final hymn. Not a sound came from the organ — the organist signalled helplessly from his post. Then I noticed the verger disappear at speed out of the church, to return in a few moments with an embarrassed organ blower — one of the old characters of Edge Hill, who, in anticipation of a 20 minute sermon, had gone, as was his wont during the time of my predecessor, to the local for a pint. Most of the congregation seemed to know what had happened, and were prepared to give judgement in favour of old West, the organ blower.

'When I saw him after the service, his embarassment had given place to indignation. He obviously thought it indecent that a sermon should last less than 20 minutes "The longer the better" said he, with a malicious wink, "they could do with it".'

Among Treacy's first acts was to deliver personally a letter to every house in the parish introducing himself and indicating that he hoped to pay a personal visit shortly. The Sunday services and weekday activities were listed and he ended, 'I want to ask you not to wait for me to call upon you, before you pay *your* visit to me.' This primary visitation may seem superficial but it yielded rich dividends. The sight of a parson sticking leaflets in letter boxes aroused a good deal of interest. The doors of most of the houses in the parish were permanently open, the children played in the streets, and the women sat on their doorsteps gossiping to each other, and occasionally addressed themselves to their offsprings. In such a setting contacts were easily made by Treacy as he canvassed the streets.

Again he encountered a less appealing sight and his attitude was noticeably different from that he adopted at Shrewsbury House.

'There would be the odd groups of unemployed squatting in a gambling school on a piece of waste land: at first they would disappear the moment I appeared on the

47

scene. I took it as something of a compliment when the time came that they no longer suspended their activities as I passed by. I felt that it meant that I was accepted as part of the local scenery. After all, who was I to condemn them? I with my secure income, my daily work to do. I, with none of the problems of tedium and poverty to face — what right had I to sit in judgement on these chaps for whom every day was one of purposelessness and boredom. Perhaps this gambling, evil as it was, brought some little excitement to them.

'It occurs to me now (1963) — as I look back on those depressed years of the 'thirties — that too many of my generation of clergy — and I must plead guilty — accepted the social evils of those days as something beyond the power of man to alter, and saw it as a situation within which to minister, rather than a situation to be attacked by every means in our power.'

If Treacy could not bring experience to his first living he could and did bring energy and enthusiasm. There was faith and hope, and charity was provided by the parishioners. May and Eric were soon taken to the hearts of their parishioners and a mutual feeling of belonging developed. Liverpudlians are warm-hearted and friendly and, except in those days when bigotry surfaced, inclined to think the best of their clergy until they have good grounds for not doing so. In this, they are noticeably different from Yorkshire people who are slower in giving themselves to strangers. They are more non-committal in their judgements about people until they have good grounds for committing themselves — as Treacy was to find out.

Word had reached Edge Hill from Shrewsbury House that the new Vicar was a wild young man. It is to the credit of Edge Hill parishioners — and to May — that the wildness was harnessed rather than tamed. He hit the parish like a whirlwind. Former parishioners, Mr & Mrs G. Standen, remember the advent of Treacy: 'He soon had a club going for the boys under 16, another for over 16 and we soon had two football teams and two cricket teams going. Then a Girls Club and Girl Guides, and a Boys' Brigade all followed within 12 months. He started a 7am service for cyclists who wished to attend before starting out on Sundays. He always rode a bicycle which had a basket at the front and he and his bike were well known in the district. One day coming back from Edge Hill station, not thinking he rode through the traffic lights on red. Somebody mentioned it to him so he stopped the first policeman he saw and reported himself.' It was not always that way. On a later occasion he was returning from a bird watching trip with Charles Raven. Treacy the fearless driver jumped a long queue of cars crawling into Liverpool and was 'run in' by the police!

When Treacy wanted something he persisted until he got it. At Edge Hill his first agitation was for a curate and he got one in 1937. He was David Mercier, now in New Zealand, who has vivid memories of his time with Treacy. Fussy matters of churchmanship always went clean over Treacy's head but at Edge Hill he had an unusual way of dealing with them as David Mercier recalls:

'The Church had had a strong Evangelical tradition, and the previous Vicar (William Ingles — who had moved to Mallerstang in Westmorland) had unwisely tried to raise its ritual standards without securing the cooperation of his people. He incurred the bitter opposition of many of the congregation led by the two churchwardens. Opposition centred on such apparently innocuous matters as candles on the altar and the celebration of Holy Communion from an eastwards-facing position. Such things were regarded as Roman and therefore suspect.

'Eric set out to rebuild the spirit of unity and fellowship in the parish, sadly eroded during the previous incumbency and to show that these liturgical trappings, which had taken on such a sinister role to the people, were quite unimportant in comparison with the true spirit of worship. So he sometimes had one candle, sometimes two and sometimes none at all. Sometimes he celebrated Holy Communion facing East, and sometimes from a Northward position. I'm sure that if there had been any other position in use he would have tried it! The congregation never quite knew what to expect next, but they came to realise that what was done was in the interests of true worship and so they accepted it as they accepted him. The atmosphere of the Church improved greatly, and St Mary's became once again the homely and beloved mother of her people in Edge Hill.

'Eric was a very interesting and exciting person to work alongside. He was so likeable and full of fun, and so interested in people and their real needs. He was completely free of all pomposity and clericalism, and in fact was rather like an overgrown schoolboy.'

Treacy's impact on the parish was immediate whether in the pulpit or in the streets or on the platform. People who only heard him preach after the war would scarcely have recognised the prewar harangues, a term he would not have disowned. 'The worst mistake was my conviction that I had the gift of tongues, which led me to preach and speak passionately on a variety of subjects with the minimum of preparation. What my sermons lacked in substance I made up for in noise and wind. And the frightening thing was that I achieved something of a reputation as a preacher, and received invitations to preach here, there and everywhere.'

James Hill kept a diary at the time and the following extract confirms Treacy's preaching tendencies.

'Sunday October 4 1936. Went into Liverpool after chapel (Shrewsbury Mission) to service at St Mary's Edge Hill. Sat with May. Eric took it and looked very tired at the end of an impossibly hard day. It was his eighth service, and after that he had a meeting and had to visit the Infirmary again. It's fantastic the amount he's doing. Can't afford a curate [ie before Mercier's appointment] and does as much as an ordinary vicar and three curates. At it at full pressure all day and most of the night. I don't see how he can go on. It was the Harvest Festival Service, and the Church beautifully decorated. Eric preached very well. He can. He didn't say all that he meant to, but got quite carried away. It was about thanks and service. I don't know how his voice lasts. He had to go and get a drink out of the font before his sermon.'

Like many an extempore preacher Treacy was in great danger of finishing before he stopped. Occasionally he would flail around searching for that final sentence which seemed to elude him. It was ever his practice from the war onwards if he had only a short time in which to prepare a sermon to spend it on preparing the end.

He was a vigorous rather than a diligent visitor. It went in sustained bouts but he collected and collated much information about the people of the parish and kept a careful card index. He recruited parish couriers who were not only Vicar's look-outs to report cases of sickness or other needs, but also beacons of Christ in the parish. Visiting brought another dimension to his ministry. He always held hospital chaplaincy work in deep regard. He was made Chaplain to Liverpool Royal Infirmary. The pastoral care of the dying was new to him and was both a privilege and a blessing. He always remembered his first experience of this ministry to an old St Mary's chorister:

'Charlie Thomas was dying of throat cancer. This was the first time that I had to brace myself to visit a man who was dying — and knew it. I went to him, apprehensive as to what I should find — would he be bitter? Would he detect my grievous inexperience and, perhaps, resent my attempt to minister to him?

'How baseless my worries were. Charlie Thomas ministered more to me than I to him. I found courage, faith and humour in that sick room. As his life drew to its end, his faith glowed like a bright light; no complaining in that room, only gratitude. My memory of him is not of a body ravaged by disease, but of a spirit unconquered.'

The memory of another Edge Hill Christian never left him: 'Clara Clarke at the Girls' Home. She was truly a saint of God — one of his chosen vessels. A little woman with a great heart and a burning faith in her Lord — and in the essential goodness of the girls in her care. May and I have never met again the likes of her. Her peace and dignity — one who lived very close to her Master. She remains a standard by which we still judge other people today.'

The overwhelming single quality that Treacy brought to Edge Hill and which informed all his actions was dynamism. As at Shrewsbury House activity was vigorous and unceasing. Two further brief extracts from James Hill's diary give the flavour and recreate two not untypical days:

'Wednesday October 7 1936. Took the Day Boys back in the evening and went on to Liverpool. Sat talking with May and Rees sometime before supper. Eric was down at Shrewsbury. I don't know how he gets through all he does. He never has five minutes to himself and never has an afternoon off. The Infirmary in itself must be a full time job. Rees thinks that if he did a bit less, he might really do more. He thinks it is not really economical, going at it so hard all the time. But I don't know what else he can do. He never says "No" to anyone, and there is so much to be done. His engagements often overlap one another. He rushed back from Shrewsbury and grabbed his dog collar and rushed from the house again putting it on as he went, to be at a Confirmation class which started before his train was even due at Lime Street. He had no supper of course and May took some down to one of his meetings. It's like that all the time. I'm sure he's the hardest working parson in England. How he writes his sermons etc Lord knows. I think May finds it a bit much trying to keep him in hand and do her work. Edge Hill is certainly a different place since he came.'

'Sunday March 7 1937. Went into tea with May and Eric in the afternoon. Had a very good tea and talked. Eric was playing hymns on the piano and I washed up the tea things with May, while Eric finished his sermon and shaved. What a queer household! Went to St Mary's for the evening service. Eric preached about Judgement and the sure fact that we *would* be judged, and in a sense we judged ourselves here and now by our everyday lives. Michael came afterwards and took us down to the Club, where Eric was talking again. Eric insisted on racing us there on his bike much to May's alarm and annoyance! He spoke well about Power. We all have immense power and it is so often misused. It may not be because we happen to control a lot of people under us, but the fact we have power to make someone's life happy or unhappy shows us what an almost alarming store we have. There was a lot more and it was very good.'

The parochial activities flourished. Boys' Brigade camps at Abergele were riotous affairs except for one tragic incident when a parishioner who had gone to cook for them sliced his hand off in the bread machine on the first day. The Men's Club football team was possessed of more enthusiasm than skill. Treacy would arrive on his bicycle with the half time lemons at a variety of grounds, all of which had one thing in common — that they were half an hour's hard cycling from the Vicarage. A Literary and Philosophical Society thrived though its lively meetings suggested debate and philanthropy rather than literature and philosophy.

Treacy wanted to put Edge Hill on the map! He did so by the sheer force of his energy and personality. Church of England life in Liverpool was weak in the industrial areas. The Anglican church-going belt existed in Mossley Hill, Allerton, Sefton Park, Waterloo and Great Crosby. Here there were thriving parishes with large congregations under good priests who made the most of their opportunities. In the poorer areas of the city, churches were not well attended and the clergy had tough jobs. It is commonplace today to emphasise the serving and servant aspects of the priest's ministry. For Treacy as a parish priest only one word sufficed — leadership.

One additional ministry required of Treacy, in common with other clergy in the City of Liverpool, was officiating at the city cemeteries for three weeks in each year at funerals which were 'without benefit of clergy'. He exercised this ministry with very great care but, as he recalls, it was not easy:

'This was a most depressing business. The vestries at those municipal cemeteries were miserable places, as were the chapels in which the burial service was conducted. They were "Local Authority" provisions at the worst, and I wonder now why we clergy as a body did not unite to insist that the cemetery chapels were given something of the attractive comforts that belonged to the Town Hall, where the Lord Mayor and city councillors did their business in a setting of cut glass light fittings, mahogany furnishings and thick pile carpets. Often, there would be as many as four coffins, and a large number of attendant mourners in the chapel, after which the coffins would be carried to the graves which were usually separated from each other by considerable distances. The officiating minister would take the committal at each grave, moving from one to the other as quickly as possible in order that the mourners at the last grave should not be kept waiting too long. Such an arrangement made it almost impossible to have any pastoral or personal relation with the mourner.'

Alas, the times have not brought about any dramatic improvement in a self-evident scandal. On the other hand we have not travelled down the sickening slope to the American way of bereavement and burial where the reality of death is camouflaged and the Christian certainties are cushioned in lavishly furnished funeral parlours against a gushy background of soothing music. Death has lost its sting!

David Mercier remembers Treacy's crematoria ministry:

'He had a special compassion for the bereaved. Some clergy regarded this as an unpleasant chore, to be got over as expeditiously as possible. Eric disagreed strongly. He felt that there were special opportunities to reach out and help those in great need, and the fact that we had never known them was irrelevant. So we always tried to give each service as much warmth and meaning as possible. From occasional letters I received I can personally vouch for the fact that some at least were helped by our ministrations on these occasions.'

Much of this work, no less and no more, was that which fell to countless parochial clergy in the urban areas of England. For Treacy 'it was a rich and full life, deeply satisfying, refreshing in spite of the fact that the physical output was heavy. The refreshment derived from the fact that all the time one was dealing with people.'

Treacy's formed personality and gathering character were more clearly discernible at Edge Hill than at Shrewsbury House. Yet to the perceptive onlooker there were many question marks. What was the intellectual habit of the fluent preacher? What foundation of knowledge sustained his incessant speaking? What were the books which fed his mind, and marked out the courses of his thinking? Was he a hard student, or a steady reader, or merely a dabbler in ephemeral literature? How far did he draw water from contemporary pools?

There are many accounts to certify the variety and humour of his conversation, the reckless charm of his personality, the ruthless nature of his temperament, and what might be termed his 'Irishness'; but good talkers and popular preachers are not always learned or even well read, and there is certainly something in the distraction of frequent talking, public and private, which is unfavourable to severe standards of knowledge and accuracy. It may be asked therefore what particular gift or developing skill emerged at Edge Hill. The answer is simple. Treacy had emerged as a communicator. Prior to Edge Hill he had been chiefly concerned with boys. Edge Hill projected him on to a wider stage. He communicated as effectively with his journalistic hand as he did with his vocal chords. It was a circle beginning and ending with *people*. This is what remains in David Mercier's mind:

'I have always considered myself very fortunate to have begun my clerical life with a man like Eric. He was a big man in every sense of the word. Not by any means the traditional parson, he was a real lover of his fellow man, and for that reason was probably a more effective instrument in the Church's work than his more orthodox counterpart. There was something of the Good Samaritan about him — a Samaritan who was also a churchman, which the original may or may not have been — and certainly more of the Good Samaritan than of the Priest or the Levite. In any case I cannot imagine him ever "passing by on the other side".'

It did not take Treacy long to learn how to gain the maximum publicity for his views. As early as at Edge Hill he found himself quoted in the local and national press and mentioned on the radio. There is little doubt that he sought publicity for his views even though he would feign surprise when he received it. A list of his pungent pieces and the controversies of the period would be a tedious undertaking. Three are selected for mention here.

Treacy's lifelong affiliation with the Rotary Movement had a stormy birth at Liverpool. He was asked to speak at one of their meetings in August 1937 and chose juvenile courts as his subject. His practice for preparation altered little over the years. Research and speech were undertaken and prepared at the last moment. In fact he bicycled to see various police constables on his way to the actual meeting. He was less carrying out research than seeking confirmation of his previously formed views. In the course of his speech he said:

'Our present juvenile courts are a hindrance to social progress. What happens to the young offender? He is taken down to nice kind magistrates who are supposed to understand children. But the young offenders are not punished but told to be good boys and join the Scouts. Young offenders are leaving the juvenile courts laughing at the magistrates and the police.

'Twenty years of the dole has meant the softening of the will of parents and a complete lack of control over boys and girls . . . I maintain that the modern boy is a healthy animal who has two vulnerable spots — his belly and his buttocks. If you punish either of these spots it will take effect.

'By the way we are going on I think there will come a time when a boy ordered to be birched will demand an anaesthetic.'

Treacy advocated a greater use of the birch and thought that the policeman on the beat might be allowed to carry a small cane.

The speech occupied a great deal of space in all the national newspapers and sparked off a vociferous debate in Liverpool itself. Counter speeches were made taking "Thrash-em Treacy" to task, and he found himself in the position of having to defend his views. Support outweighed attack. Anyone entering the public arena of debate must expect to be misunderstood occasionally and to receive the homage of people whose own views would make the speaker shudder. The insidious, when not slightly ridiculous, 'silent majority' is not a creation of the 1970s. They have ever been the apathetic writ gross, whose latent strength resides in their plausible anonymity. Suddenly, Treacy had a following of illiberal hangers and floggers. Correspondence in support reached him from all the expected quarters and with sentiments of which the following is typical. 'Hail to the parson for having the courage to tell the truth! It is time we cleared our minds of this gump about kind words etc. Boys know jolly well when they are doing wrong — and they always did — and real reform is injured, not helped, by the stuff being poured out just now, mostly from frank or disguised leftists, whose politics I sympathise with and usually approve, but whose namby-pamby ideas I find the hardest part of their creed to swallow.'

Replying to his critics in a sermon at Edge Hill, Treacy underlined that punishment 'is never an end in itself, otherwise it would be inexcusable and degrading to the child and to the giver. It is a means to an end; a stage in the training of the child. It is impossible, in every age of life, to escape the consequences of any act. Repeated escapes from the consequences of his actions causes a boy to grow up a selfish, useless and lawless member of society.'

Schoolgirls did not escape the verbal lash when he spoke at a weekend conference of youth club workers at Heswall, Wirral, 'Schoolgirls subject many decent boys to temptation. It has amazed me to see the precocity of the average schoolgirl. Girls develop in the poorer districts at an alarmingly early age, and they are a real menace to many decent boys.' He had a solid layer of Puritanism in him which was pronounced on such matters as sex. He even condemned the game of 'tig' when played by boys and girls though what he was expecting to happen is not revealed.

Reporters regularly attended St Mary's, looking up to be fed. They were rarely sent empty away. Another major debate was triggered off by Treacy's suggestion that schools for marriage should be set up in Liverpool to instruct young couples in the responsibilities and meaning of married life. He advocated the formation of panels for each district consisting of representatives of the churches and the medical profession, who would undertake to conduct a series of classes on the physical and spiritual sides of marriage, and advise on how to run a house. The galloping increase in divorce cases had led Treacy to voice his views. He attended many meetings in support of his proposals and perhaps with greater perseverance he might have succeeded in achieving what he advocated. Unfortunately his fertile mind was too active in too many directions and he moved on to other subjects.

In 1939 he contributed to the national debate concerning the evacuation of children. He gave expression to his feelings in many places but chiefly in a letter to *The Times* (3 October) and by an article in *Tit Bits* (28 October). His article touched on a number of his experiences:

'The evacuation of great numbers of school-children (and in some cases their mothers) from our large cities to country districts will have brought into close contact the inhabitants of two different worlds. I fear that there may be at first a measure of quite inexcusable misunderstanding and hastiness of judgement on the part of those who are acting as hosts to these young people.

'Already I have heard of certain country dwellers who express themselves as appalled at the behaviour of the evacuated children. Having myself had several years' experience of the children of a large industrial city, I feel able to set out something of the background and living conditions of these boys and girls.

'It must be remembered that the size of families in the poorer quarters of our cities is usually in inverse proportion to the living accommodation. It is not unusual to find as many as six to eight children living with their parents in a four-roomed house. This inevitably means that in order to relieve the congestion the children are sent out to play on their own in the parks and streets.

'Years of this produce in the child an extraordinary self reliance and artfulness — and a morality which is sometimes not far short of jungle law.

'Those of us who are fortunate enough to possess property, even in the smallest degree, must remember that to a certain extent, our respect for other's property is based on our desire for their respect of our own; the corollary to this is that those who have possessed very little (not even toys of their own as children) will treat with scant respect the rights and property of others.

'... Many housewives in the receiving areas must have been surprised to find the scant appreciation which was accorded to the food with which they provided their visitors. We must remember that in many cases the children from the cities have existed on a diet of strong tea, chipped potatoes well soaked in fat, and thick hunks of bread plastered with dripping or margarine.

'Fresh milk, eggs, butter, salads are all too often items unknown in the diet of poorer children, and are consequently little appreciated when supplied.

'Personal cleanliness and refined habits are taken for granted among those who have been fortunate enough to live in houses in which the necessary sanitary equipment is provided.

'It must be remembered that in the more congested quarters of our big cities many houses do not possess a lavatory or a bathroom of their own — consequently the street is often used as the former, while washing is considered as one of the least important of the duties of man.

'I have no doubt that a certain crudity of expression on the part of the children will have manifested itself by now. The apparently bad language of the slum children is due partly to a lack of vocabulary, and secondly to the fact that certain words have long ceased to have any specific meaning to those who use them.

'It is well to remember the background and environment of city children — busy streets with a constant stream of traffic, a cinema almost every 100 yards, fish and chip shops, ice-cream vendors, street rows, an occasional street accident, the camaraderie of a street in which, often, the majority of the inhabitants are related by inter-marriage — all of which is in such sharp distinction to the peaceful and uneventful atmosphere of the country that it is small wonder that at first many of these young people find it hard to adjust themselves.

'It is not my purpose to excuse habits and conditions which are anything but ideal — but (on the assumption that "to know all is to forgive all") to set before those whose remoteness from the towns will have prevented them from obtaining first-hand knowledge of the conditions under which so many of their young guests have had to live.

'This knowledge may perhaps be the means of creating the necessary understanding between these town and country people.'

There was a great deal of charitable activity in Liverpool at this period and the voluntary social services were outstandingly progressive. Leading the Personal Service Society was Miss Dorothy Keeling. Treacy knew her from the time that he had enticed away one of her best voluntary workers — May! Dorothy Keeling and Treacy clashed on many occasions, both in public and in private, for she abhorred Treacy's views on corporal punishment. But he admired her strength of purpose, her prodigious capacity for work, her burning concern for the underprivileged and her skill at collecting first rate people to work for her. She neither suffered fools gladly nor tolerated the condescension of those who did good works as those who conferred favours.

There were men like Sir Sidney Jones, thrice Lord Mayor, and Sir John Shute, to whom wealth and position were a stewardship. They established the work of the Liverpool Boys' Association which had one Ernest Humble as its General Secretary. Dorothy Keeling and Ernest Humble were wholly dedicated people. They were examples of the principle that the people who have the power to create movements are people who possess a kind of emotional ruthlessness that makes them independent of other people's good opinions and enables them to move towards their goal regardless of the number of people they offend on the way. Here lies the significant difference between Treacy and such people. He was not a man of and for movements. He was an individualist and strove hard to be one. Despite certain superficial signs to the contrary he did care what people thought of him. He wanted to be both controversial and popular, the one sustaining the other. This he achieved to a remarkable degree. Paradoxically his later gift of reconciliation grew from this conflict.

There was an impulsive recklessness about Treacy at Edge Hill. His restless energy was proverbial. There was little time for reflection and none for post-mortems. Action was the watchword. If one was not continually advancing then one was automatically retreating. It was difficult to move at his pace, impossible to keep in step. He was to change in some respects in the coming years, but some constants had surfaced at Edge Hill. Canon J. P. Newell, a former Headmaster of Bradford Grammar School and the King's School, Canterbury, knew Treacy from Shrewsbury House days until his death. He was moved to preach about Treacy in Canterbury Cathedral on 3 September 1978 taking as his text 'Make full proof of thy ministry' (2 Timothy 4.5). Treacy lived that text and Canon Newell's words could have referred to him equally at Edge Hill and at Wakefield:

'I saw in him a pattern and a standard for what the clergyman may be, not fanciful or idealised but robust, rugged and rough-cast, in his concern for people, in the range of his interest, in his firm grasp of the simplicities of the faith, in his forthright and independent views and in the fullness of his own warm personality. He indeed was one who made full proof of his ministry.'

6
Lime Street Cutting

About one mile from St Mary's Church was the Edge Hill Motive Power Depot of the London Midland and Scottish Railway. Threading the centre of the parish was the Lime Street cutting up which trains thundered from Lime Street Station on their journeys to London, Newcastle, Hull and South Wales. The smoke they emitted hung heavily over the streets of the parish.

It was here that Treacy was provided with the two components which led to a hobby of and for a lifetime, giving him deep satisfaction and international recognition. On the one hand there was photography. A seaport like Liverpool, with its Pier Head, river, docks and the vistas from the heights of Everton, presented endless opportunities for the photographer. Treacy had always been interested in photography and not in merely a casual way. Not for him the button pusher loading up with film and banging away at everything with no eye for composition, or of accumulating a vast number of pictures of no lasting value.

In 1932 he began to apply his photography to railways and mountains. Any specialist photographer is like a game hunter who knows what he wants to get and plans accordingly. He is never satisfied with the results, which is the great urge behind the hobby. So it was less the sea and the physical contours of Liverpool that drew him but the smell, the noise, the dirt and the atmosphere of the steam engine. He wrote:

'I doubt if there was any more impressive setting for the steam engine at work than the long cutting from Lime Street Station. It reminded me of the nave of some great cathedral with its succession of high arches. The trains plunged straight into it from the platform end of the station. With regulators wide open, a long cut-off, and sanders working, the locomotives went slowly up the hill, their exhaust echoing against the cavernous walls of the cutting.

'There was a wonderful interplay of light and shade, made mysterious by the mist of steam and smoke which could not escape from the depths of the cutting.'

Treacy left Liverpool before electrics whipped up the hill at 50 miles an hour.

Treacy's regular visits to Shrewsbury School gave him other opportunities for steam sniffing. In his diary for 30 June 1936 he records:

'Perhaps fortunately I missed my connection at Crewe on my way back from Salop. I had a very happy hour on Crewe station watching the trains. Nothing gives me greater pleasure or deeper satisfaction than the sight of a modern express locomotive — I sometimes fear that it may be a materialistic side of my nature that is so deeply stirred by the mass of metal so often shrouded in steam. Today I saw the Royal Scot arrive and depart at Crewe. She was drawn by one of the LMS latest Pacific engines; she glided so gently to a standstill: she looked so graceful and shining: but how different her departure. No more gracious and polished — but now a vicious monster belching out a cloud of steam out of which the engine emerged looking bigger than ever, roaring like some fantastic dragon. Verily a sight for the gods!'

Although Treacy began his photographic hobby with a Box Brownie the first camera he would admit to owning was a Soho $\frac{1}{4}$plate reflex with a swing front, which he purchased second hand. The difficulty with that camera was that focusing was awkward and needed at least five minutes' notice before it took a picture! This was before the railways were ready and willing to 'oblige' for Treacy. Later one wondered if *Bradshaw* was planned around Treacy's photographic itinerary.

In 1936 when Treacy left the crowded streets of Scotland Road to become

Vicar of St Mary's, Edge Hill the other dimension to his hobby disclosed itself. The Edge Hill Sheds — the old 8A — was a remarkable railway community and it was not long before Treacy numbered drivers and firemen among his friends, as well as signalmen, permanent way men, inspectors and superintendents. The two aspects—men and camera—were to lead to the mini-canonisation in steam of Eric Treacy. The two are inextricably interwoven.

He always regarded the three years leading up to the outbreak of World War II as ones when the performance of the steam locomotive reached its peak. There was healthy competition between the major railway companies, and the four outstanding engineers — Stanier, Gresley, Bulleid and Churchward — were producing some superb and exciting engines. In particular Treacy never forgot a summer's evening at Edge Hill when he spotted 'a magnificent engine with an enormous boiler and a squat chimney and chromium hand rails on the smokebox door. It was the first of Stanier's "Duchess" Pacific - No 6230. What an engine! Surely no more impressive locomotive came out of the steam age?'

Stanier engines always had a special interest for Treacy. He had met Sir William Stanier, whom he regarded as 'a man open to other people's ideas and easy of approach. A simple man in the sense that he never developed that repulsive sophistication which so often goes with success.' Stanier's range was wide. There were the working class 'Black 5s' whose motto Treacy always thought should have been *'Ubique'* like the Royal Regiment of Artillery because they went from Penzance to Thurso and Wick. The 'Black 5s' could travel like the wind on their 6ft driving wheels. They were too numerous to rate as highly in the beauty stakes as the 'Jubilees' but in some ways they were more reliable engines.

It was not long before Treacy was permitted to 'footplate' from Liverpool to Crewe. Sometimes he needed a prayer to sustain him. He reflected:

'I recall some pretty rough rides especially one on a "Baby Scot" which did its best to throw the three of us off the footplate. The noise, clatter and shaking left me deaf and bruised for the rest of the day.

'I remember riding on a "Royal Scot" from Crewe with Lawrie Earl, to whom engine driving was a perpetual joy. I suspect that he rather liked having an audience. That day we hopped it from Crewe at a fantastic pace. At one time, as we came down the hill into Lime Street station, I thought that we should end up in the St George's Hall but we came to a beautiful halt at the buffer stops, ten minutes before anybody expected us!'

Before his days were out Treacy experienced most of the delights and dangers of riding on the footplate. He had been near suffocated in tunnels, shaken to bits and bruised on some piece of run-down machinery. He knew what it was like to have his top end frozen and his bottom end roasted on the footplate. Alas, the weather-beaten faces of railwaymen have vanished for ever.

It was through footplating and forming friendships with railwaymen that Treacy discovered that a steam engine had a life of its own. Outwardly they might be huffing and puffing, dirty or clean, slipping or priming, shunter or special, in shed or station, blasting up hill or coasting down hill. Inwardly, the engine could be a moody devil yet a machine that man could understand and tame, one that would limp home under a firm hand if anything went wrong under the bonnet.

Even its dirt, and that more often than not it was facing the wrong way; even its draughts and evil habit of occasionally blowing back, had to be treated as the higher moods of a creature that had a will and personality of its own and which often defied human efforts to make it behave.

Like a curvaceous woman the steam engine was the right shape for the job. In a chauvinistic way the charm of the engine was that it possessed the quality of capriciousness and though unpredictable it responded to good treatment.

It was the people who had to manage the individual to whom Treacy was drawn in filial affection. The age of steam produced a strong community spirit and loyalty which he found at Edge Hill. He always held that the railwaymen he knew there were amongst the steadiest and most responsible characters he ever knew. Like a mining community, the railways engendered a strong and close comradeship. When tragedy struck the whole community was affected.

In May 1937 two Edge Hill men, driver Ball and fireman Higgins, were on the footplate of a Liverpool express from Euston when, shortly after leaving Euston station, in Primrose Hill tunnel, near Camden Sheds, there was a blow-back of the fire. They were both very badly burned but they stuck to their engine and continued to drive the crowded train safely four miles to Willesden Junction. They walked off the footplate into a waiting ambulance, to die two days later of their burns.

Treacy organised a Memorial Service at St Mary's and later unveiled a commemorative tablet at Edge Hill loco sheds. 'Let us not call these men "Heroes" ', he said, 'so much as men who did their duty according to the best traditions of their company and vocation.' He listed five motives of human behaviour and would not have changed them 40 years later: '(1) Sense of honour. (2) Pride in fine workmanship. (3) Sportsmanship. (4) Love of adventure. (5) Living for the approval of the Highest.'

The corporate attendance of railwaymen at the Memorial Service was so great that they asked Treacy if they could have an annual railwaymen's service. Treacy was only too willing to oblige. He was becoming as well known to the wives and children of the men as to the railwaymen themselves.

Meanwhile his photography was proceeding and improving apace. George Hedgcock was a footplate man at the time and remembers Treacy:

'More as a friend and not a Vicar, except when one of our workmates passed away and then we had the "Reverend Eric Treacy". He would be present whenever he could at all our functions, retirements etc. The London passenger trains would leave Lime Street with a huge loco hauling 400-500 tons and it was a heavy gradient. About three miles to the curve at Wavertree Junction. This curve was one of the best on the LMS Railway and the loco would work very heavily and it was here that we would see Eric Treacy with his camera. He knew we were coming (he couldn't see us due to the curve) by the roar and smoke. He took some wonderful pictures here and we would wave to him as we went by.'

Sometimes Treacy achieved a good photograph by sustained perseverance. Occasionally it was luck, though the camera was rarely too far away. He later recalled an early occasion in his photographic life.

'In 1936 I was teaching in my church day school in Edge Hill: the time was about 10.15am, when almost from under my feet, I heard a noise akin to an earthquake. At first it was as distant thunder; then it rose to a violent crescendo and it seemed as if the very foundations of the school must collapse. Down the road I detected a cloud of sulphurous smoke emerging from what seemed to be a great hole in the ground. It was none other than the "Merseyside Express", behind a "Royal Scot" engine, blasting its way up the cutting from Lime Street to Edge Hill station; 400 tons of train lifted from a dead stop, up the 1 in 90 incline. What a noise and, I discovered in due time, what a sight.'

He might have added — and what photographs!

Some of Treacy's best and favourite shots and which first appeared in print, thus launching him as a railway photographer, were not completely natural! One personal favourite appeared in his first published booklet, *My Best Railway Photographs* — No 1 in an ABC Locomotive Series (Ian Allan, 1946) dedicated naturally to 'My friends of 8A the Edge Hill (Liverpool) Shed'. The photograph is of the 11.15 Liverpool to London train — the 'Manxman' climbing out of Lime Street. The engine was a 'Royal Scot' 4-6-0 No 6130, *The West Yorkshire Regiment*. By way of comment Treacy adds:

'The light is never good in deep cuttings, especially round Liverpool, when there is a high sulphur content in the air. For this shot I had been trying on and off for a couple of years, but had never been lucky. The sun is only right about a month in the year; and that is not all, for there is very heavy traffic through this cutting into Lime Street station, which makes it difficult to get the other roads clear. Indeed, a second or two after I had taken this photograph another train thundered into the scene, deluging me with dust and fumes.'

Treacy loved the railway and his approach to photography was emotional rather than scientific. Perhaps that is why he was such an outstanding photographer. Writing on the *spell* of the railway in *Steam Up* he refers to it as 'a form of magic — an abstract. For its effect it depends upon the capacity of the enthusiast to experience it. —— A spell will invest a certain place with a certain atmosphere at a certain time, and all attempts to capture it again will fail . . .' His own success was due in no small measure to capturing the moment in the lens and letting the photograph cast its own spell on the viewer. Often Treacy helped Nature to provide the perfect atmosphere and the result could be interpreted conspicuously differently in the eyes of different beholders. The Lime Street Cutting photographs are a good example. To the enthusiastic amateur or steam buff, the spell is complete. Like Wordsworth's daffodils:

They flash upon that inward eye —
then my heart with pleasure fills

But, as Treacy comments, 'When I showed one of my most satisfying photographs to a nameless expert he, observing a magnificent cloud of smoke, snorted "That's bad firing!" — which it probably was (little did he know that I had arranged it with the fireman!). But the critical eye of the expert was blind to the feeling of movement and life expressed by that gorgeous cloud of smoke.'

As Treacy's interest in railway photography grew he ventured to contact the well known photographers of the day such as Maurice Earley and E. R. Wethersett. Some of them were generous in giving advice but perhaps their benevolence was not wholly altruistic for they often ended their letters by saying 'It so happens that I have for disposal . . .'

Two further cameras were added to Treacy's collection — a Zeiss Contessa press camera (9cm x 12cm) in which he used a 7in Cooke Aviar lens interchangeably; and a Zeiss Superikonta $3\frac{1}{4} \times 2\frac{1}{4}$ film camera with Compur shutter and 3.5 Tessar lens.

He was beginning to have photographs published in a number of periodicals such as *The Railway Magazine*. From the outset they were regarded as being special and different. If Lime Street Cutting was one setting for successful and exciting photographs, Shap was another. Treacy had begun to explore the wide open spaces of Shap Fell on his holidays. Armed with a lineside permit and his pushbike he would start from Oxenholme and pedal and walk to Penrith. Farmers and shepherds, signalmen and permanent way men along that glorious stretch of line came to know Treacy well. He drank gallons of tea in gangers' bothies and signalboxes. His visits were anticipated with joy for the coming of Treacy meant fun and laughter. Occasionally there were personal or pastoral problems to sort out too. At this time, more than in his later railway exploits, he was Chaplain of the Line. In *Roaming the Northern Rails* Treacy describes Shap:

'To the west of Oxenholme are the hills of Lakeland, with the Langdale Pikes easily recognisable. In steam days engines worked hard up the hill to Grayrigg, then eased off through the Lune valley. Over the water splash at Dillicar troughs, through Tebay, an ugly little railway town at the foot of Shap Bank. Then the hard work started — 1 in 75 all the way to the top, and the driver hoping against hope that he would not be stopped half way up at Scout Green. When this happened, there could be trouble in restarting, especially if there were wet rails. Then on to one of the best known bits of line in England, past Shap Wells to the Summit.'

Throughout his life he never tired of Shap, ever finding new angles for photographs.

By now steam had entered Treacy's blood stream. He could never quite explain to his own satisfaction why the railway and all that appertained to it held him in its power. He wrote: 'What is it that in every town I go to draws me to the Railway Station? What is it that causes me unconsciously to step on it when my car is approaching a main line? What is it that causes me secretly to hope that every level crossing gate will be closed? What is it that invests all the noises of the railway — especially at night — with the quality of music that soothes?'

Treacy never quite found the answer so his enthusiasm remained a riddle and he kept on taking wonderful photographs. He was never in danger of becoming one of those railway nuts, or enthusiastic bores, whose minds go on a single line and they have neither the wit nor the vision to see that it is a siding. Sidings were a sore point with Treacy! On one occasion shortly after the war he was returning from London to Yorkshire and took his seat in the train standing at Platform 7, St Pancras, although the train was suspiciously empty. 'After a few moments it began to move out of the station on its way to the sidings — I just managed to get out in time; and I am supposed to know something about railways!' On a later occasion he was not quite so lucky. He dozed off in a train which he thought was heading for Leeds but he was prodded to life two hours later by a railway official. Yes — he was in a siding.

The war was to interrupt his hobby and his plans. He had thought of embarking on a joint venture with a doyen of railway writers, Cecil J. Allen. The intention was, in Allen's words taken from a letter to Treacy, 'to do something on the lines of *Famous Trains*, largely pictorial, with full-page plates from your collection, and each train described in a separate chapter, with brief notes on its locomotive, stock, speeds, route and other interesting features.'

At the Edge Hill shed, in the local Labour Club and particularly with the local Territorial Regiment, with which Treacy was associated, the talk began to be of war. Treacy, ever addicted to bouts of patriotism, took a simple line with his friends. Munich represented expediency and expediency meant a sacrifice of the Luther spirit of 'I protest'. The real struggle was between reality and sham, the choice between moral rearmament or national decay. Pacifist in declaration, Treacy nevertheless knew that the country would have to take up arms and fight if it chose light rather than darkness. He said:

'No one in his right senses can believe that armaments and war are right, and yet if we believe that in certain circumstances these are the only things possible we shall come in time to believe that they are right. We are breaking our pledges because we believe in expediency above everything. If the armaments race continues we shall have to sacrifice social services for armaments, and things that have taken thousands of years to build up will be annihilated. The times through which we are passing cannot, however, be everlasting and if we hold to our faith the dawn must come.'

Treacy's ministry at Edge Hill and link with Liverpool were coming to a close, although he little realised it at the time.

7

Man Among Men

Treacy's telephone rang late one evening within a few days of war being declared.

'This is Wavertree 1247' he replied.

'This is Douglas Crawford' said the voice at the other end of the line. 'Well what about it old boy? We need a padre, and we could do worse than have you'.

Douglas Crawford, a friend of Treacy's, was then Second-in-Command of the 59th (4th W. Lancs) Medium Regiment, Royal Artillery, the first Liverpool volunteer artillery unit.

Treacy comments:

'I suppose that Douglas Crawford would be embarrassed if I said that, for me, this was the word from God: but it was no less. I had been waiting for some sign as to where my duty lay, and this was it. For me, it was a clear call.

'It all seemed so simple at first. Here was a regiment that wanted me as its chaplain: here was I ready to go. But, I did not realise the weird and stubborn ways of the Army Chaplains' Department of those days.'

Treacy's problems started earlier when he went to Gieves to order his uniform. When he went for his fitting he found the uniform fitted perfectly. The only snag was that it was naval uniform. He had forgotten to mention which Service he was joining.

Much to Treacy's bewilderment and Douglas Crawford's chagrin, Treacy was posted to another unit. Every string in the marionette theatre was pulled and when that failed personal pleas were made but to no effect. The Chaplains' Department made it clear that they were not going to be told where their chaplains should go. Treacy was sent to the 68th Medium Regiment which was the second line of the 59th.

The 68th was stationed at Bolesworth Castle in Cheshire, to which Treacy reported in February 1940 after an emotional au revoir at St Mary's. He hoped to be back in the parish after his war service. At first he found it hard to reconcile the three pips on his shoulder with the dog collar round his neck. The three pips were going to leave a permanent mark on him and his personality. The beginning was different from the end as he well remembered:

'Well, there was I, loaded with kit, feeling like a fish out of water, reporting to a unit in mid-Cheshire, which didn't particularly want a chaplain, and hadn't a clue what to do with him when it got one. But, let me not give a wrong impression. Everyone was very kind and my welcome left nothing to be desired. The trouble was that they were all very busy with their training programmes and I just didn't fit into what they were doing.

'I found it a humiliating experience to be surrounded by men, all of whom had clearly defined duties to perform, whereas I had none. At first, I felt sure that I had made a mistake in volunteering for the Army. I had left a parish in which there was a lot to do for a setting in which there appeared very little to do. In a parish, my vicarage and my church were my headquarters: in the army I had no headquarters. In Edge Hill, the people had known what a vicar was for: in the army, no one seemed to have the faintest idea what a padre was for. For a few weeks I floundered miserably. Then, gradually, it dawned upon me that if I wanted anything to happen, I had to make it happen. A lesson that has been of great value to me. And, if I wanted things to happen, than I had to earn help and not demand it.'

This is an over-simplification of what was involved. At this stage of his ministry Treacy was more parson than priest. He had not the high view of his priesthood that he came to have in later life although he always placed ministry above priesthood. When he joined the army he was eager to be sharing in its general purposefulness. The result was that he found himself busier than anyone else. The activity had little to do with being a clergyman. Most of his time was spent doing things that could perfectly well have been done by a layman. He became Mess Secretary. This involved the control of the kitchen staff, the ordering of food and drink, the arranging of menus with the Mess Sergeant, and a good deal of accounting. It also meant getting brassed off by the Colonel when the food was not up to standard. This was a lackey ministry not a servant one. Further it fixed him more firmly in the Officers' Mess than was right or good for him. Later he could admit: 'As a priest I was a wash-out — just because I had not thought out what the priest's work in the army should be, I had no priorities.'

In his desperation to be serviceable Treacy could not see that he was becoming an odd job man, taking on the work no one else wanted to do. He was rapidly ceasing to be a minister of the Gospel. Always busy — and withal doing nothing — meant that his prayer life was suffering and his studying was non-existent. For the first time in his ministry Treacy felt lost, helpless, almost bitter. In theory he knew that the role of the priest is never changing, ever sure. It is to preach, teach, communicate and interpret the Gospel; to exercise pastoral care and oversight and to celebrate and administer the sacraments and to be responsible for the ordering of worship.

What to the mind seemed firm, to the heart appeared faltering. How could he fulfil his role in the army? With no church and no colleague his spiritual discipline collapsed. He felt futile and ineffective. Although his discipline in spiritual matters was not prodigious he had learned to regard the Daily Offices of Matins and Evensong as his anchor. Without them his spiritual foundations were in danger of disintegrating.

After two months of agonised frustration and despair two people came to the rescue in quite different ways. They rescued Treacy from crumbling ruin. The first belonged to that lonely and despised breed of humanity — Regimental Sergeant Majors. Treacy wrote:

'The RSM of the 68th was a worthy called Joe Ryan. Joe realised what I was up against and took me under his wing. In no time I got a truck and a batman, church parades were laid on. Various men were suggested to me as needing help and, bit by bit, I began to feel that I had a parish again.

'I was very fortunate to get a vehicle, because at that stage in the war, the Army was very short indeed of motor transport. We were requisitioning tradesmen's vans, decrepit lorries, anything on four wheels, to augment the totally inadequate supply of vehicles issued.

'Mine was an old one that had belonged to a laundry in Chester. It went, but only just. After a time, its performance began to improve and I observed that every time we visited the car park in Chester, the vehicle ran better. Not for a moment would I suggest that my driver "improved" my vehicle at the expense of some other machine in the car park. The thought just crossed my mind — that's all. There are times when you just don't ask questions.

'However, when it was discovered how sweetly my laundry van was performing, it was impounded for the use of the Adjutant. I then got a Pheasant Margarine van and the whole process started again.'

The outward expression of Treacy's ministry was rescued and encouraged by Joe Ryan. The inward reality was earthed again by the Archdeacon of Chester (R. V. H. Burne) who was Rector of Tattenhall, where Treacy was billeted in an inn, by name the Bear and Ragged Staff. Archdeacon Burne was shy and scholarly. After a time Treacy's spiritual plight became known and obvious to Burne. From that moment 'he was a good friend to me, and the hospitality of his Vicarage remains a gracious memory. He had qualities of mind and spirit upon which I drew to my lasting good. I needed such companionship.' Treacy had someone to whom he could unburden himself and with whom he could say his Daily Offices. He was anchored again. As he later reflected, 'Thank God, I saw what was happening and realised that I should be lost if I did not hold on to my Daily Offices'. Of clergy who openly confessed that they did not say their Offices he simply said 'Perhaps they have deeper spiritual resources than I have, but I cannot help wondering how they keep going without them.'

Treacy's comments on other people are always interesting and usually significant not merely because they indicate his preferences but for the light they throw on him. Here are his observations on his superiors:

'Ken Dimoline and Bill Napier, the CO and 2nd in Command were an interesting blend. Both Territorial Officers, but each with a different attitude to the Army. Ken Dimoline was as keen as mustard and determined to succeed as a regimental commander. Bill Napier, by nature easy going, and with an abundance of charm, was, I suspect, a good deal out of his depth. Ken, I felt, had to prove to himself that he was a success: whilst Bill wasn't bothered about being a success. He just lived each day as it came, and enjoyed it.'

Treacy's problem was not to get in the way when the troops were undergoing training and yet he had to keep in touch with them. As a non-combatant, he could not train for war, but he went where they went and learned to do most of their jobs so that he came to know what they were talking about. How did Treacy see himself? The following observations are self-revealing:

'I was learning fast, and I needed to. I had been thrown into regimental life by the Chaplains' Department totally ignorant of the ways of the army. There are, in the Services, so many unwritten laws and conventions that it is very easy to make a fool of yourself if, by chance, you should ignore some well established tradition. I am not clever; far from it. In some things I am unbelievably slow: but I possess two qualities which have served me well. I am a good imitator, and I am quick witted. I realise that these two qualities would have fitted me for a life of crime, but they were very useful in my early days in the army.

'Carefully, I watched other people: what they did, I did. I took care never to be the first to do anything. And when I was caught unawares, I usually exercised my wits to rescue myself. I must confess it was something of a strain.

'We had our Sunday services wherever we could get them. Sometimes in mess huts, sometimes in the open air, and wherever possible in local churches. Occasionally we joined with the local congregation at their normal morning service, but more often we were allowed the use of the church for our parade service. The problem about joining in the normal morning worship was that very often the form of service was a long florid Matins lasting well over the hour, which was a bit more than the troops could take. Sometimes it was sung Eucharist which was scarcely the most appropriate service for a lot of fidgeting and mostly unconfirmed, gunners. So, we had our own services, taken by me in the form of a truncated Matins. I was never happy about worship in the army: except for the celebrations of Holy Communion, which were voluntary and attended by men who had been, for the most part, regular worshippers in civilian life.

'These church parades were compulsory, but that is not to say that everyone came. It was easy enough to find some excuse for not going, but those who did were formed up, inspected, and marched to church. Scarcely conditions best designed to create the right atmosphere for worship; nor was the potted Matins provided in the Army Prayer Book an inspired act of worship. Preaching was not easy. Nine or ten minutes was about the maximum for which one could hope to keep their attention.'

Treacy's fellow officers were not exactly merciful about his preaching when they met him in the mess after a service. James Knoch, the Scottish doctor, had considerable, and, for Treacy often embarrassing theological insights. This was good for Treacy and had a decisive effect on the course of his future preaching. Henceforth he was never in danger of returning to the Edge Hill style, if 'style' is not too polite for the windy hectoring prating that there took place. Treacy frankly admitted the lesson learned:

'I had always rather fancied myself as a preacher in my parish, but I soon discovered how much I had to learn about the business of having something to say, to say it in 10 minutes, and in language understood by the average soldier. I came to the conclusion that in the pulpit of my parish church I had ranted rather than preached. I had prided myself on my flow of words; on my ability to preach without notes. I had mistaken noise for conviction. Now, I discovered how little I knew of preaching, and how little use my prewar pulpit antics cut with the troops.

This early period of the war was difficult for the home-based units of the army. I the 68th most of the men came from the Liverpool area and they were too near home to feel that they were going to war. The Chaplains' Department exercised no pastoral care over its chaplains at this stage and their organisation was ill-prepared to cope with the clergy who were volunteering for service. Treacy was not impressed with the situation or with some of the men who were volunteering:

'There were good and bad. There were some who had seen the army as an escape from the day-to-day toil of parish life, and who hankered after the glamour given by uniform and rank. There were others who came out of a sincere conviction that God was calling them to a ministry in the Forces.

'At first we were free to volunteer if it seemed right for us to do so. After a few months, the Diocesan Bishops woke up to the fact that the situation was getting out of control, and took it upon themselves to nominate clergy for chaplaincy service. Bishops, being only human, tended to hold on to their best men, and to nominate the ones they could most easily spare. The result was that the Services received younger and untried men, when, in fact the need was for older men who had developed spiritual stability and had the authority to stand up to authority. Let it be said, however, that some of these younger men developed fast and became first rate chaplains, and many of them, amongst whom I would count myself, would say that their most valuable pastoral training took place in the Services.'

In April 1940 the 68th moved to the small town of Melksham in Wiltshire where Treacy succeeded in billeting himself in the Vicarage. Again he was strengthened by the support of the local Vicar, who, Treacy remembers, 'affected a slightly surprised attitude to the world and its unregenerate ways, but he had little to learn about humanity.'

Suddenly they were ordered to France, but the day before they were due to sail the French collapsed so they did not go. Instead they moved to the Fens of East Anglia waiting for the invasion which never came. At the end of August they were sent to High Wycombe. Here as elsewhere local churches and various voluntary organisations were active in helping and providing canteens, and providing links with life outside the army. They also sewed and darned for the men and sometimes did their washing. Only occasionally did Treacy encounter the female grandee who treated the canteen work as a kind of necessary service to the lower orders. He recalls one aspect of this work which left a sour taste in his mouth:

'Certain of the religious organisations which sponsored canteens felt it consistent with their principles to have epilogues in the canteen on Sunday evenings, and, not unnaturally, they thought that I was the natural person to take them. I wish that I had had the moral courage to refuse for it was about the last thing that the troops wanted. They felt that they had been caught. Imagine the scene. A crowded canteen, chaps writing letters, reading magazines, playing darts, listening to the radio, swilling tea and munching sandwiches — and then, a voice raised calling for silence, and the summons to prayer. I cannot believe that by such means religion is commended. I remember the surly looks and the muttered comments.'

During September it was again announced that the Regiment was going overseas.

War at last! Not for Treacy. As he wrote to his sister Mary at the time 'To my great disappointment I failed to pass the medical examination so I was unable to go with them. My old trouble for which I had an operation before had recurred. I tried all sorts of dodges to wangle it — but it was no good.' In fact Treacy had undone the surgeon's work on his first hernia in January 1937 by push-biking round Liverpool too soon after the operation. He had not disclosed this to the MO when he had been examined for the Army. The Western Desert was no place in which to have a strangulated hernia so the second in command of the Regiment, Barney de Robeck and the first in command of Treacy, his wife May, decided that some abdominal repairs should be undertaken. The 68th left for the Middle East and their Padre entered a Liverpool Nursing Home.

What a richly disguised blessing this proved to be. First, he had to endure the German blitz on Liverpool whilst he was in the Nursing Home:

'Night after night bombs rained down on Liverpool, and there was I lying helpless in bed with my tummy stitched up. Not only that, May who visited me with courageous regularity had to find her way home to Hoylake through the bombing.

'I have no hesitation in saying, nor am I ashamed to, that I was more frightened during that bombing than I was at any other time in the war — Normandy included. It was the helplessness, the waiting for the bomb to arrive, the tingling of every nerve in the body, the noise of buildings falling and, occasionally, the agonised cries of the injured, that all added up to make this a time in which one came to realise, and with some shame, that although Christians believed in life after death, they were very keen to hold on to life before death.'

When the doctors decided that Treacy was fit again he made sure that he was available for another posting. This time, with the assistance of a co-operative Deputy Assistant Chaplain-General in Southern Command, Captain Treacy reported to Douglas Crawford and the 59th Medium Regiment at RHQ near Cambridge. Thus began a memorable association with an exceptional regiment. Its officers and men were almost wholly recruited from Liverpool. As a Territorial unit it had a splendid record in the King's Cup, and its officers were all business men in the City of Liverpool.

The CO was Douglas Crawford (now knighted and Lord Lieutenant of Lancashire) of biscuit firm fame, of whom Treacy wrote:

'He is a Scotsman with all the canniness of his race. He was a skilful team builder with a genius for getting rid of those who didn't fit into his team, and for attracting those who would. He was a very good regimental commander who succeeded in maintaining a very high level of morale during the long years of waiting. He had a fertile mind and produced one good idea after another for keeping us on our toes. Like most Scotsmen bred in the Presbyterian tradition he had a strong streak of Puritanism. Regimental binges were always followed by a period of what we called "alcoholic remorse", during which there was a marked abstemiousness in the mess.

'His cousin Keith, who became second-in-command, was even worse in this respect. He believed that there was positive virtue in being uncomfortable. If the regiment, on an exercise, had the choice of spending the night sleeping in a damp ditch, or in an empty house in the vicinity into the ditch we went, on the grounds that there was some kind of redemptive value in roughing it. He was something of a pragmatic theologian.

'Douglas and I grew very close during the four years we were together. No Commanding Officer could have given his chaplain more encouragement and facilities than he gave me. In some respects we were ahead of our time. We started voluntary church parades in 1941 but were smartly called to order by the Chaplains' Department, who quoted King's Regulations at us. I was conducting Padre's hours with the troops long before they became established by the War Office.'

The Crawford-Treacy relationship was mutually important and rewarding. Douglas Crawford admits that he used Treacy as a sounding board for many of his ideas and regarded Treacy as his 'personnel' or perhaps 'industrial relations manager' in modern parlance. Contrariwise Treacy learned lasting lessons. When he proposed a bright but shapeless plan Douglas Crawford would listen patiently and then say:

' "And what's the follow-up?" And I would realise that I had laid an egg with no yoke in it. How many schemes in church and state come to grief because those who have hatched them have not thought in terms of follow up.

'Douglas and I had our own code. If either of us started by saying "My dear chap, if I may say, with the greatest respect . . ." it meant that we were going to be as rude to each other as a Colonel and a padre could be without a court martial. We would knock each other's ideas to bits. I was a bit weak on logic, and Douglas was, I venture to think, a bit adrift in assessing human reactions to some of his ideas. In spite of Uppingham and Cambridge I think Douglas was something of a Philistine. Golf, shooting and the TA were his addictions. The Arts were a closed world to him. It was amusing to watch his reactions to a subaltern posted to us, who was, in civilian life, a music critic. He and Douglas inhabited two different worlds, between which there was no communication. "What's a music critic FOR?" he would ask; "you either like the stuff or you don't. All this stuff these fellas write won't change my mind about what I like and what I don't like."

'And that was that!'

From November 1941 until June 1944 the Regiment moved up and down England. Cambridge, Battle, the Cotswolds, County Durham, Selby, Hunmanby, Tonbridge were all visited and the last move before the invasion was to Alnmouth in Northumberland. Treacy was already showing outstanding qualities as Padre. He had emerged from his initial slough of despondency a stronger man in every way. A fellow officer, Alan Buchanan, puts his finger on this new 'strength'.

'It did not take long before one realised that whereas Eric was a very special man among men he was also someone with something extra. There was an "Otherness" to him which seemed to grow so that although he was immediately with one in conversation and dealing with any specific problems he never was as close as an ordinary fellow would become. This "Otherness" was a quality I had not experienced in clergy or padres at the time and so did not immediately identify it. I was suffering at the time from severe doubts about my faith and had become something of an agnostic but I was drawn to Eric and the message he was putting across.'

Treacy's teaching of the faith became at once more simple and more profound. He was not unaware of the change. Some officers asked him to give a series of talks on the Christian Faith. The talks were prepared with great care. During the discussions that followed he discovered something. 'It is the compelling power of Jesus Christ. I never anticipated the reaction of the Group. It was as if Jesus came through as bigger than any of us and seized our minds and imagination, so that decision seemed more appropriate than discussion. I have found the same thing to happen repeatedly. Certainly, in preaching, to speak simply of the Jesus of the Gospels is to compel immediate attention.'

Stories of Treacy's activities are legion. I quote a few for the light they throw on his principles and his faith, his banter and his escapades. There was an evening when an ENSA concert party did a series of items of sordid vulgarity. Greatly daring Treacy brought the proceedings to a dramatic end which he recalls:

'A step which, rather to my surprise, gained general approval from the troops and which caused alarm and dismay on the part of the entertainers. So alarmed were they that they called on me the following morning to beg that I did not report the incident to ENSA headquarters.

'Their explanation was interesting, and I could not help sympathising with them. "I don't suppose you realise what an exhausting business entertainment is" said their producer. "Night after night we bump around in a 3-tonner from one unit to another. Often we haven't time for a meal, and we arrive on the stage dead beat. What we need to get us going is a laugh, and the quickest way to get a laugh is a dirty crack or a smutty joke."

' "Be that as it may", I replied, "but I think you need to realise that the men you are entertaining are, on the whole, a decent lot of chaps with wives and kids at home, and not a lot of licentious soldiery wallowing in dirt." And, with this exchange of views, we parted each the wiser, and with greater understanding each of the other.'

Treacy was critical of George Formby for the unnecessary lewdness of some of his pieces and wrote to tell him so! He much preferred his weekly date with Tommy Handley's ITMA. Woe betide anything or anyone who came between him and Frisby Dyke, Mr So So, Mona Lot and Chin Strap. Once, a well-intentioned worthy in Cambridge did so by inviting Douglas Crawford and Treacy to dinner and afterwards as a very special treat they were taken to the Ballet through which, except for the first few minutes, the ungrateful guests slept soundly. In an understatement Treacy later commented 'Ballet never has said anything to me'.

One incident is embedded in the Regiment's history and is perhaps best retold by the principal participant — the Padre of course!

'One of the side-shows laid on to induce our aggressive spirit in the Home Forces during the waiting years were Battle Schools. They originated at Barnard Castle, whither Regimental Commanders went to be initiated. Douglas Crawford went and came back with a dangerous glint in his eye. We knew we were for it.

'A young officer was appointed as Commandant of the Regimental Battle School. This young warrior's name was Bob Taylor, who had the time of his life devising and operating a series of physical tortures through which the regiment went in groups of about 30. I will swear that young Bob paid off a lot of old scores during this home based campaign. The trouble was that it didn't make us aggressive but so tired that the Germans could have walked over us if they had landed. Like everybody else, I went through this particular mill. Torn to bits on barbed wire, soaked to the skin crawling through stinking culverts, bruised as we fell off walls and jumped out of windows, scared out of our wits as they fired Bren guns a few inches over our heads, our arms wrenched out of their sockets as we clung on to ropes, and all the time the directing staff making rude remarks, such as "What are we waiting for?" as we emerged gasping from a wet ditch; "They wouldn't have a shower like you in the Home Guard", as we emerged blinded and weeping from a smoke filled house.

'The average age of my group was fairly high, and we were determined to give a good account of ourselves, and although it nearly killed us, we did. We did the assault course like stags and returned the best average time for the whole course.

'It so happened that Douglas Crawford took a particular, and I would say, sadistic interest in the course I was on. He haunted me. In my blackest moments, there he would be, immaculate, asking me what I was waiting for.

'There had been a good deal of bad language in the mess at this time, and I had instituted a swear box, for which there was a tariff. It so happened that one afternoon, I emerged from a culvert with my trousers full of muddy water, cold and stinking, to find my revered CO standing on the bank with his usual words of exhortation. By chance, I had a shilling in my pocket. With more joy than was decent for a man of God, I handed him the shilling and said "Bugger off!"

'I don't suppose I have ever uttered two words which (a) gave me greater pleasure, or (b) gained a greater degree of support throughout the regiment.

'He did!'

Whilst on the subject of language, several members of the regiment including J. C. Bingham recall another occasion which 'serves to illustrate Eric's fearlessness and blunt opposition to anything of which he disapproved. I remember a Church Parade Service when the time came for Eric's sermon he embarked on five or ten minutes of abusive and largely inconsequential talk with swear words punctuating almost every other word. He then stated that he was fed up with this sort of language which was pointless and expressed the hope that the members of the Regiment would restrain their language in the future, at any rate in his presence. It certainly made a big impression at the time.'

This kind of forthright expression did not alienate affection or admiration but drew men to him. One soldier, Jim Scott, writes:

'My recollection is of someone who was down-to-earth, and an awareness of all the life styles with their faults and virtues. To me he had an impish, puckish face with twinkling, humorous eyes, and a smile which easily turned to infectious laughter. Although he mixed freely and put people completely at ease, giving the impression that he was not easily shocked, he also had a quality which prevented anyone putting it to the test.'

Harold Sills remembers him as:

'Never sparing of himself, always ready and willing to give of himself in the interests of those spiritually in his care. The welfare of the men was always his first concern. He found the time and the inclination to enter into the life of the Regiment, not excluding those bêtes noires, assault courses and cross-country runs. But first and foremost he was the Padre, and many a lad with a problem found in Eric "a very present help in time of trouble". '

If Treacy regarded the Regimental Battle School as violent, it was like a Sunday School outing compared with the Battle School organised by the Chaplains' Department for its members serving with the 2nd Army. The brain — if that is the right description — behind the exercise was John Youens, later Chaplain-General, but Treacy did not hold him responsible for what happened, as he here describes:

'I was certainly nearer death on this course than ever I was from the activities of the German Army in the Battle for Caen, which was a pretty bloody business. The purpose of this exercise in home-spun savagery was to give us a taste of what was to come. It was run by three combatant officers whose performances remain vivid to me today. It was as if they said to themselves "Right, here we are with thirty parsons at our mercy for a week: we'll find out what stuff the martyrs are made of. We'll see how they stand up to the burning fiery furnace."

'And I am proud to say that we did show them what stuff the martyrs are made of. We stood up to their tortures like men, even though some of us bear the marks of the ordeal to this present day. One chaplain, Geoffrey Treglown, then a Methodist minister, now an Anglican priest, was blinded and lost an arm: another chaplain broke both his legs, and there were a number of minor injuries.'

During the Regiment's movement throughout the country Treacy sampled many churches but not always in the way he expected. One recollection comes from Colonel A. I. Crawford:

'When he was invited to preach at a church in Polegate, which he didn't know, he left insufficient time to get from his previous service (a not uncommon experience) rushed in late, put on his robes, sat down to compose himself and only realised it was the wrong church when the Vicar walked over to him and whispered "Who on earth are you?".'

The official Regimental History records that on 23 November (1941) 'at Little Compton Church he (the Padre) began to play an organ voluntary while the collection was being made, when he realised something was wrong. Apparently the collection bags were missing. He went on playing, eventually giving a solemn rendering of *Three Blind Mice*. Only the organ blower recognised it, and the collection bags were found. The Padre was sitting on them!'

Some Treacy errors were potentially more serious. There was one brittle cold night spent in the precincts of Canterbury Cathedral, waiting for the Regiment which did not turn up because Treacy, not for the first or last time, had a wrong map reference. It was manifestly absurd to expect a gunner regiment to rendezvous inside Canterbury Cathedral, but that is how Treacy read his map, so with the blind obedience that was the making of the British Army, he waited there in his truck from 00.00 hours until 07.00 hours. Afterwards he thought it well worth being paralysed with the cold to spend the night watches in the company of the glorious building.

On 17 August 1941 the Regiment was allotted a BBC Morning Service Broadcast. Treacy conducted it and gave the address. Douglas Crawford read the lessons. There was quite a 'fan' mail afterwards — more than was usual after such broadcasts. Treacy received a letter from the BBC (18 August 1941) expressing their view that it 'was one of the best services we have had for a long time. Unlike the morning service on the previous Sunday, we could hear your men simply singing themselves out and the effect was thoroughly invigorating, even though the Organist was rather fond of his tremulant. Of your own part in the service I hope you will not think it patronising if I say that it seemed to us in every way excellent — virile and moving.'

Monk Fryston Hall, near Selby, is a very pleasant hotel possessing a good restaurant. During the war the building was requisitioned by the Army and housed a WOSB (War Office Selection Board) centre. To this place of assessment came men who had been recommended for commissions. Treacy was allowed to attend one of the Selection Boards as an observer. The agenda of the course would be familiar to anyone today who has had a surfeit of management courses but during the war such courses were in their infancy in this country. The course consisted of intelligence tests, psychiatric assessment, discussions, tests of leadership under stress, and a morning engaged in 'situations'. Treacy asked if he could be part participant as well as full time observer, which was agreed. Treacy vividly recalls the occasion:

'The psychiatrist who attended this course was the sort of man with whom you couldn't win. Everything we did was watched and duly noted. If a man talked too much at a discussion group, he was likely to be assessed as too bombastic, and a poor listener; if a man didn't talk enough, then he was lacking either in ideas or self confidence — or both.

'The "trick-cyclist" was a nice little Scotsman, but he had us all in a panic; we felt that we were revealing all sorts of things about our "psyches". One chap confided to me that he daren't be caught looking at "Jane" in the *Daily Mirror* for fear that he would be rated as a sex maniac. Now Jane was a delightful young woman who appeared daily in the *Mirror* and kept the whole British Army on tenterhooks throughout most of the war lest she lost all her clothes. Each next instalment promised the inevitability of this, but always she managed to keep covered, if only just. Jane became quite an institution in the Services, and I am sure, that in her coy way, she did quite a lot for the war effort. She was a great leveller, in that her following knew no bounds of rank. From general to private, she had her admirers, but, somehow, I don't think Monty was amongst them.

'To return to these WOSBs. One of the tests consisted of the candidate being sent out on a march along the country lanes in this not unpleasant part of

Yorkshire. On this particular day, the sun was shining, the birds singing, and it all seemed very peaceful, when — suddenly — a Bren gun opened up on this happy band of pilgrims. For a moment, there was consternation, then, flat on our faces in a ditch. Obviously, no natural leaders amongst us!

'Gradually, it dawned upon the candidates that this was all part of the system, and that somebody was expected to do something. As the morning proceeded, one unexpected situation followed another, and, before long, there was considerable competition to display leadership potential. I could not help observing that the most effective men in these situations were the ones who made least noise about it.'

Treacy was going to have a great deal to do with the selection of candidates for the ordained ministry in later years as a bishop. Although he did not realise it at the time, some seeds of discontent with this 'system' lodged in his mind.

At the beginning of 1944 it became clear that the long wait was coming to an end. They were named the British Liberation Army, censoring of letters was introduced and the southern areas of the country were sealed off. It was the beginning of the end.

8
MBE

The effectiveness of any priest's ministry, to be incumbent or padre, archdeacon or bishop, can only be dimly discerned in human terms. One sign that Treacy's ministry to the 59th was having a spiritual effect came when a number of men requested Confirmation at the beginning of 1944. Douglas Crawford allowed Treacy to organise a Confirmation School in the Regiment. To Treacy's surprise no less than 150 men and officers offered themselves for preparation, as he recalled:

'This was very nearly 25% of the Regiment. Douglas gave my candidates what amounted to a week off for the preparation, but, let it be said, none of those who offered themselves knew this when they came forward. I spent a busy and, to me, exciting week moving from group to group to give them instruction. I had to reduce my preparation to the essentials of the Christian Faith. A very good exercise for me; a time when I learnt things in the art of communication which have been the greatest use to me ever since. It was a wonderful experience to encounter the desire of these men to learn of the Christian way of life.'

The Confirmation took place in Tonbridge Parish Church and was conducted by the Bishop of Rochester, Christopher Chavasse. 'He knew just what to say and how to say it. No one who was present at the service will ever forget it. The fire of the Holy Spirit was there that Spring evening.'

Of Christopher Chavasse, Treacy retained respectful and happy memories:

'He made a very great impression on me. In all my wanderings about England, he was the only Diocesan Bishop who showed any pastoral concern for me. I reported my presence in his Diocese to him, and was immediately invited to lunch at Bishopscourt, Rochester. When he found that we were a Liverpool regiment, he promptly invited himself to dinner in the mess and was a tremendous "hit" with everybody. (Chavasse's father was Bishop of Liverpool from 1900-1923). Subsequently, I made several visits to Rochester and we became close friends. This man, small in stature, was in every other way a giant. Every inch a bishop, the personification of authority, a bonny fighter where his principles were concerned, and a man with whom liberties just were not taken. In some ways, coldly formal, yet by his actions revealing a warm heart. A man of immense courage who throughout his episcopate, suffered grievously both physically and morally.'

After the Confirmation Eric and May Treacy wrote to the incumbents of all the home parishes from which the men came. Treacy comments ruefully: 'I am sorry to say that we received acknowledgements from less than half the clergy to whom we wrote. Why is it that clergy are so bad at answering letters? —'

Then — an extraordinary thing happened. The Regiment was ordered to proceed up the Great North Road to Northumberland. Confusion and disillusion reigned amongst the ranks for they thought they were in Kent ready to cross the Channel. As the regiment moved North they saw an endless queue of units going in the opposite direction. In fact they were taking their place in an enormous armoured crocodile embarking for Normandy from the South Coast. From Alnmouth in Northumberland, along the Great North Road, staging at Doncaster, the Regiment moved to Wanstead Flats where they were, like animals in a cage, cut off from the world outside, waiting their turn to embark from Tilbury.

From June 1944 until March 1945 Treacy kept a journal from which extracts are taken in this chapter and it is well to begin at the beginning:

'June 6 1944. I was dressing — the wireless had just finished "Lift up your hearts". I wasn't paying much attention to the news as I thought it would only be a repeat of what I had heard at midnight. Then I realised that something startling was happening. The announcer was telling the British Nation that D-Day had come. The invasion had started. My heart missed a couple of beats and came up almost into my mouth. I wonder how many other amateur heroes had the same feeling. I was in this; there was no escape for me — did I want an escape — would I be any good in action — what about May — how would she be taking this morning's news? But very soon I got myself orientated — and in a peculiar way found a measure of real peace. After all, I had known this *had* to come — and it was the shortest way home — even if it might be a rather uncomfortable route. As my emotions settled down, I found that my chief fear was for May — as this would be so much worse for her than for me. Let us make no mistake — by far the greatest burden of this war has been borne by the wives of the fighting men.The greater their love — the greater the suffering. It's they who deserve the decorations.'

Moving along the crocodile from North to South, Treacy records one or two events of interest. On one occasion he had gone into Newcastle to collect some welfare stores and he went into the Station Hotel for a cup of tea.

'Place crowded with prosperous civilians. On this great day the conversations around me consisted of (a) a fat Jewish gentleman who had been to the Music Hall, repeating the more lurid jokes to his friend; (b) a group of overdressed youngish men discussing their previous week's betting; (c) a heated discussion of the relative merits of certain ladies of easy virtue by a group of commercial travellers.
    'I couldn't help feeling that all this didn't match with the general tone of the day. A day of tremendous effort and sacrifice for so many young Englishmen. Lives laid down that this sort of Englishman might back his horses, patronise his prostitutes, enjoy dirty stories.
    'June 25, Sunday. The Doctor and I were just putting our razors together for a shave when the Camp "hailer" announced that we should move in 20 minutes. At last the moment had come — we were sailing to war. Real full-blooded war after four years of playing at war. At 9.15pm we set off for France. We had an enthusiastic send-off by a slightly intoxicated East London who were just being emptied out of the pubs. I must confess to a feeling of contempt for the maudlin sentimentality of crowds. How little there is behind it. The Passion story of our Lord is a terrifying instance of what a crowd of feeble-minded people can do. But obviously the troops greatly enjoyed having notice taken of them, and threw back as many kisses as they received.'

Enough has been written about the landings of the Normandy beachhead for me to limit myself to one solitary detail noted by Treacy in his diary. 'We actually landed at a small placed called Comselles. Owing to the protracted sickness of Jock Hamilton, the CO's driver, I drove his truck off the ship.' It was not that simple, as Colonel A. I. Crawford recalls:

'The CO's driver had been violently seasick on the way over and had lost all his dentures. He was not feeling very well. The CO called for volunteers to take his place. The Padre immediately volunteered.
    'In fear and trembling, for his reputation as driver was not very high in the Regiment and he knew all anticipated he would tip the CO into the water. However, with great concentration and a steady nerve he went over the stern and into 4ft of water and all went well.'

The Regiment landed with a canine stowaway. Whilst in England a particularly unattractive mongrel dog had attached itself to one of the gun troops.

'It had been christened 'Blanco' because in its original state it was white. It was not good on personal relationships, as individually it did not seem to have any affection for its two-footed brothers! But somehow it appeared to find security in our midst. For at least two years it had stuck to its local branch of the RSPC to Dogs in 236 Battery. Our Colonel, who was not particularly attracted to this nondescript and not very responsive animal, had said, shortly before we embarked, with characteristic terseness "Get rid of that bloody dog". It was a source of great joy that within minutes of landing, Blanco was seen sprinting up the beach, and at our first stop, lifted its back leg against the rear wheel of the Colonel's car. How he got there no one knew — or did they? A good example of the cunning exercised by the British soldiery in the matter of animals.

'Sat July 1. We move to action stations just outside Camilly overlooking Caen. It appears that Monty's plan is to use 2nd Army as a bait to draw the main German attack, while the Americans have a go at them in the South ... Saw Monty in Lenilly this morning. He's a pleasant looking chap. I saluted him from my Jeep and in the effort all but fell out — and in trying to recover myself caught hold of my driver's arm which caused him to swerve violently. We near as anything rammed the great man's car amidships — which would not have been popular.'

They were in the Beachhead for several weeks. Although mortared and shot at regularly, with a certain amount of aerial activity at night, they were surprisingly fortunate in casualties. The most terrifying of the enemy's horror weapons were the *Nebelwerfers*; multi-barrelled mortars which sent mortar bombs in clusters making a disgusting noise as they descended on their targets.

Treacy's work as Padre necessitated his moving around the gun positions, with occasional visits to the Base Hospitals. On 10 July he had his first burial in the field. It was of the remains of 'Tiny' Jack Soper, who had been killed by mortar fire. The service was taken to an obligato of furious shell fire. For Treacy this was the first of all too many. Sometimes the Regiment stumbled across dead bodies in the cornfields. Treacy recruited a burial party and it mattered not whether the dead were British or German, they were given a Christian burial. It was ever a painful duty. 'It was a heart-rending business sorting out their personal effects. These nearly always contained photographs of the family and affectionate letters from their wives and children. Nothing was more unpleasant than extracting human remains from a truck that had been "brewed up": there was not much left to extract after these enforced cremations.'

Treacy conducted services as often as circumstances permitted. He planned each of them carefully even though they were held at short notice. They were conducted in a gun pit, at the back of a command post or under a tree. What they lacked in outward dignity and finesse was made up in the simple devoutness of the men. They stood in a semi-circle but knelt to receive the sustaining sacrament of the Body and Blood of Christ. '13 July. Service in the open at half hour's notice. The chaps sat in a ditch and I stood at the base of a tree. It was entirely voluntary — and 30-40 came. We sang two hymns, said the 46th Psalm and had three prayers. It was unique in that at the service, we had one very strong RC, one Jew, a number of Non-conformists and C of E.'

Of all the deaths in the 59th none was as tragic as those which occurred on 15 July (1944). One of the gun positions suffered a direct hit.

'I sped to the gun position in the doctor's jeep — the first place I called at was the CCP — which was congested with dead and dying but no sign of the two majors (Arthur Toosey the Battery Commander and Keith Crawford the second-in-command). Clearly there had been a very nasty accident — the injured looked very bad. Sgt Lloyd was already dead — so I went to the gun pit where I found Arthur and Keith blasted against the back of the pit — around them were the remains of the gun detachment. They were so blasted and burned as to be almost unrecognisable. It appears that the shell had gone off before it had been placed in the breech. It killed 10 and injured four ... One of the most poignant aspects for me of our fatalities was to find in the chaps' pockets the testaments and prayer cards that I had given them only 24 hours before. How little I thought when I gave them how soon they would come back to me.'

The cards which Treacy had had printed were headed 'Into Battle' and consisted of five prayers 'offered to you in the hope that they may help you to make your needs known to God during the days ahead'. They were a Soldier's Prayer, a Lover's Prayer, the Worker's Prayer, the Lord's Prayer and a Salute to God.

Douglas Knight-Gregson remembers the Regiment's blackest day and of Treacy giving spiritual comfort. 'When there was nothing else that could be done I took him into my dugout because by this time he was overcome with emotion, which was quite natural under the circumstances. I felt that a drink would not go amiss and I poured out two and offered one to the Padre. He declined my offer and he proved to have a strong sense of purpose and relied on his faith whereas I needed that drink to bolster my courage'.

The earthly remains of the July dead were buried in a Normandy field. Of his experiences at this time Treacy later frankly admitted:

'One thing I discovered about myself during these days in the Beach head. I was not of the stuff of which heroes were made. I don't think that I failed to go anywhere that I should have gone, but only I know how much I had to screw myself up to do it. How difficult it was to walk nonchalantly in the open when the temptation was to run like a frightened rabbit from one slit trench to another. Only I know how hard it was to remain standing when a shell was whistling in our direction, and not to throw myself flat on the ground.'

He was not on his own, as a diary entry for 22 July makes clear: 'I wish I weren't so frightened: but I am comforted to find that everybody else is. When they get talking I find most people are longing to confess how scared they are most of the time.'

Treacy and the Regiment continued to live in dugout holes which were as uncomfortable as they were unclean. One wag suggested that they might be called the BUM — the British Underground Movement.

There were occasional meetings with other Chaplains. One came to see him in a very dispirited state as Treacy noted in his diary:

'Apparently he is not finding that active service conditions are creating a desire for services amongst his men. I think this may be due to the fact that he gives the impression that he is ashamed of being a parson. For instance, he refuses to wear a dog collar — which over here I think to be *most* important. I hate the clerical collar — but I have worn it every day since getting to France.

'Already we are getting one or two cases of exhaustion. In the last war they were called "shell shock" — the uncharitable in both wars call them "wind up". I must admit that I am rather surprised at the type which is cracking. They are the hefty toughs — and not the weedy little men — as one might have anticipated.'

Eventually the 59th moved by stages to the point south of Caen at which the British, Canadian and American forces met to cut off the German army from the Seine. Those German units that managed to escape, or so they thought, were slaughtered by rocket firing Typhoons. The result was ghastly to behold. Mile after mile of dead Germans, overturned tanks and transport and an enormous number of dead horses. They crossed the Seine at Les Andelys and then started their ride to Belgium. Treacy's sense of direction failed again on 1 September:

'I was responsible for leading a small group of six vehicles and at one point I missed my way and I had to find my way back by cutting through two little villages well off the beaten track. I think I can claim that I and my little column liberated these villages. We were the first troops they had seen since the Bosche departed. And what a reception. The Curé organised the local school children on the village green — and the children curtsied and handed us bunches of flowers hastily picked in the local gardens. Several of the drivers were soundly kissed. Drinks were handed round ... We then passed through some dense woods in which large numbers of Germans were hiding — we could see them every now and then peering at us through the undergrowth. It was here that we took our prisoner — he darted out of the wood and insisted on being picked up. So we gave the poor devil a seat in one the cars: but we were all very puzzled as to what we should do with him. His name was Martin Vögel; he was a poor harmless hungry specimen — nothing of the Herrenvolk about him. He seemed delighted when I greeted him *Guten Morgen mein Herr* — I think he thought the first officer he saw would give orders for him to be shot. Our chaps were greatly intrigued with their first captive. They shared their rations with him and plied him with cigarettes.'

Treacy realised that the end of the war was in sight and his thoughts had turned to his postwar ministry on many occasions, of which more shortly. Naturally he expected to be with his Regiment until the end. But on 11 September 1944 he received a 'teleprint' ordering him to go as Senior Chaplain to 9 L of C area. He immediately left to see 'Freddie' Hughes, the Deputy Chaplain General (later Dean of Ripon), 21 Army Group in Brussels, to persuade him to let him be; and Douglas Crawford tried his luck with the 12 Corps Commander, Neil Ritchie. Of his visit to the DCG Treacy records:

'I was charmed by him. He is 'petit' and volatile and a very reasonable person: but he was quite firm that I must go from the Regiment. He said that the very fact that (a) my Regiment did not want me to go and (b) that I did not want to leave my Regiment — strengthened his conviction that I was the type of person that he wanted. He said he was sick of appointing SCF's whom no unit wanted to keep, and was starting promoting men who would bring to the RAChD unit experience and gifts of leadership. He offered me, as an alternative, SCF 11 Armoured Division, but I refused on the grounds of health.'

On 13 September Treacy said goodbye to the Regiment. After four years living in such close contact relationships were very deep. As he went round all the gun pits saying his farewells there were many red eyes for *The* only Padré.

The 9 L of C sub area was miles behind the fighting, somewhere back in France at a place called Coconne. As Treacy frankly records:

'There started about my most miserable and useless spell in the army; I had about four chaplains for whom I was responsible: they were good chaps, doing their best, but, with good reason, feeling that they would be better employed in their home parishes. After the strong family atmosphere of the 59th, the L of C gave me the impression of a Chamber of Trade organisation. A number of shop-keepers banded together for mutual protection but, when not protecting, in fierce competition. On the headquarters were the Senior Officers of the various services operating the L of C; Signals, Transport, Civil Affairs, Education, REME. They were a flabby lot, and morale was not very high. To me, it was humiliation to come back into the back areas, and to feel that I was achieving nothing.

'In fact it was very good for me, as I see now. It knocked some of the conceit out of me and brought home to me the fact that the ministry has to be worked out in situations in which people are in personal difficulties. In the 59th I had had the immense advantage of being a close friend of the colonel: everything, within reason, that I wanted, I had. I was on the terms of close friendship with officers and men.'

In his new position Treacy became alarmed and depressed at the amount of general moral laxity, and sexual laxity in particular, in conversation and in practice that existed among the officers. One major boasted to Treacy of his sexual proclivities and the Brigadier 'at lunch today (Oct 6) asked PK to draw a picture of our four ladies at their ablutions in the mobile bath unit. The Brig is an RC — I suppose they have pretty elastic standards in this kind of thing.' His diary contains many such entries. 'On Monday I had my chaplains' meeting at which poor old Rice — a rather holy Baptist — reported that he had been issued by the Pioneers to whom he was attached with a "French letter". I told him it was outrageous that these things should be issued wholesale to everyone whether they wanted them or not — and that he was to make a detailed report of the whole business.'

Above all Treacy was vehemently opposed to the Army's method of checking venereal disease. In his diary for 27 August he refers to the subject prompted by reading Archbishop William Temple's address on 'The Church's approach to the Problems of VD' (in *The Church Looks Forward*) in which Temple asserts: 'Governments affect the conduct of their subjects far more by the principles implicit in their acts than by the severity of the penalties attached to the neglect of those requirements.' Treacy comments:

'He (Temple) instances this in the Army's method of checking VD by giving instruction in the use of prophylactics; the implication and the suggestion being that the authorities expect a considerable number to practise fornication.

'I have said this continually since I have been in the army. I am certain that this is the wrong approach. The army's reply is to offer the padre the opportunity of following up the MO's lectures on anti-VD measures with a homily on the moral aspect of the problem; thus suggesting that the problem is a medical one with a moral aspect, whereas it is fundamentally a moral problem with a medical aspect. At first I used to avail myself of this opportunity, but latterly I have refused — as I think it bad tactics to allow myself to be turned on by the Army as a means of softening the crudities of the doctors' talks.'

After three months of this posting Treacy was sent to 11 L of C Area at Lalmes as Senior Chaplain. Here he had four senior chaplains serving with him of whom he was *primus inter pares*. These chaplains were Geoffrey Lampe (now Regius Professor of Divinity in the University of Cambridge), Gordon Calvert Lee (until his death Vicar of St Barnabas, Hove), Harry Bailey (later Rector of Stoke Newington) and Jack Bishop (later Vicar of Mexborough). Together they had responsibility for over one hundred chaplaincies in North-West Europe.

Treacy's primary task was to provide facilities for the chaplains to meet for short periods of mental uplift and spiritual refreshment. This was made possible by the requisitioning of Talbot House. Canon F. N. Robathan, Treacy's superior at the time, writes:

'As soon as I knew Poperinghe was liberated I hurried there to prevent Talbot House being taken over as a military HQ. All the contents which the inhabitants had taken and hidden from the Germans, were returned and Talbot House (which I had known in 1916) was restored to use under the new conditions. Retreats, conferences etc, etc were constantly held there. I myself met "Tubby" Clayton at Dieppe and he became a constant visitor. It was in this connection that Eric Treacy with his knowledge of clubs etc was most helpful. As a result of this and other good work I submitted his name for a decoration and was delighted when he was awarded the MBE.'

Treacy's plan was to withdraw the chaplains from their units in groups of 20 for the inside of a week and invited from England experienced clergy to conduct these retreat-conferences. In his innocence he thought that the clergy would respond wholeheartedly to such an opportunity, but he did not reckon with the stubbornness of some of the chaplains who made it clear that they resented being told by authority that they should participate in spiritual exercises. It is due to Treacy's determination and enthusiasm and disarming manner that those who arrived indignantly departed in peace.

Professor Lampe reflects on this period:

'I was always immensely impressed by Eric's cheerful and happy approach to pastoral work at a time when, with the end of the war, there was a great deal of anxiety on the part of everyone, including chaplains, about demobilisation and future prospects, and much (to use the contemporary term) bellyaching. We had older chaplains, for the most part in our areas, ministering to hospitals, rest camps, reinforcement depots, supply bases, POW camps and so forth and some who had not hit it off with fighting formations or, in one or two cases, had been recalcitrant about the ludicrous "non-fraternisation" policy in occupied Germany, and had been posted back. They wanted to get out and suspected that bishops at home would overlook them. Eric was admirable at keeping up morale and renewing spiritual life and pastoral concern among these people. He looked often, at first sight, like a hearty, joke-cracking, stereotype of an Army Padre; but of course there was much more depth to him than that, and it was his down-to-earth commonsense and shrewd judgement of people, as well as his genuine friendship and concern for them, that made him, to my mind, such an attractive character.'

Selection Conferences were started for the large number of potential Service candidates for ordination. The procedure was that a group of candidates lived for a few days with four selectors each of whom interviewed every candidate, storing up his comments until the selectors' meetings at the end. Canon Frank White, an army chaplain who later worked with Treacy in the Wakefield Diocese, observes:

'This was a work at which Eric was supremely good. The process of interviewing was harder than in normal life because the preliminary sorting out which ordinary parish life and work achieves was absent and, mixed with the good candidates, were some very strange ones, including some who were adept at "putting up a good show". Often timid men, or those struggling against difficult army conditions, needed encouragement, but sometimes there was false piety or humbug to expose and rebuke. Eric was good in both these directions. No one kinder than he or more patient with human frailty and no one sharper than he to detect and expose deceit or self-deception. This intuitive understanding of human nature and motive always stayed with him to the end of his life. Coupled with his outspokenness it sometimes led him into error, yet it was also the means of helping many to understand themselves.'

Professor Lampe's memories are of a similar nature:

'Eric showed that he had a good nose for picking out likely ordinands. I remember that he spoke to them remarkably frankly, and, by his own account, could be somewhat brutal. I remember him telling us at the final meeting of selectors on one occasion about an interview at which a pretentiously pious young man had enlarged on his own prayer life in terms of "basking in the sunshine of the Infinite", or some such phrase. Eric had interrupted "You're a liar; you never take the trouble to say your prayers at all" and the candidate had crumpled up and acknowledged that his professions were phoney. I was not very happy about that particular episode, which is perhaps why I remember it clearly. But, generally he was a sympathetic and exceptionally trouble-taking pastor.'

The question of Treacy's own future had become a pressing anxiety. He was one of those clergy who had resigned his benefice. He had left Edge Hill in March 1940 leaving his curate behind to run the parish. However, as he wrote to the new Bishop at Liverpool, Clifford Martin, on 27 September 1944:

'After a year in the army it became quite obvious to my wife and myself that the only straight thing to do was to resign the parish in order that another incumbent should be appointed. When I first made the suggestion, both Dr David and the patron were against it. But time proved to the then Bishop the wisdom of our intention, and ultimately my resignation was accepted, in spite of the fact that the patron (Canon Potter) was against it. Both my wife and I realised at the time that we were burning our boats in the sense that when the war ended we should run the risk of being jobless and homeless. I must give full credit to my wife for accepting so readily what was a most uncertain future without hesitation; in fact, it was she who was more sure of the rightness of the step than I was.'

Resigning had not been without incident. Treacy signed a deed vacating the benefice, for which he was charged four guineas by the ecclesiastical lawyers. This he refused, on principle, to pay. Despite what was to follow he never regretted his decision. How could it be just to have the benefits of an incumbency, namely a house and an income, when one was quite unable to discharge the duties to which those benefits attached.

Throughout the war May had continued to support and share Eric's ministry. A former sergeant known as Shippo witnessed this and writes:

'They both worked for the welfare of the Regiment. Mrs Treacy helped to organise the wives and friends of the Regiment in Liverpool especially during the difficult times of the bombing of Liverpool. Men were frantic about their families at home and the Padre and his wife co-operated by phone and obtained news and sorted out some difficult situations, for example, one gunner had a young wife and baby in Liverpool and when the bombing was happening, some of the selfish public in Liverpool bought up all the baby food to use as dried milk. This left the poor woman with no food for the baby. Eric was told of the situation and he phoned his wife and she arranged for the baby to receive a regular supply from a local Chemist. Little things, if you are not in the middle of it, but they helped such a lot. Mrs Treacy helped Eric also when she stayed with him in some of the different places in this country before the Regiment went abroad. They set up canteens together and organised many social activities.'

Earlier in the war the Bishop of Rochester, Christopher Chavasse, who had taken to Treacy as Treacy to him in a deep way, tried to obtain his services for the Rochester Diocese. In January 1943 he offered him 'the most important Church in the Medway towns', St Barnabas, Gillingham. Treacy refused on the grounds that he would not be able to take up the appointment until after the war. Inwardly all he wanted was to return to Liverpool.

In May 1944 Bishop Chavasse approached Treacy about the parish of St Nicholas, Strood, the vicar of which ranked with the Rector of Chatham and the Vicar of Gillingham as a 'persona' in the Diocese. Bishop Chavasse was prepared to keep Strood open until after the war but as he wrote to Treacy on 3 November

1944: 'For an important parish like Strood the Army Authorities are willing to release a Chaplain, if another clergyman from the Diocese can be offered in his stead. This means that as you are browned off by being a Chaplain on lines of communication, and if you would like to come and work at Strood as soon as possible, I believe, I can work your swift demobilisation.' He added significantly, 'I don't think I have ever wanted anything more in my life'.

There is no doubt of the regard in which Bishop Chavasse held Treacy: 'One of the most promising men in the Church of England'. Had Treacy gone to Rochester he would have risen fast in the Diocese, but perhaps not in the wider Church.

However, Treacy's chief desire was to return to Liverpool where he now felt his roots to be implanted. In the summer of 1944 he had been approached about the living of Garston in Liverpool. After some agonising he wrote to the trustees saying that he would be willing to leave the army by the end of the year if the Bishop of Liverpool could obtain his release. After two months' suspense he heard that someone else (G.R. Lindsay) had been appointed. Lindsay was reluctant to accept and wrote to Treacy telling him so but Bishop Martin had pressed him.

During this period Treacy was in constant touch with his friend the Bishop Suffragan of Warrington, Herbert Gresford Jones. After the Garston disappointment he put Treacy's name in for the living of St Michael's, Blundellsands, but Treacy regarded it as 'a suburban backwater which I don't fancy at all'.

Treacy's frustration was in danger of leading to bitterness. It was not helped by seeing his friends and acquaintances moving onwards and upwards; for example, Roger Wilson who left Holy Trinity, South Shore, Blackpool to become Archdeacon of Nottingham in 1944.

The basic problem was that Bishop Martin, who had succeeded Bishop David in 1944, had not met Treacy and Bishop Gresford Jones conveyed to Treacy that he should no longer expect to return to Liverpool, saying: 'The *Diocese* does not matter. I've been in six! What outstanding man is there who has kept all the Ministry in *one* Diocese? What matters is being *in* the Church of Christ and trying to do His blessed Will.'

Treacy needed those words and he replied saying:

'I must reorient my mind and get used to the idea of going elsewhere. I cannot pretend that it is not a tremendous disappointment to us both. In these long five years of war May and I have so often thought of our return to a parish, and have based all our thinking and planning on the assumption that it would be Liverpool that claimed us. I suppose that I have been rather stubborn in my desire to get back to the diocese. The reason is that being away so long I have thought a lot about home and homecoming, and always in my mind I have identified somewhere in Liverpool with my thoughts about home. But I do realise that I have been guilty of imposing terms on God. After all, it is obviously wrong to ask God to guide one in a situation like this, and then add — almost in brackets — "But Lord, mind you make it Liverpool". And that is rather what I have been doing. As doors shut in Liverpool, they seem to be opening elsewhere, which I suppose is God's way of showing me what He wants me to do.'

Treacy's personality changed perceptively during these war years. He emerged stronger and surer. The war had a remarkable effect on him and he had had a marked and lasting influence on a host of people in the Regiment who never forgot him and learned lessons which influenced their future lives. If there had been no war experience it is unlikely that he would have achieved high office in the Church. Richard Bingham, an officer during the war and now a County Court Judge sums it up:

'I always thought that he gained greatly in self-confidence as he found increasingly during his time with us (in the 59th) that he was both liked and respected not only as a minister but as a man. He would probably also agree, were he alive, that no man suffered more than he did in resisting the many temptations to reduce his own high standards which war conditions continually put before him. His attitude to swearing is an example of this. Although swearing was not a major vice in the Regiment, there was in his view too much of it, and against it he waged a relentless and effective war. But the irony was that, in moments of exceptional stress, on no one did this war rebound more than on himself for everyone knew that when it came to ventilating his feelings he could do so as well as the next man, and many a time have I watched in quiet amusement the battle, in such moments of stress, between his Irish aptitude for self-expression and his consciousness of the imperative need for self-control. The result was usually a purple face, followed after a moment or two by a great gust of laughter.

'He was in truth a very human man, full of frailties which affect us all, which he had determined to overcome, and full of the standards to which we all aspire and to which he greatly helped us to continue to aspire.

'Quite apart from this, but not entirely disconnected was that quality of his which can only be called "charisma", and which so affected my wife when he married us that to this day my wife becomes weak at the knees when she remembers the feeling, or charisma, which he then generated.'

Treacy was awarded the MBE. To the 59th he was always OBE 'Our Beloved Eric'.

Above left: Mother and Son.

Above: Boyhood. *A. W. Dron*

Left: The Insurance Salesman. *Vandyk*

Top right: At Camp with Shrewsbury House boys.

Right: First camera.

Far right: Padre having a bath.

Left: 'Woodbine' Treacy.

Below: Institution as Rector of Keighley, 15 June 1945 (l to r) Bishop's Chaplain; Canon E. E. Peters, Rural Dean; E. T.; Alfred Blunt, Bishop of Bradford; F. A. T. Mossman, Registrar; F. G. Ackerley, Archdeacon of Craven. *W. Speight*

Right: Remembrance Day, 1945. *W. Speight*

Below right: Halifax Parish Church, St John the Baptist. *Eric Treacy*

88

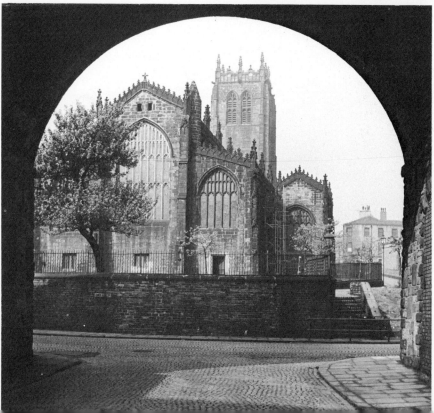

Above: The Parish!   *Eric Treacy*

Left: Thistles to keep the Archdeacon awake.
Daily Express

Top right: The Vicar's Vigil.   *Yorkshire Post*

Right: Bishop Suffragan of Pontefract. In centre
— George D'Oyly Snow, Bishop Suffragan of
Whitby; Archbishop; E.T.; John Ramsbotham,
Bishop of Wakefield.   *K. Pettinger*

Left: Enthronement as Bishop of Wakefield with Chancellor G. B. Graham and Registrar Cecil Coles. 27 March 1968. *Yorkshire Post*

Above: Emerging from the pit, 28 March 1968. *National Coal Board*

Above right: Receiving Honorary Doctorate of Laws at Leeds University from its Chancellor, the Duchess of Kent, 23 May 1968.

Right: Consecration of Gordon Fallows as Bishop Suffragan of Pontefract at Wakefield Cathedral, 11 June 1968, by Donald Coggan, Archbishop of York.

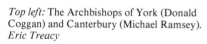

Top left: The Archbishops of York (Donald Coggan) and Canterbury (Michael Ramsey). *Eric Treacy*

Left: Free Ride. Helme Parish Church. *Huddersfield Examiner*

Above: Gaitered Friends Stride Out — E.T. and Roger Wilson.

Top right: Eric and May. *Yorkshire Post*

Right: On the Air.

Above: With Love from Love Lane. Portraits presented from inmates of Wakefield Prison, April 1974.   *Wakefield Express*

Left: Nearing Retirement.   *Ray D. Clarke*

Top right: At Treacy's memorial service. *R. O. Coffin*

Right: Evening Star heading for Appleby. *D. Eatwell*

9
The Church in Action

The door which opened as the Liverpool one shut was across the Pennines in Yorkshire. The new Provost of Bradford, John G. Tiarks (later Bishop of Chelmsford), was a close friend of Treacy's from the Liverpool Diocese and he was keen to help find a parish for Treacy and capture him for the Diocese of Bradford, which badly needed new life. Tiarks was a remarkable Provost of Bradford who filled his Cathedral with people. He combined in an unusual way, a high degree of efficiency, paying meticulous attention to detail, with a pastoral ministry. He was brilliantly original in his methods, and though cold on the exterior, had a wonderful gift of attracting people, and harnessing them to the service of the Kingdom.

Tiarks tried to get Treacy appointed as Vicar of St Barnabas, Heaton, an area in which there was a high concentration of Bradford 'brass'. This came to nothing. On 8 November 1944 Tiarks wrote to Treacy mentioning another possibility:

'The Rectory of Keighley, one of the three large centres in the Diocese has just fallen vacant. The resigning Rector, Canon J. C. F. Hood, is DACG Southern Command, I think. He ought to have resigned five years ago. At any rate I wrote this week to the Duke of Devonshire who is the Patron putting your name in. I told him that I had not consulted you, so I will be glad if you will let me know what you feel about it. There is a tremendous job to be done as the whole work has gone to pieces since the outbreak of War and the life of the Anglican Church there is at a very low ebb. It will need a man of determination and vision to pull things back again.'

A month elapsed before Treacy heard everything officially. Then, sitting in a dingy room in some old French Barracks in Rouen he received the following letter:

> The Mayfair Hotel,
> Berkeley Square,
> London W 1
> 5th December, 1944

Dear Mr Treacy,

I believe that you have been told by the Provost of Bradford that I should be approaching you with a view to asking you to accept the Living of Keighley in Yorkshire.

I write to say that the way is now clear for me to make you the formal offer and I hope most sincerely that you will accept it.

Keighley is an important parish, and I gather that things have not gone altogether well there recently.

I should be very glad to see you about it at any time if you could get leave to come over and talk about it, but this is a formal offer and I hope very much you will be able to accept it straight away.
Yours sincerely,
Devonshire.

Thus a patron exercised his rights!

Treacy accepted almost blindly for he saw neither patron nor parish though May went over to Keighley to have a look and said 'Accept' which he did with relief and enthusiasm.

Keighley is situated in the valley of the Aire. Within the Borough boundary is the village of Haworth, famous for its Parsonage, the home of the gifted Bronte sisters. It is midway between Bradford and Skipton and it was then a thriving town with a population of about fourteen thousand. A combination of canal, railway and road had opened up Keighley and made it into an industrial town. The Leeds & Liverpool Canal at Keighley was opened in 1773 and the railway came in 1847. Until then the town clustered round the Church as the village had done for centuries.

The parish contained five Anglican places of worship, the number in no way suggesting any measure of religious vitality. As Keighley had expanded, the Parish Church of St Andrew, a building of little character outside and even less inside, seemed to have been pushed off centre from what vitality the town possessed. In addition there were St Mark's, Utley; All Saints, Highfield; St Matthew's, Braithwaite; and St John's, Newsholme. The church at Newsholme was part of the farm buildings belonging to the Ogden family. Here was a complete village community which became Treacy's favourite part of the parish. At Braithwaite there was a combination of new housing and village life; at Utley dwelt the 'better-offs', and the professional folk; Highfield was a thickly populated residential area; and the Mother Church, surrounded by shops and offices, had all the problems of a non-residential area to face, which, in practice, meant that the poor old Mother was accused of sheep stealing from the daughters.

Above all Keighley was a materialistic town and Mammon had bitten deep into its soul. 'Where there's muck there's brass.' The people were almost literally dyed in the wool. They were dour and even went about their many material pleasures with a gruff manner and miserable demeanour. Keighley people — who found it difficult to believe that any good could possibly come from outside Keighley — were not lavish with praise and seemed almost frightened of showing too much enthusiasm.

Such religion as existed was Nonconformist in fact and temperament. The Church of England had made little impact. Treacy summed up the position like this: 'Their sturdy independence causes them to resist the influence of anything established — religious or otherwise.' He was too optimistic in thinking 'that there is a very strong Christian life in Keighley — stronger perhaps than can be measured by the size of the congregations attending the various churches. 'More realistically, he added 'The West Riding folk do not by temperament find it easy to worship, but they have it in them to be stubbornly loyal to any cause that they have made their own.'

When Treacy's appointment was announced the Parochial Church Council requested him to obtain an immediate release from the army. He refused on the grounds that like everybody else in the Services he must wait until his release group came round. On 8 February 1945 Treacy noted in his diary:

'Received a rather unpleasant letter from the senior curate at Keighley (C. P. L. Dennis). From the line of it I suspect that he is jealous of me; being an older man and more learned than me, I think he feels that he ought to have been offered the living. His complaint is that I am being instituted to the living and then returning to the Army. He says this will cause grave dissatisfaction in the parish, and that they are very critical. I cannot believe that this is a fair indication of the parish's attitude; it may be the view of a small clique of which he is a member. I wrote him a long letter explaining the reasons for my early induction (chiefly, that it would make it easier for the Bishop to effect my release when the war was over) — but decided not to send it on the grounds that it was a bad beginning to start explaining one's actions to one's curates. Instead, I sent him a rather formal note of acknowledgement and wrote a full explanation of my position to the Secretary of the PCC. I can see that the parish have some grounds for complaining that their new Rector cannot come straight to them, as they have been without a Rector for $5\frac{1}{2}$ years, but I think that the more thoughtful of them would rather wait for a man who had seen the war through than have a man who pulled strings to get out. Personally I am convinced that I ought to go to Keighley straight away — and I have asked the Bishop, the Patron and the MP to ask the War Office to release me. But they have not succeeded.'

Curate Dennis had a PhD, which in his case meant a crammed up knowledge of an obscure Russian poet. He worked this for all it was worth but it repelled rather than attracted the people of Keighley Parish Church. Treacy was correct in his assumptions for he heard from the Church Council 'in the warmest terms saying that they fully appreciated the position. As I suspected, all the opposition comes from Dennis — who seems from his letters to be a *most* awkward man. I have heard privately that he will be leaving within the next 3 months, which will save me the trouble of getting rid of him'. Dennis was shortly appointed to the Dales parish of Tosside.

On 16 March Treacy caught his first glimpse of Keighley — and of the Parochial Church Council face to face. In a borrowed car he and May set out to view their new charge, having a picnic lunch on the moors above nearby Silsden. Later he reflected: 'I had heard much about the Yorkshire character from my Lancashire friends; that they were blunt, suspicious and Nonconformist. My first impressions of the West Riding bore these judgements out. My welcome to Keighley was scarcely hearty. On our first visit we had to find accommodation in one of the shabbiest hotels we have ever stayed in. No hospitality was offered us.'

At the meeting of the PCC Treacy offered to withdraw his acceptance of the living in view of the fact that he could not get to them immediately. His offer was rejected. He returned to the Army and back to Keighley on a quick visit for his Institution by the Bishop of Bradford (Alfred Blunt) on 15 June. The old Institution Service used in the Church of England has a good balance between striking awe into the heart of the new incumbent, and promising him strength and inspiration for his new task. Bishop Blunt warned the congregation 'You churchgoers in Keighley must be prepared to lay aside your prejudices and consider innovation.' The warning was apt as Treacy had been thinking a great deal about his future ministry in Keighley and if inspired perspiration could win the day then Treacy was the man! He had drawn up the following plan — it was to be the last time he ever concocted a plan in advance of taking up a new appointment or initiative.

'1. Bill Naylor once said to me of the army chaplain's work: "Nothing ever happens in the army unless you make it happen". The same goes for a parish. So I go to my new job prepared to *make* things happen — and not just to keep it ticking over as I find it.

2. James Welsh (Religious Director of BBC) said that "Power follows clearness of purpose and efficiency". Substitute "achievement" for "power". I must go there with my purpose clear and I must subordinate all my energies and bright ideas to that purpose. A purpose carries with it a discipline. For me the efficiency part of it will be difficult, because I am *not* by nature efficient or methodical — but that will be part of the discipline. If I am to be a leader of my people I must have my purpose clear. What then is to be my purpose? To make the Christian Faith a living reality in the life of Keighley: to make my parish not only a place where the Gospel is preached but where it is lived — so that the Church shall be what the town should be. To explore every means whereby the Church may make an impact on the town. In a word — to aim that the Church shall take the place of God's son in Keighley. That it should love the people as He would have loved them; that it should challenge evil as He would have challenged it; that it should give itself in sacrificial service as He did; that it should have unquestioning Faith in God's Power as He had.

3. It is as fatal to be in too great a hurry as it is to be too slow. The best plans may fail if they are presented tactlessly and unintelligently. Whatever I set out to do must be supported enthusiastically by the people. After all — it is they who will do the work. Therefore they must be made to feel that what they are doing is what they want to do. It is no use flogging an apathetic congregation. It may take time to do this but it is time well spent. To achieve this I plan to organise a week-end conference for the parish at which — after an opening talk on the Task confronting the Church, the Conference will break up into four syndicates which will consider:

(a) *Worship*. Do we need new forms of worship to meet 20th century needs; or greater efforts to teach people the significance of the Prayer Book.

(b) *Propaganda*. To explore means of putting the Christian Faith — directly and indirectly — before as large a number of people as possible. To devise an up to date advertising campaign — and to inaugurate a parish magazine which will be unrecognisable as such, but will present the Christian point of view on important questions and topics.

(c) *Youth Work*. To plan a drive on the young people in the Parish — in the schools — secondary and elementary; in pre-service organisations etc. To plan first class youth clubs and camps. To survey the work and methods of the Sunday School.

(d) *Bringing them in*. To discuss methods of visitation in the parish. To think out new methods of getting in touch with the people — and what to do with the fish that is nibbling at the bait.

'I shall try to get the syndicate leaders from outside the parish and shall use only first class people. If possible they and I will have a weekend discussing our aims for the parish so that they will know how to exert their influence in discussions.'

Treacy finally arrived in the parish in October 1945 in his demob suit. He was ready; but was Keighley? He wrote:

'My first encounter with the twelve churchwardens of the parish was a pretty hostile one in which they tried to tell me how to deal with my staff. I dealt with them in a matter of minutes and I am pleased to say that all twelve of them became close friends during the years that followed. Not a thing was done in the Rectory to welcome us. All in all — not a very charming welcome.

'They were very suspicious of me at the beginning; they were blunt but so was I. Gradually, the clouds lifted and we began to understand each other. Two things, I believe, helped to bring the breakthrough.

'One was that they saw that I was prepared to work; the other was that they began to realise that I intended to Captain the Ship. Two things Yorkshiremen cannot stand are laziness and weakness in the exercise of responsibility. I have a theory that Yorkshiremen rig situations with the single intention of seeing whether the man in question (a) has the wits to spot the situation which they have set up; and (b) the strength of character to deal with it, and them. If he does both he is home and dry; if he doesn't and they get the better of him, he will never recover.'

There was a healthy quality in this temperamental attitude of Keighleyites to their Rector. Church of England clergy in central or large parishes tend to be flattered by their people, which exposes them to the dangerous democratic passion for eulogy, for giving and receiving compliments.

Treacy started his ministry using as his maxim 'You take people as you find them, and work with what you've got.' If the bracing air of the Pennine moors had bred an energetic and healthy race of people, they seemed singularly unprepared for a dynamic and energetic Rector. Moreover Treacy had both cheek and charm and knew increasingly how to use both. Kenneth Law, an inherited curate (and now Vicar of Ossett in the Wakefield Diocese) admits that 'At first Eric may have given the impression of a young man in a hurry which was understandable in view of his army service. We, at Keighley, may have appeared, to him, to be in a rut.' Another curate, Duncan Philips, describes him as, ' "The Church in Action" as his detractors — or leg-pullers — would say in our Keighley days together.' And the Church in Action it was to be.

Complacency was punctured, if only temporarily. Within the first 12 months or so Treacy appealed for what seemed an impossible sum of £450 for urgent renovations to the Church. He sat in the Church porch for eight hours and received £464; an Evangelistic campaign was held in Keighley with the irrepressible, challenging and effective Joe Fison (then Canon of Rochester, later Bishop of Salisbury) leading at the Parish Church; three services were broadcast by the BBC; a Parish Festival was inaugurated and a Parish Magazine was started. The first issue of the monthly magazine appeared in April 1946. It was arresting and lively, the best in the Diocese. Besides the usual round of parish pump paraphernalia and recording of hatches, matches and despatches, outside contributors were invited to write articles on a variety of subjects. Articles on national and international affairs were culled from periodicals in an attempt to add another dimension to Keighley's insularity. Above all it was the amplifier for 'his master's voice'. A 'Modern Rector's Diary' was a chatty but stimulating individual account of the parish and Treacy's selective doings and misdoings. I pluck a few times at random to give the flavour of the Diary, showing the mixture of the serious and not-so-serious.

'1946 November 19. Notice in this morning's *Yorkshire Post* an Appeal for the fabric of Canterbury Cathedral; the space in the paper being presented by the Brewers' Association. Surely, it is a pitiable thing that the Mother Church of England should have its needs commended to the public by an Association whose products are doing so much to undermine and contaminate the morals of England. Mr Dean — think again!

'1947 January 1. First letter of the New Year from the Income Tax Collector! Not a demand note, but a charming letter replying to a Christmas Greeting that I added to a cheque that I recently paid him. His words are worth quoting: "However, I believe you to be a man of sufficient Christian spirit to wish happiness to publicans and sinners — and even Tax Gatherers. I therefore heartily reciprocate . . ."

'1947 March 13. The Rev Kenneth Law's Institution to the living of Allerton took place. A sudden thaw made the roads appalling, with the result that the two bus loads from Keighley arrived twenty minutes late for the service. When I arrived at the West Door of the Church I was delighted to find Mr Law waiting (as I thought) to welcome us: I was greeting him (somewhat noisily, I must confess) when I noticed the Archdeacon and Rural Dean looking at me rather reprovingly — then I realised what a brick I had dropped. At that moment they were in the act of inducting Mr Law to the living. Keighley certainly made an impression on Allerton: forty people in the middle of a service cannot be ignored!

'1947 December 9. Crisis due to the non-arrival of trifle and cakes for the Women's Meeting Christmas Party. Caterer found in the nick of time. Two dishes of trifle loaded into back of car; on unloading it was found that a large amount of the trifle had decided to remain in the car! This had unfortunate results later on in the evening when I gave two gentlemen of Morton a lift in the car after addressing their Brotherhood!'

There were stirrings of new life in the Parish but Treacy did not limit his activity to the Church of England. With the object of advancing co-operation in worship and action, a Fellowship of Christian Congregations was formed in January 1946 at a meeting convened by Treacy. This subsequently became the Keighley Council of Churches with Treacy as its first President. The Council met regularly and produced its own printed quarterly newsletter. One of the first tasks of the Council was to address a letter of protest to the General Purposes Committee of the West Riding County Council with regard to the granting of a licence for a dog-racing track at Keighley. The unsuccessful protest was made on two grounds:

'(1) The moral and social deterioration which follows from the institution of dog tracks in any town through the increase of gambling and drunkenness; and (2) on the grounds of the diversion of materials required for constructive effort to a purpose which cannot be other than harmful.'

The Council of Churches conducted open air services and held meetings in factories. They acted as hosts to European Voluntary Workers resident in Keighley. They were fortunate in having an Austrian curate, Heinz Helmuth Arnold, at one of the Keighley churches. He had suffered great tortures during the war. The Council kept up a pressure of opposition to the continued retention of German prisoners of war in the country.

Fundamentally, Treacy was a puritan with a sense of humour. The first rather than the last ensured understanding and co-operation by most of the Free Churches in Keighley. He was always strong on Sunday observance and he led the opponents of Sunday cinema opening in Keighley in 1946. At a public meeting in the Municipal Hall, Treacy and his supporters won the day by 275 votes to 136. He was chairman and moving force of an exploratory committee which led to the setting up of a Marriage Guidance Council in Keighley. There was one exception to united friendliness amongst clergy and ministers as Treacy recalls:

'I was told by many people that Keighley was a Nonconformist stronghold and that the Church of England did not count for much. It is true that Methodism was strong, but it was beginning to lose its strength. The Methodist ministers were without exception friendly and co-operative. The most active opponent of the Church of England was a Congregational Minister called Nicholson Balmer. Balmer was an able man, an excellent preacher, and his congregation contained many of the leading figures in Keighley. He was a bonny fighter, but often he was fighting issues which were fantasies of his own imagination. In fact I think he was as suspicious of other Free Churches as he was of the Church of England. Of one thing he was quite determined, and that was that in no circumstances was he going to acknowledge any primacy to the Church of England. Actually no one wanted him to, as we all felt ourselves partners in the Lord's work, but nothing that we could say, or do, would convince him that we had not some cunning plot to undermine his influence in the town. He was a character, a man of considerable ability, who would have done well in politics, provided that his party could always have been in opposition.'

Treacy was an innovator though not one to light the touch paper and then run to observe the effects from a safe distance. If something he had initiated was faltering he tried to give it new life by frequent challenges. Preaching in Temple Street Methodist Chapel on 22 August 1948 he wondered if all things were well with the Council of Churches which, having emerged from its first romantic flush, seemed to be floundering. 'I think that we are now in danger of relapsing into a state of contented apathy — satisfied that we have started something; pleased that the churches of the town have "got organised".'

The unity that Treacy desired was the unity of harmony rather than unison. 'I don't think many of us would want uniformity — my church has traditional forms of worship which I love and should hate to lose; so have others. Rather do I think that what we want is a matter of relationships and attitudes — plus a readiness to allow God to guide us — and not to be obstructed by prejudices.' Within a few years he moved away from this rather lukewarm position, perhaps against his own real feelings.

Treacy soon began to make his mark and his reputation as a preacher and speaker. His sermons, addresses and speeches were now usually written out word for word. Another Keighley curate, Roger Vallance, writes: 'Eric was a great talker and even when he hadn't much to say of particular importance one always felt that he managed to say it beautifully and that made up for the slim content. Consequently, his preaching was not always profound but it was never dull in presentation.' Herein lay a gift and a temptation. Treacy's manner of thinking and speaking was lay rather than clerical. He had a layman's mind, and with its many excellences possessed also some of its limitations. His preaching at Keighley often had the freedom, directness and vivacity of conversation. His understanding of the people to whom he was preaching was born of personal knowledge, and inspired by genuine sympathy. His scorn for whatsoever was unreal, or ostentatious, or merely conventional, added a cutting edge to his phrases. He pointed his moral by reference to familiar experiences.

This type of preaching was eminently reportable. If the telling phrase left an impression or, better, challenged the listener, Treacy was satisfied. Yet he constantly questioned his own power of persuasion and was genuinely worried about being superficial. His topical sermons were better than his strictly biblical ones at Keighley. As an evangelical this tall, craggy, plausible man preached for conversions but he did not find it easy to make the personal appeal. No Billy Graham he!

Much effort went into the preparation of sermons. On 2 November 1947 he noted:

'I had a bad day with my sermons. I had spent more time than usual preparing them too — yet as the day went on I got progressively worse. At one point during my sermon at Evensong, I lost myself completely. In the middle of a sentence I forgot what the sentence was about. I was seized with a cowardly desire to flee the pulpit. Sermons are unpredictable — often when there has been but little preparation the sermon comes alive from the first few words, and thoughts and words flow freely and fluently. At other times, in spite of the most careful preparation, words stick and thoughts wander and the whole thing is a real ordeal. I am certain that the the attitude of the congregation has a lot to do with this. The presence of but a few hostile and critical people can affect the morale of the preacher. Yet, I do not think the effectiveness of the sermon always depends upon the preacher's feeling that he has succeeded. God can and does work through the most halting and unskilful sermons.'

Treacy's preaching changed over the years. He knew that the Christian preacher has failed miserably however well he has succeeded in filling his church, who so preaches that the congregation is amused, attracted, excited, but never moved to repentance, or strengthened in good living, or lifted from earth to heaven. Cowper draws the portrait of one method of preaching:

He that negotiates between God and man,
As God's ambassador, the grand concerns
Of judgement and of mercy, shall beware
Of lightness in his speech. 'Tis pitiful
To court a grin, when you should woo a soul;
To break a jest, when pity would inspire
Pathetic exhortation; and to address
The skittish fancy with facetious tales,
When sent with God's commission to the heart!
So did not Paul.

Self-knowledge prompted Treacy to beware of giving amusement rather than religion, or of giving a commentary on contemporary affairs rather than help and comfort in the difficult ways of duty.

When all the sermons have been preached, the meetings chaired, the organisations attended and new schemes initiated, the chief work of the Church and its deepest claim to the gratitude of the people lies in the quiet round of ceaseless ministration by its parochial clergy. Keighley was unmarked so far as the effects of enemy action was concerned. But as in places throughout the country there were the marks of war which were not visible to the eye. There were many families which had suffered bereavement during the five years of war. Men were returning from the prisoner of war camps, and many there were who came back suffering from the wounds of war. Treacy recognised and tried to meet the needs for pastoral care and understanding which would help these people to build up relationships which had so seriously suffered by reason of the long separations caused by the war.

The geographical inconvenience of the Rectory helped him in his pastoral ministry. The Rectory was a large house situated about one mile from the Parish Church. This gave Treacy the opportunity for exercise when he walked to Church to say his daily offices and thus provided him with contacts with people in the streets of the parish. Although he loved motoring and fast cars he never sealed himself up in them. He recalls his walks to and from the Church and the people he met:

'These contacts grew to large proportions with the passing of time, and although they made time-keeping difficult, they were the means whereby I was able to discover what was happening in the parish. People came to know that I would be passing by at the same time each day, and I would often he told of someone in hospital, or called into a house to see a parishioner who required my services. Sometimes such visits were of a serious nature, and, sometimes, to do no more than sign a pensions form. These daily walks brought me into daily contact with the police, the postman, the men who emptied the bins, and kept the streets clean and a variety of people going to and from work.'

At first congregations increased quite dramatically and records were being broken. For Treacy's first Easter in 1946 there were 700 communicants at the Parish Church, a record 52 at Braithwaite and the largest number since 1919 at All Saints. The temporary boost soon passed off and a normality returned which meant a church half full for Evensong and rather less than that for Matins. Yorkshire people were not great churchgoers. Very few people went twice on Sundays and even fewer every Sunday. Treacy's report of the year 1947-1948 showed that collections were up and communicants down. The attendance at those functions which he designed to help people understand their faith better, were bad. The need for a devotional core to the Church was constantly stressed.

Of all the Churches for which he was responsible he had a special favourite — the one at Newsholme, as he writes:

'Services were attended by the whole village. Doris Ogden, whose father owned the farmbuildings of which the church was part, played the organ with great gusto, and her brother David blew it with even more gusto. Our repertoire of hymns was limited, but we knew what we were singing, and let fly. Ernest Page, the verger-caretaker, was about as typical a bit of Yorkshire grit as you would find however far you searched the county. An old age pensioner, a widower, his word in the village was unquestioned. Intensely cautious in his reactions to people, he looked you up and down, suspicious that you were going to suggest some change in, or reorganisation of, local habits.

'It took Ernest a long time to make up his mind about me; he arranged one or two situations designed to force me to a decision that I could not win, but, rather to his disappointment, I failed to see them. Well, of course I saw them, but I didn't "let on". After two years during which he withheld judgement, one afternoon, pointing with his thumb over his shoulder to where I was standing he said, tersely, to me "Yon's real" which I suppose was something of a compliment.'

These Yorkshire towns and villages often produced patriarchal characters who exercised remarkable authority in the places in which they lived. This authority had nothing to do with social standing, education or wealth. It was a triumph of character and personal force over the local tribe. By 'character' I do not necessarily mean personal virtue or integrity, as some of these people were ruffians, but they possessed an indefinable capacity for leadership. Treacy remarked: 'There are places in the West Riding in which, if you want to get something done, or to win support for a project, you don't go to the Mayor or the Town Clerk, you go to the local patriarch and if he says "Yes" everybody else says "Yes". How this particular grapevine works, I haven't the faintest idea, but of its effectiveness, I have no doubt. Although Newsholme was a hamlet with a population of less than a hundred, Ernest Page stood in this kind of relationship to the place.'

Throughout his time at Keighley Treacy had three curates. Although he never chose 'Yes' men there was no mistaking who was running the show! His relationship with his curates was mixed. Duncan Phillips recalls that 'he was the sort of person one could have followed anywhere even if one disagreed with him. I kept a diary — because I was told I had to! — and I had to show it to him, for initialling once a month.' Among random reflections he recalls 'Phillips you *make* work!' and in a typed letter 'Sound less fierce on the 'phone', which says Phillips, I had stuck to my own 'phone for many months. One Monday he rang me up 'Phillips, go away for a week. I don't want to see you around till Saturday. Several of the congregation say I'm killing you." '

The curates met daily with their Rector for Matins at the Parish Church. 'Every Wednesday morning,' recollects Duncan Phillips, 'I had to have my sermon in manuscript and preach it to him in the Parish Church. (I don't think all his curates enjoyed this as much as I did.) He got bored with the sound of my voice eventually. But in the meantime gave good advice. Over some theological points of variance he sometimes said: "Phillips, fundamentally, I'm a Prot" to which I could only reply "Well — fundamentally, I'm a Cath".'

Roger Vallance remembers:

'I found him so much more friendly than many of the incumbents of the day; for example, I left a curacy where I had been Vallance from the day I started to the day I left and the idea of fellowship between vicar and curate did not exist. But here at Keighley was someone with a great sense of fun and warmth. Of course there were times when he was irritable — especially if one didn't agree with him. I recall two occasions when I differed in matters where I felt one was entitled to a point of view about his intentions for a third person and he sent me a letter through the post expressing annoyance, despite the fact that we met daily. He was a good man, beneath the external charm and seeming self-assurance was plenty of shyness and uncertainty. He loved his Lord in those Keighley days and from what I have known since I doubt if he changed except to become even more simple in Faith and even more compassionate towards his fellow men.'

In 1947 Bishop Blunt appointed Treacy as Rural Dean of South Craven and an Honorary Canon of Bradford assigning him to the stall of King Edward. These duties and honours respectively widened the scope of his pastoral ministry and integrated him into the general life of the Diocese of Bradford. It is a small Diocese with under 150 parishes. The Cathedral city is at the southern extremity of the Diocese, which extends northwards for about 50 miles, reaching to the Cumbrian border. Although its name suggests that it is an industrial diocese, it is, in fact, except for Bradford and Keighley, a largely rural diocese, containing within its boundaries market towns such as Skipton, Otley, Settle and Sedbergh; the beautiful villages of the Wharfe and the Ribble; undulating dale as well as Ilkley Moor ba'tat; and the three peaks of Pen-y-Ghent, Ingleborough and Great Whernside. Its size makes it possible for a bishop to enjoy a close relationship with his clergy and people although it is not entirely convenient having the bishop residing in Bradford.

Treacy came to have a great regard and respect for Alfred Blunt, second Bishop of Bradford:

'When I first met him he was a tired man and was obviously suffering from the loss of one of his sons in the war. At first, I found him reserved and of few words. When I was appointed to Keighley I wrote him a letter introducing myself. In reply I received a letter of two lines. By modern standards, he was not a good Bishop, because he was not here, there and everywhere in the Diocese. He was not given to easy and "pally" relationships as are so many of the Bishops today. He possessed a dignity which bore no relationship to his inches, which were few. He was a man with authority.

'Alfred Blunt was a wise man: he possessed a shrewd, salty and slightly cynical approach to human situations, to which would be added — like soda to whisky — a pastoral kindness and understanding which issued in the sound practical advice that so often I needed from him, and which I never failed to get. Alfred did not run about the Diocese like a peripatetic Father in God; as an ex-parish priest himself, I think that he realised that men, on the whole, preferred to be left to get on with their jobs, and not to have blasts of episcopal breath down their necks.

'But, for any who were prepared to make the journey to Horton Hall, Bradford, there was always a welcome and through the mists of pipe smoke would emerge words of wisdom delivered in a queer gutteral accent. I did not sense that his marriage was one from which he derived much companionship; indeed Mrs Blunt frequently gave the impression of mocking him in public, and I do not think there was anyone in the Diocese with whom he had relationships which were at all close.

'Blunt was an excellent preacher, but his matter was better than his delivery. His best sermons were delivered at Institutions, when he drew on his grasp of theological principles and his pastoral experience to give both laity and clergy something with bite and substance. These sermons were short, but they never failed to hit the target, and to this day I remember how skilfully he made the truths of the Bible relevant to the everyday life of the parish.'

Unfortunately, because Bishop Blunt's hand on the organisation and administration of the Diocese was light, little men with power complexes set up internecine friction within it. Attempts were made to lure Treacy into these unedifying activities but he refused to be persuaded. From this he learned the need for a Diocesan Bishop to give positive leadership and be master in his own house in order to keep such factions in restraint. He noted 'Firmness at the top does not need to be autocracy; all that is required is that there be sufficient control to keep a balance between the various power structures that exist.'

Treacy took his duties as Rural Dean of South Craven very seriously. It housed some of the most difficult parishes in the Diocese. No one told him what to do as Rural Dean. His immediate superior, the Archdeacon of Craven, F. G. Ackerley, lived the life of a hermit at Long Preston and only emerged from hiding when fetched. As Treacy remarked, 'He certainly gave me not the slightest help. It was a case of learn as you go.'

There is something pastorally inept and irresponsible in the fact that the Church of England gave, and continues to give, men increased responsibility, and practically no assistance in the exercising of it. The Church simply hopes for the best — and usually gets it!! It is no credit to the Church however when it leaves behind disillusioned sceptics and dispirited pastors. Here was Treacy, a rural dean at 39 and comparatively new to the parish and the diocese. Initially, he was in danger of becoming aggressive and unbending. In the absence of any guidance he started visiting the clergy in the deanery. What he found was both disturbing and illuminating. Some of the clergy were rampant individualists whilst the enthusiasm of others had been neutralised by lack of outward success. There were congregations in the deanery which were hotbeds of malice, bickering and quarrelling, and some found little encouragement in being a holy huddle of ten.

In the parish of Cowling, the most difficult in the Diocese, the Chapel reigned supreme. Relations between Church and Chapel were systematically unfriendly and un-Christian. In another parish the vicar was sent for trial regarding irregular accounts. Another incumbent was at war with himself and with most of his parishioners. In another parish there was a vicar in name only. His overbearing wife ran it — and the people fled before her. Alcohol occupied one incumbency and matrimonial problems another. There were idle clergy and lonely clergy and some hard working pastors too. Treacy made a discovery which was confirmed repeatedly in his subsequent experience. 'The clergy who complained most about loneliness were those who most consistently refused to support any efforts which were made to create fellowship amongst the brethren. It seemed as if they cherished their loneliness and resented any measures to remove the cause of their complaining.'

Treacy's vigorous parochial and diocesan activity was supplemented by no less vociferous movement in the town and beyond. As Mayor's Chaplain during his first year at Keighley, Treacy took every opportunity to project himself into the civic life of the town. He never refused an invitation to appear on public platforms. The outreach of the Church was extended under Treacy's leadership. Rotary was an example. Rotary is scoffed at because of its addiction to platitudes and its tendency to think that nobody else thought of community service until it did. Treacy was not blind to its deficiencies and frequently faced Rotary gatherings with a few home truths. Even so he preferred to see the tremendous possibilities, as he notes:

'I have been to meetings at which there has been a lot of fuss made about very little in the way of service. They pass a lot of high-sounding resolutions which often deceive them into thinking that they have done something. With their little bannerettes festooned over the top table, their birthday greetings to each other, the reports they make of having visited another club for lunch no more than three miles distant — they give the impression of not having grown up.

'When all that has been said, I have always found them a jolly good lot, sympathetic to any call for help. I never refuse an invitation to go and speak at their meetings because (a) I like being with them and (b) what parson can or should refuse the opportunity of talking to a gathering of 50 or 60 men? It is generally true that in most towns, the Rotary Club includes the best type of laymen from all denominations. They talk much of their fellowship, and there is no doubt that they achieve a high level of friendliness, but, as I often tell them, so they should when every potential member is carefully screened and classified before he is invited to join. In comparison, the Church has a much greater problem in creating fellowship, as it has to take all and sundry without any process of selection, and do the best it can with what it gets.'

Besides being an entertaining yet provocative speaker Treacy was developing some skill as a reconciler of conflicting opinions and gaining the qualities that make a good chairman. This was nowhere needed more than at a famous public meeting of Keighley's Member of Parliament, an event which will be ever remembered in the town's political history. Ivor Thomas (later Ivor Bulmer-Thomas) had been Keighley's Labour MP since 1942. Following the nationalisation of the iron and steel industry, with which Thomas strongly disagreed, he crossed the floor of the House of Commons and announced that he intended to remain in Parliament as an Independent Member. He subsequently became a Conservative.

Ivor Thomas came to explain his action to an over-capacity (1,200 people) audience in the Municipal Hall in December 1948. Labour feeling against him ran understandably high and such was the demand for tickets that many counterfeit tickets were for sale at black market prices. Treacy was asked to chair the meeting and records his impressions of it:

'Ivor and I arrived at the meeting to find the hall crowded to the doors, and the approaches blocked by angry ticket holders unable to gain admission. The atmosphere was "tense and full of bubble" as Sam Small would have described it. I realised as chairman that I was not going to have a very easy evening. I introduced Ivor Thomas and the meeting started. He then launched an attack on the Labour Party, its policies and its leaders which was astounding in its impudence. It really was an amazing performance and very courageous. He was confronted with an audience most of whom were out for his blood, and he spat straight in their eyes. At first they seemed to be stunned by the bitterness of his attack, then they began to react, and I feared that there might be an attack of violence. Mercifully, when things were beginning to look critical, Thomas asked a rhetorical question (he ought to have known better!) and he got a very prompt and earthy answer from a large woman sitting in the front row — given in a strident tone which was heard all over the hall. "Aye — and he bloody well done reight", was the answer. Who "he" was, and what he had done, I cannot recall, but that splendid nameless woman, with miraculous timing, lowered the temperature of that meeting in a flash. Her comment was greeted with loud laughter, and from then on, all was under control. I wish I knew who she was, because I would have liked to take her out to dinner; she certainly saved us from a rough house, and if there had been a rough house in that overcrowded hall, the consequences would have been extremely serious.

'When Thomas had finished, the attack was led from the Labour side by a man whom I should guess was a lapsed Methodist local preacher. No man had a better wicket to bat on, but he threw his wicket away. Unfortunately for him he made much use of biblical parallels to what Ivor Thomas had done. It was a cleverly mounted attack, but it badly misfired, because he had reckoned without the fact that, on the whole, the public instinct is offended when cheap use is made of the Scriptures. I can remember vividly how he lost the sympathy of the meeting as he persisted in his near-blasphemous attack on Ivor Thomas' defection from the Labour cause. This meeting took place at a time when the majority of people had grown up in Sunday Schools, and had, therefore, a respect for the Bible which, I fear, we should not find in a similar situation today.'

1948 was the centenary Year of the Parish Church and provided new opportunities for evangelism which was Treacy's constant theme and challenge. He never lost an opportunity of making the presence of the Church and its ministrations felt by imaginative means. At the beginning of 1948 he persuaded the Parochial Church Council to spend money on a well produced booklet for all couples married in the Church. It contained a pocket for the marriage certificate, space in which to enter particulars of the wedding, some prayers for use together after they were married, a message from Treacy entitled 'A word about your Marriage' and space to enter the names and dates of the baptism of any children.

He introduced an annual service for all those who had been married in the Church. A servers' guild was started designed principally for senior choir boys whose voices had broken. Many a boy kept his church allegiance who otherwise might have drifted away. Keighley's Confirmation Service was always held on Palm Sunday. Treacy was unhappy with the casual ease with which candidates were trained and accepted for Confirmation. He drew up a scheme which was enthusiastically approved by Bishop Blunt. Names of would-be candidates were required a year in advance. Three months' preliminary preparation was given, followed by six months' 'apprenticeship' during which the candidates became part of the worshipping life of the Church, and then there was a final three months' preparation, but only for those who had shown during the middle six months that they were prepared to take membership of the Church seriously. It was not easy to become a full member of the worshipping community at Keighley Parish Church but the survivors were keen disciples for life.

During the autumn of 1949 there was a general 'exchange of pulpits' in Keighley. Ministers of the Free Churches preached in Anglican Churches and the Anglican clergy in the Free Churches. A *Church Times* correspondent reported this event with a tart note that 'Catholic friends will learn with regret that a preacher from the local Holiness Mission occupied the pulpit of St Peter's Keighley'. St Peter's had had an Anglo-Catholic tradition and there were those who accused Treacy of trying to undo the work that a faithful priest had built up and maintained over a long period of years. There was correspondence and much acrimony in the press and elsewhere. Treacy wrote to point out that the preacher at St Peter's was not the Minister of the Holiness Mission, but a Methodist Minister from the neighbouring Methodist church. Unfortunately the attack became bitter and personalised. Another local priest tried to lift the argument away from the personal attack to Treacy's views of which he did not approve: 'I believe his theology to be unsound, his thinking sentimental, and his action ill-advised.' The vitriolic correspondence continued and it was not aided by the fact that his departure from Keighley to Halifax had been announced, causing many heads to shake in the Wakefield Diocese which was regarded as an Anglo-Catholic Diocese.

This sour note was insufficient to eclipse the personal and public ministry of Treacy in and beyond Keighley. A member of the congregation describes the period as 'exhilarating'. It was under Eric Treacy — the Church in Action.

10
By Worth

The war years had been bleak ones for Treacy's railway photography. He had risked and succeeded in taking a few photographs at times and in places when and where photography was strictly forbidden during the war. It was part innocence but in larger part mischievous naivety similar to the occasion when one of his letters had been censored. Writing to his friend John Tilney (later knighted and Member of Parliament for Wavertree) during the war he said 'We spent our night just outside Abergavenny — and while there I discovered a secret which even Parliament doesn't know judging by the number of times it asks for an answer in the House. I discovered where Rudolph Hess is. He is in a ... Censored ... Now don't put that in your diary!'

Once Treacy arrived in Keighley he resumed his hobby with typical Treacian gusto. Keighley was a declining station and was a long way from becoming the famous home of the Keighley & Worth Valley Railway, of which more in a later chapter.

Treacy contacted Maurice Earley of the Railway Photographic Society and other steam friends of the prewar period. The Society was small but select. In October 1945 there were 47 members. Folios of photographs were circulated to members for critical comments and members were expected to write in note-books of their photographic aspirations and exasperations.

The postwar railway network had a hard recovery from the ordeal of six years' bombing, worn out track and engines and a depleted and dilapidated coaching stock. Half of their experienced staff were in the long queue for demobilisation. Treacy was itching to be active again and needed renewed permissions and permits for his footplate activities. Ronald Taylor, newly appointed District Motive Power Superintendent at Leeds, sat down in his office on his first day in his new job. Not five minutes elapsed before his secretary said 'There is a clergyman to see you'. In walked Eric Treacy who remained in and out of Ron Taylor's hair and life until Treacy's death. They were good friends, and were partners in steam. Ron Taylor, like so many other Motive Power Superintendents and like officials, contracted that disease for which no antidote or cure was known — MEFET — Making Excuses for Eric Treacy! On one occasion a senior railway official had seen excessive smoke coming from an engine and Ron Taylor was asked who was responsible and to investigate the matter. He did not tell me what his reply and report was, but he did say what it wasn't, namely the truth — that Treacy was photographing and had arranged for the usual smoke effects.

Treacy was happier enveloped in smoke than ever he was in incense, but that was something he would have to get used to. Years later the Deputy Editor of the *Wakefield Express*, E. A. Walker, remembers attending a High Mass at Horbury Parish Church (celebrating the parish priest's — Milton Lindleys, fortieth anniversary of his priesthood) and wrote '. . . the incense was wafted with telling effect. Afterwards I walked outside with Bishop Treacy and commented that it was nice to see so many of Father Lindley's former curates at the altar. He looked at me and wryly asked "Could you see the altar for smoke?".' He never appreciated that incense to worship is not quite the same as smoke was to his photographs.

Steam had its enthusiasts in this early postwar period but not yet its fanatics. A whole literature of very mixed quality is now available but it is of comparatively recent enterprise. After World War I there was the monthly *Railway Magazine* and the Locomotive Publishing Company produced *The Locomotive* and some ephemeral literature. By the end of World War II the *Railway Magazine* appeared only bi-monthly and was subordinate to other publications by the same company aimed at the professional railway readership. With the reawakened interest in railways caused largely by the advent of Ian Allan's locomotive 'ABC' stock books, colloquially known in the North as 'refs', the scope for an adventurous new approach by an enterprising publisher was virtually unlimited. Treacy was in a way midwife to a new venture which was to carry his name far and wide. It was another rung on the ladder which ultimately led to the Railway Bishop. The new born was Ian Allan Ltd and the contact came about by an unusual mixture of the religious with the temporal, the latter in its most literal meaning — Cecil J. Allen, nonconformist preacher and train timer extraordinary, who had had both spiritual and railway connections with Eric Treacy over the years.

Cecil had become one of Ian Allan Ltd's first directors and brought about the introduction of the 40-ish Canon with the 20-ish Ian Allan in a rather seedy cafe in Vauxhall Bridge Road, Victoria, approximate to where Allan had set up his first office in an ancient and bombed out building.

From this meeting Eric Treacy's and Ian Allan's first pictorial book emerged, in fact it was probably the first purely railway picture book of its kind ever to have been published and was the forerunner of so many more. *Steam Up* was printed in photogravure, case bound and retailed at the exorbitant price of 10/6 but much to everyone's surprise and delight was an instant sell-out and Treacy donated all his royalties to worthy causes — as indeed he so often did with his later books.

Thereafter he was a regular contributor of both literary and illustrative material to Ian Allan journals until the onset of the first of his major works, *Lure of Steam* which set the pattern for the future though he became more and more testy as an author, as time went by, no doubt the result of his rising status in the railway fraternity and his being nobbled by critics.

Allan says he was always easy to deal with in the first stages of publication but as production of the book went on he would get more and more pernickety, demanding often to have one perfectly good photograph replaced with one almost exactly similar and insisting on getting his own way. In fact so much so that eventually the relationship between him and his publishing firm was only held together by his dealing personally with Ian Allan through every stage and with design and layout being done jointly between them either on the floor of the episcopal study (Treacy usually sat on the floor for these sessions) or on the table at Craven House, Hampton Court whither Ian Allan had moved from London.

The later Treacy works were designed professionally at Shepperton (but still under the strictest supervision of the principals) where the designers and printers shook with apprehension at the advent of Treacy who invariably turned their work upside down and equally invariably followed a highly convivial visit with a snorting letter of complaint that two or three reproductions in a book containing hundreds had been overinked or underinked. But the bluster was quickly turned aside for basically he loved being published and was one of the greatest critics of his own work, though his self criticism was rarely shared by others.

It was all good fun both for Treacy and for Ian Allan, especially the latter as during the last years, the House of Lords was the usual rendezvous for author/ publisher meetings and it was by no means infrequent for the selection of railway photographs to take place with the bishop fully regaled in surplice and frills in a small meeting room from which some noble lord had been gently persuaded out.

Keighley was not Liverpool! But the Midland line from Leeds to Carlisle threaded the Aire Valley just below Treacy's Keighley Vicarage. This was a line that he was going to know intimately. There is a strange magic about the footplate that can more easily be explained than captured. It never failed to seduce Treacy. Even the camera took a tender seat. It was ever the same. He started out with the intention of observing carefully the engine's performance and the methods of handling her, then suddenly all was forgotten as the footplate cast its spell. The swaying of the engine, the absorption of the driver, the warmth of the fire, the sight of the track stretching mile upon mile into the distance, the metallic clang of the fireman's shovel, the smell of hot oil and steam — the intimacy that comes of minds concentrated on the same thing. He often wrote of footplate journeys but nowhere does he better catch the total experience of a particular journey than in the following description taken from *Steam Up:*

'My first postwar footplate trip was from Leeds to Carlisle, over that gruelling stretch from Settle to Appleby. The engine was a rebuilt "Royal Scot", No 6117 *Welsh Guardsman*. She looked a picture, newly painted and spotless. The crew were Driver Rose and Fireman Warr, both of Holbeck, Leeds. Tim Wood, the District Locomotive Superintendent, stationed at Holbeck, came down with us on the engine from the shed to Leeds City, where we awaited the arrival of our train from London. The train was the 9.45am St Pancras to Glasgow (St Enoch), and it arrived 27 minutes late. We backed on to our train, which was a fairly light one, only about 300 tons, and made a good start. It was immediately apparent that the engine's mechanical condition matched her outward appearance. She rode well and steamed well. I wedged myself, more or less comfortably, into the corner of the tender, between the brake handle and the door, whence I had a good view of everything in the cab, and of the track as well. Soon the murky suburbs of Leeds gave place to the more pleasant country which is but a foretaste of the magnificent countryside of the Craven District through which the line passes. From my vantage point I kept an eye on Rose, Warr, and the way ahead. I would see a signal far off, on an inside curve; Rose would be looking across the cab at Warr, awaiting his tip that all was well. It is interesting to watch the teamwork of a good crew on the footplate. There is seldom need for much talk between "top link" men. The enginemen know their jobs and the work goes on in silence, in mutual confidence of each other's efficiency. Rose had his regulator half open and his cut-off at about 18% and between Leeds and Skipton we didn't exceed 55mph. At Shipley, Bingley, and Kildwick there were speed restrictions — at Kildwick to

5mph because of a temporary bridge over a troublesome beck which had shortly before washed the piers of the permanent bridge away. Warr was a model fireman, "little and often" was his motto, and because of this he didn't need his seat much, so I ventured across the cab and sat down on the little wooden tip-up seat, which was far more comfortable than it looked. Skipton was ahead, and beyond that the Pennine hills climbing away into the north. To me, they had a certain artistic appeal; to Warr they were a barrier that had to be climbed and that meant more work for him, but in spite of this, as a loyal Yorkshireman, he thinks a lot of them.

'At Skipton we found that one minute of the 27 had been regained. During this short stop we took water, which necessitated Warr's hopping off the footplate to operate the water-crane. Next stop was Hellifield, after a gentle climb most of the way with the steepest stretch (1 in 132) at Bell Busk; but this was a further foretaste of what was to come. For this Rose set his cut-off at 20%. By now the rainy skies of Leeds had given place to blue skies and sun; as we passed through the pastures of Craven, I detected the fragrant smell of newly cut hay. The boiler was steaming well and Warr had no difficulty in keeping pressure nicely above the 200 mark — I felt that the engine was enjoying itself and was game for anything. By Gargrave we were doing a steady 60. At Hellifield I just had time to nip off the footplate and take a photograph of the engine. It was a hurried shot and I omitted to notice some cows standing on a hillside behind the engine — the resulting photograph showed two cows walking along the top of the boiler towards the cab.

'We made a smart get-away from Hellifield, for as far as Settle it is downhill, which gave Rose the chance of a flying start at the big climb which comes thereafter. As we were leaving Hellifield I pushed my camera as far as my arm would allow out of the cab and took a blind shot which came off. From Hellifield to Settle, Rose had the regulator half open and his cut-off at 15% which was sufficient to produce a speed of 60mph. As we flashed through Settle, I could just see the roofs of that charming village nestling below the line in the trees, with something indefinably Swiss about it. Then came the long grind up to Blea Moor — 14 miles at 1 in 100. And now Rose began to work the engine harder — regulator wide open and 30% cut-off — and Warr started to shovel with a vengeance too; much and often was the method now. What a glorious deep-throated roar the engine was making! Now we were in the bleakest of all the Yorkshire Dales, Ribblesdale, and the river from which the dale takes its name wound its way over a boulder-strewn bed to the sea. After Horton-in-Ribblesdale we were out to the open moor with Pen-y-Ghent like a crouching lion on our right and the flat topped Ingleborough ahead of us. Over the Ribbleshead viaduct, the piers of which are, I believe, sunk on wool, under the shoulder of Whernside, and then ahead of us gaped the Blea Moor tunnel, with the climb behind us.

'Having reached the summit at last we all relaxed. Warr straightened his back, mopped his brow, swept up the footplate, had a swig of cold tea, and lit a cigarette. There was a general sense of relief in the air, and the cut-off came back to 15%; ahead lay an easy 58 miles to Carlisle. Rose had done well; we had picked up another five minutes and now we were only 21 minutes late. Soon after emerging from Blea Moor tunnel, Warr motioned me away from my corner behind the driver, and prepared to operate his scoop at Garsdale Troughs. And so we bowled along at 60mph across the roof of Yorkshire. Below us was the wide and beautiful prospect of Dentdale — a prospect unbelievably lovely. Came Ais Gill and then down the hill to Appleby. Wild Boar Fell towered above us on the left, and on the right the wide expanse of Mallerstang Common, studded with some of the loneliest farmsteads in Britain. We were coasting now, and Rose made frequent applications of the brake to prevent speed from rising too high. At one point we touched 80, and even at this speed the engine rode beautifully; the motion seemed very smooth and unobtrusive in action. We stopped at Appleby only 17 minutes late: it was pretty good to have recovered no less than 10 minutes since leaving Leeds over a stretch of line infested with slacks, including 14 miles at 1 in 100. After Appleby things were relatively quiet on the footplate, which gave me the opportunity of savouring this lovely corner of England. To the west the Lakeland mountains made a wonderful horizon, with Saddleback easily recognisable. In the east, Cross Fell and the long line of the Pennines, and below us, one of the loveliest stretches of river scenery in all England as the River Eden wound its way through the red sandstone gorges which abound in this part of Cumberland.

'We made Carlisle only 15 minutes late. Here I had to say goodbye to Rose and Warr, for I was spending the night in Carlisle, and rejoining them the next morning at 12.5 for the return journey to Leeds. We were rather disconcerted to find a Press photographer waiting for us at Carlisle. Apparently my trip had leaked out — a parson on a footplate is news, whereas a parson in a pulpit isn't. Perhaps an engine driver in a pulpit would be worthy of recording, too. However Rose, Warr and I had our picture taken — and a very good one it was, too. It was a great run; one couldn't have wished for a better engine, or two better companions. My wife joined me from the restaurant car in which she had partaken of a dainty afternoon tea, and suggested rather bluntly that I needed a wash. Somehow or other, I was considerably dirtier than either the driver or the fireman, but I valued that dirt. I felt rather like the small boy who wouldn't wash his hand after shaking hands with the King. So long as I could remain dirty I felt that I belonged to that world in which a dirty face is the passport to a natural kinship with all other men with dirty faces who dwell on footplates. Space does not permit of my telling you of my return journey, or how I, all unknowingly, gave Fireman Warr a winner for the 2.30 at Lincoln. That's another story.'

Traction Inspector G. Gordon of Carlisle has a story of this line from retired driver W. Watt for whom he fired in steam days at Kingmoor Motive Power Depot. Driver Watt possesses two beautiful Treacy photographs showing a Class 8P 'Duchess' locomotive, one hauling the down 'Royal Scot' leaving Carlisle station and the other hauling the same train up Beattock Summit. Pride in having the photographs almost led to a fall when he showed them to the Locomotive Inspector at Carlisle. He had not appreciated that the excellence of the Treacy photographs was not limited to the 'Duchess' alone. They also showed an assisting 'bank' engine in the rear of the nine-coach train, which was underload and well within the capacity of the Class 8 train locomotive for a run through Beattock to the Summit. The Inspector remarked 'I have been trying to catch you stopping for a bank engine at Beattock unnecessarily: I never thought the Good Lord would provide the assistance of a Bishop to obtain the evidence — the camera does not lie. That locomotive looks in good condition with steam escaping at the safety valves.' The driver retorted as quickly 'The Bishop's a very good friend of mine and that is why his camera did not show how much water was in the tender before I stopped at Beattock for water.' The Inspector concluded by saying, 'Yes, but you were still underload for starting away from Beattock.'

It happens that the 67 miles running from Floriston Troughs to Strawfrank Troughs required very careful handling by drivers and economical shovel work by firemen. However, the real problem was from where had Treacy taken the photograph? It transpired that he had stood on the verandah of Greskine Signalbox which was half way up Beattock Summit on the left hand side of the Down line. But how had Treacy materialised at the signalbox as road access was almost non existent? The answer comes in these words. 'The Bishop's human touch had endeared him to one burly Beattock driver because he knew how he had travelled to Greskine, and is quoted as saying "That man just came into the messroom. I commanded an engine and crew, and the Good Lord provided".'

The onlooker may wonder what exactly was the main attraction of steam to Treacy? Was it simply that engines were good subjects for photography? His interest came long before anyone thought that steam would be replaced by diesel and electricity thus creating an artificial and romantic interest in steam, the stuff of today's activists and their passenger flocks. To a large extent the answer lies in a different direction and can best be understood when set against the character of the man.

Treacy liked the steam engine because it was massive and noisy. It was temperamental and hard to tame. It had a lovely shape and it was primitive in that it visibly united the elements of fire and water to produce power. There was always the risk that it would blow up, but it seldom did. The steam engine expressed something of the violence that is in human nature and in a way that is constructive.

Treacy's other joys and delights were in the main simple, emotional and basic. Give him a brass band playing Handel's *Largo* or some martial tune. He liked church organs with all the stops out playing music that was rich, fruity and obvious. He liked a few hymns a lot and the congregations of Keighley and Halifax soon learned what the few hymns were! His sense of adventure was reflected in his reading. He liked books which told of man's struggle to make friends with the wild things of nature. He once said: 'I like to read the stories of those who have had the courage to break with the conventional and to do the things that most of us want to do, but have never had the courage to do.'

In quite a different way Treacy himself was going to be recognised as a railway photographer who broke away from the existing conventions. Following publication of *My Best Railway Photographs* in October 1946 he received what can only be called a 'fan mail'. He was able to bask amongst the congratulatory 'How ever do you do it' missives. From the letters he received it is clear that he had already made his mark in railway photography during the late 1930s and a Treacy photograph in a magazine was instantly recognisable for its distinction and excellence. There was the aesthetic appeal as distinct from the technical although the latter could seldom be faulted. Then there were the thrilling view points which he chose, with natural effects of the gradation of lighting and usually ample sunshine.

Ian Allan had latched on to a sound investment, and a further booklet in the ABC Locomotive Series appeared in 1948 — *Still More of My Best Railway Photographs LMR*. In this publication Treacy had some advice for budding railway photographers:

'A good picture has to be planned. It may take years to achieve the result desired, but discipline in this matter of button pressing will certainly add tremendously to our enjoyment of the hobby. I have in mind, as I write, a dozen or so places at which I am going to make a picture. I have decided on them after careful observation over several years — my plans have taken into account such things as (1) the scenic setting, (2) the type of locomotive and the method in which it is handled, (3) the time of year with special regard to position of sun, and temperature. When the opportunity arises I shall go straight to my vantage point — resisting all other temptations en route — and I *shan't* take my photograph unless the engine is doing exactly what I want it to do, and looking as I have intended it shall look.'

This is Treacy the artist and the results were never displayed to better effect than in his first major work *Steam Up* which many critics regard as his finest book. For an estimate of Treacy as the supreme artist I turn to Derek Cross, himself a distinguished railway photographer:

'The innovator is not necessarily the artist, but Eric Treacy was both. Perhaps the only parallel which comes to mind is the Venetian composer Monteverdi, who broke the strict and rather sterile rules of polyphony and launched music into the glories of the Baroque on a sea of screaming trumpets. An exaggerated illusion? I don't think so, for the early composers in the strict polyphonic mould were very competent men, just as were the early British photographers of the railway scene. They were experts in their sphere. Where Monteverdi broke from tradition was not in altering the technical competence of those who had gone before, but in totally altering the framework in which these skills were used. Eric Treacy did exactly the same for railway photography. He didn't try to create a "new wave" with injudicious use of gimmicks such as long-focus lenses, he didn't try to abolish technical excellence in terms of composition, exposure or focus. He took the basic concept of a train photograph and added one new and very significant dimension — background. What is more, he made this background as important a part of the picture as the train itself. Thus the concept of the train in its environment was born. Nowhere was this realisation of the train as part of a scene, rather than the one and only feature in a photograph, better shown than in Eric's early work around Liverpool, when Lime Street cuttings took on the aspect of Dante's Inferno with a "Rebuilt Scot" as the wretched victim. I shall never forget the impact of his first, and in my opinion his best book, *Steam Up*. To those of my generation just beginning to realise the complexities of photographing a train in action, often with primitive equipment and even more sketchy technical knowledge, this book came as a bombshell. We knew we did not have the equipment to stop a "Castle" dead in its tracks at 70mph on Goring troughs. What Eric Treacy showed us was that a "Duchess" on Shap with a rivet or two out of focus could make a more interesting picture than a pin sharp "King" in the featureless wastes of West London. It gave a great many of us hope, confidence and the will to try. Much is talked these days of the "generation gap" — a glorious excuse for sloppy thinking on the part of our elders and over-confident ignorance on the part of the young. But there will always be bridges over this gap, and Eric Treacy's art and work were one such bridge. To those of us who had the time to assimilate the basic concept of a Treacy picture before the end of steam, there can be no doubt of his influence. Some of us, myself included, may have taken this landscape approach too far — our fault, not his. This was his genius, he never went too far. Shap Wells is a case in point; a Treacy picture from where he stood was near-perfection. Twenty yards further from the line was an interesting picture in a different way — twenty yards further was a damned awful mess. His approach to photography might be summed up as innovation with moderation, and somehow this summed up Eric Treacy the man. By his examples he taught many of us a great deal. Above all he was the most "human" man I have ever met. He was the innovator who was superbly the artist'.

11

Ecclesiastical Mayor

The entry in Treacy's diary for 24 July 1949 includes the following; 'To Mexborough (South Yorkshire) to preach at their Patronal Festival: the Vicar (Jack Bishop) there is an old army friend of mine. In a very ugly mining town it is something of a surprise to observe a really old and beautiful Parish Church. Observed some unexpectedly attractive country between Wakefield and Barnsley. On the way back, slipped in for a cup of tea with the Bishop of Wakefield (Roger Wilson) who was found looking most unepiscopal weeding in his garden.'

This innocuous entry masks the fact that it was on this occasion that Bishop Wilson invited Treacy to join him as Archdeacon of Halifax. Treacy was overwhelmed by the offer and after some thought, but only a little agonising, he accepted. On the day of the public announcement — 13 August — the front page of the *Keighley News* carried an advertisement for a film called *The Amazing Adventures of Dick Tracey* — an augury?

Treacy's predecessor as Archdeacon was Arthur Harold Morris who had become Bishop Suffragan and Archdeacon of Pontefract and was later Bishop of

St Edmundsbury and Ipswich (1954-1965). As Archdeacon of Halifax, Harold Morris had received his stipend from the Cathedral revenues, but as they were proving inadequate to pay three Canons it was proposed that the new Archdeacon should derive his income from a benefice. Bishop Wilson completes the picture:

'In my first year as a bishop, the prospect of having Eric's companionship was almost more than I dared hope for. But there were difficulties. The Archdeaconry consisted of two large deaneries, Halifax and Huddersfield, and the previous archdeacon had held the post with a Cathedral Canonry and no parochial commitment. This left him rather in the air. For the intense local patriotism of West Riding towns meant that nobody, yes, nobody counted for much ecclesiastically in Halifax and Huddersfield but their own vicars. This kind of situation would not have suited Eric, who was accustomed to his own area of command, and already had a big responsibility — at Keighley. However, a vacancy at Halifax Parish Church, which the Crown was prepared to offer him, altered the scene.'

It was not quite as easy as it sounds. (Sir) Anthony Bevir, the Prime Minister's Appointments Secretary, took some persuading of the rightness of this dual appointment and wondered if Treacy had enough 'bottom' for the job. The absence of a degree would not have escaped Bevir's notice either! However, Treacy was appointed. The announcement appeared on 2 December, although he was not instituted until 4 February 1950.

When Treacy attended a meeting of the Halifax Parochial Church Council on 13 December 1949 he wondered if it was to be Keighley all over again for he noted: 'It was a deadly meeting — completely lacking in warmth and spontaneity. Individually they seemed a nice lot but collectively they gave the impression of suspicious wariness. Not even a cup of tea laid on to welcome the new Vicar and his wife.' Apparently the Parochial Church Council felt aggrieved that they had been insufficiently consulted, yet Bevir had travelled all the way from London to discuss the appointment personally with the churchwardens. Later Treacy discovered that the troubles were 'due to the weakness of the Churchwardens who apparently funked telling the Council that they had agreed with the Bishop and the PM's Appointment Secretary, that a Vicar of Halifax who would also be Archdeacon would be acceptable to the Parish. On these interviews they had been strangely silent. The Wardens are a nice couple but lacking in guts. I shall want new ones.'

Treacy's dual appointment was increased by one when he was subsequently appointed Rural Dean of Halifax. This whole arrangement was not without its critics in Halifax and in the Diocese. There were those who thought that this 'young man' would spend more time on his archidiaconal duties than on his parochial work. Others were proud that the Vicar of Halifax was gaitered. In the Diocese Treacy's predecessor but one at Halifax had not been forgotten. George Horsfall Frodsham, one-time Bishop of North Queensland, was Vicar of Halifax from 1920-1937. He was a powerful figure in his own right and he used his real standing in the community to the full. Further, one of the results of the breaking up of the Ancient Parish into so many new ones had been that the Vicar of

Halifax was the patron of 26 benefices in the area thus having the responsibility of appointing vicars to them as and when required. Bishop Frodsham almost created a diocese within a diocese and not infrequently the Bishop of Wakefield had difficulty exercising his episcopal ministry in Halifax. Consequently the sturdy and independent spirit of Halifax was fed, pampered and prospered.

Frodsham's successor and Treacy's predecessor, Percival Ernest James, came to Halifax from New Zealand. James possessed those qualities of steadiness and quiet faith, of sympathy and inner strength which led to a more tranquil though none the less active ministry than Frodsham's. James left Halifax to return to New Zealand as Dean of Dunedin in 1949 primarily because of the poor health of his wife.

Halifax was at the time a slatternly looking town but not a poor one. It had its millionaires and its Bentleys; it also had nearly full employment, great diversification of industry, with machine tools quite as important as the famous woollen and worsteds, and an exceptionally high proportion of women at work. Here was the setting for Treacy's work, an enigma of a town — prosperity with a grubby face. The shadowy outlines of bare moorland at the end of the streets, gaunt mills, and steep cobbled streets of stone cottages were the traditional standbys of the 'trouble at t'mill' school of regional novelists. So were the smoke-blackened public buildings in Victorian Gothic and the old sages in flat caps with names like Murgatroyd, Crossley and Gaukroger, supping their ale and grunting our terse wisdom between strange oaths.

The mists of change were gathering, although the much and justly criticised soulless developer was more than a decade away. Nevertheless, 'For Sale' bills were beginning to appear on some splendid Nonconformist chapels, carrying their own message and indictment.

As a town Halifax was less materialistic than Keighley. The people were thoughtful and had been brought up in the belief that 'you don't get owt for nowt, and not much for a tanner.'

The Parish Church, dedicated to St John the Baptist, stood in good shape, suggesting that successive generations of Halifax people, not only Anglicans, had expressed their pride in her, and their love for her in hard cash. It is a large, solid and noble building situated at the bottom end of the town and it was then surrounded by factories, mills, shops, offices, the gas works, the electricity generating station and coal yards. All pretty dirty. There has been a church on the site since 1098 but the present building dates from the 15th century and is built in early Perpendicular style. It contains some unique Commonwealth windows, an Elizabethan font cover, Jacobean pews and altar rails, a superb Harrison four-manual organ and a north wall dating back to the 11th century. When the Diocese of Wakefield was created in 1888 there was some debate as to whether Halifax or Wakefield should provide the Cathedral. Treacy described the Church in the 22nd *Annual Report 1954-55*, Society of Friends of the Halifax Parish Church as:

'Handsome rather than beautiful. Some of the ancient churches of the South are beautiful with their willowy architecture in limestone with the light that pours through a profusion of windows destroying all sense of mystery. Some modern churches are pretty with all their fussy ornamentation and their rich colours. But

Yorkshire churches and none more than ours, are handsome. They are solid and stubborn buildings, their stone work grimed and weathered, sometimes dark and sombre, and for that reason yielding an atmosphere of mystery, suggesting that all may not be known at once, but they have to be persuaded to yield up their secrets. I have seen prettier and more beautiful churches than ours, but none more impressive, none that speaks by atmosphere and appearance more of the past, giving to those of the present a sense of the continuous life of the Christian community within its walls.'

Treacy often quoted Bishop H. Hensley Henson on 'The Respected Clergyman'. 'You will have to win whatever measure of respect you will have — You will surely be "despised" if you have no other ground for claiming respect than your official character. Respect for your office may grow out of respect for yourself but it will hardly precede, and rarely survive it. — With us I hold it to be certain that unless the clergyman is respected as a man he will not be accepted as a minister of Christ.'*

Treacy left Keighley as a 'respected clergyman'. The Duke of Devonshire had written to him: 'You have the great satisfaction of knowing that your work at Keighley will be a lasting memorial to your time there.' He left Edge Hill in a similar way. A *Liverpool Daily Post* reporter wrote at the time:

'He will be remembered in the city in which he was an incumbent of marked personality. I never heard him preach, but I listened to him once outside his church and the impression he left with me was altogether favourable. The thought which struck me at the time was, "here is a man as well as a cleric, and the church needs more of this type".'

Some major parish churches such as Leeds and Portsea were like bishops' preparatory schools. Not so Halifax. At first the living was a rectory but of its vicars since 1274 more had been murdered than had become bishops. Only one, in the 16th century, had been raised to the episcopate, William Rokeby to be Archbishop of Dublin. A few had become deans. It appears that Halifax was more a pinnacle than a plateau.

Treacy was relishing the thought of increased responsibility. He was now firmly committed to the Church of England as the National Church. Its churches stood in the midst of the community not only to serve the people but also to recall people from the servitude of time to the freedom of eternity. An old parish church like Halifax is ever the eloquent symbol of eternity. It stands, solid, austere and challenging, attesting the changing fortunes of the generations who have lived and toiled and sinned and suffered and rejoiced and found peace around it.

The actual parish was incredibly small, densely populated during the day but with few residents. The subject of his first sermon was 'The Functions of a Parish Church in the 20th Century'. This was typically Treacian — bold, almost breathtaking. Most new incumbents commence their cures tentatively. Not Treacy. This relatively young man of 42 was not going to 'hide his light under a bushel'. One incumbent in the Diocese said to a curate 'Mark my words, that man

From Bishoprick Papers p182 Oxford University Press, 1946.

has all his goods in the shop window', words more unkind than untrue. Yet this was part of the attractive and refreshing directness of Treacy.

Years later, writing in *Church Times* (9 March 1973) Treacy gave his job specification for a vicar of a 'down town mother church':

'To do work of this kind demands a particular kind of man, and such men are not always easy to find. Men with a genius for mixing with all sorts and conditions of folk; men who can stand up and speak sense on almost any subject, often at very short notice; men who can touch the world at all points without the world touching them; men with minds that can "zoom" — that is to say, alter focus from near to far without difficulty; men with a confidence that is not arrogance but a confidence in the God whom they represent; men with the facility to challenge without giving offence, with a Pauline bluntness in saying what has to be said without destroying relationships. And the capacity to work sixteen hours a day without collapsing.'

Treacy's vicariate in Halifax is the story of how he himself fulfilled and carried out that specification in the fullest measure.

Treacy realised that some changes would have to be made but his hope was that he would be able to persuade or cajole even if not convert outright. It was not easy. The pew population comprised three groups. There were the old loyal sweats whom nothing would shake off, but as they were old they were a shrinking asset. Then there were the committed casuals whose first loyalty was to another church but who liked the services at the Parish Church. Finally there were members of the Waterhouse Almshouses who had to attend as a condition of living there. His first challenge was the choir, as he recalled:

'Halifax in those days was a church with great musical traditions. An excellent choir rendered florid choral services, in which the congregation played very little part. This was something that caused me a great deal of anxiety. I took the view that we were not a Cathedral but a Parish Church, and that we ought to behave like one. The choir was good, but not perhaps as good as they thought they were. The organist, Shackleton Pollard, was a superb musician, and a humble Christian, for whom I came to have a deep affection. I realised that it would not be easy to persuade the choir that the services should be made more congregational, but I knew that it had to be done.

'Shackleton Pollard, although regretting the need for change, with great generosity, saw the point, and cooperated with me. The choir were not too pleased, but they accepted my suggestions although there were one or two who never forgave me for interfering with their long established habits. We did, in fact, effect a compromise. I let them have their heads at the morning service, but I insisted that Evensong should be a simple service with maximum congregational participation. I allowed them an anthem, but it had to be a short one.'

Relations with the PCC were not always easy or good. Like all good Yorkshiremen they were suspicious blighters. However, although they could be a bit gruff they were anything but direct in their speech. If you ask a Yorkshireman to have a drink he will answer 'Ah'm not bothered'. How is a stranger to know that he is dying of thirst and is desperate for a drink. Mr P. A. Womersley, who was on the PCC at the time, comments 'I didn't approve of Eric's attitude to a PCC as being a rubber stamp for the incumbent's whims nor as being a captive audience for a mid-week sermon'. These were not so much 'mid-week sermons' as Treacy facing the PCC with some unpalatable facts about the parish and themselves. After some time there he thought it right to turn the parish's attention to the future. He was concerned at the smallness of the reliable nucleus of regular churchgoers and he was not deceived by the large congregations which frequently occurred on some Sunday evenings. Although the people worshipped together there was little means of bringing them into relation with each other and with the clergy. The Sunday School met in a parish building called the House of the Good Shepherd, but were cut off from the worshipping life of the Church and the older youths tended to float away.

Treacy set out to train his own people and equip them for evangelistic activity — for mission! From the start he insisted that they must develop a congregational 'Action Group' based on the fact that membership of the church carried with it obligations of service and Christian practice. He wanted open air evangelistic services with an address in the centre of the town during the summer months. He advocated a Christian lunch club to be addressed by only the best speakers, the aim of which would be to express the Christian point of view on important social issues. He was determined to alter and improve the parish leaflet. He would have liked to have seen the formation of Trade Guilds with their own chapels in the Parish Church. Further, he wanted to develop a monthly 'Parish Pump' which would be an open meeting for the discussion of the affairs and future planning of the parish followed by a common meal together.

If he was going to revitalise the parish and equip the people for outward-looking activities — in short, for *mission* — he knew that the Vicarage would have to be a focal point of informal gatherings. Here May was the key and Bishop Roger Wilson reflects on this development:

'The hospitality which May provided was at that time something unique. The tide of friends, callers, connections flowed in and out of the vicarage, while every organisation in the town counted on their interest and indeed their presence. It was the kind of situation in which Eric excelled; he made contacts so easily, and so widely, from the representatives and ornaments of Halifax society down to the ordinary folk in the pew and the street. For all his love of the country he was urban in sympathy through and through, as was May. Indeed the human scene came to him so naturally that he found it difficult to understand why some of his fellow clergy seemed so church-bound and limited in their horizons. No doubt he trod on toes; he could be abrupt and rude, he didn't hide his feelings, he fell asleep unashamedly in his chair, regardless of his visitors. But all this was superficial, and in any case May was always there to pick up the pieces, to keep the conversation going and to assuage the puzzled and aggrieved. In such things the test is a clear one — "by their fruits ye shall know them". These two gathered friends and kept them, the snowball ever increasing as each change of scene brought new ones without their losing touch with older associates.'

In fact, May often wondered if they had too many friends but questions of this sort were brushed aside by her husband!

The staff of the parish church was small, normally one curate, an 'honorary' curate, a lady worker and a multi-tasked verger. In someways Treacy was not an easy person to work with as he ran his own show in his own way. Consultation was frequently little more than a cosmetic. He was not unaware of his faults in this regard but did little to curb them even though he regretted them on occasions. In the sad case of one curate he did quite a lot of breast-beating. The curate was a late ordinand, having been some years in business:

'Alas, something went badly wrong. After a few months he showed signs of losing confidence, and wishing to avoid me. It was a case of my trying to do too much too quickly, with the result that he felt that I was crushing him personally. I confess that this was a great sadness to me, because I held him and his wife in great affection, but it was clear that he ought to go to another vicar to complete his training. I fear that I used too little imagination in my efforts to train him. The fault was mine and the memory of this unhappy experience deters me from being too dogmatic in the matter of curate-training.'

Treacy's effect on another curate, Colin Docker (now Bishop Suffragan of Horsham) was the reverse, but he had had the advantage of having served a first curacy before alighting on Halifax. They first met in 1949 when Treacy, then Rector of Keighley, conducted the Wakefield Ordination Retreat at which Colin Docker was made deacon. What stays in his mind:

'... was the deep impression made upon me by the wholeheartedness of his commitment to a priestly life. Wholeheartedness in the sense of his infectious and attractive enthusiasm and of his obvious enjoyment of his ministry; but also in the literal sense that his whole heart belonged both to his Lord and to the people whom he served. There were no half-measures about Eric and it was this that came across in those three days of retreat in such a powerful way that I believe it has affected the whole course of my ministry.

'It was three years later when I was offered the opportunity of serving my second curacy under him at Halifax. It was an exciting prospect and the reality proved to be in every way as exciting as the anticipation — and as exacting! For not only did Eric expect the same dedication and thoroughness of those who worked with him as he himself showed, but he drew it from them through the magnetism of his own example.

'Working with Eric Treacy was always an enjoyable experience, for his innate sense of fun was never far beneath the surface — he would never, in my experience, make fun of people, but was always ready to get some fun out of the most unlikely situations.

'Eric was very skilled too in keeping the perfect balance in a working relationship which combined friendship with the limits which make genuine authority possible. So it was possible, as soon as I left Halifax, for a more intimate and life-long friendship to develop.'

Charles Tremayne joined Treacy in 1950 as Honorary Curate and remained in Halifax until his death in 1960. He had been an incumbent of important parishes in the dioceses of Bradford and Wakefield. He was a burly old man with white hair, the complexion of a ripe pippin, and a delightfully simple outlook in life. He was stern and at times a bit peppery, and if anything riled him, he would explode like a bomb. However, Treacy was not the only person to regard him with considerable affection:

'He had fixed ideas of what the ministry should be. Always dressed in black, he was meticulously punctual; with a strong self-discipline of his own, he expected discipline in others. None of this hearty Christian name business with him; we were all known by our surnames, but with me, he would occasionally relax and address me as "Laddie", otherwise I was always "Vicar". His sermons were short and to the point; his attitude to people was akin to that of the captain on the bridge dealing with a rather scruffy crew. As he had spent his early years at sea this was not surprising.

'His days were inflexibly planned. Up at 6am, to do the housework, an activity to which Mrs Tremayne was not particularly partial. Parade in Church for Matins at 8.30am, back home for reading and letters; hospital visits before lunch. After lunch, visiting. Back at Church for Evensong at 5.30pm and then to his evening meetings. This was his timetable in retirement! He walked to and from church, a total distance of 5 miles a day, and he always carried a small bag which we jokingly called his midwife's bag. None of us ever discovered what was in it, but we suspected that it was empty, and that he simply carried it for company. He believed that the strength of the Church lay in persistent and unceasing visiting, and the simple proclamation of evangelical truth. He abhorred sloppiness and laziness on the part of the clergy, and disliked emotionalism of any kind. This I believe, was due to the fact that he possessed an affectionate nature, which his marriage failed to satisfy, so he shut off that side of his life, and developed an emotional coldness as a protection against the language of the heart. A period piece? Yes. But of a splendid period in the Church's history.'

Treacy regarded the Church Army Sister — Sister Ward — as 'pure gold'; never once in 12 years was she other than cheerful and willing. Young and old loved her. She was the best type of woman worker with none of the 'touchiness' that afflicts many women who undertake whole-time church work. Day after day she footed it round the parish visiting from early morning to late at night. She was one of the best known figures in Halifax.

Sister Ward, now retired, thinks the success of Treacy's ministry was due in no small part to May working unsparingly with him. She notes that 'he was very human and needed to succeed, being on top of his job; knowledgeable with much to share with his fellow men; suffering very much when meeting opposition. He worked and expected everybody around him to work: for repayment — a job well done.'

Another former curate, Stuart Pearson, now Social Responsibility Officer for the Wakefield Diocese, has a similar recollection:

'Eric Treacy led by example. He worked so hard that I tried to work as hard. He expected one to get on with the job under his umbrella of supervision. He said "If you don't want an unpopular decision, don't ask". I had to make 25 visits a week and he wanted to see my visiting lists. He wanted, almost demanded, obedience but he gave massively in return. When I arrived at Halifax Parish Church I lacked self-confidence and had a slight stammer. He helped me enormously over this, for example, by asking me just before a service to read the first lesson. This was very good for me.'

Whenever there was a need Treacy responded immediately and practically, without fuss. There are many examples. Sister Ward has one; 'An old clergyman, a bit confused, turned up in the middle of the night to visit the General Hospital. The Ward Sister rang the Vicar of Halifax (Treacy) who got up and went down to the hospital. On arriving he said "Hello James, are you visiting too. I will give you a lift home". This he did without anybody losing face.'

Another occasion relates to an old man who went around doing odd gardening jobs, cutting people's trees and so on. Everyone knew him. He slept rough, cut the trees rough, and at the end died rough. In the ordinary way he would have had a normal pauper's funeral with a parson off the rota. But Treacy got to hear of it and it was typical of him that he intervened and took the service at the graveside himself.

Treacy soon drew people of an increasingly wide divergence of opinion and background to the Parish Church. They were attracted by his preaching and his character, the two being inextricably linked. A former Town Clerk of Halifax, Richard de Z. Hall — on whom was conferred the Honorary Freedom of the Borough together with Treacy on 13 December 1973 — recalls:

'A number of private meetings with Eric with respect to my own position as a frequent attender with my wife at the Parish Church, but as a lifelong Unitarian. Our talks were frank and searching, but did not reach the results that Eric was hoping for. At the finish I asked Eric what his attitude was to my continued attendance at the Parish Church, as a Laodicean, or Eclectic, or whatever, and his answer to me revealed his general attitude to the role of the Church of England as he saw it. He thought that if I wanted genuinely to come to his Church, it was to be welcomed, and he viewed the Church of England as being truly catholic and under the duty of welcoming and serving all within its parish so far as it could offer, and they receive. I can well imagine that some of the clergy might have taken a strict attitude of "he who is not for us ... etc", or of resentment against those who took what was convenient and rejected what was inconvenient ... There were at that time a small handful of those who felt glad to be able to shelter under Eric's very commodious tent.'

If Unitarians found peace in the pew, at the other end of the spectrum the Orthodox were at ease before its altar. The Ukranian community in Halifax was a sizeable one and Treacy arranged for the Ukranian Orthodox to use the Parish Church under their priest Fr A. Zacharchnko.

Treacy's own 'pull' was that combination of his humanity and his preaching. He built up a good congregation who knew that he would be 'proclaiming' on Sunday evenings. He did not hesitate to be topical in his preaching because he believed that people sat up and took notice when they found that he was talking about something that had been in their minds the previous week. Henceforth his style of preaching (as opposed to his devotional addresses) did not change. Like all forceful preachers he found it difficult to make himself decrease so that God increased but God used him in a remarkable way. His sermons may have been full of topical allusions but the aim was always to lead his hearers from the topical to the teaching of the Gospel. Although his sermons were written out in full, as at Keighley, he had succeeded in developing the art of reading without too obviously appearing to read. This is not difficult if you can read your own writing (and he could), and do not leave the vital page at home (as he did more than once) or if you do not post it with the evening's letters (as he did twice, only to have them delivered the following day to the Vicarage by the Head Postmaster). Little wonder that the Post Office was a more enlightened institution in those days.

The great advantage about a sermon that is written out in full is that the preacher finishes at the last page, whereas those who trust in ad hoc inspiration never finish. Or rather they are in danger of concluding well in advance of stopping.

At a man's ordination the Bishop delivers to him the Bible saying 'Take thou authority to preach the word of God'. That is why Treacy took his preaching so seriously. He had been entrusted with a solemn and heavy responsibility and he had a strong sense of the opportunity that was his in his preaching ministry. He was taught that the subject of a Sunday sermon should be in the mind the Monday before it has to be preached, and that one should meditate on it during the week, and have it on paper at least by Thursday. Although he was rigorous in expecting his curates to abide by this ideal, he rarely realised it himself. Many was the time when a Sunday morning sermon was unfinished when he went to bed on Saturday night. A Sunday evening sermon was frequently just about ready to take out of the oven at 5.30pm. When later as Bishop of Pontefract and of Wakefield, it was not unknown for him to pull in to a lay-by on his way to a Service to prepare a Sermon. There are countless stories of the Treacy method but one will suffice to illustrate a tendency. Malcolm Robinson (now Vicar of Dent) remembers a Treacy visit to St Peter's, Shipley, 'He came into the vestry about one minute before the service was due to begin. He said to me "You start Evensong, Malcolm, while I prepare my sermon." He then proceeded to do this in the vestry and by the time he was due to preach he had everything he wanted to say at his finger tips. He came into the church to join the rest of us and went on to give an excellent and provocative sermon.'

Sometimes his personal allusions were too cheeky for comfort. Colonel Freddie Crossley, his next-door neighbour, recalls one shortly after Treacy's arrival at Halifax. Colonel Crossley commanded the local Territorial Regiment and Treacy called to see him about a Church Parade. It was the Saturday before Remembrance Day when the Festival of Remembrance is televised from the Royal Albert Hall. 'It started at 7.00pm' writes Colonel Crossley, when Treacy called on him 'so I asked him if he minded if we switched it on and he said not at all as he would have to dash off for his boiled eggs which would be ready. (He didn't).

'The programme duly started and I asked my wife if she would like a drink and so she said she would have a gin and tonic. I then asked the vicar who asked for a bitter lemon so I got the drinks and we settled down to watch the programme. During the course of the programme I think he had two more bitter lemons and we had two more gins. The programme finished at 9.00pm whereupon the Vicar stood up and said he must leave as he was already late.'

The parade service followed on the Sunday with Colonel and Mrs Crossley sitting in the front pew in front of the Regiment. 'Eric Treacy mounted the pulpit steps and proceeded to talk about the evils of television and especially on those people who when the vicar called to see them, switched on the television and started to drink! My wife and I simply couldn't believe our ears as we were the only ones who knew what he was referring to. He then went on slamming television in general and said he wouldn't have one in the house. As we left the church I said to my wife "That man has either a tremendous sense of humour or he's not fit to be a vicar." ' About a week later the same neighbour received another visit from Treacy:

'He said he was so cold, the vicarage had no central heating, could he come in and get warm as his wife was out too. I invited him in and made him a coffee, the time would be about 9.00pm. He took up his familiar sprawl in one of the easy chairs and we talked in general about the town and people. At about 9.30pm, he suddenly said "You haven't got the television on". Without thinking I said "You cheeky devil, after all you've said" and he burst out laughing. As soon as he started to laugh I felt that I really knew this man. We chatted on and about 15 minutes later he said "Aren't you going to put the television on?" so I said "I don't even know what's on." He said, "I do, there's a cowboy starting at 10.00pm" I switched it on and he sat through the whole of the cowboy like a young lad and really enjoyed it. These visits became quite frequent, especially if there was something on the television he wanted to see.'

Treacy knew how to attract attention by the vivid language he used to make a particular point. One example comes from a speech at the Annual Dinner of the Royal Society of St George on 21 April 1961. He remarked that it was significant that the poodle had replaced the bulldog as the canine symbol of the British character, adding 'This silly little dog with its absurd name, its beady eyes, its mincing walk, its silly little tail with a knob at the end; its permanent waves and shampoos.' Tongue in cheek, the day after the event, he noted in his diary:

'I suppose I ought to have realised that the press would seize on this at the expense of everything else I said. Furious poodle owners are after my blood and various reporters have been after me all day. One woman has challenged me to enter her backyard one night and brave the attack of her poodles.'

Treacy needed a desk as well as a pulpit from which he could air his views on most subjects under the sun. The Parish of Halifax did not boast a conventional parish magazine. There was a monthly four-page leaflet. Over the Treacy years the space given to the announcement of the music rendered by the choir diminished and the space was occupied by the Vicar until in 1959 a first class quarterly was produced entitled *The Vicar's News Letter*. His views on parish magazines never changed:

'I never have seen the point of publishing one every month for the sake of it. This is responsible for some of the drivel which appears in parish magazines. The poor vicar scratches around for something to say as the due date comes round each month, and, even if he hasn't got anything to say, he takes about a page to say it. The rest is filled up with lists of flower arrangers, sidesmen's rotas, reports of the Mothers Union meeting, the CEMS outing, the annual bazaar, the amounts of the collections for the previous month, and so on. Come what may, the magazine must appear each month because it is under contract to the advertisers.

'Parish magazine advertisements always seem to me akin to blackmail. Local tradesmen are pressed to advertise as a kind of impressed support for the parish. I doubt if many of them can say that these advertisements are the means of bringing them any new business.

'The aggregate circulation of parish magazines in the country must be several million copies per month; what an opportunity for the presentation of Christian truth and standards this affords, but is it used properly?'

Treacy regarded the News Letter as a periodical compulsion. He used it for making comments on local and national issues, with the result that the press quoted from it at length. Here it is worthwhile including something about Treacy's high regard for the Press and their craft. It was heartily reciprocated and they all thought that Treacy would have made a good professional journalist. In Halifax he was seldom out of the news. Christopher Spafford, formerly a priest in the Wakefield Diocese and now Provost of Newcastle, tells how he once asked Treacy:

' "Why is it that whenever you write or say anything at all even if it . . ." and he interrupted me to say "is nonsense". I went on to say "even if it could hardly be said to be worth quoting, you always get the headlines in the Press." He replied "Don't you know why it is, Christopher? It is because I am basically common".

'Certainly he had more of the "common touch" than most people holding the offices which he held. In many ways, I think that although he was much admired by his clergy, it was to the laity that he appealed. He had a no nonsense down to earth way with him.'

George Beddoe, a former Editor of the *Halifax Evening Courier* and who was its Chief Reporter in Treacy's Halifax years writes:

'It was characteristic of Eric Treacy's superb qualities as a communicator that he came over to Halifax and introduced himself to the *Courier* before taking up the appointment. After his interview with Charles Ramsden, the Editor, to which I was called in, Mr Ramsden said to me "There's a man worth cultivating — he's a spellbinder." Few people in Halifax during the next 12 years would have quarrelled with that assessment.

'In those 12 years ET made a mark on the community life of the Ancient Parish of Halifax (now Calderdale Metropolitan District) matched by few before him in any sphere of public life. That influence derived only in comparatively small part from his ecclesiastical office but in greatest measure from his own personality and presence. But I would suggest that he would have been the first to acknowledge that this influence was greatly fostered and his personality projected by a recognition of the value of the media as an arm to mission.

'What moral and spiritual stands he took — and they were many, all positively championed but certainly not all universally popular — he saw as being worthy of a wider audience than the few hundreds of a congregation. He used the media — but in such a way that the media was happy to cooperate and recognised that such "usage" was of a nature that did not demean the editorial ethic.

'At the same time his co-operation with the media was always on his own terms. When he was reported he required that he should be reported accurately — and offered the fullest co-operation to see this was achieved — by supplying the complete manuscript ... Many times in the 1950s did I arrive in the newsroom shortly after 8am to find him the sole occupant, waiting to hand over a manuscript and dictate a succinct report of a meeting we had been unable to attend.

'This emphasis on accurate reporting he also directed towards telephone inquiries seeking a statement or a comment on some contemporary issue. "Ring me back in ten minutes — how many words?" he would say. And in those ten minutes he would draft a considered statement and dictate it and generally be unwilling to add any further comment.'

Treacy criticised his fellow clergy who regarded reporters as potential enemies and who grumbled when they were misreported or had had some small item from the parish magazine quoted. Gentlemen called 'stringers' comb parish magazines for newsy items, and feed them, for a few pieces of silver, to the media. It is the unusual the Press is after. The Churchwardens counting the collection is not news, but the Vicar pinching it is. On this basis Treacy had no quarrel — although he was sore — when the Press plucked some trivial matter from his News Letter, overlooking something of substance.

When he bared his soul about dozing in public (News Letter September-October 1959) the item was reported in several countries. He made a plea 'I would be grateful if anyone could tell me what to do when the eyelids begin to droop. I have tried everything including pinching myself, asking my neighbour to prod me when he sees it beginning to happen, sucking acid drops — but all to no avail.' Treacy slept on as many public platforms as a tramp on park benches. Two recollections illustrate two different ways of dealing with the snoozing dilemma. One comes from his Keighley curate, Roger Vallance:

'He had a persistent habit of going to sleep at meetings and many was the time when I felt his weight gradually increasing against me as he dropped off and started to breathe heavily. On one occasion he was asked to propose a vote of thanks at a meeting where the speaker was a titled lady. He was on the platform and in full view of the audience he dropped off to sleep. The applause when the speaker had finished woke him up. With all the charm of which he was capable he openly confessed that he had slept through a good part of the address, pointed out to the people the delicate task which confronted someone who had to propose a vote of thanks in such circumstances, reduced the speaker and audience to helpless laughter and received a great round of applause at the end of his little speech. One was left with the feeling that the speaker would have had it no other way!'

Treacy's alternative method was more subtle. He recalls a meeting of the local Moral Welfare Council addressed by the Bishop of Wakefield (John Ramsbotham) 'when in spite of all my precautions I dropped off as he began, and woke to hear the clapping which marked the end of his address. If that were not bad enough, it was made worse by the fact that the Mayor then called upon me to propose a vote of thanks to the speaker! I could only thank him by saying that we were grateful not so much for what he had said, but for the fact that he had found time to come and encourage us with his presence. I don't think that anyone was deceived.'

Treacy was beseiged with letters from fellow sufferers begging him to share with them any remedy that he might have or find. One chap confessed that when he proposed marriage to his 'intended' he dropped off to sleep before she had given him his answer. As for cures? Three children from the Channel Islands sent some thistles and told him to sit on them. He was advised to carry a wallet full of money on his lap or try to keep his feet off the ground until the end of the last speech. Pills came from Australia, a letter of sympathy from Boston, Massachusetts, and most impertinent and colosally untrue in Treacy's case, he was told that if parsons worked harder they would not be so tired.

Another topic aired in the News Letter (August 1956) and which hit the headlines related to the Roman Catholic Church. He wrote:

'By the year 2000 this country will quite probably be Roman Catholic ... a nation with a predominantly Roman Catholic population will, by then, have taken steps to have the constitution of the country changed so that the cathedrals and ancient parish churches are made over to the Roman Catholics; so that the King (or Queen) of this country is crowned by a Roman prelate, and the Anglican Church and its clergy deprived of the privileges that now belong to them as ministers of the establishment.'

Treacy based his observation on mathematics. Roman Catholics pursued an inflexible policy in the matter of the marriages of Roman Catholics to non-Romans; family limitation was not easily practised in view of the Church's ban on all methods of birth control, except what is known as the 'safe period'; the Roman Church made the retention of her Church Schools a priority and full use was made of them for grounding her young people thoroughly in the Roman faith. Whilst Treacy admired the strength of the Roman Church's discipline and the consistency of her tactics, he felt uneasy as to where it was leading. In his ecumenical thinking at this time Rome played no part and it was a long time before it did so, and then only in personal relations, not in discussions. He was distinctively Protestant in this regard. The Roman Catholic Church in England was the Italian Mission. Having worked in Liverpool he had seen the hard but effective face of Rome. Although he had been on friendly terms with one or two Roman Catholic priests through his youth work, it was a period when the Roman Catholic Church was exclusive and her members were discouraged, even forbidden, from associating with fellow Christians in public! In his Halifax article Treacy ended with a challenge:

'Let us give Roman Catholics full marks for the vitality of their churchmanship; but do not let us be blind as to their objective. Logically, could they have any other? God will grant religious leadership of this nation to those He sees worthy of it. On our present showing, are we of the Angican Church worthy of the position, the opportunities and the authority which God has bestowed upon us? And if we are not, we shall lose it, and we shall deserve to. The burden of this article is to suggest to whom it will pass.'

The Church of England has often been in danger of becoming a decrepit formality but equally has as often been rescued by new and revitalising leadership. Treacy sought to and succeeded in giving leadership as Vicar of Halifax. It was the kind of leadership that the mass middle classes in particular yearned for, yet just when their ecstatic approval reached fever pitch Treacy would admonish one of their favourite pastimes. 'Moral Leadership' differs from the generally accepted view of leadership, in that it has no justification other than that it is goodness in action. It has no force to support it, other than the consent of those who recognise it. Its speed of effectiveness has always been disappointingly sluggish, but in the end it must prevail. The secret of it is to be found in character, in being rather than doing, and this Treacy found very hard. Its activity is in influence rather than coercion; its justification rests in its quality rather than in its results; its appreciation is in the future rather than in the present. It is not so much the formulae that people proclaim as the expression of their own convictions.

With views like Treacy's he was an obvious candidate for the Oxford Group Movement, more commonly referred to as Moral Rearmament. They tried to recruit him but failed, not because he did not agree with their spiritual credentials but rather because he was hesitant about joining any Movement. He expressed dismay at the Church of England's 'official' attitude towards MRA as it disclosed itself in a *Church Assembly* debate (February 1955): 'As I sat listening to it all, I was sad that the world outside should know that the Church of England was spending the best part of a day criticising cruelly and unkindly, a movement that had done much that the Church of England failed to.'

Treacy's dislike of Movements extended to a supreme suspicion of 'specialists'. In this respect his view never changed. It was always 'gut reaction' to use a colloquial phrase. It was not that he was adopting a rigorist stand based on conviction or prejudice which argument could not dislodge. This could have produced an unbending personality but in Treacy it was always softened and sweetened by a large compassionate heart. Even so, he would not easily be labelled, for he was conservative in some of his views but liberal in others. His 'gut reaction' is seen clearly in his opposition to all forms of gambling. When a report *Gambling — an Ethical Discussion* was published in 1950 he launched a frontal attack beginning with the composition of the committee which produced the Report — 'specialists' and 'moral theologians'. (Who better? one might ask). Speaking to clergy in Leeds, 22 January 1951 he said 'The report smacks too much of the ethical hair-splitting of the casuists: it contains, what seem to me, too many false and glib parallels — some of them intellectually unanswerable — *yet which violate one's deepest feelings.*'

For Treacy all forms of gambling were, quite simply, wrong. He never accepted the view that to gamble — or to drink for that matter — in moderation was completely harmless and innocent. They were social evils to be judged by their consequences as much as by their intrinsic qualities. Many of his friends indulged in mild flutters on the Boat Race, Bridge and the Pools. He had a word for them: 'These comparatively harmless excursions do not spring from an evil character — they may well be done in all innocence — but innocence of the person doing a thing does not prove the innocence of the act.' And his general view was 'that the distribution of money by chance is a socially wrong principle — it should altogether be repudiated'.

Treacy would countenance no form of gambling, whether raffles or tombolas at Church Fairs and Bazaars or wicked Bingo as a means of augmenting the weekly income. He was later to write, when Bishop of Wakefield 'I think that such forms of raising money for the work of the Church, are an insult to God, and a most unworthy offering to Him. Can a parish which depends for its financial survival on Bingo really maintain that it is expressing the spirit of a stewardship that should govern the use Christian people make of their money?'

On all the issues of his time Treacy had something to say. He chaired a public meeting on the subject of capital punishment and later expressed his view that: 'On the whole I find myself on the side of those who feel that it must be retained in some cases as a deterrent. So long as it is retained, I plead that some less brutal way (than hanging) of administering it should be adopted.'

Treacy was *the* figure in the town but he earned that position. Before going to Halifax, he had understood that the Vicar of Halifax was a lesser Vicar of Leeds in that he was, ex-officio, on everything. This was not the case. He was not a Governor of any of the town's main Grammar Schools, nor on any of the Hospital Management Committees, nor on the Borough Education Committee. In fact, he began by having very little official connection, except for all the voluntary organisations and charities. He ended having effected a marvellous transformation. His successor as Vicar of Halifax, A. G. Hardie (afterwards Archdeacon of West Cumberland) writes: 'He carved out a deep niche, not only in the parish, but also in the whole life of the town. I soon discovered that his influence and his presence still remained a reality years after he had left to be Bishop of Pontefract. Such was his influence on many people's lives that they found it hard to think of anyone else as Vicar of Halifax.'

Initially, Treacy was disappointed that he was not a card carrying member of the Ex-Officio Club, but his unofficial and personal contacts soon enabled him to bring influence to bear. During his twelve years in Halifax he was Chaplain to seven Mayors. The opportunities afforded by this position differed with the Mayor. Some treated their chaplains as friends and confidants whilst others saw as little of them as possible. But Treacy made the most of the slightest opportunity. It was the Church in Action again, Richard de Z. Hall recalls:

'It was Eric who initiated the proposal that Council meetings should open with prayer. When first mooted the idea sparked off some initial resentment but that was quickly dispelled ... When prayers were first said, it was noticed that two, may be three, members came in immediately after Eric had concluded, and for a couple of (monthly) meetings thereafter, the same members (known for their beliefs or unbeliefs) came in seconds after conclusion of prayers. But that seemed to be the end of the demo. Eric had to my judgement, set a simple, unaggressive format and style, and I think such people came quickly to realise that they had no need to be scared. I think that members thought that Eric's introduction of prayers added to the dignity of the proceedings, though whether it helped to assuage the high feelings of some of the members, may be open to doubt.'

Treacy's version runs thus:

'It was clear from the attitude of some of the councillors that they did not feel the need for any wisdom other than their own, and some of the debates showed that commodity to be in lamentably short supply. I appreciated the opportunity of taking tea with the councillors and sitting in at the proceedings.

'There were times in these debates when I despaired of the democratic processes which put such idiots in charge of the town's affairs, but, in a curious way, after steam had been let off, and various petty points scored off each other, they would come to a conclusion that was essentially sound. But we had some narrow escapes. One might say that it was answer to prayer.

'I could not help observing that the Conservative and Liberal Councillors were more cordial in their attitude to the Mayor's Chaplain than those who represented Labour. These seemed to nourish a suspicion in their attitude to the Church; perhaps it went back to the time when the Church of England was the Church of the bosses. Or, perhaps, they resented the Church as a power structure in the life of the nation.'

Treacy was co-opted as a member of the Executive Committee of the Halifax Council of Social Services — and May Treacy was too. This was the natural successor of the Citizens' Guild of Help, founded by a group of prominent Halifax citizens in 1905. Along with Bradford, Halifax was reckoned as amongst the pioneers of the Guild Movement. The aim was to provide an organisation to give material help and moral support to the poor and needy. Halifax was divided into 23 districts each with its own committee presided over by a captain. He, with a team of helpers, found work for the unemployed, pruned the town of 'cadger' beggars, distributed clothing, arranged for invalids to go to convalescent homes, set up work yards for the 'won't works', organised allotment gardens, assisted families to emigrate, served meals to schoolchildren and assisted in forming and helping the Health Association which provided lady visitors for 'poor and ignorant mothers during childbirth'. With the coming of National Health Insurance, the Labour Exchange and, later, the whole panoply of the Welfare State, the work of the Society adapted and diversified with need.

Treacy was convinced that the Welfare State had developed so rapidly that its scope outpaced its ability to produce the right people to run it. Further, it discouraged voluntary effort. State responsibility has ever tended to destroy personal responsibility. Treacy lent his name and gave his time to every effort of the Council as it pressed for changed conditions and refused to allow itself to be merely ameliorative.

Treacy was involved in an affair which made national headlines in April 1957. It concerned the former General Manager of the Halifax Building Society, Fred Bentley, who had risen to that position from that of junior clerk over 40 years during which the assets of the Halifax grew from £5 millions to £265 millions, making it the largest Building Society in the world. He resigned to become Chairman of the Building Societies' Association with which the Halifax was in dispute. When Fred Bentley was proposed for the Board of the Halifax this naturally caused a furore which took on rather a personal nature. Treacy attended the meeting and spoke in support of Fred Bentley, who was elected.

Towards the end of Treacy's time in Halifax it seemed as if he had his finger in every pie in the town. They are too numerous to list but two in particular should be mentioned. He was Honorary Chaplain to the Loyal Georgian Friendly

Society which, with one exception, is the oldest friendly society in the country. Treacy wrote:

'This Society, which now consists of most of the leading business men in Halifax, and who, by no stretch of imagination, could be said to be in "need of benefit", meets once a month in the Oak Room of the Old Cock Inn, in order to engage in refined but steady imbibing, snuff taking and conversation. Proceedings are occasionally enlivened with a "turn" from one or other of the members. Perhaps a dialect recitation, a song, some conjuring, or even a talk from me. These were delightful evenings of old fashioned pleasure, leisured and civilised, which I greatly enjoyed.'

Before the cut-back in the armed forces, Halifax was a garrison town of the Duke of Wellington's Regiment, with headquarters at Wellesley Barracks. This brought a good deal of social significance to the town, which took a great pride in its own regiment. A large number of men had served in the 'Duke's' and the Regiment had its own Memorial Chapel in the Parish Church. The Waterloo and Dettingen Colours are the church's proud possession. Treacy was appointed Honorary Chaplain. When he left Halifax in 1961 he was asked by the then Colonel of the Regiment, Maj Gen K. G. Exham, if he would do them the honour of becoming Honorary Chaplain to the Regiment — an appointment which was unique as it was unofficial (in military eyes) and personal. Treacy greatly appreciated the honour and the annual service of the Duke's in their All Saints Chapel in York Minster was always earmarked in his diary.

For Treacy this was but another part of his 'parish' for the men of the Regiment called on him for pastoral care as well as official duties. Major J. H. Davis writes of his daughter:

'Margrethe was born in June 1949 and we got to know Eric when I was in command of the Depot of the Duke of Wellington's from 1952-54. We returned to Halifax in August 1959 with Margrethe who had cancer in her arm — later she had an ablation (removal of the arm) and removal of an infected lung. Her love for Eric increased and she was seldom disappointed if he didn't reach out a hand to her as he progressed to or from a service in the Parish Church. Eric, knowing she realised where her path was leading, missed a Convocation in order to take her funeral in Frederikborg Church in Copenhagen on 11 February 1962 which she had asked if he would.'

Major Gen D. E. Isles, Colonel of the Regiment, knew Treacy for 30 years and recalls the occasions when they met:

'He used always to give me his views on the great topics of the day; these varied from race riots through the Arab-Israeli troubles to the Old Age Pension. I never argued with Eric — for the simple reason that he was always right. For sure he was a man to be listened to and a man whose advice was always sound. Often he would ask my advice on strategic defence matters, but more to confirm his own ideas, rather than the need to know, for he had a shrewd notion of all that was going on. Eric filled me (and all of us in the Regiment) with envy for his obvious faith. He never "pushed" religion at anyone; he didn't need to for it shone out of him. He was all good and that is why I envied him. Wise too, wise in all matters. We all miss him terribly.'

Treacy was not always wise. He spoke too often and on too many subjects with insufficient time for proper research and preparation to do so. Anyone who frequently fires from the hip is bound to miss his target, or worse, hit the wrong one, occasionally. When he did he was as quick to apologise. At a public quiz in Halifax when asked his opinion on whether Britain should renounce the H-bomb he replied that the 'crews of the USA bombers carrying nuclear weapons over this country should get the hell out of it'. His comment was widely reported and as widely denounced. It takes a kind of courage to apologise publicly and this put Treacy high above the moral standing of many public figures not least politicians. In a letter to *The Yorkshire Evening Post* (6 February 1958) he wrote:

'I regretted these words the moment I had uttered them. One of the dangers in appearing in these panels of "Any Questions" type is that one has to answer "off the cuff".

'I regret those words because they are harsh and unkind. They are crude — especially coming from a clergyman. I am not concerned to excuse myself so much as to offer my apologies to any Americans who may have read those words.

'It is ungracious to the extreme to utter such words as I did on Tuesday, and I wish to withdraw them. These men are here as part of the Western defence line.

'In my answer to this question, I was trying to say that I do not believe that there is a real danger of this country becoming an advanced airfield for American nuclear bombers. If Britain is to renounce the use of the H-bomb, as I hope she may, she must be prepared to request the United States Government to withdraw her nuclear bomber squadrons from these shores.'

Another example arose in 1960 when Treacy appeared to criticise the Archbishop of Cape Town (Joost de Blank) on the question of 'his courageous and single-handed resistance against the policy of Apartheid adopted by the South African Government. Without wishing to detract in the least from his sincerity in the stand that he has made, I cannot help wishing that he had not decided to 'go it alone' — There are some situations in which it is not easy for Christians of different loyalties to work together, but, surely, this is one in which positive leadership could unite all men of goodwill in effective action.' This came from the 'Halifax Pontiff', as a friendly rival called Treacy, writing in his News Letter (December 1960-February 1961). By this time in Halifax Treacy's comments were quoted more widely than ever and they found their way into the South African Press. On this occasion Treacy was mistaken on all counts, for Joost de Blank was not the only arch-opponent of Apartheid but it was he who sent Treacy a stinging rebuke on 4 January 1961 which Treacy later published in full. The Archbishop referred to the lead the Anglican Church had taken and the prominent part it had played in the activities of the Christian Council of South Africa which rallied together all the English-speaking churches except the Roman Catholics. He went on to ask Treacy:

'What, in God's name, ought we to have done besides? I hope you will write and tell me, and if you agree we have done all we can, perhaps you will say in the next number of your magazine. Only Anglicans have been imprisoned for their witness.

'It really hurts when a spectator from the touch line who has apparently not been watching the game properly indulges in superficial criticism, particularly when for us it is not a game but a life and death struggle in which hatred and bitterness are part of the daily lot we have to bear because of our witness. It hurts even more when these criticisms are made in public without referring first to those situated to check the facts. And even more still, when made by one whom I have always regarded as a friend and supporter.'

Treacy accepted the rebuke, adding 'I hope, too that the publication of this letter which hits one pretty hard will be seen by the Church in South Africa as a penance. To the Archbishop I can only say, "May I be forgiven".'

There is an interesting footnote to this particular issue. Treacy had in fact written to the Archbishop of Canterbury (Geoffrey Fisher) about the matter and he received a letter from the Archbishop agreeing with his criticism of Joost de Blank and revealing some of the difficulties 'created by de Blank's impatience and impetuosity'.

Treacy always had wide vision. He often told his parishioners, as later his diocese, that the cosy and well fed West, cushioned in affluence, had suffered a hardening of the spiritual arteries so that the power to respond to need and suffering had become deadened. He told a Church Missionary Society (CMS) Jubilee Rally in Liverpool in 1971: 'It is the poor who respond to the needs of the poor. That is why old age pensioners living on a pittance give more generously to the work of the church than the rich business men. It is my experience that the more affluent people become, the less they feel the need of anything — that much less are they capable of responding to the needs of others.' Giving to the Church overseas was the prime example of what he meant. And giving could not be confined to money. To Treacy the Church was entrusted with the Gospel that people needed. The need was in Halifax. It was even greater overseas. He was once referred to as a 'frustrated missionary'. The label is not inappropriate. He was frustrated because he was divinely impatient for the extension of God's Kingdom. He spent a great deal of time speaking at CMS meetings, summer schools and the Northern Congresses and he was on the Executive Committee of CMS. The regular prayer group at Halifax involved earnest commitment to the missionary cause.

For Treacy there was no question of coming to terms with the rapid and ruthless extension of Communism or with other religions such as Islam. On the other hand he was well abreast of contemporary missionary thinking. He readily accepted that the missionary had to be concerned with standards of living as well as standards for living in the face of materialism. Archdeacon Leslie Fisher, a former Home Secretary of CMS, remembers Treacy's 'tremendous vision of the world-wide Church and deep sense of commitment to the world-wide mission of the Church.

'Bishop Treacy had a keen analytical mind which could take him to the heart of a matter very rapidly. He had no use for cant or hypocrisy, so where the mission of the Church was concerned mere words were not enough. Our commitment to our Lord and his mission to the world must be measured in deeds, in hard work and sacrifice. To hear him preach at a Northern Congress was to be left in no doubt of the fact that Eric Treacy put Christ and His mission to the world in the first place in his life and everything else had to be related to that. I well remember one phrase, which he often used — there is only one way for missionary giving to go, and that is up.'

His Halifax curate, Colin Docker, says:

'It was from Eric that I caught a vision of what if means for our ministry to be exercised in the context of the world-wide Church, and it was his influence which had much to do with my spending five years of my ministry on the staff of CMS.'

The joy in Treacy's heart when a member of his own parish volunteered for missionary service with CMS was overwhelming. An answer to prayer! But he was careful never to force anyone in that direction as Ruth Walker recalls: 'When I was considering offering myself to CMS they (Eric and May) did all in their power to help me with the practical details, without in any way making me feel pressurised into going — in fact it wasn't until much later I began to realise how much it meant to them that the parish had produced a missionary. Eric was a great pastor for me. His insights enabled him to see the question behind the question and some of his advice could be pretty tough. More than once he made me see things about myself I would rather not have faced.' Ruth Walker, working in a hospital in Pakistan, was followed by another CMS recruit and then a Church Army recruit, taking their places amongst that band of men and women who felt and answered Christ's call to 'Go! Preach in all the world'.

Ask anyone today who knew or met Treacy at Halifax what most lingers in their memory and the answer is his 'humanity' or versions of 'what a character' and 'What a pastor when one was in trouble'. There are other memories too. Mrs Dorothy Holdsworth's 'outstanding memory of him is his enthusiasm, a gaiety in everything that he did and the courage which allowed him to speak openly against social wrongs and injustices'. Frank Marsden was his verger and close friend. In some ways he was a kind of batman to Treacy. Perhaps Treacy needed a batman figure. Treacy recalled Frank Marsden as having 'a remarkably shrewd capacity for judging people, and a pithy way of expressing his judgements. One of Frank's great joys was showing parties of school children round the church, in the course of which he ventured on historical details of the history of the Church in Halifax, which occasionally, a teacher might question. Frank was never outwitted, and always, with unquestioned authority, produced his own version of the event in question, which bore more resemblance to *1066 and all that* than to Trevelyan.'

After daily Matins, Frank Marsden usually walked with Treacy to the Vicarage. Treacy regretted the absence of working class people from the Church and as Frank Marsden recalls: 'He loved his parishioners of high and low bearing and oft he would remark that the man with the dirty finger nails was just as important to him as the others.' When Treacy was desperate to see *Cockleshell Heroes*, which was showing in Halifax, he wanted to go with Frank Marsden but did not want them to be seen walking to the cinema together. 'Meet me in the foyer' said Treacy — and they went their separate ways after the show. This was the *Vicar* of Halifax rather than Eric Treacy.

A description which Bishop John Ramsbotham, who succeeded to the See of Wakefield in 1958 when Bishop Roger Wilson was translated to Chichester, used of Treacy after seeing him in action at Halifax was 'Ecclesiastical Mayor'. Treacy later wrote, 'I think that he meant it as a compliment, but at the time, I thought that it suggested that I was better at the secular than the sacred.' It *was* a compliment for Treacy had not only renewed the life of the Parish but he himself had become a focus of Christian endeavour in the town. It was probably the happiest period of his ministry although not its fulfilment. The parish was only a portion of his work and we must now consider his advent as archdeacon and emergence on the national scene.

12
Lowest Form of Gaitered Life

Treacy's predecessor as Archdeacon of Halifax, Harold Morris, described his own view of his later episcopal ministry in a letter to this biographer (3 July 1971). 'I regarded my work very definitely as a pastoral charge and it was my hope that I should be able to visit all the clergy, understand their difficulties and help them in any way possible to do their work efficiently. In other words I regarded myself as a friend of all. Undoubtedly what I felt to be the chief function of my episcopate was to be behind the clergy in proclaiming the Gospel of Jesus Christ.' What Bishop Morris aspired to he accomplished as archdeacon and bishop. Accordingly he was not an easy person to follow, and in particular because he was still in the Wakefield Diocese.

Treacy used to quip that an archdeacon is 'the lowest form of gaitered life'. Technically that may be accurate but lack of power does not annihilate influence. The boundaries of influence depend in small part on the individual's own will, determination and character and in large measure on the particular Diocesan Bishop for whom he is the *oculus episcopi*.

Treacy squeezed every atom of authority from the archidiaconal office and extended its influence. By legislation in the 19th century archdeacons had been deprived of most of their old powers and with the increase in suffragan bishops they had less of a pastoral function. In history they are known to have existed before the Norman Conquest. The bishop's deacon of the third century is the ancestor of today's archdeacon. He used to administer the revenues and discipline of the Church. The Office had its first development in the assignment of a local area for the Archdeacon. Prior to the Act of Uniformity in 1662 he did not have to be in priest's orders. There is a sound argument in favour of reverting to lay archdeacons again. Until 1868 the Archdeacon could levy a repair and building rate. During the Middle Ages the Archdeacon's Visitations and Procurations were unpopular. As judge of the moral delinquencies of the laity, Mediaeval Archdeacons' Courts had an unsavoury reputation.

Looking back on his archdiaconal work Treacy felt a little balked!

'I fear that I was not a particularly good Archdeacon, not for any lack of intention, but simply from the difficulty of balancing the claims of my incumbency, and of the Archdeaconry.

'As Archdeacon, I was an ex-officio member of Convocation and Church Assembly. This meant three spells of two days per year in York, and three spells of four days in London. In the Diocese of Wakefield the Archdeacons shared the chairmanship of Diocesan Committees. My share included the Youth Council, Children's Council, and the Diocesan Church Schools Committee. This last committee was an onerous one because it involved endless consultations with Local Education Authorities and School Managers about the retention of Church Schools with Aided Status. In addition to that, I was responsible for seeing that the churches in my Archdeaconry were regularly inspected by the Rural Dean, but as I was also Rural Dean of Halifax, there was a certain amount of this that I could not delegate.

'I had to keep my ear to the ground, and keep the Bishop informed of anything that he ought to know regarding his clergy. Where I failed most was in the pastoral care of the clergy in the Archdeaconry. I did my best, but it was an impossible task to fulfil the pastoral work of the parish, my administrative and committee work in Wakefield, and to attend Convocation and Church Assembly.

'Yet, this is an unavoidable situation so long as the Church fails to recognise financially the Office of Archdeacon. The Church Commissioners make an allowance to Archdeacons which is so small that they need to hold some other appointment to produce a stipend sufficient to live on. If the Office of Archdeacon is a necessary one within the structures of the Church of England, then an adequate stipend should be attached to it, so that he can give his whole attention to the work. My own view is that Archdeacons are necessary, although the development of omni-competent, and sometimes omniscient, diocesan secretaries tends to erode the office and the work of the Archdeacon. Clergy, I find, prefer to deal with a man in orders about their houses, stipends, and other administrative matters than they do with a layman.'

That was how the bishop's eye saw it! Now the episcopal head of Roger Wilson who himself had formerly been Archdeacon of Nottingham:

'Eric did not see himself as the venerable, nor was he fond of gaiters, yet like other archdeacons he had to turn his hand to anything in the diocese, and represent an authority not his own. A good deal of this was a heavy diocesan addition to an already heavy programme. But the sheer routine of Boards and Committees, dilapidations, schools, finance, readers and the like, was cheerfully discharged. He was too human to like much of this. "Can't you spare me from —————" he would exclaim, "he never stops talking"! He could not be spared, but I am bound to say that however critical he was of colleagues who were pompous or cheap or voluble or slovenly, he always stood by his men when they were in need.

'Of course his real contribution to the diocese lay in the originality and drive which he brought to its counsels and not least its Bishop.'

By 1961 Treacy served on more than seventy committees and ruefully reflected:

'There seems to be a kind of snobbery current these days about administration, as if it were an inferior order of work in the Kingdom of God. A fairly long experience of the church leads me to say that administration can be done to the Glory of God as much as preaching or visiting. If the clergy can rely on the administration behind them, they can get on with their jobs without anxiety. So much of the Church's work is concerned with money, buildings and plant in general, that these things must be seen as sacraments. Committees are a nuisance and often a bore, but what is the alternative to them? Surely the centralisation of power into very few hands, and that is far worse for the Church than a proliferation of committees. At their best — they are a good way of obtaining a corporate mind on problems; at their worst, they are a rest from the ceaseless activity of the parochial clergyman's life.'

The only outward sign of Treacy's different status was sartorial. The Archdeacon's habit of gaiters, breeches, apron and frock coat dates back to the time when his venerable-ship had to cover large areas on horseback. When four wheels replaced four legs as a form of locomotion, the skintight 22-button gaiters remained as a distinguishing mark. After hearing a young woman saying to her companion of him 'Ee, look at yon chap in his rompers' Treacy wrote a short piece in his News Letter (June 1957) beginning with a limerick which had been sent to him.

There was an Archdeacon who said
'May I take off my gaiters in bed?'
But the Bishop said 'No,
Wherever you go
You must wear them until you are dead'.

'I wonder what prompted it. Perhaps it is that someone thinks that I do not wear my gaiters as much as I should. That may be true. There are three very good practical reasons why I do not wear them more than I have to. The first is that my present rig is wearing out, and as they cost about £70 to replace, I am taking care of them. The second is that they are extremely uncomfortable to wear, and, in hot weather, intolerable.

'The third is that they are so embarrassingly conspicuous. It is not that I am ashamed of my office, far from it, but I do get rather tired of the smirks and stares which are directed at me when I thread my way along a crowded thoroughfare.

'Many of us dislike these external signs of rank, and there is a marked tendency to discard them as being expensive and uncomfortable anachronisms. In the modern world they are pointless and out of place as normal garb.'

However, in typically crafty Treacy fashion he had it both ways for he maintained on the other hand, or foot, that the Office had a certain dignity that must be sustained. 'Their out-of-dateness carries a certain charm and suggests the genius of the Church of England for combining the ancient and the modern. The dress of an Anglican dignitary is attractive and dignified.

'Certain formal occasions in Church and State deserve that we should wear the dress appropriate to our office, and the laity, rather more than the clergy, expect that we shall.'

Treacy transformed the chores of his new office into a gracious and essential ministry to the household of God. He was much more than an inspecting eye. By direct contact with that excellent and devoted body of men, — churchwardens — he obtained much personal and pastoral knowledge. People before things were always at the top of his priorities, at the core of his interest. He soon knew the clergy and their families as well as an ever-widening circle of lay people.

Treacy was also the bishop's quickening eye. His visits to a parish were converted from a formal and legal affair into a grand occasion of heartening revival.

At Shrewsbury House, Edge Hill, and at Keighley and at Halifax an initial guardedness, even suspicion, of Treacy quickly gave way to warmth, affection, respect and ovation. He had to go through the same process as Archdeacon. Bernard Pawley, now Archdeacon of Canterbury, was Rector of Elland. He had met Treacy at Keighley and so, unlike most of the clergy, he knew what manner of man was domiciled in Halifax. He remembers Treacy as:

'. . . a bit brash when I first met him. He used to make me think of a certain prelate of whom Hensley Henson said that "his powers of expression exceeded his powers of understanding". We were all rather young in those days and I think a certain amount of jealousy and intellectual snobbishness was part of my make-up. But from the first I reacted very favourably to his friendliness and had to revise my opinions about his intellectual capacity. I don't think that he had ever had the benefit of a university education and his great enthusiasm and energy did indeed make him express opinions with greater vehemence then was warranted by the information at his command but he was reading hard in those days, perhaps trying to make up for lack of previous opportunities and I believe he developed quite a lot in that sphere.'

The Halifax Archdeaconry comprised the Rural Deaneries of Halifax and Huddersfield with 47 and 50 parishes respectively. The clergy of the Halifax Rural Deanery included some remarkable men and some awkward ones as well as a few wayward priests. Meetings of the clergy were like minefields for Treacy until he knew his ground and had proved that he knew it. Then they were minefields for everybody else. Bernard Pawley comments: 'He was very good in administration and quick at repartee. I remember once asking a rather saucy question at a rural dean's meeting, blandly, hoping to catch him out: "Mr Rural Dean, I think we asked you to visit Canon W. and ask him to change his mind, did we not? Have you been and was your visit a success?" Eric's reply came very quickly: "You did and I have and it wasn't." '

Treacy often railed against fleeting incumbencies. Before he could get his feet under the parish table the parson was moving on. It was not a complaint he could sustain at Halifax. In the two adjoining parishes of Northowram and Lightcliffe the Vicars, Canons George Watkinson and H. L. Taylor, served for 48 and 41 years respectively. Canon Watkinson's private wealth built the beautiful church of which he became its first Vicar. He had the parish boundary altered when he found that he had built his Vicarage in another parish. He was the kind of man whom somehow one thought death would not have the impertinence to claim. Watkinson, who had graduated at Cambridge in 1894, used to say of Treacy, 'That man at the Parish Church — he hasn't even a degree, just an MBE'.

The bachelor Vicar of St Thomas, Claremount, Halifax, Roy Machon, served in that parish for 28 years. He was notorious for being dirty, which was made worse by an old war wound which discharged with a terrible smell. A red setter dog had been dead ten days in the vicarage before it was discovered. Treacy went out of his way to befriend Machon and sat next to him at meetings where he was shunned by some of the brethren.

Treacy's outward — and not always merely outward — autocratic and authoritarian manner met resistance from time to time. He was at All Saints, Elland, one day when the Angelus was rung and the devotion recited. Two days later the priest-in-charge received a letter from Treacy asking him to cease forthwith this un-Anglican practice. Treacy was bluntly told that 95% of the devotion was Biblical and the ancient and traditional practice in that place would continue.

Treacy certainly tried to give the people on his patch a feeling that they were members one of another. There were opportunities for encouraging this in unified action. Treacy took a leading part in the appeal to raise £30,000 in ten years for a new Church of England Secondary Modern School (Holy Trinity Transferred) in Halifax. In a carefully planned and sustained campaign the Chairman of the Committee, John Priestley, visited the parishes with Treacy to solicit support. John Priestley remembers Treacy's 'wholehearted commitment in time and energy to the project. He was the motive power behind it'. The Appeal had all the marks of a Treacy stamp — a well-produced brochure, effective advertising, a committee of enthusiasts. He always seemed to know where to get the best that was available. They were like a travelling road show, sometimes Treacy making the appeal whilst John Priestley filled in the details. At other times John Priestley put the request for money and Treacy glossed over the details. It was difficult work. Some parishes had the money but would not part with it; others were broke or in debt. The ripest plums were the parishes that had had stewardship schemes and to their amazement found that they had money. The Treacy-Priestley duo relieved them of it. Treacy continued his assistance after he had moved to Pontefract.

John Priestley recalls a visit to Roy Machon's successor at St Thomas's, A. G. ('Sandy') Kesseck. The purpose of the visit was to ask, or rather attempt to persuade Sandy Kesseck if he and Treacy could visit the parish to talk about Holy Trinity School. Living in his one up and one down cottage and ironing when John Priestley arrived, he said 'I don't want any bloody bishops in this Church'. Treacy came to have a warm regard for Sandy Kesseck who served in numerous parishes in the Diocese. He was far from popular but he could not be ignored. Glancing at the derisory collection offered to him on a plate on one occasion he decided it would be insulting to offer it to God, so he flung it back at the congregation.

Although Treacy was not a thoroughbred Evangelical and was visibly broadening all the while at Halifax, he had arrived with a reputation of being something of a party man. Canon John Brumpton (Rector of Barnsley, but then Vicar of Hepworth in Treacy's Archdeaconry) captures the feeling:

'I came to the Diocese in 1944 and remember Eric's appointment to Halifax. A note of caution was sounded among the junior clergy of my ilk (ie sensible Anglo-Catholics) that an Arch-Evangelical was with us, and no doubt, keeping an eye on us! Some of Eric's contributions to the *Halifax Courier* were of a very anti-Roman kind and there were those who felt that they were, in fact, anti-Catholic. They received, like so many of his pungent utterances, wide publicity at the time.

'My first personal encounter with Eric was when he asked me to consider the benefice of Holy Trinity, Halifax, of which the Vicar of Halifax was then Patron. He and May interviewed my wife and me at their Vicarage and were, as always, very charming, with Eric full of the blarney about the parish! To be frank we both found the joint-interview technique a bit off-putting and I am pretty certain that I felt that a Catholic under an eagle Evangelical eye in Halifax might not fare too happily. Only in later years was I to learn just how different things might have been had I accepted, though I am bound to say that I think his own attitudes mellowed and even changed with the years, from those days and the time when he expressed the view that Pope John lived at Wakefield!!'

[The reference is to John Ramsbotham, Bishop of Wakefield].

The 'mellowing' was not a weakening, It was an enlarging of the base. There were a number of factors which led to this. One was his emergence in Convocation and Church Assembly. The Convocation of York met at St William's College, York. The Upper House comprised all the 14 diocesan bishops of the Northern Province. The Lower House consisted of a good deal of gaitered glory — deans/provosts, archdeacons and a suffragan bishop or two together with proctors for the clergy elected from each diocese. Presiding over the Convocation was Cyril Forster Garbett, Archbishop of York, who, as Bishop of Southwark, had shown no interest in encouraging Treacy to exchange a collar and tie for a clerical collar. The personalities of the two men were incompatible. Treacy regarded Garbett with a mixture of irritation and respect. 'Garbett was not, by nature, a democrat and his handling of Convocation was authoritarian'. Treacy may not have observed that when he looked in a mirror, but it was the view of many people about *him*! Continuing about Garbett he writes:

'It would not be fair to say that he had his favourites, but he most certainly had his non-favourites. When members of this unhappy brigade rose to their feet, he made no attempt to hide his reactions to them... Undoubtedly there was greatness about Cyril Garbett, but he often failed in generosity with those he disliked. Certainly, those who were close to Garbett had a deep affection for him. I cannot claim to have known him at all well. Such contacts as I had with him, were freezing. If he was not interested in people, he made no effort to break the ice. I remember one occasion when he visited Halifax and was entertained by the

Mayor in the Town Hall. He was obviously bored by the proceedings, and stood aloof from the Halifax citizens, making no effort to engage in conversation. On another occasion May received him at Halifax Vicarage after some Diocesan occasion and provided him with tea. When I arrived, I could see she was desperate. His Grace sat hunched in a chair in a gloomy silence defying all her efforts to engage him in conversation. Some would say that this was due to shyness: I think it was boorishness.

'Yet when all this has been said, he was the end of a line of prelates who gave distinguished leadership in Church and State. He had authority, style, a consciousness of who he was, and however clumsy he might have been in certain relationships, he remains a giant in the episcopal scene of the 20th century.'

Cyril Garbett was most certainly a great Archbishop. When he died he was succeeded by Arthur Michael Ramsey, to whom I return in a later chapter.

Of other Northern Bishops of this period he respected but was wary of the influential bishops such as Leslie Hunter of Sheffield and F. R. Barry of Southwell. Alfred Blunt was still at Bradford but well past his peak. Anglo-Catholic Noel Hudson of Newcastle he did not like and Geoffrey Chase of Ripon was too legalistic for comfort. Of the others he liked best Thomas Bloomer of Carlisle and had a growing regard for Clifford Martin of Liverpool. He would have liked to have known William Greer of Manchester a great deal more and he never felt he knew the glamorous Bishop Gerald Ellison of Chester, a man who has been wrongly assessed and vastly underrated.

The Convocation of York had something of the atmosphere of a club, particularly when the Lower House met separately. On 14 January 1958 Treacy supported a suggestion of G. W. O. Addleshaw (then Canon Residentiary of York and later Dean of Chester) that they should sometimes have debates without the necessity of a resolution ending. He said: 'Some of us are prepared to open our mouths here, when we might not be so prepared in another setting . . . and I would have felt that this collection of clergy in the North having in common so many of the problems peculiar to the North, might well engage themselves in dealing with subjects which arise from our ministry in all its aspects, here in the fellowship.'

Treacy's interventions in debates during his time as Archdeacon reflected his passionate interests. On 6 July 1955 there was a debate on a *Report on Church Relations in England.* Amongst the resolutions which were carried was the significant one 'That this House respectfully requests his Grace the President to consult with the President of the Convocation of Canterbury with a view to opening conversations with the Methodist Church on the lines of this report.' Treacy spoke forcibly and impatiently. He was tired of hearing those who said nothing must be done to harm the prospects of reunion with Roman Christendom. He said he was tired of limited permission for the interchange of pulpits; of going round and round in circles of united fraternals; of those self-conscious joint services where they patted themselves on the back because they were able to do it. Ought they not to be moving on from discussions and tentative approaches to separate non-conformist bodies? Ought they not to be undertaking quite definite steps towards the clear objective of organic unity within this country with the established Free Churches? It might take 30 years, as it did in India, but unless they held before themselves that ideal, then he believed all those approaches to separate non-conformist bodies, all their conversations, would produce a paralysis of will, and tend to give the impression of much greater degrees of friendship than did in fact exist.

On 1 October 1957 an important debate took place in the Lower House on the Report of a Committee on the *Supply and Employment of the Ministry*. In a number of interventions Treacy revealed his position on various topics. He expressed concern at the number of church families who discouraged their own children in their desire to be ordained — there were some such in his own parish at Halifax. One amended resolution, 'that each year the ordinands available should be placed at the disposal of the dioceses in proportion to their needs', attracted vigorous exchanges. Treacy's observation reveals his natural antipathy towards directed authority — unless he was the one directing. It smacked of the ways of the Scarlet Lady. It was another example of his 'gut reaction'. He admitted it was hard to be intelligible because he had an instinct about it and the instinct was hard to express. But he felt that, in the matter of direction, the House would be doing something which was quite contrary to the *ethos* of the Anglican Church:

'Something of the Anglican Church's glory is that it is able, even after making mistakes very often, to develop its own understanding of the Will of God without too much application of external authority. This might be lost if the idea of direction is accepted too readily. The resolution says "some" direction but I know how easily "some" direction becomes "total" direction. It seems to be an attempt to find a tidy answer rather too quickly. The answer, it seems to me, will come in time if the right foundations are laid; and if more is expected of the younger clergy, I believe that the clergy will ask for direction rather than have it imposed upon them. The Church too rarely makes claims on those who wish to serve it.'

He was critical too, of theological college principals who, in over-protecting their ewe lambs, influenced where the men served.

Of all his speeches in Convocation as Archdeacon, none attracted wider publicity in the press and on the radio than that on 17 January 1961 when he moved a motion noting with concern the situation disclosed in a report of the Ministry of Health for 1959 regarding the moral standards of young people and commending for serious consideration the comments made about venereal disease. Dean G. W. O. Addleshaw recalls the occasion: 'The speech showed his forthrightness and directness and vigour; but also an inability to see the delicate nuances of these moral questions. He saw things too much in terms of black and white. He could get on with Yorkshire business people. His extrovertness and geniality was a tremendous help in this. But I have often wondered what was behind his geniality. Were there genuine spiritual depths and sensitivity? Or was it too much on the surface? He was inclined to play to the gallery. His strong suit I would say was his Christian common sense.' Treacy spent more time than was usual in preparing the January 1961 speech. There were several stabs at it the preceding week as, for example, '11 January. Spent a lot of time on my address to Convocation next Tuesday. I always feel that one never talks to a more critical audience than one consisting of one's brother clergy. Thank heavens it is to the Lower House, so I shall be spared an audience of Bishops!'

It is as well that he prepared this speech thoroughly and word for word, in view of the distractions of the day. His diary entry is self-explanatory:

'17 January. To York for Convocation — shock to see crudely chalked placard saying "Archbishop of Canterbury to retire" — confirmed on the 1 o'clock news. When the lads foregathered in St Williams College there was much tongue wagging. The runners in the Lambeth stakes reduced themselves to six about whom most people were unanimous. The thought of Geoffrey going is bleak — he may not be great by all standards, but he has infused the Assemblies of the Church with a warm humanity — and — with the passing of the years — mellow humility. I moved my Resolution in Convocation with knocking knees — I think it went fairly well. Charles Blackburn (Charles Claxton — Bishop of Blackburn) as junior Diocesan had to read the Litany in Latin in the Minster — which he did skilfully, hiding his faulty quantities behind a throaty cough assumed for the occasion. Pleasant evening at the Station Hotel based on an enormous dinner — quite a pleasant change from High Teas. (F. W.) Dilliston (Dean of Liverpool) joined us for a cup of tea — followed by Thomas Carliol (Thomas Bloomer, Bishop of Carlisle), Archdeacons (E. H.) Evans (of Warrington) and (C. E.) Nurse (of Carlisle).'

Bishop Claxton who tried to persuade Treacy to succeed him as Rector of West Derby, Liverpool, in 1948, himself remembers Treacy as 'voluble in his talk, not always fully informed, impulsive, generous and lovable. He and May used to hold court, during York Convocation, in the Station Hotel in the evening, dishing out tea and coffee to all comers.'

Returning to the Convocation speech, Treacy concentrated on the social sickness of which the incidence of venereal disease and existence of promiscuity were symptoms:

'My hypothesis is that a good deal of this social, moral, and spiritual sickness stems from the conditions of life which are developing in our ever growing centres of population. Vast areas of population must always depersonalise those who live in them.

'There is no natural centre for the life of the community. The city becomes the place to which people go to earn their living, and out of which they get as quickly as possible. A place to which they owe nothing and have no feeling of belonging. The modern city generates no values or conventions which influence people's behaviour. In them, each man lives to himself because the community is so large that it is impossible for him to observe the effects of his behaviour on other people.

'. . .Our young people are starving for lack of real tasks and vital opportunities. They are well fed and physically strong and with a dormant idealism — a longing to create and cultivate. But the life of the city frustrates all this, and many of them live like sleepwalkers; doped with mass produced unrealities, their energies turn to mischief and sexual adventure.

'The average new housing estate is a place without a centre, populated by people without roots, and the universal tendency for such people is to return on every possible occasion to the centre of the city which bred them — to such bright lights as they can find. There they mooch in aimless gangs — displaced people, not only physically but emotionally — for the provincial city has little to offer that will engage their better instincts.

'. . . The young of our cities form an instinctive group because they do not feel that they belong to anything but themselves — and it is not a big jump from that to an attitude of rebellion against the accepted standards of the community — against those who are older than themselves and who would seek to guide them. They find unity in a common war against authority. And I believe that one explanation of so many of the things which cause us anxiety today — violence, drink, sexual promiscuity, resulting in illegitimacy and venereal disease — is not that many of them like it, but that they are a form of protest against being displaced, and are instruments in the war that they are conducting against a society whose pattern they resent, and which has deprived them of personal significance.

'The novelist and playwright has a good deal to answer for in the matter of creating wrong moral standards. To claim that something is a work of art seems to be a reason for lifting it above all standards of moral judgement. Muck is muck however beautifully it may be wrapped up, and a dirty story remains a dirty story however beautiful the English in which it may be written.

'With very few exceptions the modern novelist and dramatist conveys the idea that life possesses no constructive purpose — that all is for nothing — that chastity is out of date, that sensual pleasure is the only form of happiness. It is not so much that they have produced things that are morally sterile and worthless, but that they have expressed a barren philosophy of life; not so much that they have suggested a decline in moral standards, as that they have presented a positively amoral standard.'

After paying tribute to those who were helping young people he added: 'Nor would we forget that great army of good, honest, but inarticulate citizens who know in their bones that something has gone seriously wrong, but can neither diagnose the trouble, nor understand what to do about it. I am quite sure of this. There exists in the country, a tremendous body of opinion which is deeply concerned about this problem — which recognises this moral sickness — but I do not think that this body of opinion is articulate or co-ordinated.' Articulate Treacy was to become a self-appointed spokesman for them.

'One of our tasks as parish clergymen is, I believe, to encourage, and mobilise the forces of righteousness in the communities in which we are set. My experience is that this kind of leadership, when offered humbly, is always accepted and wins a ready response.' Referring to the Ten Commandments, he said: 'They still remain, with appropriate interpretation, the expression of the law by which we must live. I am not sure about this, but I do wonder whether the fact that the weekly proclamation of the Commandments in our worship has very widely been abandoned, has something to do with the fact that we are a lawless society.'

It was at Halifax that Treacy achieved a reputation as an after dinner speaker. It was not a natural gift but he quickly developed a technique which demonstrated that the profession of the Christian and the appearance of gloom did not necessarily go together. He learned the skill of wrapping up some downright statements in a coating of amusement, the full weight of which only struck those who had heard them after the event — but then it did strike. I have received countless letters from people whose only contact with Treacy was at a dinner but who had remembered something he had said — and it was not the funny story. It had made them think hard! During the winter season of annual dinners Treacy's diary carried several bookings in each week. He was usually given the worst speech of all to make, the response to the toast of the Guests. This always came at the end of the proceedings, at a time when the inebriated company was getting restless and whose collective eye had roamed from the bar, now closed, to the clock. It followed a succession of speeches, and if they had been long and dull, the atmosphere was scarcely encouraging; if they had been short and brilliant, his was a tedious epilogue. But Treacy always scored a few sixes before the innings closed. The sincerity of the congratulatory messages received afterwards of the 'we have never had a more stimulating and provocative speech' variety was proven when he was invited to return to the dinner year after year. His enjoyment of these occasions was marred by only one thing. 'For a cleric, there is often the embarrassment of having to sit through a succession of risqué stories. This is the worst of bad manners: my impression is that no one likes it very much, but their dislike is not strong enough to prevent sufficient laughter to encourage the offender to do it again.'

Treacy prepared a speech for the occasion even if usually at the last moment and because he was teetotal he was never in danger of becoming like Rolls-Royce cars — well oiled and going on for ever. His teetotal reputation gathered pace after an incident shortly after he arrived in Halifax. When orders were being taken for drinks he asked the wine waiter for a 'pinta milk'. In due course it arrived and often when he attended a dinner in Halifax, and whether he wanted it or not, a pint of milk was ceremoniously brought into him. On another occasion recalled by Mr M. R. Hewitt of Brighouse he mischievously asked for 'Gorple 62' (Gorple being a local reservoir). Away went the waiter, only to turn to one of his colleagues and Treacy heard him say 'That silly blighter has asked for "Gorple 62" and I can't find it on the wine list, do you know it?' Eventually the bewildered waiter returned to say he could not supply that particular wine and would he take another to which the reply was 'Never mind, just bring me a jug of water'.

It may be asked what was the practical effect of all this talking. Treacy admitted to 'speaking immoderately on every subject and at a wide variety of occasions. I am sure that I spoke more often than I should have done. I know there were many who criticised me for frequent appearances at public dinners. I went to these functions when they did not clash with my parochial engagements because I thought it right to use the opportunity they gave me to meet people'. Meeting people, extending the influence of the Church, was a form of evangelism. He would not otherwise have met these people.

When Treacy had been at Halifax for ten years he felt he was getting stale. He was certainly tired and, looking at his diaries for those years, it is a wonder that he did not have a breakdown in health. Every moment of the day, evening and some of the night was booked. Although he richly enjoyed all this activity — and to an extent needed it — there was the element of sacrifice. It sometimes meant that personal inclination had to be subordinated to ministerial duty. A priest is one who cannot do exactly what he likes; he has to fulfil people's expectation of him. Public duty outclaims the private person. His personal freedom is at the mercy of pastoral demand. He has to maintain inviolate the Christian moral standard because he is to be an example to the flock of God. Because Treacy, like any priest, was a servant of God and His people, he had no protection from those who used or exploited him. He saw his friends in other spheres of life pleasing themselves in the things they did in their leisure, knowing that 'pleasing himself' was a luxury not often allowed him — but, frankly, not often sought either.

By 1960 Treacy was 53 years of age. The Diocesan hierarchy had changed. John Ramsbotham had followed Roger Wilson as Bishop of Wakefield and George Clarkson had succeeded Harold Morris at Pontefract. Treacy was in the dangerous years for a priest — and perhaps for men in secular life too. In that period there may come a staleness of spirit, the danger of automatic priestly and pastoral acts, of going through the motions though the heart is not touched. There is the corruption of perfunctoriness. Added to this, and there was in Treacy's case, perhaps a touch of unfulfilled ambition as a man's contemporaries are preferred to higher office and he may judge them to be of less ability than himself. Treacy did not have the desperate feeling that he was a forgotten man, yet he was at that point at which he saw a long road ahead. He was not in danger of relapsing into boredom or bitterness which are the plagues which destroy priesthood. Fortunately he recognised what was happening but he continued to fret below the surface.

Treacy felt the need for a change. Once clergy surrender themselves to the squalid ambition of place hunting, little or nothing can save them from pastoral failure. Self seeking for self aggrandisement can only be spiritually debilitating. Nevertheless the change which Treacy was hoping for was upwards, which meant to the purple! This is not surprising for as he had got on top of his threefold task as Vicar, Archdeacon and Rural Dean of Halifax he felt the pull towards further responsibility and exercise of power. It was natural that he should be led to think ahead towards a whole jurisdiction of his own. After all his whole life had been one of movement outwards from more local to wider ranges and there had never been a period of just digging in. His growing desire for a Bishopric (observed by many people) was part of his extroverted, activist nature, never content to be static, and it is an ambition felt by many vigorous natures. When the announcement of Donald Coggan's move from the Bishopric of Bradford to the Archbishopric of York was made public in January 1961 there was many a hope and rumour that Treacy would succeed him at Bradford, a move which Treacy would have loved. What his heart yearned for his head denied as he noted in his diary 'Oh! these well meaning people who keep on telling you that you ought to be the next Bishop of Bradford. It's difficult to know what to say to them when secretly you think it wouldn't be a bad idea, but know that it will never happen!'

There were some signs that Treacy was becoming disgruntled. Another diary entry reveals this as well as showing how very much he was at odds with Bishop Ramsbotham: '10 March 1961. To Bishop's Staff Meeting at Wakefield at 8am. I find myself increasingly out of sympathy with his autocratic conception of the Episcopal office. I suppose it is part of the theological conception of the Bishopric, which seems to me to be dangerously feudal. It may please him but it is producing a couple of browned off archdeacons — George (Clarkson) and I have between us 17 years of experience of this Diocese but we are rarely asked for our advice on anything.'

A few of Treacy's episcopal friends had been aware of his desire for and need of a move for some time. In January 1959 the Bishop of Carlisle, Thomas Bloomer, needed a new Archdeacon on the elevation of S. C. Bulley to be Bishop Suffragan of Penrith. 'For this there is no one whom I would like to have more than yourself' wrote Bloomer. 'West Cumberland is increasing in importance as an industrial area and we are establishing a West Cumberland Archdeaconry from Maryport to Millom, and coming inland to Keswick and Ambleside.' There were several reasons why this offer was declined but perhaps chiefly because it was rather less than a sideways move. Treacy replied candidly 'As the junior Archdeacon in your diocese I should not have a place on Convocation or in Assembly. Although I do not consider myself indispensable in either of these bodies — as a member of the Assembly Standing Committee and of the Northern Assessors I feel that I have a small contribution to make. This is a contraction which I do not feel it would be right to make at this time.'

A little later in 1959 another attempt was made to lure Treacy away from Halifax, and from the North of England. Shortly after Bishop Roger Wilson's accession to Chichester, the Bishop Suffragan of Lewes (G. H. Warde) retired. It was pretty well known that before George Bell retired from the See of Chichester he laid on the Archdeacon of Lewes (J. H. L. Morrell) to be the new Bishop Suffragan and it was also strongly suspected that the Vicar of Brighton (D. H. Booth) would become Archdeacon. When such matters are arranged by a combination of diplomacy and stealth in the Church of England they are not easily cast aside. Accordingly the appointments came to pass. There were those who had protested that all the gaiters in the Diocese would be on Anglo-Catholic legs. A revered and influential Evangelical, D. F. Horsefield, had pressed Roger Wilson to appoint a broad-visioned Evangelical as Bishop Suffragan or Archdeacon and named John Tiarks and Treacy as the kind of men he had in mind. As it happened Roger Wilson was left with only a free hand for the remnant of the appointments, namely the Parish Church of Brighton. He tried to persuade Treacy to accept the living of Brighton but did not really expect Treacy to accept, as it would mean moving several rungs down the ladder. Amongst other reasons for declining, Treacy mentioned his age and the need for a less exacting sphere of work. Tiredness inspired this contradiction. Such a clay pigeon was easily shot down by his friend Roger Wilson who wrote:

'I don't believe it is a lighter task than Halifax though it would all flow outwards from the one centre, rather than be divided between two focus points, and that is a real mental relief. But then I don't think you should necessarily be thinking of a lighter job at 53. I know you are both weary and therefore want some temporary break. But I do also believe that there is, in a complete change of circumstance, a stimulus, as well as a shedding of some old chains, which you would sense. I remember you felt the same when it came to leave Keighley where you had also bogged yourself down with commitments — As you know we (& esp. you two) create our own commitments, through sheer love of work.'

Again the answer was 'No'. Temporary tiredness and fraying edges were continually being restored after short breaks and then he was off at full pelt again. But he confided this to his diary on 16 January 1961: 'Had a strong feeling last night that I was beginning to fade. It may not — as yet — be apparent to my people, but it soon will be. The signs of the fading are a fear of tackling anything new — a fear of people who make demands on you — a decrease in one's confidence to see through the things one undertakes. To add (sic) is that you see the signs that the work is standing still.'

There is something unsettling about 'offers' when they are not promotions however delectably and persuasively wrapped. Should he remain in Halifax? He loved his work and his multifarious activities and could not have coped with a partially-filled diary.

There is one further important point that should be mentioned and which cannot be dismissed in explaining Treacy's apparently slow march to the Bench. Pre-eminently it was due to his lack of a degree or whatever a degree was held to signify. It may sound surprising now but the image of the theologian or the 'High Administrator' elevated from his professorial chair or the Headmaster's dais to the Bench died hard. University, moreover, for a long time meant Oxbridge. It is different today but in the 1950s this was still prevalent. Further, Treacy also gave the impression of being primarily a pragmatic individualist critical of the Establishment; or at least unpredictable in his judgements and actions. He could not be labelled and was therefore difficult to place. Further, as a close friend observes, 'Perhaps too for all his gifts, he matured late, acquired gravitas slowly with a suggestion always of the rogue elephant about him'.

13
Purple Shadow

The whole ramshackle procedure of preferment in the Church of England is enveloped in fog. The Church has an ambivalent, even hypocritical, attitude towards the subject. Publicly the talk is of vocation, and coyness takes over when professional advancement is mentioned. God will call and put his clergy where He wants them. But privately the feeling is different when honesty intervenes. In a Church in which there are so many forms of status, 'important livings', rosetted canonries (where have the rosettes gone), the gaitered ranks of Archdeacons, Deans and Bishops, there is a natural tendency for men to covet these offices. The fascination of the gaitered life is as strong as it was when they were properly worn. Treacy was quite honest with himself:

'If there are top jobs to be had then somebody has to have them, and why not ourselves? Is it sinful to be ambitious? I suppose the answer depends on what form your ambition takes. If it is for power and privilege then surely it is wrong for a clergyman. If it is for the greater use of your talents, and for greater opportunities to exercise the ministry then I do not think it is wrong. If it is for money and material possessions, I think it would be very dangerous.

'It is odd that a Christian who is a schoolmaster can apply for a headmastership, and it is not thought to be inconsistent with his vocation in teaching, yet, if a clergyman applied for a job of greater responsibility, and may be, of increased remuneration it is thought to be scarcely decent. Not at all a thing for a priest to do! Instead he has to contrive some cunning way of getting his name brought before those who have the appointment to make. Bad for the priest, and not very good for the Church. Oh! how muddled we are in these things.

'The promotion game is one that is played in all professions. It is a technique which involves being in the right place at the right time, saying the right thing when the right people are listening, being "in" with the right people.

'Perhaps it is true that some men have arrived at the top positions in the Church by their skill in the Promotion Stakes, but I think it would be much more true to say that a number of men of undoubted ability have failed to achieve their ambitions because it has been all too evident that they were more concerned with recognition than with the work of the ministry. In spite of the method employed by the Church of England in the matter of preferment, it is a fact that in a curious way it sorts out the good from the not-so-good.'

Even though Treacy's nostrils were always finely attuned to ecclesiastical gossip he did not sniff anything in the air when George Clarkson, the Bishop Suffragan of Pontefract, was surprisingly appointed as the first Dean of Guildford in 1961. The whole Church, and not just the Diocese of Guildford, had been rocked by the 'Boulton' affair. Walter Boulton was Provost of Guildford and on completion of the new Cathedral it was generally and justly expected that he would be Guildford's first Dean. Scarcely a month before the Consecration of the Cathedral on 17 May it became clear that Boulton was to be overlooked. He subsequently resigned as Provost and was appointed to country livings in the Diocese of Peterborough. The whole episode was decidedly distasteful if not outright scandalous, particularly because reasons were not given. Even the Church press was unanimous in its criticism.

George Clarkson wrote to me some years ago: 'I was shanghaid into the deanery of Guildford more as a troubleshooter than as a Christian minister. I was not even aware whether the bishop himself (George Reindorp) would have to be shot or not. However, it soon became clear that he wasn't.'

Shanghaid or not, when the summons came, Clarkson was on the first available train to Guildford whilst his difficult widowed sister, Dora Braithwaite was packing their belongings.

George Clarkson succeeded magnificently at Guildford. He ironed out the difficulties and set a good course for the cathedral's future. Treacy wrote of him:

'It will always be a surprise to me that Clarkson was not translated to a Diocesan Bishopric, for he was a man of outstanding ability. Perhaps he found it difficult to suffer fools, but only fools who thought they were clever. To those who needed help and encouragement he was the soul of kindness. He had a wonderful gift for pithy comment and could express himself with a great economy in words. Although he gave the impression of being unemotional and indifferent to people's opinions of him, I believe him to have been a sensitive person, who needed affection, but who found it difficult to reveal himself to people.

'Naturally, on his departure from the Wakefield Diocese, there was speculation as to who his successor would be. In all the guessing that went on, as far as I know, my name was not mentioned. My money was on Philip Pare, the Provost of our Cathedral; I had known for some time that John Ramsbotham felt him to be of episcopal calibre.'

In 1949 Treacy had been offered the Archdeaconry of Halifax by Roger Wilson in the garden of Bishop's Lodge. In July 1961 John Ramsbotham took him a-walking in the same garden and invited him to be Bishop of Pontefract. Treacy was surprised, even staggered, and enlarges:

'To say that I was surprised is not to assume an unnatural modesty, because there were good reasons why John should have looked in other directions. Insofar as the Church needs a learned episcopate, no one could apply that description to me. I had not graduated; I was not a natural student; and my preaching I knew to be more entertaining than edifying. Furthermore, I did not think that I had a very high rating in the "spirituality" stakes.

'From the way in which John put the invitation, I think that he anticipated that I would say "No", on the grounds that I should feel that a Suffragan Bishopric was a poor exchange for the independence that I had as Vicar of Halifax. Indeed, at first, that was precisely my reaction, and I was inclined to refuse his offer.'

Bishop Ramsbotham records that he chose Treacy:

'... because he was clearly the most outstanding personality in the diocese and because his churchmanship was different from mine. As a Catholic, though not in the party sense, there was hope that the clergy and parishes with that background would be understood by me, but the many good ones with an Evangelical background needed someone who was more familiar with that background than I was. Also Bishop Treacy clearly had gifts which not only complemented what few I had but which would be of great value to the Church as a whole. I had spent two days with him going into all sides of Halifax town's life, of which he had a wonderful grasp, and it seemed to me that he would both understand and help me to work out what I believed and believe to be an essential part of the pastoral ministry of Bishop and Incumbents in a diocese today. Very briefly that is that, whereas traditionally the Bishop was and still must be the pastor of the clergy, the pastors in the parishes, with the vast development of jobs which carry pastoral responsibility for people with them, Bishops and Incumbents who are entrusted with the cure of souls have now a whole network of secular colleagues. Their pastoral ministry is to the pastors of these colleagues, which involves a relationship in which they themselves are recognised as colleagues to such an extent that they win their way to becoming their pastors.

'Bishop Treacy could see this, and was a wonderful supporter, even if he couldn't go all the way with me.'

There was a genuine reluctance to accept. Although he wanted to be a bishop this was not quite the patch of purple which excited his interest. For one rather obvious reason, it was a number two position and John Ramsbotham was not Roger Wilson! John Ramsbotham was associated with the Parish and People Movement and reforming if not radical policies for the Church. Treacy was diametrically opposed on most of such issues. He consulted the new Archbishop of York (Donald Coggan) and his episcopal friends Roger Wilson and Harold Morris, who counselled acceptance. And accept he did!

The official announcement was made on 8 August 1961 to a chorus of praise and acclaim. Maybe only a Bishop Suffragan but a bishop none the less! His Consecration took place on the Feast of St Luke (18 October) in York Minster, alongside George D'Oyly Snow the former Headmaster of Ardingly College who was to be Bishop Suffragan of Whitby. It was Dr Coggan's first Consecration service. The sermon was preached by the Archdeacon of Lewes (D. H. Booth) whom Treacy had been asked to succeed at Brighton. He referred to Treacy's natural gifts, 'a warmth of heart, a persistence and a divine impatience coloured by the variety of his experience.'

Later Treacy reflected, 'Can any man ever forget his Consecration as Bishop? There was the glorious setting of York Minster, the consciousness of being held up by the prayers of one's friends, the feeling of being set apart, the reality of the succession, and the solemn responsibilities of the office of a bishop in the Church of God. Often I return in pilgrimage to York Minster to find a quiet corner where I can relive the solemn moments of my consecration. Whenever I am privileged to share in the consecration of a new bishop it is, for me, a re-consecration.'

After the uplifting of the Consecration 'came the hardest part of all — this was the departure from Halifax: in one way, it was a comfort that I was to remain in the Diocese and that, as a Bishop, I should still be in touch with them; and, in another, it was painful to return to them as Bishop and not Vicar. Not unlike returning to a wife whom you have left for another woman. They were wonderfully generous to us both, and, I think, derived some pleasure from the fact that their vicar had become a Bishop'. Treacy received an emotional send-off from a crowded Halifax Parish Church the Sunday before his Consecration. There were many tears. Gifts for the presentation had come from all over England. Besides a cheque he was given a bishop's pectoral cross, silver crosier, a tape recorder and May was presented with a pair of antique silver George III candelabra.

As Bishop and Archdeacon of Pontefract, Treacy's large area included Barnsley and the neighbouring mining areas; Batley and Dewsbury; Castleford and Pontefract; as well as Wakefield, Cleckheaton and Heckmondwike. He did not want to become embroiled in the tittle-tattle of Wakefield itself, or so he said. The nearer truth is that he wanted to retain something of his independence away from the prying eyes of the Wakefield curia so he chose to live in Dewsbury. With a typical impulsive gesture he decided on a house in Oxford Road, Dewsbury, opposite that of the new Vicar of Dewsbury, (E. ('Ted') C. Henderson). He went ahead without diocesan approval! It was his way.

Treacy's purple debut coincided with a dramatic change in the fortunes of the Church of England. During the 1960s the Church underwent a considerable collapse of confidence. It came after a long period of quiescent buoyancy under the leadership of Archbishop Geoffrey Fisher. Yet below the surface a cauldron of frustration had been bubbling.

It cannot have been easy for Geoffrey Francis Fisher to succeed William Temple who died so suddenly in 1944. Fisher did much to oil the squeaking machinery of the Church and showed that administration tackled sensitively can be an area of pastoral potential. He was a man usually off-guard but his personality was not free from complexities.

Treacy preferred Fisher to Temple — and similarly Coggan to Ramsey although his view of Ramsey changed dramatically. He thought that history might allot a higher place to Fisher than Temple, a view which, strangely and I think erroneously, is gathering force. Naturally he did not underrate Temple yet the opinion on hearing of his death was later considerably modified if not reversed. In his War Diary he had written: '26 October 1944. William Temple of Canterbury passed away. *What* a disaster. There is not another leader of the C of E today in the same class. In his two years at Canterbury he went a long way towards reinstating the Church in the regard of the masses.'

By 1957, after seeing Fisher at close quarters at an Oxford Conference for Public and Grammar Schoolboys he wrote:

'When an assessment is made of the four Archbishops who have presided at Lambeth since the beginning of the century I should not be surprised if the present Archbishop is acclaimed the greatest. He may lack the compromising genius of a Davidson, the polished dignity of a Lang, the intellectual brilliance of a Temple, but he possesses a down-to-earthness which the church sorely needs. Dr Fisher has guided the C of E through a period of revolution with a steady hand and a clear mind.

'The firm relations that now exist between Church and State, without any loss of integrity by the Church; the improving relationship between the Anglican and Free Churches; and the greatly increased solidarity of the Anglican Communion throughout the world — all these things are due to the wisdom and vision of the present Archbishop of Canterbury — He may not have written much but he has achieved greatly.'

Fisher combined a generous humanity and completely unaffected manner with a passion for order and efficiency. His strong personal faith underpinned his life and his work. It was all very English — unemotional and matter-of-fact. Spirituality was not displayed like peacocks' feathers. His personal religious practices were hidden from view. What Treacy saw and knew he effusively admired. The two carried on an intermittent private correspondence until Fisher's death. There were traits in Fisher's character that drew Treacy. In a way Treacy was describing himself in the following private notes written when he was Bishop of Wakefield.

'It was abundantly clear that Fisher enjoyed being Archbishop, but I do not think it was the power of his office that he enjoyed, as much as being at the centre of things and having the scope to use the many gifts with which the Almighty had endowed him. He believed in discipline; He believed in his own capacity to get things done.

'He was supremely a layman's Archbishop. There were times in the Church Assembly when he appeared to fathom some of the issues about which the clergy felt strongly, whereas he was much more in focus with lay reasoning.

'In some ways Fisher was a good chairman in that he got through the business efficiently. He had done his homework and grasped the essentials of the business; he had also, I suspect, decided how he hoped the business would be dealt with. And, herein, lay his weakness as a chairman, because he could not disguise his irritation when some villain frustrated his intentions. Speakers in the Assembly were left in no doubt when they had struck a wrong note as Fisher would turn his gaze upon them with ill-concealed disapproval. But my abiding impression of him as chairman is that of good humour, shrewdness sometimes verging on cunning, and of a strong sense of purpose. I admired him tremendously and I wish that I had become a Diocesan when he was Archbishop of Canterbury.'

The geniality of a kindly autocrat fascinated Treacy for it was something he could understand, appreciate and admire. How totally different were the outstanding and subtle gifts of Fisher's successor in 1961, Arthur Michael Ramsey. The Church Assembly was not Ramsey's idea of a pleasant and fulfilling day out!

Treacy was about to embark on the most personally frustrating and unhappy and in a way, unsatisfying, years of his life as Bishop Suffragan of Pontefract. But, as we shall discover, they were by no means unimportant years. The difficulties began with the clash of personalities and views between John Ramsbotham and Treacy. It also went deeper than that.

The relationship between Diocesan and Suffragan Bishops was and remains the most difficult in the Church of England despite the fact that some Suffragans are given over to a specific area completely. There are only a few Dioceses where area delegation really works, notably in London. More generally, it is a situation in which jealousy is unpleasantly easy; a position in which loyalty can be dangerously strained. The difficulties are inherent in the situation. Here are six problems:

1. The Suffragan is equal in Orders but inferior in status.

2. He has nothing that he can call his own. All his episcopal acts he does by delegation. If his Diocesan is not much given to delegation, he may well feel himself starved of those things that belong to his episcopal office. This is particularly true in the matter of Ordinations and Institutions. One can well understand that a Diocesan feels that these essentially belong to him, but inevitably, a Suffragan longs to exercise his ministry in these things.

3. He is constantly reminded that although a Bishop in every sense of the word, he is thought to be a second class kind of Bishop. If he is not also an Archdeacon, he has no place by right in the higher councils of the Church. If he seeks a place by election, he is reminded that he is taking a place that should go to a parochial clergyman.

4. Various theologians say in public that he is a theological nonsense, but, in spite of that, he is a practical necessity.

5. If, because he has nothing of his own, he makes a world of his own, and

perhaps in so doing, becomes well known, he has to be careful that he does not become better known than his Diocesan! He has to practise the art of self-suppression.

6. Because he is a Bishop, he is chosen from the ranks of those who have made the grade in their own field. This usually means that he has exercised responsibility and authority. As a Suffragan he finds himself with little responsibility to exercise, and not much authority. Although he has to be of the calibre that is adequate to run the Diocese in an emergency, when there is not one he has nothing to run.

It can be seen that such a situation demands from the Diocesan Bishop a considerable amount of imagination and understanding, and from his Suffragan loyalty and a willingness to lose himself in another man's ministry. That Treacy was not by nature a Suffragan or number two requires little explaining or underlining. Nevertheless the Pontefract years were going to be years of growth in all kinds of ways. Some words of counsel given by Austin Pardue, Bishop of Pittsburgh, preaching at the Consecration of Mervyn Charles Edwards (Bishop of Worcester) in 1956 are relevant. They were simple: 'Grow but don't swell.'

14
On the Boil

The 1960s saw the Church of England on the boil. Preaching in Great St Mary's Cambridge, on 26 April 1964 Treacy described it thus:

'If you have ever watched a steam locomotive with its water on the boil, you will have observed that certain things happen. If the water boils too much the safety valves blow off, and there is a deafening row and a great deal of energy is wasted. Another thing you will notice about steam is that when it mixes with the atmosphere it condenses and forms cold water.

'I think there are certain parallels that we can find between the machine which generates steam for purposes of movement and the Church of England, which generates a lot of steam but not always for movement! In all my ministry I do not remember any time when there was such a sense of urgency and pressure within the Church. In so many ways one feels that pressure is building up, rather like steam in a boiler, which is leading towards a situation which could be explosive if it is not handled and directed properly.'

He might have added that in the more primitive days of the steam engine, in order to get a greater degree of pressure, drivers were guilty of tampering with their safety valves — so that occasionally the engine blew up altogether, with painful results to everybody in range. Such was the fate of some radical proposals of the decade. It was a decade of Reports and Treacy's time at Pontefract was conterminous with the major ones. He had much to say on the various issues or, to him, the principles at stake, but there was a built in frustration with his new post. His word did not have the authority of the Diocesan edict. He had no platform as he had had as Vicar of Halifax. The Diocesan leaflet and machinery were not at his disposal. For his views to find the widest circulation he had to resort to the best publicity machine of all — himself.

To appreciate the extent and diversification of the subjects flung at the Church during this period I list the more controversial reports. (Those marked SR were published by the excellent Board for Social Responsibility and those marked BCC by the British Council of Churches. Others were official Church of England Reports.)

1959	*Ought Suicide to be a Crime?* (SR)
1962	*Soundings* (Essays concerning Christian Understanding) edited by A. R. Vidler (Published by Cambridge University Press)
	Sterilization: An Ethical Enquiry (SR)
1963	*Conversations Between the Church of England and the Methodist Church*
	Honest to God, by John Robinson, Bishop of Woolwich (Published by SCM Press)
	The British Nuclear Deterrent (BCC)
1964	*The Deployment and Payment of the Clergy*, by Leslie Paul (The Paul Report)
	Crown Appointments and the Church (The Howick Commission)
	The Failure of a Mission, by Nicholas Stacey, Rector of Woolwich (Article in the *Observer Colour Magazine*. Also his *Observer* article *How the Church Might Survive* — 23 May 1965)
1965	*Alternative Services* (First Series)
	The Church's Needs and Resources
	Decisions about Life and Death (SR)
	The Future of South Africa (BCC)

1966	*Putting Asunder* (A Divorce Law for Contemporary Society)
	Government by Synod (The Hodson Commission)
	Abortion (SR)
	World Poverty and British Responsibility (BCC)
	Fatherless by Law (The Law and the Welfare of Children designated illegitimate) (SR)
	Women and Holy Orders
1967	*Partners in Ministry* (The Morley Commission)
	Christians and the Common Market (BCC)
	Towards Reconciliation (The Interim Statement of the Anglican-Methodist Unity Commission)
1968	*Intercommunion Today*

The seeming effect of this deluge of words in print was to produce more student Christians than believing ones and many frustrated church people. The unconcern of the arbitrator was in danger of replacing the keen interest of the disciple. There was certainly an impressive absence of reserve in the discussions. Yet there is a reserve in religious discussion which grows from reason and charity, as well as the reserve which has no better roots than the proselytiser's craft or the time server's timidity.

There is some misunderstanding of Treacy's position in this turbulent confusion. Outwardly and superficially he became the champion of the parson in his parish and the lay person in the pew. On the whole *they* did not believe that if only the Church could achieve Unity, reform it ways of worship, system of government, parson's freehold, pay and deployment of clergy, be on more than a nodding acquaintance with permissive morality, all would be well. These were exhilarating times, these were depressing times. It was an era of the Spirit, it was an era of wind. The decade was motivated by inspiration, the decade moved by perspiration. It depended on which side you stood in that age of labels. The radical asserted that those who were not for them were reactionaries. Those for the status quo appeared to move backwards for shelter in the Ark.

In the face of this, was the Coroner's verdict on the Church of England likely to be 'Suicide while the balance of its mind was disturbed'? Not a bit of it! The maddening aspect of the Church of England to revolutionaries, radicals, reformers and reactionaries alike is its passion for balancing extremes. There, rightly or wrongly, lies its secret of survival. The Church plods on absorbing into itself the slaps and proddings of the extremists. It has the best set of springs and shock absorbers in Christendom. Evolution has ever been its watchword.

Treacy was unequivocal in his admiration of the way in which the Church drew the sting of its rebels and integrated them and their thinking into the growing treasury of Anglican theology.

Two sentences in Treacy's Obituary Notice in *The Times* (15 May 1978) give a partial clue to his position: 'Though regarded widely as a cleric of middle ground views, Bishop Treacy expressed himself pungently on a wide range of matters, many of them topics drawing a considerable amount of contemporary discussion'; and; 'Highly articulate as he was, both as a speaker and on paper, his pronouncements often served to conciliate widely differing standpoints within the Church Assembly'.

Addressing the Leicester Evangelical Clergy Fellowship on 8 June 1966 Treacy spoke on 'the position of the evangelical in the light of modern developments in thinking and practice in the Church.' He admitted to being out of sympathy with Conservative Evangelicals who were then in the ascendant and who had a text or a formula for almost every situation and tended to simplify issues and problems. Further, as he said:

'I find many of them more concerned with obtaining a blessing than with the social implications of the gospel.' His views on Liberal Evangelicals are important for he admits 'That this is essentially a self portrait. As I see it, the Liberal Evangelical today is really the Broad Churchman. By that I mean that he is suspicious of extremes. He is not committed to a particular view of the Eucharist; he is prepared to wear vestments if asked, although he might not know how to put them on — copes and mitres don't worry him. He gets on well with Free Churchmen. He does not like too much definition because he believes over definition leads to exclusiveness. He tends to a certain Erastianism and is not worried by the problems of Establishment — rather is he prepared to put up with any inconvenience arising from this on the grounds that the State needs the Church more than the Church needs the State.

'He is not quite sure where he stands in matters of conversion — he secretly recoils from the Billy Graham approach, but feels rather guilty for doing so.

'He is a bit uncomfortable at Retreats but can just manage a Quiet Day, provided that it is not too quiet. He is at home with Rotarians and the local ex-Servicemen — he is hailed as "Padre" by the local businessmen, by which they mean that he would be a nice person to have in the mess.

'He makes a virtue of compromise on the grounds that the ethos of the Church of England is to be a Bridge. He is sometimes in danger of being suspended in space on a bridge that is crossing from nowhere to nowhere.

'He is more interested in sociology than theology.

'He hasn't really decided where he stands in relation to the world, the flesh and the devil. He doesn't believe in the Devil; he lives in a no man's land between the opposing claims of the flesh and the spirit, and he finds the things of the world so pleasant that he often mistakes Mammon for God. He has never knowingly converted anyone, and would be a bit embarrassed if he found that by chance he had — he justifies this by saying that such things are hidden with God.

'But — basically — he is a nice chap — and whatever else he lacks, he does not lack charity. On one level, he does quite a lot to commend a kind of Christianity by being so nice, and by upsetting so few people. He tends to draw people to himself rather than to our Lord — and he will build up quite a good congregation in a parish, which will disintegrate when he leaves.

'Ministry means more to him than priesthood.

'He is blunt where he should be sharp — he does not disturb because he is not disturbed — he is too easily comforted with false comfort. He believes in the original goodness of man rather than original sin.

'Would it be true to say that the Liberal Evangelical does not hold a strict view about the inspiration of Scripture — but he does hold firmly that the Cross is the supreme example of God's Love rather than of God's merciful justice.'

This tells us more about Treacy than about Liberal Evangelicals. As usual the label eludes him. Even when he claims to wear one it is fashioned in his own image. Although his observations go some way to explaining parts of his character they fail to be a reliable guide to the stand he might take on any given issue. With the stirrings of the nineteen-sixties he recognised, however reluctantly, that he had been forced to ask himself a lot of important questions that otherwise he might never have asked. 'It has done nothing to undermine my faith' he later reflected. 'At first I thought that it had, and I found that some of my anchors were slipping — but, in the long run, the ferment that it set up in my thinking has had the effect of strengthening me where I was weak. Simply because I was forced to re-examine and re-think things that I hadn't looked at critically for 25 years. And I think that has been true for many people — I think therefore that the Lord has been at work in all this.'

Whatever he said the 'New Thinking' had done for him, he was in no doubt of its general effect. On the publication of *Honest to God* he had no hesitation in saying to the Press: '(It) is a dangerous book likely to disturb the faith of more people than it will stimulate. It will cause a great deal of pain to faithful Christians who may not possess the Bishop's intellectual approach to theological matters.' It was about this time — 1963 — that Treacy was becoming more widely known as a champion of the parochial clergy. He was already known as the layman's bishop and by the time he became Bishop of Wakefield he was pre-eminent in his defence of the parish priest. Thus, he was prompted to write to the *Church Times* (5 April 1963) on the subject.

' . . . I feel constrained to write this letter because of the effect some of this modern "thinking aloud" is having upon those men who are the backbone of the Church. I refer to the parochial clergy, from whose ranks I moved but 15 months ago.

'Recently many of them have spoken to me of the bewilderment they feel. As one said to me this weekend: "We feel that the ground is being cut from under our feet." As they slave away at their sick visiting, in the Sunday schools, taking their confirmation classes, running their clubs and organisations, preparing their sermons — and the rest — they have the feeling that the foundations are being eaten away. Things which they have held to faithfully all their lives are being questioned; things that they have done with devotion all the years of their ministry are dismissed as obsolete, unnecessary, and ill-conceived.

'It may be that our fixed points have to be questioned; it may be that our "image" as a Church is out of date; it may be that we "stick-in-the-muds" who have been faithful to the Articles to which we subscribed at our Institution, and the Prayer Book which we promised to use "and none other," have failed in our mission to the flock committed to us.

'Maybe — but there is something that ought to be said, and, though but a junior suffragan, I would venture to say it. It is this: The parochial clergy have the most difficult of all tasks in the Church. Of all people, they are the most vulnerable. They are shot at from all sides.

'This so-called clever generation of secularists assume a lofty indifference to them; within their own congregations they have to fight a constant battle against apathy; the pressures of materialism are all round them, particularly threatening their work amongst young people; the lowered moral standards of today are creating a climate in which the Church's witness is constantly being questioned. They are harried with demands for money for Church schools, Church training colleges, the central administration of the Church, the Church overseas, diocesan quotas, etc.

'They do battle in the front lines with problems of which the advocates of the New Morality and the New Theology are only vaguely aware. This is not sob-stuff, but simple truth.

'My conviction is that these men, to whom the Church owes so much, need encouragement. They need to be told that what they are doing is worthwhile; they need to be assured that the battles they are fighting are the battles of the whole Church.

'There has been far too much talk of the Church's failure. No one in his senses can be satisfied with the Church's impact on society today — but I want to say emphatically that the Church is succeeding in thousands of parishes today. And the secret of that success is that she is faithfully manifesting that love of which the modern prophet speaks; not a love of *eros* but *agape*.

'It seems to me that our modern bishops are saying "Now what is it that modern people are finding difficult to do and believe? Let us find a doctrine to justify and make respectable what they are doing and believing, rather than remind them of the absolute standards of what they ought to do and believe."

'May I then be allowed — and I hope none will think me patronising — to speak a word of appreciation and encouragement to the countless clergy in this land who, understaffed and overworked, are doing daily battle for their Lord and his Church, who are contending with daunting difficulties, and who may have begun to wonder, in their more weary moments, whether it is all worthwhile?

'The victory in this present situation will be for those who love and care for their people, who make the sacrificial ministry of our great High Priest a reality in the streets and homes of their parishes, rather than with those who write books or preach sermons that make headlines.'

Treacy appeared to be emphatic in his unease, even condemnation, of *Honest to God*, but it was not that simple. He realised that the demand for doctrinal restatement was not unreasonable because the times had witnessed a rapid and extensive accumulation of new knowledge with the result that the traditional versions of Christian truth had become largely unhelpful, and even perilously misleading to many people. The Church was required to undertake again the difficult, invidious, but in the end salutary, task of setting forth the Gospel, in right relation to the sum of knowledge, and thus commending it to the acceptance of informed and considering people. After all the Church of England is at once Catholic and Reformed, bound loyally to maintain and hand on the great tradition of Apostolic witness, and, at the same time, pledged to receive and follow the teachings of the Spirit of Truth as they are disclosed in experience. This does not make the task of theological restatement an easy one. Treacy could write in *Anglican World*:

'Whether we like it or not, something exciting is happening in the Church of England. Some fearless new thinking is being done by men who count their reputations, and, may be, their futures, as nothing, compared with the need for making the Church's message relevant to the modern situation.

'These men have come out of the trenches, in which they found their safety demoralising, and moved into an intellectual No Man's Land, in which, alas, they are being shot at by both sides; but the most wounding fire is that directed at their backs by their own side.

'But I would rather that there be some wild shooting, wide of the target some of it, than that there should be the sort of phoney war in which neither side moves against the other in the hope that the war will be called off.

'John Robinson and many of the contributors to *Soundings* have recognised something to which many of us in the Church of the England have been dangerously indifferent, namely, that there exists a world of intellectual scepticism, which is a world into which the Christian Church must be looking with sympathy, and with a concern that is fundamentally our Lord's, in an endeavour to make His Gospel speak to their needs.'

This may appear to contradict other observations by Treacy. He was faced with a threefold conflict. His head told him to be realistic. If the history of Christianity contains many warnings against reckless innovation, it is also charged with warnings against theological timidity. As one who was himself prepared to rock the boat on certain issues even if he was in danger of getting a ducking Treacy felt bound to admire those who put truth (as they saw it) before self. Preaching in Battle Parish Church on 21 July 1963 he said: 'To our shame, many of us, in the pursuit of peace at any price, have flinched from taking steps that would upset the Establishment — far too many have thought that conformity to the traditional line was the surest way to preferment in this caste ridden society which is the Church of England.'

On these counts he approved of what he believed to be the motives of John Robinson in writing *Honest to God*. The Church should be ready to accept theological conflict as a condition of progress. His instant and hasty judgement of the book was revised after a second and third reading. He then referred to the 'New Thinking' as Theological Impressionism — 'no more to be understood by detailed and conventional criticism than is an impressionist painting'. Using this metaphor he described his attitude in this way: 'At first my reaction was one of shock, even horror, then of irritation that the artist should perpetrate such an outrage, but, if you are patient in your viewing, it gradually dawns upon you what was in the artist's mind. The shapes and colours form a synthesis, and it begins to have meaning for you. Yet the picture is not obedient to the accepted and conventional standards of artistic criticism.' In later life he constantly told clergy how he had been permanently helped by John Robinson's chapter on Prayer (Wordly Holiness). Nevertheless, reading between the lines he found in some of John Robinson's comments a justification for walking his own prayer path which he felt guilty about, finding the more rigorous forms of praying very exacting.

Then there was the third conflict which had prompted his letter to *Church Times*. In true heart and mind Treacy was not a radical. He was convinced that certitude must ever be the true note of discipleship, not uncertainty, speculation and misgiving. Accordingly he appears to be a mass of contradictions. He admired the 'New' Theologians but complained that too often the note of personal conviction was absent in their writings. He defended their right to speak, and then said that the effect of their preaching was mischievous. Men are saved by faith, not by doubt. This was the missive and his slogan.

It was because Treacy's pastoral heart ruled his head that he was far too quick to 'sound off' when the succession of books and reports were published. Within 24 hours of their appearance there was a sermon, a speech or a statement. What he said was always spoken in refreshingly direct language that was both appreciated, understood and applauded. There were dangers too. Oliver Tomkins (Bishop of Bristol 1959-1975) observes: 'I always admired his gift of saying and writing plainly what many people thought but were in no position to say. As one who, for my own part, is so addicted to balanced statements and qualifying clauses, I had an affectionate admiration for the way he was ready to stick his neck out and risk being misinterpreted by speaking simply on complex questions. Sometimes this made me cross, as when he could condemn a book he had not read, but even then I was glad that one of the bishops was prepared to be a fool for Christ's sake when he thought that something needed to be plainly said.'

1964 opened with the publication on 17 January of a Report by Leslie Paul, *The Deployment and Payment of the Clergy*. Among his sixty-two proposals he included the abolition of the parson's freehold; the end of the centuries-old arrangement by which independent benefices, each with its own benefice income, supplied incumbents with part at least of their income; the end of the whole system of patronage (Crown patronage excepted) by which the clergy were appointed to parochial cures.

In place of the existing system Leslie Paul recommended that an incumbent of a parochial cure should have a limited 'leasehold' only, of ten years, renewable for a further five years and no more (and that only at the bishop's discretion). In future there would be two groups only of clergymen — assistant curates for three years, staff priests thereafter. All alike would be appointed to parochial cures or non-parochial posts by new regional staffing boards to be set up for the purpose — each responsible for the territory of several dioceses, and each with its own secretariat.

All clergy under what Leslie Paul called 'the new dispensation', would be paid from a central stipendiary fund on a nationally negotiated scale, with fixed increments at various points, and with agreed extra payments for special responsibility, for example, for the post of rural dean, and for family commitments.

True to form Treacy was preaching about the Paul Report at Bingley Parish Church two days after its publication. The contents of this Report, perhaps more than any other, stuck in his gullet. He flayed everything in sight, accusing Leslie Paul of betraying 'left wing sympathies' because of the irrelevant information as to the schools attended by bishops and particulars of the number of bishops who were related by birth or marriage to the peerage or the landed gentry. He slaughtered the obsession for statistics, equations and sociological exercises and 'busybodies running about with questionnaires probing into those areas which should be private'. Of course there was much in the Report and in its recommendations that Treacy not only recognised as sound but also welcomed, such as 'the direction of assistant curates to areas where they are most needed during the first five years of their ministry'. Again a contradiction of his previous position!

But, and it was a colossal 'but' — 'the thing which frightens me more than anything in the Report is the suggestion that the Parson's freehold should be replaced by a leasehold'. The benefits of a long ministry in a parish where the parson becomes the father of the people, and the independence of the Anglican parson far outweighed any inherent disadvantages there were in the freehold. From schemes and schemers, plans and planners Good Lord deliver us, was Treacy's private litany.

It was standing room only at Church House, Westminster, in February 1964 when the Paul Report was debated. All the star names of the Assembly spoke, as well as those with vested polarised interests. The Archbishop of Canterbury (Michael Ramsey) suggested that more young clergy should accept celibacy as a vocation for a limited time and paid special tribute to the clergy labouring in the industrial North, whilst the Archbishop of York (Donald Coggan) declared that the emergence of the Paul Report should not blind the Assembly to wider issues such as mutual responsibility and interdependence, and Anglican-Methodist Relations, which had been the subject of a Report the previous year. Bishop John Robinson of Woolwich believed that the Report, though masterly, was 'not radical enough' yet it 'represented a moment of truth for the Church of England if the Church could bear to see and face it.' What he and other radicals feared was that the Report would be allowed to die the death of a thousand qualifications so it would be emasculated with compromise. 'To refuse this revolution would be to connive in a situation which is already slowly destroying the Church.'

Treacy made a rather emotional speech about his love for the Church and admitted that his first reactions were of the strongest opposition 'But on sober reflection I see that it is equally wrong to be strongly opposed — as it is to be strongly in favour — of this or that change in the Church's machinery. If we honestly believe that the Holy Spirit works in and through the Church — how can we say "Ah yes — but not in this way — or perhaps in another". We cannot and must not impose our wills upon God.' He then turned his attention to his underlying unease that 'one of the great dangers facing the church is worldliness. When we think of worldliness, we tend to think of it in limited terms — such as the worship of money, the pursuit of pleasure, the lowering of moral standards. But are there not more subtle forms of worldliness — ways in which the world's methods and remedies eat into the Church's thinking. For instance, the idea that the work of the Church can be evaluated and expressed by means of figures, returns and graphs. The suggestion that the work of the spirit in the wills and spirits of men can be measured by surveys and sociologists' questionnaires. Surely this is worldliness — that the calling of the priest can be subject to a career structure or a promotion ladder. Surely this is worldliness — any more than the health of a parish can be measured by a balance sheet.'

If not by a balance sheet, by numbers? Nicholas Stacey, Rector of Woolwich, thought so. In December 1964 he created a stir with an article in *The Observer Colour Magazine* describing the failure of his four-year mission in Woolwich to bring the Church into the life of a working-class community. The article opened with the words 'We have had a remarkable opportunity of making a breakthrough in getting people to come to Church. We have played every card in the pack. We have done everything we set out to do. But we have achieved virtually not one of the modest things we hoped for — We have no excuses. These have been the most dramatic and exhausting years of my life. We have laughed and occasionally wept. We have tried to pray and to love. We have been as brazen as a Fleet Street publicity agent and we have tried to be humble and sensitive. We have raised a fortune and spent it. We have quite obviously failed.' Together with another article (in the *Weekend Review* of *The Observer* published 23 May 1965) on *How the Church Might Survive* Nick Stacey brought down upon himself much wrath. The day after each of the articles appeared Treacy's vocal chord's were straining. 'Is there no end to the hammering which these faithful, battle scarred clergy have to take from these relatively inexperienced Radicals? Surely, we owe it to each other to strengthen each other's hands in the fight — not to stab in the back' he declared in his Wakefield Archdiaconal Visitation Charge on 24 May 1965. He knew how grievously hurt were many parish priests within his jurisdiction at 'these irresponsible, barren and unsatisfying jejeune outbursts'. He could not understand how any churchman could have a doctrine of the Church which used the word 'might' in connection with its survival. 'This is the Church of our Lord — and it "will" survive because it is His and not ours.' When speaking to clergy groups he aimed to send them away encouraged in their work and ministries. This approach meant that some of the serious issues were not faced because they were not presented.

But the balance was in danger of tilting in the radicals' favour. In a letter to Treacy in January 1967 Geoffrey Fisher, then Archbishop Lord Fisher of Lambeth, wrote 'In my part of the world, here in the West, the Church of England is in fine shape! Doing its job faithfully without trying to *count* its failures or its successes. Why should one? As with politics, so with the Church, more than 50% of the unsettlement is due to publicists of one kind or another crying their own wares or decrying the wares of others ad nauseam. Down with public discussion I say!! I agree with you that there is no firm lead of the right sort from Church House or Lambeth. That is due partly to muddled thinking by earnest people like the Bishop of Bristol, Oliver Tomkins, and partly to the old danger of schemers covering up their real motives and purposes and so deceiving the faithful.'

Treacy was just as vocally active on other issues. In sum, and quite simply, he was wanting to exercise leadership. He was a popular leader. He discerned the currents of social, moral, political or ecclesiastical tendency, read the signs of the time and then gave clear and forceful expression to the aspirations or anxieties of his coevals. A popular leader finds in this representative function his worst and nearest temptation. It is easy to seek a short cut to power or popularity by echoing the baser demands of the multitude. Democracy is the parent and the victim of demagogues who are its own parasites but do not survive the moods which evoke them.

Treacy himself was fully aware of the dangers and knew that popularity divorced from principles and ideals is short lived. He wrote:

'Those of us who speak in public places, and are from time to time given the benefit of being reported, have experience of the unhealthy response that is evoked whenever we are unwise enough to indulge in criticism, condemnation or sweeping denigration of some national institution, some public figure, or some group of people. In public speaking this is always a "winner"; it is easy to do, it is based on generalisation (which can be, and often is, uncharitable and not true to all the facts), and, in the long run, achieves nothing, except the bolstering of the speaker's ego. But the response is nearly always the same. Either loud applause punctuated with "Hear, Hears" or letters of thanks for having struck a blow for righteousness and giving much needed moral leadership. I suppose it is that people think that something is being done about things which they are powerless to deal with. How little, in fact, is achieved by public denunciation of people and situations! Denunciation is a never failing source of strength to the thing which is denounced.'

Treacy did not always heed what he summarised so succinctly. Similarly, in an article on *Leadership in the Church* in *Church Times* (1 October 1965) he wrote: 'We live in an age which is hungry for personalities; this is a cult which is, I am sure, better not encouraged.' Yet, to a degree he fed this hunger and revelled in it. His public ministry was the triumph of sheer character.

In 1963 the 'Profumo affair' produced a collective chant, a chorus of cant, to which English people are prone. They relish a scandal and behave abominably and are nauseatingly hypocritical. John Bull becomes Mr Pecksniff. *The Times* thundered 'It *is* a moral issue' in a famous leader. Treacy retorted by a letter to *The Times* (15 June) in which he criticised those who were clamouring for moral leadership outside themselves. As for those who cried for the raising up of some prophet to conduct a puritanical mission to the nation, and for a return to the Christian faith, he wrote: 'The Christian faith is not a kind of national prophylactic; it is the truth about God, and is to be accepted and practised for no other reason.'

One of Treacy's anxieties on leaving Halifax was the thought that he and May would not be earthed in a parish. This was considerably softened by his friendship with Ted Henderson, Vicar of Dewsbury. They were neighbours and said their prayers together every morning at 8.30 in Dewsbury Parish Church. Ted Henderson went direct to Church but Treacy organised himself a four-mile walking circuit. As at Keighley and Halifax, he built up quite a constituency in Dewsbury consisting of people going to work or at work with whom he had conversation. There were one or two hatchet-faced Yorkshiremen who defied his efforts to provoke a greeting at first but it was not for long. 'Digger', a milkman from Thornhill, was his most cheerful contact, in his battery-operated milk float.

Ted Henderson and Treacy sat in the same pew near a window where they could hear the traffic outside. They prayed for individual people with their trials and tribulations, and sometimes their joys, commending them and their own day's work to the use of God. Ted Henderson remembers one occasion when prayer was disturbed not by the hand of God but by that of Treacy coming down heavily on his shoulder. 'You've got it' said Treacy. Startled Vicar followed Treacy's finger, which was pointing to a death watch beetle. This dramatic interruption was greeted by 'You daft lump'.

Treacy needed to start his day in this way before the rough and tumble in Wakefield and beyond. Albert Nurse, long serving Diocesan Secretary until 1971, remembers Treacy's

. . . 'Enormous capacity for work and he seemed capable of doing more than one job at a time. I remember having a meal with him during which he ate, talked and revised the proofs of one of his railway books at the same time. — He was an excellent chairman — vital and decisive — always giving all members a chance of expressing their views and summing up a discussion at the right point. As Chairman of the Diocesan Dilapidations Board, the body responsible for the selling, buying, improving and repairing of parsonage houses, he used to invite incumbents whose cases were of major importance to attend the meetings to put their points of view. This must have given these clergy the feeling that decisions were not taken by bureaucrats or "them" but only after the local point of view had been heard and understood. — Occasionally we had our disagreements. I remember the case of an incumbent who wanted to carry out extensive and expensive reconstruction and improvement of his over-large parsonage house. Eric sanctioned this and promised a Church Commissioners' loan of £10,000 (I think it was) before the approval of the Board or the Commissioners had been obtained. He and I were summoned to the Church Commissioners and faced a committee of about seven and asked to explain our actions. At the end of the discussion, Lord Silsoe, the Chairman, said that on that occasion the Commissioners would sanction the work and the necessary loan but we were not to do it again!On leaving the meeting and going out into Millbank, Eric said to me —"I would do it again if I thought it advisable!" 'And he did—again and again.

Albert Nurse adds, 'Eric could be very impetuous and sometimes very stubborn. But these attitudes never broke friendships. I remember an occasion when he had a strong disagreement with a member at a committee meeting on a matter of fact. At the next meeting he came back full of profound apologies. He had been wrong about his fact! This willingness to admit errors endeared him to those concerned and strengthened friendships.'

Treacy was travelling more than ever before to fulfil speaking engagements. He had become a very well known person in the Church and, where much was expected, much was given. In the Diocese of Wakefield his position was unassailable. Unfortunately his relations with his 'boss' John 'Ram', as he was known, were only formally and outwardly satisfactory.

Treacy had written to his old friend Douglas Crawford as early as 1964 saying that 'these last three years have not been easy ones for me. I miss having a unit of my own to run. I have to play 2i/c to a pretty muddle headed bird — who rollicks about like an unguided missile. I have to hold my peace when I want to blow up and have to file most of my bright ideas for future reference — but goodness knows when that will be! However — someone has to do the job I am doing, and I suppose it's good for me to have to knuckle under. I can admit to you, but to few others — that I feel I am being wasted in this present situation. That sounds a bit conceited but I think you will understand.'

Below the surface Treacy was permanently unsettled. He had hoped that Pontefract would not be for long or for life. His mind was not helped by the appearance of his name in gossip columns when bishoprics became vacant. He was mentioned in 1964 for Southwell when Russell Barry retired and for Carlisle when Thomas Bloomer retired. More than speculation had surfaced when his friend F. W. Dillistone moved from the Deanery of Liverpool in 1963. Treacy had reason to think that the appointment would come his way. Canon Harold Kirkman, then Vicar of Oldham and a member of Church Assembly for the Manchester Diocese remembers Treacy telling him about approaches. Dean Dillistone himself records 'that it was my hope initially that he might have succeeded me as Dean of Liverpool but I am confident now that the post which was later to be his was the one in which his buoyant leadership and pastoral concern could gain its richest fulfilment.'

Treacy battled on, having to assume the full reins of the Diocese during John Ramsbotham' illnesses, particularly in 1966 and 1967. During the summer of 1967 John Ramsbotham suffered a stroke and announced his resignation of the See of Wakefield of 23 October. Treacy wrote:

'This resignation is in no sense an end of a ministry. It will be, under God, the beginning of a rich and valuable ministry towards which the experience of nearly 40 years in Orders have been leading him. The ministry of counsel and spiritual direction which is greatly needed within the Church of England to-day, and in which Bishop John will give that which he is so wonderfully equipped to give, and more so in view of the suffering through which he has passed in these latter years.'

The Ramsbotham-Treacy relationship was not always an easy one but it was good that Treacy had to work with and under someone whose spiritual gifts, ecclesiastical outlook and reforming enthusiasms were different from his own.

15
Tha's Made It

The steps leading to the selection and election of the new Bishop of Wakefield began with a visit to the Diocese by the Prime Minister's Patronage Secretary (John Hewitt). He met the Cathedral Chapter, who made known to him the qualities that they hoped to find in their new bishop. Hewitt also consulted a number of clergy and leading laity of the diocese. The 'qualities but no names' rule was severely breached. There was only one man they wanted or was thought possible — Eric Treacy.

The Archbishop's Secretary for Appointments (W. 'Bill' H. Saumarez Smith) met the Diocesan Vacancy in See Committee of which Treacy, as Suffragan Bishop, was Chairman. Treacy recalls the occasion:

'In the course of the meeting I was asked to vacate the chair, and it was suggested that I leave the room. It would be hypocritical if I did not admit to some suspicion as to what was afoot. The meeting dispersed after a short time, but a discreet silence was maintained.

'Although I suspected that my name had been suggested as a possible successor to John Ramsbotham, I did not attach much importance to this. I knew that there were many good reasons against promoting a Suffragan within the diocese in which he was already serving. Furthermore the Suffragan in the Diocese of Carlisle (S. Cyril Bulley of Penrith) had been appointed Diocesan only a short time previously, and I doubted that the authorities would do the same thing again.

'There were other reasons which led me to think that this would be out of the question. I was not a graduate and I could not pretend to any kind of intellectual attainment; I was over 60, and there was a very strong case for appointing a younger man. Furthermore, after 20 years in the diocese, it could be said that I knew the diocese almost too well. A stranger with new ideas and an entirely fresh approach to the diocese would, I thought, bring a much needed stimulus to the life of the Church in Wakefield. For these reasons, I had put out of my mind any possibility that I should be seriously considered for the Bishopric.'

The questions of Treacy's age and status were raised, as was his lack of university education and a degree, quite apart from a theological training that had been at best cursory. It was pointed out to those taking 'soundings' that Treacy was about to receive an Honorary Doctorate of Laws from the University of Leeds. This was conferred on 23 May 1968. Fenton Morley (then Vicar of Leeds, later Dean of Salisbury) was a member of the University's Honorary Degrees Committee at the time and he writes 'I know that the committee was unanimous in its decision and further we decided that the LLD was appropriate in recognition of Eric's services not only to the Church but to the whole community.' The parishes gave him the money to purchase his treasured Doctor's robes. On the great day he arrived at the University and when he opened his robe case there were no robes but a collection of electric light bulbs. He had taken the wrong case. In presenting him to the Chancellor, the Duchess of Kent, Professor Ruse addressed the Congregation in words both simple and moving — and true. 'No award of an honorary degree by this University can ever have given more widespread pleasure in Yorkshire than that you will shortly confer upon Eric Treacy, Lord Bishop of Wakefield, so great is the admiration and affection felt for him. During his 22 years in the county he has indeed become identified with all that is best in its enterprising people. Truly he is one whose light continues to shine before men.'

All avenues of enquiry about a new bishop led to a single cul-de-sac bearing the name of Eric Treacy. No other name was mentioned or considered, which was a rare occurrence. Nevertheless it was with genuine surprise that Treacy received an envelope ominously marked 'Prime Minister' with a pile of Christmas cards. The invitation written on 20 December 1967 was couched in familiar language. A few Prime Ministers made their 'invitations' personal but not in recent times.

My dear Bishop,

It is my duty to recommend to The Queen the name of a successor to Bishop Ramsbotham as Bishop of Wakefield. After the most careful consideration I have decided, if you are willing that I should do so, to submit your name for the succession to this See.

On hearing that this is agreeable to you, I shall be happy to recommend your name to The Queen, and I trust that you will treat this proposal as confidential until her Majesty's approval has been sought.

Yours sincerely,
Harold Wilson

In July 1976, shortly before his retirement, Treacy made a note:

'Sir Harold Wilson opened, and I dedicated, the new Featherstone High School. I do not belong to the anti-Wilson brigade. I have always found him easy to talk to, without the high and mighty airs of Harold Macmillan, who talked *at* you and not *to* you. I reminded him that, as Prime Minister in 1968, he had proposed my name to Her Majesty the Queen for nomination to the See of Wakefield. He needed no reminding; he not only remembered his share in my elevation, but was able to speak with considerable knowledge of all the other episcopal appointments in which he had had a hand. He revealed a quite remarkable knowledge of the men and their qualifications, as well as the needs of the various dioceses. There was more than a formal interest; there was a deep concern about the wellbeing of the Church, and clearly, on his part a sincere desire to exercise his responsibilities in the matter of Crown appointments with considerable care. A most encouraging conversation. I would guess that a similar approach to the appointment of Diocesan Bishops will have been taken by all the Prime Ministers of the 20th century, with the possible exception of Winston Churchill who looked upon the Church of England as a Department of State, and was impatient with Bishops who questioned the ways of Caesar. But to be fair to him, he had a war on his hands, and pigheaded prelates who tended to say the right things at the wrong times, made life more difficult for him than he liked.'

When Treacy received the letter he asked for a week to consider the suggestion and it was a time of agonising uncertainty. May and he prayed desperately that there might be some sign as to what they ought to do. They did not seek advice from friends because Treacy had learned that one's friends always advise acceptance of positions of greater responsibility. The decision was made on Christmas Day as he records:

'Pontefract Parish Church is without an incumbent, so I took myself there this morning to celebrate and preach at the Parish Communion. Good, un-fussy service — parish worship at its best. After service set out, up the Great North Road, for Applethwaite, where we are having a few days rest. Had the road to ourselves all the way.

'First chance May and I have had really to discuss the PM's letter. After a long discussion the following points emerge:
FOR
(a) the fact that the Diocese wants me, and that this is something that I have, in no wise, sought.
(b) If I am to have a Diocese, then it is this or nothing.
(c) That I know the Diocese, its parishes, clergy and people so well, there will be no time lost in learning my way about, or in assessing the men.

(d) That after 22 years in the West Riding, I know the area and understand its people

(e) This is to speak very humanly — but after spending six years as second man, it is attractive to have a show of one's own.

AGAINST

(a) There is my age. I am 60 but from all accounts, a fairly young and robust 60.

(b) There is the danger that after so long in the Diocese, I shall be found stale and lacking original ideas.

(c) Is it a good thing for a Suffragan to become a Diocesan? Is there not likely to be a difficulty in that he assumes his new responsibilities with a mind pre-conditioned in his judgements of men and situations?

(d) I doubt whether my mind and temperament will suit me for the ultimate responsibility which must rest upon a Diocesan Bishop. I am said to be rash in my utterances, impetuous in my judgements, and apt to express myself too forcibly for such high office.

'Well, we talked ourselves out by the time we finished our journey, and without adding up the score of pro's and con's, we knew that the answer must be "Yes", the Lord being our Helper. Although the "Yes" opens the door to all sorts of problems, to have arrived there brings a sense of peace to both of us. We know we are committed, but whatever that commitment may involve, our course is set.'

Accordingly Treacy accepted the nomination and the public announcement was made on 9 January 1968 to an applause of popular approbation and universal good will. If any other appointment had been made then it is certain that open disappointment and dissension, even anger, would have resulted from many quarters in the Diocese and beyond. The Chapter of Wakefield unanimously elected him and confirmation of the election took place in the Consistory Court at York Minister on 8 March. Between the election and the confirmation he existed in a kind of ecclesiastical limbo and was tempted to sign himself 'Eric Featherstone' which is about half way between Pontefract and Wakefield. On one occasion he signed himself — Eric Pontefract under + John Wakefield in a parish register.

On 26 March Treacy did his homage to The Queen at Buckingham Palace. He describes the quaint and historic ceremony:

'I knelt before Her Majesty the Queen and she placed her hands outside mine as I swore my oath of allegiance to her. I completely fell under the spell of the Queen. (Then) we had nearly half an hour's conversation. She revealed a remarkable knowledge of Yorkshire and its problems. We covered such issues as Church Union, the problems of the coal field, Prince Philip's recent television interview with the press, the rights and wrongs of spending vast sums on the preservation of ancient buildings like York Minster. She was charming, so easy to talk to and so gay. This was a half hour that I shall never forget.'

The Diocese of Wakefield had been granted its desire. A man who rides to high office on the back of public acclaim has cause for unease as well as satisfaction. Throughout his ministry Treacy had been haunted by a sense of inadequacy. He was constantly praying for guidance and inner peace — in fact for signs. He had desperately wanted to be a good Padre, a good Vicar, a good Archdeacon, a good Suffragan Bishop and now a good Diocesan Bishop. The unreflecting and unknowing onlooker saw a man exuding self-confidence with a word for all occasions. It was in part a mask. Although he was ever quietly and unassumingly confident in his faith in God yet he was plagued with self-doubt about his abilities and frightened of the feeling of shallowness, even emptiness, of his spiritual life. At one and the same time he knew that he was capable of carrying out the functions, and doing the job of a bishop, whilst tormenting himself with questionings as to his worthiness. In the too few quiet moments there were the times of disquiet, depression and despondency. Fortunately God enables whom He calls.

As we have seen, Treacy made no pretension to genius or learning. Neither an academic nor a specialist he! But he was temperamentally fitted for the work of a father-in-God to his clergy. He had a keen intelligence, a quick sympathy and a pastoral heart. His excellent gifts of nature had been improved and strengthened by his wide and varied experience. Above all he knew Christ and loved the Diocese, its parishes and its people. Gradually inner confidence came. When 'Digger' the milkman from Thornhill saw the appointment he shouted across the road to Treacy 'Ee tha's made it.' Perhaps with the conferring of the doctorate and later membership of the House of Lords Treacy himself realised that he had indeed made it!

At his Enthronement in Wakefield Cathedral on 27 March he shared his thoughts very directly with the Christian Family who had gathered, not to witness the enthroning of a prelate but to welcome one who had been called to be Head of the Family. Of the Diocese he said:

'I know its parishes and people; the clergy are my friends; I have walked its streets; I have rattled along its roads. Since I have been in the Diocese, I must have drunk enough parochial tea to fill a small lake, and I must have eaten several tons of parish buns — but these have all been meals of fellowship that I have shared in the Diocese.

'Yes, indeed, I am greatly blessed and privileged. But what of you, to whom I come as Pastor Pastorum? You have my sympathy — you deserved better. You deserved someone young in mind, as well as in body. Someone of greater intellectual powers than I possess; someone who would bring exciting new insights to the life of the Diocese; someone of greater spiritual depth than I know myself to possess.

'And what have you got? An ageing man with the will to serve you, and the heart to love you, but one whom you know so well that you will not have the excitement of exploring a new personality, and whose attitudes and performances are so well known that you may feel the lack of invigoration that a stranger would bring to you . . . '

Whatever he said, Treacy had a great deal to give and little to forget.

Nineteen hours after his Ethronement, Treacy exchanged the Cathedral and Cope and Mitre for a pit cage and miner's helmet at Crigglestone Colliery, near Wakefield. He wrote privately of the visit:

'As soon as we left the Pit Manager's Office, we were caught by a brigade of Press photographers. What is so unusual about a parson paying a pastoral visit to men in his diocese? We (Frank Fairclough the Pit Manager and Michael Doidge Harrison, Vicar of Chapelthorpe) shot down the 900 foot shaft in an open sided cage, did about a mile in the "Paddy" and then walked to the coal face, which was not very easy for me as I am six feet tall and I had to walk with my head well down. At the face, I crawled some distance on my stomach with a clearance of about six inches above my backside, to where the men were at work on the seam. Fortunately I am not claustrophobic, so it didn't worry me. What did worry me, however, was the thought that mine was only a brief visit, and that these miners had worked all their lives in these conditions. I wonder how many people realise what coal miners have had to endure to provide the nation with coal. Nothing can alter the fact that their working conditions are appalling.

'Of course, this was an old pit and many pits today have been modernised, and conditions are better, but of all the jobs that industry has laid upon men, none can be worse than that of heaving coal out of the earth.

'I was greatly touched that the men down the pit were pleased to see me. I had feared that they would think that I was an interloper, indulging my curiosity at their expense. Dust, dirt, darkness, confined space, and the ever present risk of accident, are the working conditions of the miner. Is there any wonder that there is a greater solidarity amongst them than exists in any other group of industrial workers?'

After the visit he and May withdrew from the Diocese for a month's disengagement. 'This is to enable me to stop being one "thing" and to start to be another.' He longed to returned to the Diocese refreshed in spirit and revitalised in mind and ready to grow into his new work. He was well aware that the opposite to growth is not stagnation but shrinkage. Growth is largely a matter of responding, taking risks and being on mental tiptoe, always reaching upwards.

The tasks and duties awaiting him in Wakefield were enormous. He returned eager to commence his work for which his previous ministry had been a preparation. He had no plan and no policy. He told a congregation at Sandal Parish Church on 8 November 1970, 'I live each day as it comes, do what has to be done, and I am not bothered whether I do — or do not — fulfil the role cast for me as a Bishop.'

As for the Diocese, when asked by someone in the South of England what it was like he replied, 'From the time you leave the North Road at Pontefract until the time you cross into Lancashire beyond Todmorden there is nowhere you can have a quiet pee without being overlooked.' The Diocese covered an area of slag heaps, pit heads and mill chimneys. The sun had to work hard to break through and the rain left dirty marks on the washing. The towns of the Diocese such as Barnsley, Halifax, Huddersfield, Pontefract, Castleford, Dewsbury and Batley looked like active volcanoes with their rows of little houses, and acres of slanting and gleaming slates.

In these areas of high teas and fish and chips the Yorkshireman is at his most proud, pugnacious and stubborn. Anything south of the Diocese is suspect as J. B. Priestley caught so well in *When we are married*. There is a wonderful incident when the organist at t'Chapel is on the carpet for having been slow off the mark with his Messiah and is stigmatised as being Lah-de-dah because he was a Southerner. The people lack pretensions (though they have some home-cultivated ones) and are suspicious of those who affect 'airs and graces'. Treacy, who had successfully buried his London birth and boyhood and whose Irishness was excused on the grounds that he could not help it, had always lacked sophistication. It showed in all sorts of ways. An entry from his diary is a good example: '8 April 1968. May's birthday. We went to a very lah-de-dah Hotel on the shores of Ullswater for lunch. Every room crowded with antiques and bric-a-brac with people to match. Not my kind of place — although, I must say, they gave us a spanking meal.'

There are still many people whose mouths fall open aghast if a bishop speaks to them in a completely normal and natural way. He is often avoided in case he intones a greeting. Treacy had always been able to break through these barriers with lay people. This was as important as it was appreciated in a Diocese in which certain of its valleys were dying on their feet and needed a bishop who could meet people naturally and encouragingly. Industrial decline was running parallel with local government reorganisation, miscalled 'reform'. Treacy had always believed in the small independent local community or medium sized town. Local pride begets national pride. The Diocese had many such towns that supported their own newspaper, produced their own cultural activities and were 'run' by people of the community for the community. He did not indulge in a frozen sentimentality which idolised the past in his thinking for he knew all the bad things there were to know about the narrow parochialism of West Riding people. He once wrote in the *Yorkshire Evening Post*, 'Some think this [parochialism] to be a form of admirable local loyalty. I maintain that it is a form of self-centred conceit which is an expensive luxury — Stubbornness is dangerous; the Yorkshireman is not flexible in his thinking or his outlook, and if the area is to survive, he must be. This kind of parochialism is the road to destruction, because it results in a blockage of communication in the field of ideas.'

Treacy's antagonism towards the new tiers of local government was on lines similar to his opposition to the 'Big is Better' mentality which he thought successive Governments had promoted or allowed. He saw communities disappearing as they were absorbed into larger units in the cause of administrative efficiency. He conceived his duty as stirring up industrialists and civic leaders through meetings of Rotary, Chambers of Commerce and Trade, and the like, to fight and prevent the worst excrescences of the reforms becoming realities. It was to little avail as the big state steamroller moved to flatten what it could not pattern. His worst fears have been realised, as the new administrative amorphous bodies are unloved and unwieldy. For the most part they have bred disillusionment and cynicism instead of creating a sense of unity and loyalty.

In public speeches and in private meetings Treacy encouraged thought and action on the subject. He asked young people to stay in the area, and when they had graduated, or completed their professional training, to stay in the North and revitalise it. He told council officials to encourage civic pride and make the towns look as if they were coming to life and not dying. This required hard thought and an individualistic approach to planning rather than the cosmetic effect of tulips on roundabouts and geraniums hanging from lamp posts, when the hinterland was decaying. Many a rotating Rotary meeting was challenged to act, slumbering

Soroptomists were given a vision and Commerce was invited to leave its Chambers for wider horizons.

Treacy spoke, wrote and provoked because he cared. This is nowhere better observed than in a privately circulated Ad Clerum in 1970 in which he wrote:

'Recently, I accepted the invitation of a Brother Diocesan Bishop to spend a day visiting his Diocese. It was an invigorating experience. I saw new churches, a wonderfully renovated Cathedral, a new Teacher Training College, a new University with a magnificent Chapel. I heard of new projects of an exciting nature. As evening fell, I returned to the Diocese of Wakefield. On my journey I passed one mill after another, either for sale, or in the process of demolition. I passed coal mines that had been closed, slag heaps standing like gloomy monuments to a dying age, and I could not help feeling envious of my brother Bishop with so much happening. Here, in this Diocese, I thought, there is so little that is glamorous or exciting. Then, I thought of the clergy ministering in some of these drab areas, and I felt a sense of pride.

'Here, in this Diocese, in which there is more ending than beginning; in which there is more talk of the past than the future; in which there is not the stimulation of new and exciting developments; we labour on without hitting the headlines. There are moments, for all of us, when we should like to be involved in new and exciting projects.

'Yet, I believe that it calls for faithfulness and steadfastness of a high order to stick at it in areas in which there is not much to stimulate. Those who dwell in the Wakefield Diocese cannot but be depressed as they see their mills closed and many of them demolished; their pits shut; to see an almost complete absence of economic development; and to live under the shadow of redundancy.

'We have a tremendous opportunity to give encouragement; for getting alongside those whose future is in question. And, furthermore, I believe we have a duty in some areas to bring pressure to bear upon local and national government in situations where the needs of the local community are being overlooked.

'The great thing is that they should know that there is someone who CARES, and who is prepared to understand their problems.

'As most of you will appreciate, I have a deep love for the Diocese of Wakefield after 21 years' ministry in it and it is for this reason that it causes me deep sadness to see the run-down condition into which so much of it has got. I find people in the area depressed because they cannot see much future for it. I would venture the opinion that it is one of the most challenging dioceses in the country in which to work. For us, this is an opportunity — an opportunity to give it the best we have got; yes, and to be stimulated by the needs of our people.'

Responding to opportunity and being stimulated by the needs of others were marks of Treacy's own ministry.

A selection of Eric Treacy's Railway Photographs

Above: Ex-London & North Western Railway 'Prince of Wales' No 25804 heads a freight at Edge Hill, Liverpool, in prewar days.

Below: Eric Treacy's classic wartime photograph of LMS 'Duchess' Pacific No 6230 *Duchess of Buccleuch* on Shap.

Above: Eric Treacy enjoyed a number of footplate trips and here has caught the concentration displayed by Driver Sowry of Neville Hill shed, Leeds, at the controls of the LNER 'A2/2' Pacific No 60501 *Cock o' the North* on the 'North Briton'.

Below: LMS rebuilt 'Royal Scot' 4-6-0 No 46146 *The Rifle Brigade* making a stirring climb out of Holyhead with the up 'Irish Mail' in early BR days.

Left: Eric Treacy took comparatively few pictures on the former GWR territory. Near Royal Oak in the early 1950s, 'Castle' 4-6-0 No 5070 *Sir Daniel Gooch* sets out under the bridges with a down express.

Below left: One of Eric Treacy's favourite locations in Leeds — Whitehall Jn. 'Jubilee' 4-6-0 No 45565 *Victoria*, a Leeds Holbeck engine, headed westwards.

Above: Another Eric Treacy classic. Sunlight picks out rebuilt LMS 'Patriot' 4-6-0 No 45527 *Southport* in the depths of Lime St cutting, Liverpool, on the up 'Merseyside Express'.

Below: Carlisle Upperby shed yard. Two LMS '3F' 0-6-0Ts and a 'Duchess'.

Above: The roundhouse at York shed, now incorporated in the National Railway Museum. Three of the home shed's engines — left to right — 'B1' 4-6-0 No 61084, 'V2' 2-6-2 No 60918 and 'A1' Pacific No 60126.

Below: One of Haymarket, Edinburgh shed's immaculate Pacifics, 'A1' No 60161 *North British* leaves Waverley with the up 'Queen of Scots' in the mid-1950s.

Above: Edge Hill shed was a favourite locality for Eric Treacy. In the late 1950s 'Princess Royal' Pacific No 46208 *Princess Helena Victoria* is prepared for the up 'Merseyside Express'.

Below: From the footplate: double chimney 'A3' Pacific No 60081 *Shotover* approaches Blea Moor box, with a freight waiting in the adjacent loop, with the 10.35 Leeds (City)-Glasgow (St Enoch) in the early 1960s.

Above: Border City. Contrasts in motive power: 'Princess Royal' Pacific No 46204 *Princess Louise* (left) on an up express, station pilot, '3F' 0-6-0T No 47292, and a diesel unit on the Newcastle service.

Below: We owe Eric Treacy a debt for his care in recording diesel locomotives at work in the 1960s and 1970s. Here is the short-lived prototype 2,750hp diesel electric No D0260 *Lion* passing the deserted Copley Hill sheds, Leeds, with the up 'Yorkshire Pullman'.

Top right: The down 'Flying Scotsman' passes Hadley Wood in the 1963-5 period behind 'Deltic' No D9008 *The Green Howards.*

Right: Steam finale. Latter days at Nine Elms shed with the home shed's rebuilt 'Battle of Britain' Pacific No 34082 *615 Squadron.*

16
Issues and Principles

A number of issues dominated the Church of England's corporate agenda during the first few years of Treacy's Wakefield episcopate. These included the introduction of Synodical Government, the changes in the Church's structure proposed in the report *Partners in Ministry* chaired by Fenton Morley, and the possibility of moving into the first stage of Union with the Methodist Church. These issues occasioned much mental agonising by bishops, clergy and laity alike. Treacy's position was usually unequivocal.

Treacy was no enthusiast for Synodical Government, preferring things as they were with a Church Assembly, Convocations, Diocesan Conferences and Ruridecanal Conferences. The General Synod was born in 1970 although it had been conceived in 1966 within the folds of a commission's report, *Synodical Government in the Church of England*.

Meetings of the General Synod became grey letter weeks for Treacy except for the opportunities it gave him for pursuing trains. Kings Cross brew was much better than Church House, Westminster, tea. After six years of Synodical Government he articulated the feelings of the majority of churchgoers when he wrote 'The Church has not been helped by the coming of the General Synod, which costs far more than it justifies; which breeds more "bumf" than any reasonable person with a job to do can hope to read; and which allocates to itself more time than it needs, with the result that its agenda expands into the available time. This means that it is increasingly finding new areas of the Church's life in which to interfere and breed unsettlement.'*

This was typically a populist view. But was it true? Any high hopes for the General Synod have long since receded except for the bewildered, the blinkered, the bureaucrats or the blind — a contemporary Pool of Bethesda! To understand its frustrating failure it is well to consider its ancestry. Following the publication of the Archbishops' Commission on Church and State in 1916, William Temple became the inspired and inspiring leader of an organised agitation called the Life and Liberty Movement. It was the chief campaigning instrument which led to the full orchestral trump of the National Assembly of the Church of England (Church Assembly) in 1919. What a triumph for William Temple and his fellow players! In terms of what they achieved it was. And it is important to remember that William Temple, like his successor Geoffrey Fisher but unlike *his* successor Michael Ramsey, was an ardent institutionalist, believing in the power and effectiveness of deliberative assemblies. Donald Coggan has been more in the former mould though rather more in the manner of a managing director than Geoffrey Fisher's headmaster.

The Church Assembly developed in a way very different from the aspirations of

Wakefield Diocesan News, August 1976.

the Life and Liberty group. They wanted it to be a prophetic body as well as a recommending and legislative assembly. It was a forlorn hope. The Assembly — like the General Synod — soon became an 'Oh what might have been'. It was an area in which ideals became institutionalised, prophecy lost its amplifier and the leaven became lumpish. The Enabling Act of 1919 became a disabling measure as committees waxed, initiative waned and the Garden of Eden was strewn with red tape.

William Temple's vision was right but he did not foresee that although the laity were given their mouths, and the clergy their heads, the Assembly would fall into the welcoming hands of those legalistic clergy, partisan clerics, professional ecclesiastical lay people and some purple-bibbed bureaucrats who suffocate their victims by points of order.

When the Church Assembly gave way to the General Synod, and Diocesan Synods replaced Diocesan Conferences, and Ruridecanal Conferences bowed out in favour of Deanery Synods, great again were the general hopes for these multifarious bodies. But it was like looking through one of those distorting mirrors in a fairground. The image changes, but not the reality.

Treacy never had any illusions about the process. His deepest anxieties were not limited to practicalities. 'The new system of Synodical Government will limit the powers of the Bishop — but, we remain an episcopal church, and in the last analysis, authority in things "lawful and honest" remains with the Bishop.' He was fond of quoting Bishop Christopher Chavasse's remarks on the subject, made when instituting a new incumbent in his Diocese of Rochester. 'There is some confusion in the Church as to the nature of lawful authority', said Chavasse, 'but so long as you are in this Diocese, I am IT.'

Canon Theo Wetherall, a former Vicar of Huddersfield, observes of Treacy:

'The Bishop's responsibility seemed to him like that of a Colonel. He became a diocesan bishop shortly before synodical government was introduced. It was against his own natural style, but he tried to make it work. Every now and then impatience made him relapse, and for about a month he resorted to autocratic decisions; then he used to repent, and went back to consultation. It was rather confusing for the members of diocesan committees.'

The authority of the bishop as a ruler, his claim to the obedience of his clergy and their duty to render it have been problems in Church government from the beginning. The bishop exercises paternal authority as in a family rather than coercive authority as in a civil state. Christian 'polity' is centred in the balance between the spiritual autocracy of the benevolent tyrant, the Bishop, and the spiritual democracy of the Holy Spirit, the brotherhood of believers. The imbalance can be seen historically in the aggrandisement of the benevolent spiritual tyrant in the Church of Rome (pre-Vatican II) and the over emphasis on the democracy of the Holy Spirit in the Free and Non-conforming Churches. It was ever the glory of the Church of England to maintain this Polity long before Hooker wrote his Ecclesiastical Polity; maintaining such a balance involves tension.

Treacy was a natural benevolent despot of a bishop. As father-in-God to his clergy he was seen as an understanding, compassionate, affectionate and caring figure. At the same time he carried an aura of character and strength — of authority — that was conveyed to those around him. He had a sense of the dignity of the Office of Bishop which covered many matters, including dress as he confided to some notes written in 1975.

'I grew up in a church in which Bishops, Deans and Archdeacons wore the uniform of their respective offices [reference to gaiters, etc], I think we have lost something in adopting our present sartorial permissiveness. Bishops in pullovers, berets and corduroys [reference to Richard Hare, present Bishop Suffragan of Pontefract] are all very well in times when to be scruffy is fashionable, but we can't have it both ways. If we want to be thought to be "one of the lads" then we mustn't mind if we are treated as one of the lads.

'I suppose that is all part of the revolution which has expressed itself, curiously, on the one hand in a much greater consciousness of status, and, on the other, with a determination to remove the traditional marks of status. I liked the authority framework which existed in my younger days, and the outward observances which accompanied them. It gave me a sense of security to know where I stood in relationship to them.'

How did Treacy see himself? Quite simply, as 'Head of the Family; Father in God, Pastor Pastorum; Defender of the Faith; but, above all, as in the Apostolic tradition, sent by our Lord with the good news of the Gospel, and with authority to send others forth with the Good News.'

On 17-18 June 1968 Treacy made his first appearance at a Bishops' Meeting held at Lambeth. He noted:

'A very pleasant party over which Michael Cantuar [Michael Ramsey] presided with deceptive mildness. My brother Diocesans are a very nice lot of chaps, but I must confess that I did not feel as much out of my class as I had anticipated. The discussions were vague and often off the point. Two bishops in particular impressed me as having considerable mental bite. Ian Ramsey, Bishop of Durham, and Ronald Williams of Leicester [nicknamed St Erastus of Leicester]. They each have the power to strip all the trimmings off an issue and to say pungently just what are the fundamentals. Ian Dunelm is a joy. Small and rubicund, sharp as a needle, never in danger of taking himself too seriously, in spite of his scholarship, delightfully simple, with a down-to-earth shrewdness, all of which have endeared him to the clergy of the Durham Diocese. Noel Wardle-Harpur, the Rector of Stockton on Tees, told me the other day that no one goes to see Ian without coming away feeling better for it. The last thing you would think him to be is a Prince-Bishop, but all the better for that.

'In a discussion on theological colleges, Billy Greer of Manchester [W. D. L. Greer, Bishop of Manchester] pleaded that we might have some "men" to ordain rather than the old women who so often present themselves. I know well what he means. It is rare to have an ordination candidate who looks as if he could shove well in a scrum, or pull a useful oar, but then, the athletic, hearty cult is out. When I was a young man, the ideal was the healthy looking tough, about 6 foot in height, scaling at 13 stone, with a nice, clean, well washed look about him. The muscular Christian, dedicated to open air sports, runs before breakfast and cold baths, dressed in a brown sports coat and flannel bags, more at home in a pub than a dance hall. I am afraid that poor William Manchester is a bit out of date, for the archetype these days is very different. The young have created their own image. I don't like it, but obviously they do. The aim now is to look as scruffy and grubby as possible, to equate games playing with Imperialism, and to lurk in dark corners listening to barbaric music. However, in defence of those whom William dubs old women, some of them are first class in spite of their appearance, and may well have a clearer grasp of spiritual realities than the hearties of my generation.'

Bishops' Meetings are much suspected of being secret gatherings at which the Diocesan Bishops gather to discuss great issues of Church and State, to plan the more important appointments within the Church, and to do in private things that should be done in the open. After attending a few such gatherings Treacy admitted that he too had been suspicious of them before he was a Diocesan but now 'At our sessions we discuss nothing that could not be known by the whole church. The business is mostly administrative, and there is no question of their lordships agreeing on a "line" to be taken by the House of Bishops on any issues currently before the church.'

Those were early thoughts. After a few years Treacy noted a subtle change which in its hidden way was both dramatic and dangerous. He agreed with a fellow Diocesan who wrote to him only six months after Treacy had retired: 'I am more and more disturbed about the manifestations of our church administration ... Everything seems to be arranged by some inner cabal [of bishops] whose membership I do not know and we are merely presented with virtually a fait accompli. In some ways I am beginning to suspect that during the last 15 years I have been "conned".' There were a few like-minded bishops whose own individualistic and independent approaches prevented them from uniting to expose and combat a strong inner clique. In any event Treacy would not have had the steely grit necessary to oppose a general episcopal trend. He might occasionally tilt at the episcopal windmill, but no more. He too much enjoyed being a member of the 'bishops' club' for which, deep inside he had longed but never expected to belong. Ross Hook, Bishop of Bradford, writes interestingly:

'I have found that in general the "bench" tends to divide on lines of the "extrovert" and the "introvert". Eric was outgoing, as his whole ministry bore witness.

'Combined, however, with his outgoing attitude to affairs and people was a humility which led to constant self-searching. This humility with regard to his own capacities was both endearing and remarkable, since the tremendous popularity which he enjoyed might well have made a lesser man complacent. It was pre-eminently a personal popularity — the briefest contact with any person elicited that person's love and admiration. Charm alone could not have made this instant but lasting impact on people from all walks of life; as well as charm he had the gift not only of caring for the individual but of making this caring interest felt; and the fact that his personality was far from lightweight gave value and substance to all these relationships.

'... Although he played along with it, he basically had no great sympathy with synodical government, finding it difficult to reconcile with episcopal authority. For all his openness he was basically conservative, and in his heart I think he found as he grew older that he resented change more than most of us do. But the overall impression that he left upon people was that they felt better for having met him. And if you can say that of a man, there is not much worth adding.'

Although Treacy felt privileged to attend the 1968 Lambeth Conference [the meeting of world wide bishops in communion with the See of Canterbury] he told a gathering of clergy in the semi-cloistered atmosphere of the College of the Resurrection, Mirfield, at a later date — and I quote from his notes — 'Lambeth Conference — described as a dull and unexciting lot of men. Thought the same myself but hesitated to say so. As far as the Church of England is concerned the episcopate today seems to lack distinction. Maybe because I sit on the Bench myself, and the distant view no longer enchants me. Maybe because one always tends to romanticise about the past. Yet — there does seem to be a lack of episcopal leadership — there are no particular episcopal voices which demand public attention. Is this because the C of E is in the shadows — or is it in the shadows because it is failing to produce colourful and compelling men?' It should be noted that there were outstanding men but some said nolo episcopari and others did not have the chance of so doing.

The Lambeth Conference provided Treacy with the opportunity of seeing the Archbishop of Canterbury (Michael Ramsey) over a period of time and his previously rather negative views about him were completely transformed; as he records, for example:

'July 26. Day of Recollection in Lambeth Parish Church, conducted by Michael Cantuar. Today, we have discovered the real man, and what a discovery it is. For here is a man of the deepest spiritual penetration, a man who is so much at home in the Gospel that you feel that he is showing you some of the most precious treasures of the Gospel Household. Basically, Michael is a simple man, who loves His Lord, and wants others to do so too. I must confess that this has been something of a revelation to me, for I have always admired Michael, but found him something of an enigma. His acute shyness makes it difficult for him to achieve social communication. But in talking of spiritual things — there is no shyness — but authority, the simplicity of a man who has really grasped the fundamentals of his subject, and the fire of a man who speaks with Pauline urgency.

'I wish that the real Michael were known to the world outside, which only sees a rather inarticulate, bumbling old parson; to some, rather laughable; to most, out of touch with the modern world.

'How wrong these impressions are. For here is a man who knows what he believes; and who knows in Whom he believes; here is a man who would die for his beliefs if ever it were needed. Whatever else happens during the Conference nothing will impress me more than the spiritual power and humble simplicity of the Archbishop, and nothing will help me more than the light that he has brought to understanding of familiar events in the Gospel.'

If the Church was not producing 'colourful and compelling men' it was continuing to produce controversial Reports which rained down on the Church like — or perhaps unlike — manna from heaven. One such was the Report called *Partners in Ministry*, published in June 1967. It became popularly known as the Morley Report after its chairman, Fenton Morley. Amongst the Commission's members had been John Ramsbotham, Treacy's predecessor. The proposals were courageous and staggering as the *Church Times* leader (2 June 1967) commented:

'At one fell swoop they have proposed the destruction of a pattern of ministry which has served the Church of England for centuries; a frontal assault on complex and long established laws of property; and massive infringement of the Royal Prerogative. All this and much more is entailed in the proposed abolition of the whole system of Church patronage, including the immemorial power of the Sovereign to present to hundreds of benefices and other Church appointments, and by the proposed abolition too, root and branch, of the freehold right of the incumbent to his benefice and of the bishop to his see.'

Replacing the existing patronage system — would be a 'Diocesan Ministry Commission' responsible for the appointment of all clergy in the dioceses apart from deans, provosts and some canons. In place of the freehold a parson's tenure would be for a fixed term of years, with the possibility of renewal by mutual consent, or without a term of years but subject to review. Newly ordained men would be 'placed' to secure a fair distribution through the country. It was the outcome of the Paul Report proposals.

Treacy was not the only bishop to express strong feelings against the proposed 'Diocesan Ministry Commission'. Writing in the *Diocesan News* (December 1968):

'Perhaps the most important aspect of the work of a Bishop is in the care of the clergy in his Diocese. Better than anyone, he will know the needs of his clergy and the conditions in their parishes. He will know their strong points and their weak points; he will know their family and personal problems; he will know things about them that no one else should ever know. As their Bishop he will advise them as to their movements; as their Bishop, the clergy may come and open their hearts to him. He will be thinking well ahead what is best for them, and will, as their Father in God, exercise his responsibility in placing them where they should be, for their good and the good of the Church. Furthermore, he will do this in consultation with those who have a wide knowledge of the Diocese. This is a matter about which a Bishop will seek in prayer to know the Will of God. Now, the Bishops are being asked to hand over this solemn responsibility to a Diocesan Commission.

'Presumably this will mean that when a Bishop has discussed with a priest what his next work will be he will have to say "Well, I should like you to go to such and such a place, but, of course, I shall have to bring it before the Diocesan Ministry Commission, and see if they agree."

'There will be factors in the situation that no Bishop worthy of his office would dream of divulging to a Committee, and if these factors are not revealed, it is unlikely that the Commission would agree to the move.

'The solution to the problem of Bishop-clergy relationship lies in the creation of smaller dioceses rather than in taking from Bishops a responsibility which belongs inseparably to their office.'

Another of Treacy's anxieties concerned the doctrine of the Holy Spirit. The Commission would have the power to move a man and to organise and manage the ministry. 'How, then, does the Holy Spirit come into this? I may be a bit simple in this modern world of management by committee but I have always believed that a man in Holy Orders places his life under the authority of the Holy Spirit, in the faith that God the Holy Spirit will direct, sanctify, and govern. It is not uncommon for the Holy Spirit to inspire a person to do something, to go somewhere, or to stay somewhere, in a way that a Committee would find it difficult to understand.'

From long experience of committees Treacy added 'that the Holy Spirit is often hard put to it to make His will known in such bodies.'

A decade later a certain amount of tinkering and patchwork has been effected but the revolution has not noticeably arrived.

For some reason a great deal of the strong feeling against the Report found its focus in Fenton Morley in a way that had not been the case with Leslie Paul — but then *he* was a layman. Treacy never personalised his wrath. He was so disturbed about what he observed that he wrote a letter to the *Church Times* two years later — 24 July 1970 — praising Fenton Morley's service to the whole Church as well as his successful ministry in Leeds, and ended by saying:

'I write as one who had considerable misgivings about some of the recommendations of the Morley Commission, but I feel I cannot let this moment pass without paying tribute to the efforts of Canon Morley in the service of his Church. Dare I express the hope that he will be accorded the recognition his labours deserve; that it will be remembered that he was given a job to do by the Church Assembly which he has done with distinction; and that he will not be penalised for having given himself with such courage and enthusiasm to piloting a report which, by its very nature, will have raised a good deal of opposition.'

Treacy's friend and Fenton Morley's Archdeacon (of Leeds), C. O. Ellison, wrote to Treacy: 'It is exactly what many of us have been thinking and saying, but it is entirely characteristic on your part to be the one actually to seize the pen and write. Thank you for doing it.' Many people had been expecting Fenton Morley to move and one diocesan bishop wrote to Treacy: 'I have been working hard to try and get some recognition for Fenton, but John Hewitt [Prime Minister's Appointments Secretary] has quite decided that he is not going to offer him anything. This is really in the nature of a scandal. Fenton is a much bigger and abler man than a good many occupants of the episcopal bench, and it is really tragic to think that he is being passed over just because his name is attached to a controversial report.'

Had the Morley Report proposals been implemented great would have been the strain within the Church. But it would not have rent it asunder as the Anglican-Methodist proposals threatened to do. Proposals for Union of the two Churches had been in the air and on the table for a number of years but in 1969 the time for voting had arrived. Treacy was a firm supporter of Reunion with the Methodists and cast his vote in favour. The clergy of his Diocese were far from united on the issue. At a Diocesan Synod on 25 January 1969 under 50% of the clergy approved the proposed Service of Reconciliation. The proposals were turned down at the Church Assembly in 1969 and when they came before the General Synod on 3 May 1972 they failed to get an overall majority of 75%, in spite of the Bishops being 85% in favour. After the vote Treacy advised a 'cooling off' period — 'We should be well advised not to rush in with any new proposals, nor to hold inquests in public. Let us settle down quietly to get on with our jobs, and give the Holy Spirit time to show us what He wants us to do.'

Treacy became rather disillusioned with talk about unity and paper schemes on reunion of specific churches. His personal view, not often publicly expressed, was that all those Christians 'who acknowledged Jesus Christ as Lord and Saviour should move to inter-communion with each other immediately — that we should be *ONE* at the one place where to be separated is sin, and that is, at the Lord's Table; that we should share the bread and the wine, the Body and Blood of the Blessed Lord, freely and naturally'.

His further interest in 'schemes' vanished. Let the Churches remain largely unaltered, offering a rich variety in religious expression rather than merging into a monochrome world of uniformity. Feeling that organic unity would produce a kind of religious multiple store of which all the branches would be indistinguishable from one another, he came to the conclusion that 'we should keep the variety and differences that exist within the Body of Christ — many of which have grown up because He has willed it so'.

Naturally, Treacy obeyed the official line of the Church of England about Intercommunion and correct areas of collaboration with other Churches, but his inner convictions remained intact. He was more interested in Christians doing things together than he was with Churches working together. One fellow Christian was the Roman Catholic Bishop of Leeds (W. Gordon Wheeler) — an ex-Anglican — who writes: 'I liked him from the start, because he was a very unusual type of Anglican Bishop in that he genuinely possessed the common touch ... But he was above all a man of God with a great sense of humour and tremendous compassion for others ... His relationship with the Roman Catholic Church was always a very happy one indeed and we found ourselves on the same wavelength of evangelical priorities in so many ways.'

One other potentially divisive issue was before the Church although it was not voted upon until Treacy had retired. The subject — the ordination of women to the priesthood. His assessment of reactions in the Church to the prospect of women priests (or lady vicars as some opponents called them), was as follows:

'There is a small hard core who are utterly opposed to the possibility. They argue that the ordination of women to the priesthood would prejudice the prospects of ultimate reunion with the Roman Catholic Church. They also produce the extraordinary argument that if our Lord had envisaged women priests, He would have chosen a woman as one of the twelve.

'There is a much larger element who don't much like the idea, but will confess that they have no valid reasons for objecting. They will admit that their attitude is due more to prejudice than anything, and their dislike of change. They know that they haven't much of a case, and are reconciled to the possibility.

'There is a third element who are convinced that it is right for women to be ordained as priests, on the grounds that in Christ there is neither male nor female, and that women have valuable gifts and insights to bring to the priesthood.

'Personally I belong to the second group, and feel rather ashamed of myself for doing so. However, I see myself moving slowly into the third group. For my part I don't take too seriously the warning that the ordination of women to the priesthood will affect our ecumenical relations. We have to do that which we believe the Holy Spirit is calling us to do, and never mind the consequences. We simply cannot go on being deterred by what others think of us.

'Clearly, women priests open the way to women bishops. We can't only open the door half way to them. The Church may find it rather hard to reconcile itself to having "Mothers in God" as well as "Fathers in God". My experience of being a Bishop leads me to the conclusion that there is nothing a Bishop has to do that could not be done equally well by a woman. Therefore, I am not deterred by the prospect of calling a future Bishop of Wakefield "My Lady" instead of "My Lord".'

One subject which forced itself on Treacy throughout his ministry was the question of the remarriage of divorced people in Church. It became an issue of perpetual and increasing torment for him. It had not always been so, for his position changed during the course of his ministry. There was a time when Treacy held that there was no such thing as an 'innocent' party in the break-up of a marriage. The regulation adopted by Convocation in 1938 satisfied this view 'That in order to maintain the principle of lifelong obligation in every marriage contract between Christians (however solemnised) and as expressed in plainest terms in the Marriage Service, the Church should not allow the use of that service in the case of anyone who has a former partner living.'

In April 1971 a Report of a Commission entitled *Marriage, Divorce and the Church* was deposited on a bewildered Church and a bemused public. The existing situation was unsatisfactory, unedifying and unstable. There was a rigid inflexibility about remarrying divorced persons in Church running parallel to an apparent policy of marrying almost anyone for the first time of asking, whether or not they were practising members of the Church and without asking too many questions. The main conclusion reached in the unsatisfactory report was: 'If the General Synod after due enquiry and consultation decided to give effect to remarriage in church, this would not be a mere accommodation to secular pressure; it would be an acknowledgement of human weakness and a declaration of faith in God's forgiveness and creative power. We believe that the grace which God may bestow in a first marriage He may also bestow in a subsequent marriage.' Although the report went out of its way to stress that Christians must recognise that they live in a plural society the conclusions suggested otherwise. It was as if the writers really believed that England was a Christian country. They led one to imagine long queues of divorced people clamouring to have their second marriage solemnised in Church. Little wonder that they headed among 'some unacceptable proposals' the one proposal that seemed to be ideally suited to post-Christian times: 'One expedient — continually pressed upon the Christian community — is to accept universal civil registration, leaving the State to devise what sort of marriage contract it will. Christian people would register their contract in these terms then go to church to solemnise holy matrimony in accordance with the doctrine and discipline of the Church.' And then came the important words: 'The union contracted in the civil ceremony would be dissoluble: that solemnised in church would be indissoluble.'

That was precisely the situation that obtains in many countries where the civil and legal ceremony is separated from the religious act. A contract is made on the one occasion and vows are made at the other. The fact that vows are made in Church neither adds to nor subtracts from the civil ceremony. That would be the one recognised by the Inland Revenue — and the Church would naturally recognise its validity.

By the time Treacy became Bishop of Wakefield — and some time before it — he was firmly of the opinion that the Church of England should provide for the remarriage in Church of the 'many devout people who have been victims of other people's selfishness, irresponsibility, and I, for one, do not feel that we can continue in our present inflexible attitude'. It pained him to have to rule on the cases which came before him. He was often asked to fly in the face of the rules of the Church and he was sorely tempted so to do.

Treacy thought that a new service should be prepared for the remarriage of divorced people in Church. Writing in the *Diocesan News* for July 1969 he proposed:

'Personally I should be opposed to such a Service without music, flowers, and the usual frills which accompany a wedding. I would not wish such a wedding to give the impression of something second best.

'To bring this matter out into the open, and to provide a properly authorised and dignified order of Service for the remarriage of the divorced would put an end to the rather hole-in-the-corner device of the short Service of Blessing in Church which many clergy, of their compassion, give to those who have been married in the Registrar's Office.

'I do not think that such a Service would imply the Church's going back on the principle of the indissolubility of marriage. It would, in fact, recognise the sincerity of many Christian people in desiring that a second marriage should receive the blessing of the Church, and that which they hope and intend should be a lasting union should start in Church.

'One obvious difficulty about this would be the burden of the decision in granting permission for such marriage. Clearly, such a Service could not be available to everyone who had been involved in a Divorce.

'Certain things would need to be established. They are:

'The sincerity of the couple's intentions.

'The circumstances of the Divorce, and the degree of innocence of the party requesting the marriage.

'The necessity that such a marriage would be contractually valid to the Registrar.

'That the couple concerned were practising members of the Church.

'The need for a penitential note in the order of Service which would acknowledge our Lord's teaching about the life-long union of marriage.'

Although Treacy's views on these issues were important, and his time much taken with them, it was in other spheres that he gained a wider audience and respect or irritation depending on the horizon of the beholder.

17
Sanctified Common Sense

Treacy was pre-eminently a communicator with his pen and his mouth, backed, or rather fronted, by his personality. His monthly contribution to the *Wakefield Diocesan News* was eagerly awaited by the media who devoured and spread its contents widely and rapidly. John Trevisick, formerly News Editor of the *Church Times*, remembers Treacy in print and in the debating chamber:

'He employed no tricks of oratory; it was commendably brief, straight from the shoulder, home-spun and relevant, invariably laced with some illustration based on his own pastoral experience as a parish priest . . . Those of us who had the task of reporting him had no excuses for making mistakes. He was clarity personified, but if they did stray he would never create a furore or complain. He made himself readily available to the Media generally and his own thoughts pungently expressed in the monthly *Diocesan News* on matters of current concern provided us all with a wealth of news stories, outpacing all his contemporaries. He had a news sense, but never pushed his wares, leaving what he had written to the judgement of the Press or whatever. There was a measure of trust between both sides unequalled in my experience.'

Treacy's impulsiveness led to some mistakes, and fellow bishops tended to groan 'Oh Eric again!' when he jumped in rather too quickly on a topical subject. The Bishop of London, Gerald Ellison, observes: 'We who were his friends and observed him from a rather detached position were also immensely invigorated by his friendship and his immense enthusiasm. It is always good to work alongside people who express their thoughts and minds forcefully and entertainingly. I suspect however there was an element of impetuousness which meant that he was apt to say things and then to question their wisdom afterwards.'

There were occasions when he spoke with his tongue well concealed in his cheek. Sometimes he spoke or wrote without adequate attention to facts and then he stumbled. Nevertheless in his public speaking he endeavoured to be aware of his responsibilities more than many public figures. There are those who let themselves in for dishing out prizes at School Speech Days, and reflect to fidgeting and unappreciative audiences on the state of the nation or the moral lapses of the young. Similarly there are those who allow themselves to be sacrificial offerings at public banquets and who have to pay their dues by proposing or responding to a toast, in the course of which they will almost certainly come round, via a number of painfully unfunny stories, to an analysis of economic maladies. Treacy was not ensnared by such traps, largely because he had a respect for those with whom he was seeking to communicate. He regarded his audience as people like himself who were not to be treated as an amorphous mass to be indoctrinated or bored at his will or to be insulted or amused by trivialities.

Treacy was ever watchful of those whom he regarded as the power figures in the world of communication, the News Editors of the daily Press and the Editors of Television and Radio who decide what shall be presented to the public, how it shall be presented and how much time and space shall be allotted. If he was not as vigilant as Mary Whitehouse, (whom he called 'that splendid campaigner for righteousness') regarding what appeared on BBC television, it was only because he had not the time to watch much television. In the *Diocesan News* for November 1972 he complained about a recent programme of *Till death us do part*:

'. . . in which that crashing bore Alf Garnett made some blasphemous remarks about God, the Virgin Mary, and the Pill, which seemed to have reached a new low in tasteless crudity. This blasphemy was defended to me recently on the grounds that people are like Alf Garnett, and say the sort of things he said in the programme. This argument could be used to justify the presentation of the most appalling conduct on the television. There are people who murder and torture small children; there are people who submit animals to the vilest cruelty, but is the public to have these things projected into their living rooms?

'I suppose that overworked word "Freedom" would be used to justify such things as these. And, herein, is something which should give us cause for anxiety. "Freedom" is the justification for every kind of debauch and anti-social behaviour.

'The worrying thing is that what men abuse, in the long run they will lose. This is a kind of judgement on them. They are found lacking in the capacity to use this great gift, and so they set in motion the processes that will take it away from them.

'The fact is that the right use of freedom calls for people of much finer character than those who live under a dictatorship. If you live under a dictatorship, you haven't much choice. What you do is laid down for you, and if you don't do it, you know what the consequences will be. Living in freedom makes demands upon us. We have to make judgements; value judgements, for which we need a scale of values.

'In the sphere of morals today my own feeling is that freedom has been replaced by the doctrine "I do what I like and if you don't like what I like, then, that's just too bad for you". People can write and talk filth and subversion; they can release all their instincts of violence and sheer nastiness and call it freedom.

'... The religion of Jesus Christ is one that makes men free because it first puts them under authority. At first, freedom and discipline seem to be mutually exclusive; but the fact is that freedom without self-discipline is the way to destruction. A life entirely outside discipline of any kind is a life without direction, purpose, or reference points, and is, I should think, as miserable as hell. Once a person is living outside a commitment, then his attitudes, standards and behaviour, derive from that commitment, and, in that, is the right kind of freedom. Take that framework away, and we are like a space vehicle that has got out of orbit, and which will fly around in space until it is burnt up.'

In January 1973 the BBC produced a study on *Taste and standards in BBC programmes* which Treacy studied carefully. He was particularly concerned about blasphemy and sex and less with violence. One of his favourite programmes was *The Sweeney.*

On 27 February 1973 Treacy wrote to Charles Curran, Director-General of the BBC about a play *The Operation* which had been broadcast on BBC 1 on 26 February. He wrote:

'On two occasions one of the leading actors of this play used the word "Christ" as an epithet. The use of this word seemed quite unnecessary to the dramatic impact of the play. One realises that the character portrayed was a thoroughly unpleasant creature, and he presented the part in such a way as not to need the use of such words to heighten the effect. The use of the words "Jesus" and "Christ" is greatly on the increase and is deplored by a very large number of people. I write to you in the hope that it might be possible for instructions to be given that blasphemous interjections of this kind shall not be permitted in the presentation of drama or current affairs interviews. I write to you as one whom I know to be a Christian, and I feel sure you will share my abhorrence at tendencies of this kind on Radio and Television.'

Charles Curran's reply of 7 March though perhaps predictable, was not what Treacy was looking or hoping for:

'About the play in question it is possible to say many things, but I will restrain myself. The odious central character, who was shot and killed by the husband of his mistress in the final scene, did indeed use the words of which you complain. The use of those words as expletives is, as you say, "as a sword piercing the heart" of those who are faithful Christians. And yet many people use these names as expletives every day. Moreover, they have always done so, even at times when the religious life of this country was very much stronger and more generally evident than it is now. Those expletives are a part — a shameful part — of the language. Dramatists of whatever quality seek to reproduce in their plays the authentic voice of real characters in the society they are portraying. We dealt with this point in the pamphlet *Taste and Standards.*

'The question we have to ask ourselves is how much verisimilitude we ought to allow writers for broadcasting. You will no doubt have observed that the range of oaths and expletives permitted in broadcast plays, whether serious or comic, is much more limited — by far — than that which can be encountered in real life.

We draw a line, and in some circumstances we are prepared to allow a writer to include harsh and even offensive expressions if we are convinced that these are genuinely needed for his dramatic purpose. But there are certain expressions which remain on the other side of the line. You would argue that expletives based on the name of Jesus Christ should always be excluded. I would sympathise with you, and press in the same general direction, but I should be unwilling to outlaw them completely, for the reasons already stated.

'At the same time I would deeply deplore and strongly resist any attempt to use them loosely and without justification in their context. It seems to me that in this play about a repellent and depraved property developer there might just conceivably be a case for saying that these were expletives which one would expect in precisely those circumstances. But I would not wish to spend too much energy on the justification, for I do not believe that the play itself was good enough.

'I can only say in conclusion that I am sorry if the use of these words in *The Operation* offended you or any other committed Christian viewer.'

Treacy's public utterances did not always reflect his private stance: coloured immigration for example, as he privately noted in February 1968:

'Listened to an interesting programme this evening on the Immigration problem. Enoch Powell MP has had some blunt words to say about the amount of coloured immigration that has, and is, taking place. The extraordinary thing is that if coloured immigrants are illegally smuggled into the country there is no legal power to return them to the country from which they came. Another problem arises from the fact that they can bring over their dependents; that is to say their wives and children under 16. A Pakistani boy of 15 is a man of marriageable age. There is a good deal of emotional and hysterical nonsense talked about these immigrants from India and Pakistan. They don't want to integrate, they keep themselves to themselves but they are very alert when it comes to claiming their rights under the Social Services. Although great efforts are made in the schools to teach them English, they persist in speaking their own language out of school. The result is that there is a language blockage between us and them. My experience in Dewsbury, where there are about three thousand Pakistani immigrants, is that they bring a curious atmosphere of depression to the community. I am quite clear that the time has come when there must be considerable limitation on the numbers of coloured immigrants admitted to this country. It is difficult to say this publicly, as one would be accused of Racialism; even called a Fascist. Yet to limit their entry would be in their own better interests, as, if they go on increasing, the English will find that they have had enough, and there may well be some unpleasant forms of Racialism. I sense that is already simmering under the surface.'

It is not an issue Treacy had dodged. As Archdeacon of Halifax he seconded a motion in the York Convocation in 1960 (moved by Donald Coggan, then Bishop of Bradford) urging the Church to consider the problems of multi-racial communities in cities. In January 1966 as Bishop of Pontefract he moved a motion in the same body asking them to recognise the urgency of integrating overseas minorities resident in the country. In August 1971 he appointed a Mirfield Father, Bernard Chamberlain, as his Adviser on Community Relations. Bernard Chamberlain admits that his work was not really Treacy's bowl of curry. but he received every assistance particularly regarding the unfortunate Ugandan Asians, of whom many found a home and a welcome from Christians in the Wakefield Diocese.

On a prompting from Bernard Chamberlain, who supplied some facts, in March 1974 Treacy publicly criticised the 'persistent refusal of the Home Secretary (Robert Carr) to allow about 300 Ugandan Asians, now exiled to India, to join their British wives who have settled in England. These wives possessed British passports, but in most cases their husbands took Ugandan citizenship in the hope of being allowed to stay there.

'These enforced separations are cruel, and unjustifiable. To me it seems so unlike the British way of doing things. It is within the Home Secretary's power to allow these husbands to be reunited with their wives and families under the rule which covers "exceptional compassionate circumstances".' After the General Election the same month the new Home Secretary (Roy Jenkins) decided to admit them into Britain, a move welcomed by Treacy as 'a piece of basic humanity'.

Treacy became much more worried by the activities of the National Front and people who seemed intent on inflaming a tense racial situation. His own encounters with Asians showed them to be gentle and peace loving, unlikely to initiate violence. In July 1976 he challenged Christians to 'unite to scotch all the lies and half truths which are spread about immigrants, much of which is deliberately mischievous, and has no other intention than to whip up ill feeling and resentment'. In asking Christians to be open hearted in their welcome to immigrants in a practical way he asked: 'We Christians have got to be honest with ourselves as to our attitudes to immigrants. Although we may, at one level, accept that as Christians we recognise them as Children of God with ourselves, do we at another level, resent them, and subconsciously "want them out"? In other words are we privately discriminators?'

In reply to a 'thank you' from Bernard Chamberlain, Treacy wrote 'It seems to have had wide coverage in the press, judging from the letters that I have had from all over the UK telling me what to do with myself! Clearly it was the right moment to say it. Laus Deo — I feel much better now.'

On one question closely related to this issue Treacy had very great anxiety, friction and opposition. The question arose over the future use of the consecrated mission church of St Mary, Savile Town, Dewsbury. The Church was declared redundant in May 1969. Subsequently the local Muslim Welfare Society asked to purchase the building for use as a mosque. In July 1970 the Wakefield Diocesan Redundant Churches Uses Committee agreed that it should be offered for sale to the Muslims. The Parochial Church Council of the Holy Innocents, Thornhill Lees (in which parish Savile Town was a mission) were unanimously opposed to the sale. Treacy met the PCC on 10 August 1970 and, after a lengthy meeting, left clearly convinced that he should support the PCC against the sale taking place. The district surrounding Savile Town had a very large immigrant population, but there remained a considerable white population. The PCC produced two reasons for their stand which were noted by Treacy:

'If St Mary's Church were handed over to the Muslims, it would make the district a centre for the immigrants in the whole area of Dewsbury and Batley, and this would make it intolerable for the English residents in the area, who have already suffered a serious decline in property values. Therefore, the PCC feel strongly that they owe it to the white population in that area neither to approve, nor to accept, a step which would virtually hand over the area to the Pakistanis. I know the area well and I believe the assessment to be a valid one.

'Their other reason is that to hand this Church over would hinder, rather than encourage, integration. The feeling would be so strong in the area that, in their view, there would be anti-racial demonstrations. There are already reports of clashes with knives, and the feeling amongst reasonable people there is that it would become a flash-point in community relations. This is a view with which I am in agreement.'

The whole question was aired again at the Diocesan Committee in November at which Treacy explained his stance, hoping that the Committee would change its mind, but it did not do so. The matter went before the Church Commissioners whose view was to let the Muslims have the building. One hundred local residents signed a protest petition and sent a delegation to the Commissioners. The Wakefield Diocesan Synod debated the matter and eventually, in July 1972, a motion came before the General Synod, several years after the building had been closed. Quite apart from the particular issue, Treacy wanted the Synod to express itself on:

'The larger issue concerning the use of consecrated buildings which have been declared redundant. I often ask myself what it is that makes otherwise reasonable, and often intelligent people, act like freedom fighters when it is proposed to declare a church redundant. What is it that causes normally Christian people to descend to all sorts of cunning and sometimes sheer distortion of facts when their church is threatened with closure? . . . In part it may be local reaction to authority from outside . . . Some group of people who are to them outsiders have decided the fate of something which is very local and very much their business. In part, this, I think, is really serious — it may be that it assaults their deep love for a building which has become part of their lives at the deepest level of experience, for in their church they have been married, their children have been baptised and possibly confirmed, and they have brought their dead for the last rites of the Church, and in losing their Church building they lose something of themselves. They may not now use it much, but the relationship remains.'

Whatever the feelings, once redundancy becomes a fact and a church is closed for worship the vandals and thieves move in. If it is moveable, take it. If it is static, smash it. It is not long before a building stands in a shocking state of dereliction, with daubed walls and providing a dangerous playground for children. There are many such redundant churches to be found. The fault rests in ecclesiastical legislation. Treacy wondered 'whether it would not be possible to decide about the future use or demolition of the church before closure actually takes place'. In 1979, ten years after St Mary's, Savile Town, had been declared redundant, the future use of the site remains undecided.

Other topics engaging Treacy's attention included 'Law and Order' and the Unions. He was a great friend to and of the Police. He was a frequent visitor to the Wakefield Police Academy which is partly housed in Bishopsgarth, the original residence of the Bishops of Wakefield from the time of the first and saintly Bishop William Walsham How (1888-1897). Treacy gave lectures on 'The Police and the Public' at police college courses. Former police officer, E. C. D. Thorp recalls 'his special brand of pithy humour and realism' on such occasions. When dealing with newspaper coverage of the police in too-obvious action, he was fond of quoting the response of the editor of a local newspaper when asked why he had not included a report on a particular procession which the police had handled well — 'Why, was there some trouble?'

Generally the police with whom I have talked about Treacy regarded him variously as a 'super bloke', 'a man's man', 'a real Christian' and someone who 'knew what ordinary people were thinking and saying'. In his lectures he used his special technique, first of tending to tell them what they wanted to hear. He believed anarchists were at work. 'Their intentions and hope is to see an ordered society disintegrate; they will hi-jack, kidnap, and murder — they will in the end, make the Nazis look like a lot of Samaritans. They will work for the repeal of every law that has made for decency and restraint — they will remove from our national way of life all the noble effects of religion and produce a nation of heathens; and they have their representatives in the highest councils of the land.' Then, as was his wont, he turned the coin over to reveal his anxiety that the reaction 'may well be as dangerous as the things against which it reacts. There will be a growing demand for repressive measures, for more savage methods to deal with these anti-social manifestations. There will be a real danger of a Police State.' The cascade of correspondence that flowed following a Treacy 'Law and Order' speech was in no danger of 'turning his head'.

Aggressive righteousness takes on an almost evil tone. Some people in public places have nasty private faces. Unfortunately Treacy's words were easily quoted and misquoted by fanatics as supporting their extremist views. In their eyes Treacy was 'setting an example' by, as they interpreted his oft-reported words, attacking the 'sickly, sloppy, sentimental brand of psychology' of the 'let's be kind to the criminal and layabout brigade.' Or 'Would that the Archbishop of Canterbury would occasionally make a public pronouncement like you on one of the grave moral problems of the day instead of doddering about kissing the Pope and trying to please everybody.' Many letters were from prominent people who should have known better!

To a large extent Treacy played into the hands of these would-be supporters who caused him such unease. They took from his speeches only that which fed their dangerous prejudices and completely disregarded the Christian challenge. He was aware that in making generalisations there was the danger of listeners or readers adopting a policy of support by selection!

When Inspector Barry Taylor was murdered by a gunman at Farsley in February 1970 a Memorial Service was held at Wakefield Cathedral on 6 March at which Treacy preached. His emotive address began, as was often his practice, with a simple, stark, arresting sentence: 'A man is killed doing his duty.' The address was reproduced in countless newspapers for it touched hearts and aroused minds as to the reality of the policeman's lot: 'Answering calls that bring them into contact with trigger-happy lunatics to whom violence is a way of life; for whom there is no longer the deterrent of capital punishment; dealing with morons who have been nourished with a diet of simulated violence on the TV screen so that the idea of maiming and killing has become one of the accepted accompaniments of crime.' He continued by listing the conditions in which the police had to do their work and added:

'We have to face the fact that it falls upon the Police to deal with the results of social and moral breakdowns in society which are our fault. If we breed a faithless and undisciplined generation of young people, the failing is in the home; if we have allowed the restraints of moral discipline to weaken, this is a problem in which we are all involved; if we have stood aside and allowed perverts, pornographers and anarchists to move in on Society, then ours is the fault, and we have landed the guardians of law and order with an impossible situation.

'The Churches cannot escape some measure of responsibility for the standards of society. Have we who call ourselves Christian, I wonder, done enough to proclaim what is good and to denounce what is evil? My own view is that during the last twenty years or so we have had a miserable record of ambivalence and uncertainty in this.'

The Trade Unions are always an easy target for abuse. In the confrontation of 1974 Treacy, like the vast majority of people in the country, felt a 'helpless victim of the power struggle which is tearing the nation to bits, and without a voice to speak for them. The people with no union to protect them; the people who have no power to demonstrate; the people who are helpless and who get pushed around by the Big Boys'. And the scenario for that winter of discontent? 'We see a Conservative Government which is prepared to acquiesce in a most unequal distribution of wealth; that does little to stop speculation in money and land development — which is making life intolerable for the wage earner. We see the large Trade Unions reacting ruthlessly and fighting for a share in the pickings. When shall we have armistice in this power struggle? And behind it all — there is one thing — GREED. Greed for power; greed for money.'

Usually, wherever he went, and to whatever kind of audience he spoke, Treacy was provocative yet persuasive. The two do not always harness easily but he achieved it. The times when he deliberately 'played to the gallery' left him gloomy and repentant afterwards. He confesses one such occasion:

'Preached in the Guards' Chapel this morning. Good congregation, excellent music, and as lush a setting as you will find anywhere in the Church of England. Interesting reactions to my sermon. Rarely have I received as much appreciation from the departing congregation as I received this morning. Obviously they had agreed with it and there were many expressions of hope that it might be printed and circulated. But, the fact is that it was a bad sermon, and didn't deserve praise. It was superficial and slick in its judgements; it was cliché ridden; it was lacking in Christian teaching; it did not demand any positive reaction from the congregation.

'And — they loved it! This has something to say about congregational reaction to preaching. The congregation was well above average intelligence and yet they fell for it. If I am to be honest, I have to admit that when I wrote the sermon I was aiming for precisely the reaction that I got. A mixture of patriotism, the 5th Column eating away the morale of the Nation etc. This all leads to the conclusion that the general public is satisfied by second rate preaching. Preaching that is stunningly obvious, powerfully delivered, full of assertions rather than reasoning, and which is destructive rather than constructive. Always, the preacher has to decide whether to give them what they will like, or what they will not like but need.'

Knowing his audience and how far he could bait them was an admirable Treacy trait, for it meant that he knew how far he could take and persuade the listeners. One reason why his appeal was to such a staggering range of people was that as a Christian he was world invading and not world evading. He felt called to show men that it was possible to have possessions, to seek security for their families, and to succeed in business, without losing their souls. He often spoke of holy worldliness and his preaching sought to give people a right attitude to the things of the world, not to renounce the world but merely its vain pomps and glories. The Holy Communion was the supreme example of the unity of material and ethereal — Wood (Holy Table), silver (cup and plate), bread (His own Body) and wine (His own Blood).

Treacy's intuitive antennae could usually seek out and collect people where they were, and the testimony of multitudes attests that he left them a little farther along the Christian road or had them considering the Christian Way for the first time. He was no evangelist, hammering away for a decision. He respected people's personalities and did not frighten them into changing their way of life. He simply presented them with the truth and let the truth do its own work. As an accomplished communicator he did this with simplicity, brevity, credibility and arousal. It was always done in an arresting manner. It might be a few provocative opinions expressed pungently or, perhaps, a series of rules or commandments for quite different audiences — nurses, businessmen, mothers, manual workers, Rotarians. These found their way into permanent form and the points were framed with the particular audience in mind. The themes came from his wide reading and experience but as he was not a passive consumer of other people's thoughts, there was a freshness about them that had the hallmark 'Treacy' imprinted on them. To one audience of Rotarians he gave ten commandments:

'1. Thou shalt not put thy trust in slogans. (Results are not achieved by incantation.)

2. Thou shalt not mistake conviviality for fellowship. (The use of an easy familiarity between people who are no more than acquaintances is cheap and undignified.)

3. Thou shalt not subordinate vision to constitutions.

4. Thou shalt neither slumber nor whisper while another speaketh.

5. Thou shalt learn to see the funny side of life in general and yourself in particular.

6. Thou shalt not under-rate thyself as an excuse for escaping responsibility.

7. Thou shalt not put people into categories.

8. Thou shalt learn the wisdom of silence.

9. Thou shalt learn the art of appreciation (which is very different from flattery).

10. Thou shalt expect the best of people for thus shall they become what you think them to be.'

A gathering of directors was criticised for tending to regard workers as a pack of misguided, misbegotten, faceless fodder for industry instead of people like themselves 'with secret hopes and fears'. Some politicians were hounded for promising the electorate happy days rather than hard days, 'promising a Harvest without the labour of sowing'. Harold Macmillan always came in for particular derision for creating a climate where rank materialism was nurtured and prospered. His ten rules for men in business given at the Golden Jubilee Dinner of the Institution of Production Engineers are here reproduced from his notes:

'1. You shall learn the art of delegation. This is difficult because it often seems that you have to watch somebody else make a mess of it. Don't be too much involved in detail — because decision making demands detachment.

2. Don't be too blooming clever. One thing that makes the ordinary chap suspicious is cleverness. You can't push people too much, and too far. If you do, they get stubborn and obstinate.

3. Never humiliate a person in public — they will never forgive you if you do. Everybody has his pride, and although people do darned silly things, and it is tempting to blast them on the spot, do it in private. It takes longer, but it doesn't hurt the victim so much, and doesn't strip him down in the presence of his colleagues.

4. In negotiation, always leave an escape route which your opponent can take with self-respect. Beware of ultimatums — all very powerful — but the result is usually deadlock. The desire to save face, and the inability to do it, have been the cause of many of the struggles that have plagued mankind. Always leave a door slightly open.

5. Don't flap. These are, I know, anxious times, for all men in business. Crises need clear heads, and sound judgement. Flaps at the top mean flaps all the way down the line. Steadiness creates confidence. We get National flaps, often worked up by the mass media — we have got one now, but, thank goodness, our Ted doesn't seem to be flapping. [This was in March 1971.]

6. Don't eat and drink too much. I just don't know how you business chaps stand up to all the professional boozing and guzzling that you have to do. Physical fitness is an ingredient of efficiency. A lot of illness is self-inflicted. Too much gin, not enough exercise, too much weight — disaster.

7. Don't put business before your family. This is too great a price to pay for success. It is a tragedy to be a stranger to your own children. Life at the top is often at the cost of the home. I don't believe it is necessary to take work home, to be too busy to sit and listen to the wife or to help put the kids to bed. Beware of the danger of being sucked into the business vortex.

8. Study and understand other people's fears, for fear is at the bottom of most people's reactions. It explains things that must otherwise be totally inexplicable. If you can understand other people's fears, you are a long way to understanding them. Fears go back into history, and are bred in the bone.

9. Don't drop big bombs on small targets. A man who explodes rarely and only on major issues is a man whose wrath is respected and effective. Better to lose small battles in order to win big ones.

10. Learn to laugh at yourself. The higher up the tree you are, the greater the danger of pomposity and infallibility. Laughter releases tension and cuts situations and people down to size. Sad sight on the Yorkshire Pullman, seeing all these grim-looking gents, talking shop, and busily reading memos. Relax and laugh.'

Sound commonsense? Yes, and more. There was always a specifically Christian word about the 'acceptance of the authority of God in our lives, the acceptance of the Christian Doctrine of man, and the dedication of ourselves to the best that we know'.

Treacy thought it a duty to be an interpreter of God to the times. It was not easy for the times were not conducive to religious overtures and certainly not to Christian commitment. It was even more difficult in the North of England. The Northerner is an essentially practical person and often lacks a capacity for mysticism or an awareness of the numinous. The reasons for this are manifold. Even the climate is involved. Somehow, warmth and sunshine induce a temperamental softness which is more inclined to spiritual response than the grey skies, high winds and heavy rainfall of the North that tends to make people tough and unresponsive. The essence of religion is dependence upon God; the spirit of the Northerner is dependence upon himself. Even if the spirit of religion had been evident the practice of Christianity would have still found it hard to attract adherents. The Industrial Revolution had left its mark and in its wake the Church of England in particular was not noticeably on the side of those who had to fight for social justice. Nevertheless Treacy was able to speak to the Northern condition and its people as could no other leading Churchman of his time. The Bishop of Carlisle, David Halsey, speaks for many when he says: 'Eric had the gift of understanding what the ordinary person felt and how he would respond, and the amazing gift of being able to express himself in a way that the man in the street understood and enjoyed — how many of us envied his ability to do that.' In a way Treacy was the man in the street whose commonsense was sanctified and used in a remarkable way.

18
Love Lane

As a parish priest, albeit writ large in Halifax, Treacy possessed that quality of imaginative tenderness which any good priest needs for seeing into another's fears and sensitiveness. He used his own strength to help people rather than to crush them. His intuitive antennae often found a soul in need that a reasoning mind had failed to notice. A large number of individual people in deep trouble were helped by one whose faith taught him that no situation was beyond redemption. The parish priest shares in the communal joy and the private griefs of his parishioners. In an Institution Sermon (Netherthong, 17 July 1968) he mentioned some of the things which the parish priest encounters and shares. Here I quote just one or two of the sorrows and burdens all of which came from his own experience:

'It means answering the man who says "I have three months to live, please help me to die as a Christian."

'It means sharing the suffering of a mother and father with one very precious daughter aged 12 who is dying of cancer, and trying to answer them when they cry in their agony, "Why, why, why?"

'It means dealing with the woman who is a schizophrenic, tortured with a persecution mania, convinced that her husband is trying to poison her, and who is destroying the life of a once happy family.

'It means going to the house of a man serving a prison sentence, and whose wife has neither visited, nor written to him, to find that the woman is co-habiting with the lodger.

'It means talking to a girl aged 15, who is having a baby by a married man, whose parents have turned her out.

'It means listening to a woman who has twice tried to commit suicide because she cannot face the loneliness of widowhood, and may try to do it again.

'It means going to the Police Court to speak up for the silly youngster in the Youth Club who got tight the night before and pinched a car.

'It means rampaging round the Town Hall trying to get an eviction order cancelled for an unemployed miner and his large family because he hasn't paid his rent.

'It means standing at the graveside, or at the door of the Crematorium, beholding and sharing the grief of the bereaved; it means the pain and suffering of the Hospital Ward; the misery and defeat of the Prison Cell. It means being so identified in Christ's love for your people, that everything that happens to them, in some measure, happens to you.

'It means having strength and confidence sufficient to give others, so that they can face life, and death, without fear.'

Such is the experience of any parish priest. It is one reason why many a bishop, though having the pastoral care of his clergy and their families, misses parochial life. This is particularly true of a Suffragan Bishop. Treacy was saved from pastoral frustration by his experiences in Wakefield Prison with which he became involved as soon as he became Bishop Suffragan of Pontefract although it did not reach its richest fulfilment until he moved to Wakefield. His ministry among offenders was one of the deepest experiences of his life. Behind the high walls in Love Lane, in which Wakefield Prison is situated, he learned a great deal about himself and God, as well as of the inmates. He had all the qualities required of an ideal prison chaplain if they are those described in a 1960 Report *The Church and the Prisoner*:

'The chaplain should be a man of prayer, of mature experience of life and of people in life, and of such clear and simple convictions that no one could ever mistake his calling, even though he himself rarely obtruded it or asserted it. He should be a "good Anglican", evangelical and catholic, having the full provision of the Church's message and ministrations in his hands, ready to use any and all of it with discretion, and precluded from none of it by ignorance or prejudice. He should be a priest whose first concern is neither services nor methods, but men, and men not in the mass, but individually.'

Treacy's initial, and occasional visits developed in a remarkable way. After a time it was arranged, by permission of the Governor, the enthusiastic approval of the Chaplain and the desire of the prisoners, that Treacy should visit the prison with his wife. From that moment they were 'Eric and May' to the 'lifers' whom they visited fortnightly on a Saturday morning. This became the most important fixed date in his diary. Eric and May shared this unique ministry. May became a 'Mother' figure in the prison. As a former Chaplain at Wakefield (1970-74), Brian Dodsworth (now Chaplain at Wormwood Scrubs), observes: 'May supported him in everything he did. In an all-male environment her charm and concern added a touch of humanity to an often hard and dark existence. She befriended many wives and mothers of the men inside, frequently writing to them and giving them encouragement and support. On numerous occasions she provided a meal and a bed for the night for a relative who had special problems, or had a particularly long journey to make in order to visit.'

Nothing was more important than the Love Lane ministry. The prison came first not least at Christmas and Easter when Treacy always celebrated the early Holy Communion. He told the Chaplain that it was for such men as were in prison that Christ was born. It was for men such as these Christ died, was buried and rose again.

John Trevisick comments:

'Bishop Treacy did much good by "stealth" — it is the most apposite word to use. At the last residential session of the General Synod which I attended (York in July 1975), I came upon the Bishop with his customary long strides and his wife by his side hurrying off the Campus after breakfast on the Saturday morning. "You are fed up with us and going home" I quipped. That lined, square-jawed face broke into a ready smile. "I shall be back", he replied. I knew his destination. General Synod was not going to deprive him of a regular pastoral duty 30 miles away visiting his captive flock in Wakefield Prison.'

The visits and his ministry are best remembered by people who were or are prisoners and who have responded to my request for recollections with enthusiasm — 'a way of repaying Eric'. Each of the contributors has committed murder and all were or are in prison for considerable stretches of time. Although most of them have authorised me to use their names I prefer not to do so. The Saturday morning procedure is described by A.

'Eric and May would arrive in the Main Prison at about 8am just as inmates were collecting their breakfast from the kitchens. Early morning in a prison like Wakefield is never a very inspiring sight, but Eric would stop for a moment or so in the centre of the four wings, ready to be accosted or greeted by whoever might be passing by. He knew many inmates by name even though they might never attend his "breakfasts"; to many he was affectionately known as "Bish" and would always make himself available for a few words. He would then celebrate Holy Communion, as a rule Series 3 (though he was happier with 1662 — and the Wakefield Propers as he called it) for a congregation of about 15 to 20.

'Communion was followed by breakfast, which two or three of the congregation would collect from the kitchens. Saturday morning in Wakefield Prison was mostly "goulash", a mixture of corned beef, potato and cereal baked hard in a tray. It was rum stuff really but Eric would always insist on having his ration, followed by bread and jam or marmalade. The kitchen, knowing that breakfast was being saved for the Bishop, would often try to do something a little special for him and I can remember on one occasion two pots of rather nice blackcurrant jam arriving. As might be expected, being rather attractive items they soon went missing — however the culprits missed the warning on the jam pots that too much might cause a certain amount of bowel discomfort. Eric heard the story and was greatly amused.

'Breakfast over, we would talk, often joined by other inmates who did not come to the service but would always listen to Eric. Subjects were wide and varied, often of course to do with justice or the lack of it. Eric would always encourage the less articulate to get their views over. He had at times very difficult and bitter comment from prisoners, and I do once remember him questioning whether he should continue to come — his group convinced him that he should but one was aware that he had the normal human vulnerability — and he was more valuable because of it. The real thing was that Eric, I am certain, saw his visits to the Prison not in any way as a duty but as a refreshment. He was in a very true sense one of John Donne's men, in that isolation from his fellow man, whatever his conditions, was alien to him.'

Another contributor, B, who obtained an Open University degree, offers some perceptive reflections:

'I remember Eric Treacy saying — declaring, rather — that the Christian Church might soon have to go "underground" in this country. It was, I think, a characteristic remark; at first sight extreme, but on consideration seen to be perfectly reasonable. Eric was above all a reasonable, reasoning man.

'My own reaction at the time was a strong temptation to remark that he was flattering the Church — that it really didn't pose any danger or represent anything important enough to go underground *about*.

'And this throws light on our relationship. I am a lapsed Christian with a powerful residual nostalgia for the atmosphere, the music and the language of religion. Therefore I responded to Eric chiefly for the man he was — witty, articulate, urbane at times, a public performer of great skill and relish. As one of the tiny minority of articulate prisoners, I became — in the discussion groups — his foil; by tacit convention, he basted me in many amusing exchanges and I fed him lines in order to achieve this. It was like being on stage with a really competent actor.

'But he passionately believed in what he said: that was no act — only the method of presentation. He was a conservative political animal, urging the values of the family and of tradition as a necessary stabiliser in society. His criticisms of (even working class) people who consigned Granny to an Old People's Home was violent; deeply felt, strenuously expressed without mincing words. He regarded alcoholism as one of the most serious social problems. He inveighed against selfishness — at all social levels. And so on. He expressed views without equivocation, giving the impression that he couldn't care less whom he offended, and with formidable debating resources if challenged.

'I think of Eric typically as a man always on his feet, talking, interestingly and amusingly, never superficially. Many prisoners went to his after-service discussion group for sheer entertainment (as opposed to the common motive of using the "God is good for Parole" ploy). He wore the mantle of authority lightly but obviously; he was very much a Prince of the Church, yet without a trace of arrogance. I think he enjoyed power and influence. I am confident that he never consciously misused it — and that makes him a very rare exception among competent and successful men.

'I often wondered what it was that attracted him to the prison community. The parallel with Purgatory? Or Hell? His interest seemed to go far beyond the traditional visitation of unfortunates. Did he perhaps wonder at God's inscrutable purpose in "allowing" inhuman crime? And inhuman punishment? It was obvious that he did not come in any sense of plain duty, but because he genuinely wanted to.

'How I envied their marriage! Eric and May were a living example of the Christian marriage which I had always considered a sugary myth of the Prayer Book. They walked *together* in the love of God, all the days of their lives. Now, in my book "God" is merely an alternative form of thinking — not an inferior one, provided that it is valid as a mode of life. And in Treacy's case it so obviously was valid. Consequently our differences of belief — which included the fundamental difference of opinion as to what "belief" consists of — were irrelevant. I admired and envied and drew enormous comfort from them.

'When I was transferred to another prison, Eric came to Wakefield Prison to wish me luck, and presented me with a book on Winston Churchill. It was his way, as a courageous man, of telling me that he respected what he saw as my courage in adversity.'

The prisoners regarded Treacy as a friend. He did not provide a shoulder to cry on but friendship without strings. From the many testimonies which I have received it is clear that he helped many men to believe in themselves, and thus to overcome the sense of failure that often, if not always, accompanies a long spell in prison. He gave them a dignity, a personal significance in circumstances which tended to deny them this. And Eric and May together brought grace and tenderness in a setting in which there could be crudity and brutality. He himself once wrote: 'We both say unhesitatingly that the hours we are permitted to spend behind the high walls of Love Lane are amongst the happiest of our ministry in Wakefield. We make a point of not knowing why the men we meet are in prison. We prefer to meet them as they are. I have no hesitation in saying that the Holy Communion services are deeply moving in their quiet simplicity. One feels the reality of worship as in few other places.'

Treacy had a grace which expressed itself in courtesy and made the men feel that they mattered and this helped to restore their self-respect. It was the look in his eye and an expression of voice that asked rather than demanded. Absent was his impatience and bluntness which sometimes showed with those who did not come up to his standards. Instead there was tenderness and understanding, never sloppy sentimentality, but understanding that was genuine because it was humble.

Another contributor, C, who was Chaplain's Red Band (he looked after the Chapel) writes:

'To me Eric was a true friend and I will always remain greatly indebted to him for the assistance that he gave me in so many ways. Eric was a man who upon the initial introduction struck one as a most sincere and caring person, a man of the people for the people. Eric's position as Bishop didn't affect his personality whatsoever, in others this can so often be the reverse situation. A person didn't have to agree with Eric's ideas, or even attend Church for him to take notice of you. On many occasions I have seen Eric come from the Prison Chapel and go straight to the "association" area where he would join a game of billiards or darts — in a way I suppose he was identifying himself to those concerned; they didn't have to go to Eric, he always went to them. He found the people and joined their activities. Eric would never challenge a man's reasoning, but instead would "travel the road" with that particular person, so as to tune-in and become one in thought with that person.

'Much respect was given to Eric in Wakefield Prison, and this respect was in sincerity, not a here today and gone tomorrow thing, as so often can occur in "walled cities". Eric never forgot a name, which means a good deal to a person lost in gaol. Eric gave the needed and valued acceptance to the offender; one could see that it was not his own personal gain, but for the re-building of the individual.

'Eric and May would take a personal interest in a man's welfare and wellbeing, always to ensure that the inmate had comfort of mind before leaving him. Yet upon his next visit, Eric would search the individual out to see for himself the man's wellbeing or progress.

'I vividly recall Eric coming to see me when I was employed as Hostel Cook at the Prison, to tell me that he was leaving on the morrow for his retirement residence. Very much moved, he stated that he would greatly miss his visits to the Prison and his valued association with the men, yet they would live on in his memory always. Eric Treacy was a much loved man and I know for sure of many men who will be ever grateful to him, perhaps only because he listened to them. I know I always shall.'

One contributor, D, remembers Treacy as 'a big man, warmhearted and radiating a zest for life. He believed strongly, I believe, for the Church and God, and I always came away from those Saturday breakfasts with a will to survive through the prison sentence and return to the family sane and well. Eating the prison food as he always did gave me the strength to see the food in a new light, not one of humiliation, as many did, but simply as it was, "food". I thank him. An amusing incident I remember him for was wanting May to run him up a shirt like the prison issue'.

Treacy never forgot the men at Love Lane and they did not forget him. Some of them kept in touch with him after they had served their sentences. Both he and May maintained a large correspondence with the men for the basis of their relationship was friendship. But he never imposed himself on any individual. Many men wanted to erase prison and all its memories from their minds. Accordingly once they left Wakefield Prison it was never Treacy's practice to initiate or even suggest a continuing link. One man wrote to Treacy on the eve of leaving Wakefield for a hostel and after that parole:

'I am very happy and thankful for this opportunity to make a new start in life. The main reason I have written to you is that when I realised that I would probably never see you again, I felt a tinge of sadness, as I shall miss the chats we had together. Your sincerity in everything you did impressed me very much indeed. In spite of all your titles I felt I could talk to you, and listen to you, as I would with my father. I can't pay you any greater compliment than this. I would like you to know that I will always remember with affection both you and your charming wife.

'Although I know you will spare me a thought during your prayers I thought I would remind you not to forget! As I will be thinking of you during my own, and also the many friends I have made during my stay at Wakefield, and also the other places I have been during my sentence. I must close now, so I will wish you and your wife a joyous Christmas and every happiness. I won't wish you a prosperous new year, because you will only give it away.'

Treacy's addresses at Love Lane Confirmations, which were always Christian family occasions and quite informal, were not cosy little homilies. He chose arresting texts that sometimes appeared outrageous in their audacity. 'Lord it is good to be here' and 'I was glad when they said unto me' must have puzzled even annoyed the few family visitors who were permitted to attend. The men thought differently as Treacy used the words to explore and explain the nature of God's purpose for them in prison or 'this place' as he usually called it!

The Prison Debating Society, which met under the aegis of the Education

Department each Friday evening, was an intellectually stimulating body. Chaplain Brian Dodsworth comments: 'During my time at Wakefield it was very much an on-going concern, and Eric Treacy was a frequent and highly popular debater, and always managed to take a strong team of people in with him. He delighted in choosing the most unlikely motion, and whether he was given to propose or oppose, he and his team usually managed to win the day.'

Whether in the Debating Society or on Saturday mornings Treacy could air his prejudices and ride a hobby horse or two. He wrote:

'The men are, understandably, keen readers of newspapers, and watchers of television (within the permitted hours), with the result that in our discussions, things that I have said and which have been quoted are thrown back at me and many a furious debate has followed. I have to keep my wits about me but it is all good fun. I find that there is a surprising lack of bitterness or self pity; in fact, I have more laughs in the prison than I get anywhere else.

'What impresses me most about my contacts with these chaps in prison, is the courage that they show in coming to terms with their situation — though that is not always the case. But, all the time, one is aware of the unhappiness that haunts many of them. The murderer must always carry the memory that he has killed someone; there are many serving long sentences who have been divorced by their wives; there is always the loss of freedom and personal identity — and yet, in a remarkable way, they manage to establish a personal identity in their new surroundings.'

Although Treacy's relationship was with individual men at Love Lane he formed and held some general convictions about prison life and the need for reform. He did not usually become involved in individual cases although he was often in danger of being persuaded or duped about a prisoner's innocence. One exception was the case of Michael Luvaglio who, with Dennis Stafford, was convicted of the gangland murder of Angus Sibbett, their partner in a fruit machine business at South Hetton, County Durham in 1967. A vigorous campaign was conducted by those who felt that they may have been wrongly convicted. Treacy was a co-signatory of a letter to *The Times* asking the Home Secretary to order an inquiry. Other signatories included Lords Chorley, Donaldson, Foot, Willis and Norwich, Baroness Wootton and Richard Crossman. In addition Treacy made personal representations to the Home Office and recruited other people to the cause, such as Lord Longford, whom he persuaded, if that is the appropriate word to use, to visit Wakefield. He also mentioned the case in the House of Lords (22 May 1975) but as he had failed to give notice of the individual case, no comment could be offered by the Government spokesman.

There were a few other cases where Treacy expressed a view, less on the conviction than the sentence. One such was John Poulson who was sentenced to seven years imprisonment on various corruption charges. 'Here was a man in his late sixties' he wrote (*Church Times* 15 April 1977) 'who had received his punishment before sentence was pronounced; a man in failing health; a man financially broken and never likely to repeat the offences with which he had been charged. If ever there was a case for a suspended sentence, it was this. But, no, Society must have its revenge and so to prison John Poulson goes, and there he still is, in spite of the fact that Messrs Pottinger and Dan Smith are now paroled.' John Poulson, who knew Treacy quite well, has happy memories of him 'and his friendship meant a great deal to my wife and myself'.

Treacy's one major speech in the House of Lords came during a debate on Prison Reform on 12 June 1974. He voiced his long held conviction that prisons were full of people who should not be there:

'The system is clogged by the large numbers of short-term prisoners serving sentences of a few months, so short a time that no remedial work is possible. There are drugs and drug addicts, many of them sick people [sic]. They are not criminals. There are prisoners on remand because the courts, I think sometimes for inadequate reasons, have refused bail; there are prisoners who are there because poverty has made it impossible for them to pay their fines or keep up maintenance orders ... In 1972 nearly 45,000 people were remanded on bail, yet 35% of these prisoners were not given custodial sentences, and 5% were acquitted. There is double punishment for some and injustice for a few.'

In his speech Treacy expressed concern at the psychological and moral disintegration that can occur, for:

'deprivation for long periods of the opportunity to make decisions must inevitably unfit a man on release to take his place usefully in society. And surely — I know this is an old one — the deprivation of sexual freedom is responsible for a great deal of unnatural vice in prisons as well as for tensions which can often result in violence and make the work of the prison officers infinitely more difficult. I scarcely dare say this because I may be misunderstood, but I wonder whether there is not a possibility of mixed prisons. Do not misunderstand me. I am not proposing sexual promiscuity in our prisons. I am simply saying that the presence of men and women in the same establishment would produce a more natural environment and remove some of the dangers of an enforced monastic situation.'

This was a theme to which Treacy returned in future speeches on the subject of prison reform, as he did with his advocacy of a full day's pay for a full day's work. This would make the meagre discharge grant unnecessary. 'Of course, it might be unwise to give them all their earnings at once, for obvious reasons; but I should have thought that what they had accumulated in this way might well be administered to them according to their needs. I should have thought it would be possible to stamp their insurance cards while they are in prison, thus improving their employment prospects and preserving their entitlement to social security.'

Although Treacy's contacts in Love Lane were primarily with the prisoners, his relations with the officers were far from formal. One officer regarded Treacy as 'always forthright with something to say — a big man and a man's man' whilst a former Governor of Wakefield Prison, Rundle Harris, remembers first meeting Treacy at the local Rotary Club.

'One of the first members I met was Eric Treacy and on being introduced was told rather casually "Oh! he is the Bishop of Pontefract". To me, this first meeting epitomised his character, quiet, gentle and not self-assertive, but having the underlying deep quality of friendship and all the while there was a merry twinkle in his eyes.

'He was a tower of strength to both my chaplain and to me and many matters we considered to be problems were easily disposed of when discussed with him.

'On his translation to Wakefield he became more than ever involved in our work in the prison. He frequently took services, so much so that I thought I had gained an assistant chaplain!'

The Chaplains welcomed rather than resented their bishop's regular presence on their patch. Of necessity their own pastoral work had to be exercised against the clinical background which a file provides. They saw Treacy's relationship with prisoners as being much more relaxed. Because Treacy never asked what crime a man had committed, sometimes he never knew. Hugh Reid, Chaplain from 1974-77, remembers Treacy's ministry at the prison as 'remarkable. He seemed completely at ease with the men, talking about anything and everything. He helped them to regain a sense of dignity in a wonderful way.'

Brian Dodsworth has a number of particular recollections of interest:

'A high-spot of the Church's year at Wakefield was the annual ecumenical Carol Service. With the addition of flowers, evergreens and a decorated and illuminated tree the Chapel looked particularly beautiful — in complete contrast to the landing beyond. Christmas in prison is always a lonely, depressing and upsetting time for prisoners, especially for those whose family links remained strong, and everything possible was done to make a Carol Service a joyful and special occasion. Despite the fact that I had reminded him one year to bring his cope (something he had never failed to do before) he mumbled something about "this High Church nonsense" and turned up quite unapologetically without even bringing his cassock. He said he had decided this year to sit in the congregation, and he delivered his usual short homily at the end of the service, standing in front of the congregation in a pin-striped lounge suit, and proceeded to tell the men that though he would not choose to change places with any of them, how much easier it was for them to celebrate the Festival in true Christmas spirit because they were freed entirely from the commercial aspects of Christmas which dulled the senses to what it was really all about.

'There is one incident which reminds me particularly of his unwillingness to accept the status quo. During my time at Wakefield it was agreed by the Prison Department that an Assistant Chaplain should be appointed to serve full-time at the prison. He was appointed in the usual way by a Civil Service Board, and then assigned to Wakefield for his initial training. The Bishop then received a formal and written request to issue the necessary licence. He rang me up and asked me if I was happy about the appointment. "Yes, Bishop, quite happy, thank you", I replied. "We were in College together". "Well, if you are not happy tell me, and I will get him to come and see me. I shall then say in my opinion he is quite unsuitable, and I shall refuse to licence him". On his very next visit to the prison, he raised the matter yet again. No priest in the parochial ministry expects to have an assistant imposed upon him without consultation; why, he asked, should things be any different elsewhere?

'On one occasion he joined forces — successfully — with his Roman Catholic counterpart, and a Roman Catholic Archbishop who were seeking to get the Home Office to reverse a decision it had previously made, and allow a priest, sentenced to a long term of imprisonment for supporting IRA activities, to say

Mass privately in his cell each day. Previously, the authorities had ruled that he should be permitted to keep his breviary only in order that he could say the daily offices.'

The Chaplain General of Prisons, Leslie Lloyd Rees, has a recollection:

'I first met Eric at the dedication of a new Chapel at the New Hall Detention Centre in 1968. The warmth of his greeting to me before the service made it possible for me to remind him that a commentary on the England v West German soccer international was being broadcast at the same time as the service and to suggest that the orderly officer, who had a wireless in his office, should be allowed to come into the Chapel during the service if either side scored, and to put up an appropriate number on the hymn board — top slot for England score, bottom slot for W. Germany. He readily agreed, but there was no score!

'Again I remember searching for him during the post-service cup of tea, thinking that I had some obligation to look after him — only to find that the adolescent trainees were doing it for me and enjoying it. How easily they related to him and how difficult it was to get him away from them!

'In subsequent years he was always keen to meet groups of Chaplains who came for courses to the Prison Service College at Wakefield and poured love over us. I used to say about his regular Saturday morning visits to the Prison for Holy Communion, breakfast and the discussion group that the Gatekeeper didn't quite know whether to give him a key or a number!'

It was neither key nor number that the prisoners presented in April 1974 but two portraits. On 6 April two men stepped forward as Treacy finished the Saturday morning celebration of Holy Communion and handed him a portrait of himself superimposed on a map of the Wakefield Diocese. Another portrait was for May, showing her against a map of Cheshire, the county of her birth. They were presented with love. The word is appropriate for *love* described the kernel of the ministry of Eric and May in the Lane of that name.

19
Railway Bishop

A railwayman with a suitable thick coating of coal dust and sweat on his face carried the bags of a lady along the platform. She thanked the 'porter' and tipped him a shilling, little knowing that the money had been placed in the palm of the Railway Bishop, who had been footplating.

The lively and rewarding interest in railways that Treacy enjoyed was in part personal, in part mechanical and in part artistic. Basically, the explanation is that he liked railwaymen with their strong community spirit and loyalty and a certain steadiness which the Age of Steam had produced. As steam became a sign and a symbol of the past so it fulfilled in different people very different desires. Treacy much preferred living steam to simulated smoke and he was patron and promoter of all efforts to preserve lines and engines. The wild life artist and owner of the East Somerset Railway at Cranmore, near Shepton Mallet, David Shepherd, recalls the exhibition of steam engines at Shildon. He took his engine *Green Knight* which, after an adventurous journey, arrived late and there was no time to clean it. It was placed next to *Nigel Gresley*. 'Eric Treacy walked straight past his beloved A4 to the *Green Knight*. There it was — filthy, dirty and muddy alongside the spick, span and polished other engines. Eric beamed "Ah! a *working* engine".'

By the time Treacy was nationally known as the Railway Bishop a whole industry, of which he was a founding father, had developed around the subject of his chief leisure pursuit. He remained as active as ever in photographing engines, always seeking perfection, never content to let the camera take control.

There were a growing number of occasions requiring the presence of the Railway Bishop. Of course he was known as a 'soft touch' for he rarely, if ever, said 'No' to a steam invitation, or any other for that matter. He refers to one such event:

3 February 1968. Great fun this afternoon. Gerard Fiennes (ex-Manager, Eastern Region, BR) and I named a steam locomotive *Matthew Murray* in the Middleton Railway Yards near Hunslet, Leeds. I named it *Matthew* and he named it *Murray*, after which we pulled a string so violently that we not only revealed the nameplate but very nearly pulled the engine over on top of us. We then mounted the footplate, and I drove the engine like the "Titfield Thunderbolt" down some fairly rough track towards a brick wall. We were romping happily along, making some 10mph, when I realised, I didn't know where the steam brake was. Visions of Bishop charging through brick wall into the thick of the Leeds traffic! However with seconds to spare I found it, and gave it all I had got with the result that we came to a standstill in our own length, nearly throwing Gerry Fiennes off the footplate. We did two or three runs for the benefit of photographers and tape-recordists, and left *Matthew Murray* gently simmering in the January sunshine. A very good time had by all!'

Something dramatic and drastic had been happening to the railways since Treacy's interest in them began in the prewar years. 1963 was the year of Christine Keeler and Dr Beeching, the one offering the other withdrawing services. Beeching was in the unusual position of being both Tsar and Commissar. Beeching proposed and Beeching disposed! Hindsight proves the disaster that foresight should have envisaged. Before Beeching the railways of the country comprised 51,000 miles of track, 63,000 bridges, 1,050 tunnels, 9,600 signalboxes, 270,000 miles of telephone wires and 532,000 telephone poles.

Perhaps the railways were like the churches, taken for granted. It is good to know they are there, even if they are not used. The *Annual Register* 1963, referring to the Beeching axe, observed 'The outcry from a nation of train lovers (and car owners) was hysterical. All of a sudden, it seemed, everyone had something to lose.'

Treacy had always regretted that the railways were pawns in a political game. He thought they should be a social service more than a commercial proposition but, realistically, appreciated that a national transport plan was necessary which would include road, rail and canals. He despaired of the Beeching proposals and predicted, 'I think the future will see a return to railway development under a rationalised transport plan,' a sensible sentiment on which action is still awaited!

In 1969 Brian Hollingsworth, a British Rail official, and Geoffrey Drury, an electronics engineer, bought No 45428 (now No 5428) Stanier 'Black Five' 135 tons engine, which had been built for the LMS in 1937. When it was purchased only one other 'Black Five' was to be preserved and that only to be stuffed. Brian Hollingsworth writes: 'Locos should be named and No 5428's ancestors had been the GWR 'Saints' — this gave the ecclesiastical connection. I also wanted to honour a man who had made our hobby respectable — the doyen of the corps of ferroequinologists. So we suggested *Bishop of Wakefield*. Eric Treacy objected that there were several of them living, could we use his name instead? And so it was.'

On 3 May 1969 the Bishop of Birmingham, Leonard Wilson, 'a bearded Bradshaw' who collected and studied railway timetables, was with Treacy at Tyseley Locomotive Depot, Birmingham. There Leonard Wilson unveiled the nameplate — *Eric Treacy* — and smashed a ceremonial bottle of champagne across a piston rod. Then the two bishops climbed into the cab of the locomotive and went off along the track in a baptism of steam. No 5428 *Eric Treacy* is now with the North Yorkshire Moors Railway. When Treacy drove the engine on the six-mile section between Grosmont and Goathland one of the passengers was part-owner Geoffrey Drury who commented 'He handled the train like an expert. There wasn't a jerk.'

There has always been an extraordinary addiction on the part of parsons to the steam engine. They join that underworld of steam enthusiasts which includes admirals and generals, dons and headmasters, organists and artists, office and factory workers and not a few women. Parsons attempting to travel incognito are as easily spotted as an A1, the last of the LNER Pacifics. On more than one occasion, in spite of a dirty disguise, Treacy was identified, much to his chagrin. One clergyman, who laboured in an unresponsive parish, made a daily pilgrimage to watch the 'Flying Scotsman' thundering through his parish, and when asked to explain his daily vigil, oblivious of the irony, said 'It's so wonderful to see something going like hell that hasn't got to be pushed.' It is easy to understand something of the release that he experienced by watching 500 tons rocketing so effortlessly.

All forms of transport, bar one, interested Treacy. The exception was trams — 'horrible things — thank goodness they are no more'. He was delighted when they disappeared, although he was tempted to have a requiem run on the last one!

Travelling at speed, driving his own car, was a joy even if the pleasure was not always shared by his passengers. He talked himself out of more than one speeding offence but his luck did not always hold. During one holiday he was caught for speeding whilst travelling from Keswick to take a Sunday morning service. When the Summons arrived he stormed in Diocesan Secretary, C. B. Beverley's room at Church House: 'I'll get a Solicitor.' Beverley (known to all as 'Bev') in the guise of concurring friend, suggested that it might be simpler, even wiser, to write a letter apologising, using such lubricating language as might be appropriate by way of mitigation. Treacy calmed down and took the advice but when he was fined £5 he said he was going to write asking for time to pay by instalments of five shillings a week. Fortunately Bev succeeded in drawing the attention of his boss to the limitless possibilities of newspaper headlines!

However nervous of speed a passenger might feel it was better than having Treacy as passenger. Again Bev recalls driving Treacy to the Lake District at the time when the M6 was under construction. 'It's open, it's open, go down there!' exhorted Treacy. Bev had a contrary view but as episcopal exhortations should be obeyed, he did so. The motorway was quiet — in fact they had it to themselves. After travelling for two miles down the lone highway, like royalty searching for red tape to cut, it became unquestionably clear that their trespass should be terminated forthwith. The road they needed was only one hundred yards away but not ahead! Before Bev had time to consider Treacy's further advice they drove up a bank, Treacy dashed out of the car to open a gate, they drove across a field and on to the main road!

To return to the Railway Bishop. His frequent journeys to London from Wakefield were enjoyed for their own sake. His natural gift of lifting the spirits of everyone around him was transparently present on these occasions. The whole of Wakefield Westgate seemed to come alive. He had a good friend in the car park attendant where banter was always exchanged, but often the conversation was on serious topics of the day. Once at and past the ticket office it was riveting repartee and friendliness. Albert Nurse, a former Diocesan Secretary, writes: 'Recently the catering Authority of British Rail decided to add a bar licensed to sell liquor to their refreshment room at Westgate. The staff there in their affection for the Bishop suggested that the new Bar be named "The Dr Treacy Bar". This would never have done, because as is well known the Bishop was a strict teetotaller! This suggestion was vetoed just in time.'

Treacy spent time on both official and unofficial business on Westgate station. Bev well remembers his early days in the Diocese when Treacy said 'Come on, I'll take you out to lunch.' It was like the Chairman of the Board taking the Company Secretary out for a slap up meal. There was one slight difference. Treacy took Bev to the station buffet for a pork pie. On expenses too!

Treacy enjoyed being encapsulated for two hours twenty minutes on the Inter-City breakfast train from Wakefield Westgate to Kings Cross for, as he wrote:

'I am totally cut off from the world outside, committed for better or worse to my fellow passengers and in the considerate hands of the best dining car crew on British Rail [although his first and best love had been the Yorkshire Pullman]. A lot of rude things are said about British Rail, but in one respect they achieve a triumph, and that is their breakfast, even if it is expensive. Although I am normally a small breakfast eater, on the train I make a pig of myself. It only happens occasionally so I am not in danger of gorging myself to death.'

There are as many different varieties of rail enthusiasts as of products claimed by Heinz. They did not all appeal to Treacy. He sometimes found it difficult to understand those whose passionate interest was in branch lines that were to be closed — the sort of people who converged in huge numbers on the last train to run on a particular track. Here the lunatic fringe foregathered to place a wreath round the engine's chimney, put detonators on the line and seize such mementoes as would stick to their fingers.

However, Treacy was always attracted to and by the enthusiasts who took over lines, developments which he followed very closely in the late 1950s and early 1960s. His patronage and support were solicited from railway preservation societies throughout the country. He usually obliged but warned against the irresponsible enthusiasm and soft headed sentimentality that surrounded the matter of locomotives and branch line preservation. His regular contact with British Rail officials and drivers kept him alert and alive to the anxieties of many professional railwaymen who were expecting a pile up on a preserved railway line. He gave a stern warning during the course of his Presidential Address to the Keighley & Worth Valley Railway on 9 November 1974:

'We are in business and are carrying fare paying passengers, and this puts upon us a very heavy responsibility. We have been going now for 10 years. The novelty has worn off and I foresee the danger that slackness will set in. Members will tend to do and go where they like, rather than where they are needed. They will tend to be rebellious when they are given instructions. After all — this is understandable, as many of them come long distances after a week's work.

'But I am bound to say, there are dangers in this attitude. I will be quite frank; I have noticed a good deal of larking about in the yard at Haworth and a lot of shouting and yelling — only high spirits, but remember that amongst those prowling around the yard are often professional railwaymen with a critical eye. Not only that — the public will not be impressed by this kind of thing. They will get the impression that we are playing at it.

'I do not need to remind you that the smallest degree of slackness could lead to a serious accident. After all, we are maintaining motive power, rolling stock and track 'part time' as against the professionals who have fitters and maintenance men on hand, day and night. This calls for a very high standard of thoroughness and concentration and no risk can be taken.

'I am also wondering about footplate discipline. I hold the view that the driver is in total and unquestioned command of his footplate — who goes on it, and what happens on it. I suspect that there is a good deal of unauthorised footplate travel, and much of it without the signing of indemnities.

'I say these things because I care about the railway and I want it to be the best in Britain. I believe it is, and I want to keep it that way.'

It was a great day for them when Treacy, as its President, approached the Director of the Science Museum in London 'to give sympathetic consideration to the possibility of the locomotive *Evening Star* being loaned to the KWVR until it takes its place in the National Railway Museum at York.

'Our line has clearance for locomotive running from the British Railways Board; the northern terminus is in fact part of Keighley Station. We have been entrusted with the care of 2-6-0 locomotive No 2700 (known as a "Crab"). '

When an affirmative reply was received on 10 April 1971 Treacy was so excited that he telephoned the home of Brian Baker, Chairman of KWVR, the minute the letter arrived, quite forgetting that it was very early in the morning.

Brian Baker thinks that Treacy, with his railway interests, 'did more for the image of the Church than other bishops'. It went deeper than a question of 'image'. One senior railway official says 'Encounters with Bishop Treacy reaffirmed my belief in God'. A railway worker comments 'I started going to Church after I met Bishop Treacy. I thought there must be something in it'. Birmingham business man and a patron of steam railways Patrick Whitehouse writes 'Such was his friendship and power of communication that to me he seemed God's Man as well as a Man of God'. He also recalls Treacy going as guest of honour 'to a small but high powered dining club with railway interests. He forgot to bring his dog collar but remembered his purple stock. Accepting the challenge as usual he manufactured one out of a huge handkerchief and we pinned it up at the back for him. I don't think anyone noticed'.

Naturally the Railway Bishop was asked to take a prominent part in the 150th Anniversary celebrations of the Stockton & Darlington Railway. There was a televised service on 17 August 1975 held at Bank Top Station. W. H. Auden's *Night Mail* was read, as was Canon Roger Lloyd's (a friend of Treacy's) *Driver Gimbert GC*, and *The Iron Road* was sung. Treacy gave the address from a locomotive tender. It was enlivened by the fact that all his notes fell out of the 'pulpit' just after he had gone into action. The situation was saved by the organist 'getting the blower on' and giving an encore to the previous hymn whilst Treacy picked up the scattered paper!

There was another service of thanksgiving at St John's Shildon, on 24 August at which, again, Treacy preached. The accompanying exhibition was a paradise for steam lovers. Treacy revelled in it and wrote:

'What a gathering of that curious underworld that thrives in Britain — the railway enthusiasts. David Shepherd, with his engine *Green Knight*; Michael Satow keeping a watchful eye on the replica of Stephenson's *Locomotion No 1* in whose building he played such a prominent part. The Reverend William Awdry, the originator of "Tommy the Tank Engine", disguised in soft collar and tie, but deceiving no one; Kenneth More, the Actor, bringing a touch of ebullient glamour to the proceedings; Derek Cross and Dick Blenkinsop hopping with joy at so much to photograph with the sun behaving itself. John, the Prince Bishop of Durham, and his family, making everything respectable, obviously enjoying themselves.

'As we say in Yorkshire "it were a reet do".

'Then about mid-day the marshalling of the Cavalcade begins. One by one, the engines are called out of the Yard and take their places in the procession. And this is veritably a photographers' joy as they move out at a snail's pace, breathing sulphurously through their chimneys. First out is *Locomotion No 1* followed by Engines red, green, blue and black.

'The crowd moves off towards the stands. Then there opens a fantastic vista; people on the hillsides, in the fields, up trees, zooming around in light aircraft — here was testimony to the magnetic attraction of Steam. There was even one television crew sending pictures live to Japan. I estimate that there were 300,000 people lining the route. A vast congregation to watch 34 steam locomotives puffing away at 5mph.

'Promptly at 14.00 hours *Locomotion No 1* led off to the cheers of the crowd. The BR crews in charge of the engines were obviously enjoying their "finest hour" (and entered happily into the spirit of the occasion). Perhaps the loveliest sight of all was Stanier's Pacific No 6201 *Princess Elizabeth*, of all locomotives the most elegant. I realise that in the world of railway enthusiasm it is dangerous to express a preference, but honesty compels me to give *Princess Elizabeth* the accolade.

'And what an inspiration to arrange for *Sir Nigel Gresley* to tow Stirling's No 1 with its 8-foot driving wheel. But what a pity that the headboard on *Flying Scotsman* should bear the words "McEwen's Brewery".

'So, throughout the afternoon, under a cloudless sky, this great Cavalcade went its way, the climax of years of planning. A sight never to be seen again; a thing of beauty to be remembered for ever. The procession ended with the new High Speed Train, which had a certain sinuous beauty of its own; the first and last time that it will make a journey at 5mph.

'By 16.00 hours, the crowd was dispersing, the party was over. The Yards at Shildon Works looked sadly empty, except for *Locomotion No 1* which stood cooling off after its afternoon's exertions, seeking sanctuary for the night.'

Treacy and his wife left to finish their holiday 'having met a lot of very nice people, and renewed a number of old friendships, and, as was fitting on the Lord's Day, attending Evensong in the beautiful Parish Church of Staindrop, but a few miles from Shildon. Verily, we had much for which to be grateful.'

Derek Cross remembers meeting Treacy on the fire escape to the offices at the Shildon Cavalcade in an effort to get above the crowds:

'This fire escape was not in its first youth and definitely swayed about somewhat However, having got an excellent vantage point we prepared to take our pictures and repel boarders should anyone else try to get in on the act. At this juncture the rotund figure of the Rev Teddy Boston started up the stairs and Eric said "Well there are two things I can do. Either "pull rank" and order him off as his ecclesiastical superior, or take a chance that with our combined weights this thing doesn't collapse — still, even if it does I probably have a hot line to heaven".'

This was a safe vantage point compared with some Treacy chose.

Anyone with any sense who was embarking on a railway photographic project discussed it with Treacy. Requests for photographs came from all over Europe Authors and photographers would call to see him and be allowed to help themselves from his massive collection of slides and photographs. He was always willing to read manuscripts, make constructive criticisms and write forewords. He did this in addition to producing further books of his own.

'Putting himself at the disposal' of other people was a deeply embedded trait of character. He was always happy to encourage young steam enthusiasts. Kenneth Preston recalls an occasion at Keighley when his 12-year old steam keen son discovered the Rector of Keighley was the Eric Treacy of steam fame. ' "Has he a friend who is also interested?" (he has) there and then, although he was very fully occupied, he whipped out his diary and said, "Look here, if you will let me come here some evening I will give these two a railway quiz. Let's fix it up now." It was booked; some days later, along he came, and gave two hero worshipping boys a series of questions and rewarded correct answers with photographs of engines he had himself taken.'

Treacy remained the railwayman's friend. Harry Greenwood, now Honorary Secretary of the British Rail Retired Staff Association (Leeds), but once District Signalman's Inspector, recounts 'one incident which I feel typifies the Bishop, took place at Leeds City Junction. In walking by the signalbox I observed a figure seated on the top of the signalbox steps "supping" a cup of tea from a galvanised mug. Yes, it was Bishop Treacy, who had gladly accepted the signalman's hospitality, partaking of refreshment spontaneously offered (and accepted), the action of a true gentleman, action that endeared him to all with whom he came into contact.'

Treacy was 'our most popular guest' at Staff Association meetings at many places. He was not only a friend of the men but of their families. They involved him in their family affairs, their joys and sorrows. When a travelling ticket inspector retired, there was Treacy to say 'thank you' to him on behalf of the travelling public. When a death took place amongst the railway fraternity, there was the Railway Bishop to comfort the bereaved and to give them Christian hope.

There was something both ordinary and extraordinary about Treacy that gave him charisma, that made him a life-enhancer. He sat down and munched his sandwiches on a railway embankment with other enthusiasts. It was simply a natural act. There was more too. John Belwood (Chief Mechanical Engineer, National Railway Museum at York) says 'If we knew he was coming to the Museum the atmosphere throughout the place changed, from the cleaners to the Keeper. A feeling of happiness, gaiety and expectancy were in the air. He was not a back slapper. He had real presence. We all felt better for seeing him again.' Treacy was particularly pleased when the Minister for Arts, Lord Donaldson, wrote to him in March 1978 inviting him to serve as the Secretary of State's nominee on the Council of the recently established Friends of the National Railway Museum. There is to be a permanent exhibition of Treacy's railway photographs at the Museum.

Treacy continued photographing even though the opportunities for steam engine photographs were rare. He photographed diesels but felt 'life' lacking in them. They did not excite his imagination. He was not complaining for, as he wrote, 'I feel gratitude that I have been permitted so much pleasure in the years that are past. Something has been; something has gone. For me, a chapter was closed. Thus let it end. Complete and wonderful in itself, we shall never see the like of the steam engine again. So, for me, no substitute joys are to be found in the new machines. Let me be faithful to my memories, and live with them.'

20
Man on the Beat

Treacy's final words as Bishop of Wakefield were 'This is OUR Church. Thank God for it. Trust it. Love it. Serve it and pray for it.' (Wakefield Cathedral, 31 October 1976).

He often referred to 'my love affair with the Church of England' and intended writing a book about 'That beloved and blessed mystery which gave me my faith, sustained me within that faith and entrusted me with a ministry which has given me the richest life that any man can expect'.

It is improbable that Treacy could have realised his vocation in any other Church. He was proud — and it showed — to be part of the most curious and chaotically comprehensive Church in Christendom. And the Church of England was — and is — a Church of which to be proud on many counts. No other Christian body in the world so consistently has tried to unite tradition and progress, authority and freedom, to bring from its treasures things new and old. For this, the Church has paid a heavy price in misunderstanding and misjudgement, in party dissension and sectional animosities, in the doubts of its friends and the sneers of its foes, for the loyalty with which it has pursued its ideal of comprehensiveness. I quote Treacy's own words from some of his Notes as much for the further unintentional self-portraiture as for their clear view of his conviction:

'The Church of England, like the British Constitution, has just developed, with remarkable resilience adapting herself to the winds of change; with a certain cunning meeting the onslaughts of Reformers and Rebels with a sweet reasonableness that has disarmed them, and blunted their weapons.

'The Church of England is a compound of the illogical English character, the untidiness of human nature, the unpredictability of the Holy Spirit, the contradictions of a mongrel nation — the aspirations of men and women who are at heart unconscious Pelagians.

'It is the expression of the non-conforming instinct of the British; it is the home of the eccentric — a mixture of cunning, laziness and peasant simplicity. It is a place of snobbery, and sometimes pomposity, with a delightful homeliness. It contains within itself the tensions which are a source of vitality. It is strong where the critic thinks it to be weak; and weak where it thinks itself to be strong.

'Maddening, yet beloved — most maddening to the planners — disobedient to all rational predictions, confounding those who prophesy inevitable disaster. Absorbent — yet impregnable. A weird and wonderful mystery, but above all, the spiritual home of the English people.

'The Ethos of the Church of England has eluded many who tried to analyse and dissect her. Many there have been who have come to look into her with pre-suppositions of their own — and so accommodating is Mother Church, that she has given them what they were looking for — yet, she has not revealed her true self. She has deceived them. She is accused of Erastianism because of the Establishment; she is accused of being schizophrenic because she does not know whether she is Catholic or Protestant.

'She is ill disciplined; her Bishops are too blue blooded, and too many of them live under the stigma of having been at Public Schools; her organisation is obsolete.

'Much of this may be true, but thank God, she is not the dull monochrome concentration camp with episcopal gauleiters that some planning geniuses would like her to be. The Church of England is the only place in which you can find the richness of the Catholic Religion combined with intellectual liberty.'

This may appear to be a romantic view but at heart Treacy was a romantic. To him the Church of England was the Church of the English people, the National Church, and not a sect. Moreover he liked the Church as it was and not as he saw it developing during the 1960s and 1970s. He made sympathetic noises towards the revised services, new versions of the Bible and the 'relevance' school of thought. There were those who claimed to have his support for such reforms. His successor as Vicar of Halifax, A. G. Hardie, is nearer the mark when he observes: 'I think he found it hard to come to terms with a good deal of modern thought and practice but his deep-rooted faith in the Church of England and his devotion to His Lord was unmistakeable and immovable.'

The new translations of the Bible did not appeal to him. He went so far as to say that the vanishing Authorised and Revised Versions were 'an immeasurable loss to the British way of life'. When the New English Bible made its debut he reviewed its performance in the *Halifax Courier* and admitted that the language was more easily intelligible. 'Yet it is a matter of opinion whether the average person would wish to hear the Scriptures in common-or-garden English. ... Is there not a danger in over-rating intelligibility? There are some things that ought to challenge our capacity to understand things that are not easy to understand. There are some things which ought not to be made too obvious lest they cease to provoke the mental effort to dig out the deep truths which are at first hidden from our understanding.'

As for the Book of Common Prayer, he had told his Halifax parishioners: 'I am convinced that the reform of our Prayer Book Services must engage the attention of the Church. However beautiful they are to us who have grown up with them, they are but meaningless repetition to the vast majority of English people today. Our worship must meet the deep spiritual hunger of people who, through no fault of their own, have grown up outside the Church, even if it means a good deal of sacrifice on the part of those who prefer things to stay as they are.'

Those were words to stir up the slumbering faithful rather than a reflection of his own views, for he regarded the Book of Common Prayer as part of the national heritage. Nevertheless he was not of the 'over my dead body' protagonists who do not see the irony of what they say — because the refusal to accept any change can indeed mean death. Writing in the *Diocesan News* (April 1975) he pointed out that attitudes to forms of service were governed by one's understanding of worship:

'If we look upon it as something which is *only* withdrawal from the world, a shutting out of the turmoil, conflict, tensions, sordidness, suffering, injustice and general beastliness, then it is understandable that we will not mind, nay, rather want, forms of worship that do not relate to modern forms of expression. We shall want something "other" and different. In a spiritual sense we shall be wanting "to get away from it all". We shall feel it right that the language of our worship shall not be contemporary, and that it shall segregate God from the human scene and emphasise His "outsideness". To me this suggests that He is not involved in the "nuts and bolts" of daily life . . . But worship must surely be penetration into the world.'

Whilst having a personal preference for the Book of Common Prayer and using the 1928 Prayer Book for his daily Offices, he accepted that some of the services should be revised, notably the hatching and despatching ends of life. What he thought ripe and right for revision in the Baptism and Burial Services did not extend to Morning and Evening Prayer or to a running series of Holy Communion services.

More than the words and ceremonial, he was concerned that worship should be at once dignified and homely. After all, worship should have a family atmosphere about it. The combination is not easy to achieve, but with perseverance it can be achieved.

One Sunday, whilst on holiday, he sampled three different services and records his impressions of them:

'First to a Parish Communion in a High Church in which the parson intoned both Epistle and Gospel so that both were quite inaudible. What is wrong with the spoken word in Church? Then to an Evangelical Church for Matins; a good service but a bit "chummy" — in the evening to a small Mission Church in the hills, where the service was taken by a Lay Reader and the sermon preached by an elderly retired clergyman. This was far and away the best service of the day. The congregation was small, about 25, but we all knew each other and there was a wonderful feeling of the family at prayer.'

After re-reading H. Hensley Henson's *Things which my soul hateth* he was prompted to observe privately:

'Amongst his (Hensley Henson's) hates are sham flowers under glass globes in churchyards; the allocation of Sundays to special objects with topical sermons; the smoking of (sic) clergymen in the streets. With all those I find myself in complete sympathy. I am tempted to draw up my own list of "Pet Hates". They are:

'1. Those who cannot bother to kneel to pray in Church, but assume the: "Protestant Crouch".

2. Notices that become sermonettes. Always noticeable when the Vicar is not preaching!

3. Extra prayers after the Blessing. The Blessing is the end of the service.

4. Small children brought up to the altar rail to be blessed at the administration of the Sacrament.

5. Smoking in vestries.

6. Intoning the Gospel at the Eucharist.

7. Choirs who think their purpose in coming to Church is to sing rather than to worship.

8. The irritating habit of extinguishing the altar candles after the third collect.

9. Churchwardens to whom counting the collection is so important that the visiting preacher is not even given a civil greeting — and who may find his bag deposited on the floor, so that the counting can have pride of the place.

10. People who pointedly pick up a hymn book and who start to read it, with apparent concentration, just as one starts to preach.'

In a Church which allows many varieties of dress Treacy had many near scrapes with his own dignity. Mr B. R. Hewitt recalls one occasion at St John the Divine, Rastrick:

'Bishop Eric had discovered that he hadn't his sermon notes, so asked me if we were "processing right round the Church". It was duly arranged that upon reaching the back of the Church one Warden would hold the Crook and the other open the door while the Bishop nipped out to his car, conveniently placed just outside, at that point. He soon reappeared waving his sermon, whispered to Mrs Treacy, who was sitting near the back "forgot my sermon, dear", and proceeded on his way. When I congratulated him on his speed, after the service, he said "You don't know the half lad!" He went on to explain that he saw his notes on the back seat of the car, unlocked the front door to open the back one, picked up the notes, locked the back door, locked the front door, found he had shut his cope in the back door, unlocked the front, unlocked the back, withdrew the cope, locked the back door, locked the front, set off to come into Church only to find he couldn't because his cope had caught round the car bumper.'

Of the outward trappings of worship and episcopal haberdashery Treacy had little interest and less knowledge. But Wakefield was known to be a High Church Diocese, so smells and bells were familiar to nose and ear. As Archdeacon of Halifax he had been largely protected from the vesture and gesture brigade. Later, as Bishop Suffragan of Pontefract he was often to be seen but dimly through clouds of incense. Milton Lindley, now retired but then a leading Anglo-Catholic in the Diocese and a priest for whom Treacy had both affection and respect, writes:

'Shortly after Eric Treacy was made Bishop of Pontefract, John Ramsbotham the then Diocesan rang me up (I was then Vicar of South Kirkby). He said that Eric was having to go to Mirfield Commemoration Day to Pontificate at the Community High Mass in the morning of that day, because John himself could not be there. He told me that Eric was very nervous about it all because he hadn't a clue as to what he was expected to do. Therefore could I help?

'I rang Eric up and asked him if he would like to come to South Kirkby one Sunday morning, and I would put on a High Mass exactly as he would find it done at Mirfield on Commem Day. He fixed a date and agreed to preach. We put on everything which was then normal for a Pontifical High Mass, and I remember being very pleased with my team of servers, and the two curates who acted as deacons for the bishop. The music was well and heartily done too. Eric preached about Unity, and thought himself in duty bound to warn my people against bigotry and intolerance! He didn't know then that we had excellent relationships with the only opposition we had in South Kirkby, namely a struggling group of Methodists, whom my people took close to their hearts and with whom they cooperated willingly and frequently.

'After the Mass was over we all trooped over to the parish hall for a parish breakfast. There were about a couple of hundred folk there, mostly miners and their families. They talked freely to him and he was very obviously taken with them.'

The Community of the Resurrection at Mirfield, known as the Mirfield Fathers, had indeed frightened him at first. Writing to Hugh Bishop (a former Superior of the Community) in 1977 he referred to the three Superiors he had known: 'I must confess that I was terrified of Raymond Raynes — that I found Jonathan Graham an icicle — but in you I found a warmth and love which was very precious.' There was another Religious Community in the Diocese. The Nuns of the Community of St Peter, Horbury, meant more to Treacy as time went on and they regarded him as 'our beloved Bishop'.

Whatever Treacy's personal inclinations and private thoughts were about some of the activities in which he was asked to indulge, he rarely let them surface. He was bishop to all. A Halifax lady, Dorothy Holdsworth, writes:

'My daughter tells a tale of him. I always kissed his ring when I met him. She says that if she saw him first at a function he would say "Is your mother here" and if she said yes his reply was "I must polish up my ring ready for her", and proceeded to rub it on his cassock. We always made a great joke of this, but I always got a blessing! He always promised me that he would bless my new house when I moved and that he would preach at my Requiem. He did the first, but it never occurred to me that he would pre-decease me — I being 84. When he came to bless the house (with May) he gave me a card with the following words: "Be always joyful. Pray continually and give thanks whatever happens". This I think is typical of the man — it was the way he lived his life and he wanted to show it to everyone he met.'

As a bishop Treacy was perfectly happy to fall in with local liturgical habits. He once asked Canon J. C. K. Brumpton, Rector of Barnsley, if he thought he was fair to the Catholics in the Deanery: 'I was able to reply without any hesitation — "Yes, you are". Indeed after the ceremonial simplifications which arrived with the liturgical renewal in the Church, he was doing much more genuflecting than we were.' Nevertheless Treacy's outwardly all-embracing style did not mean that he did not often wince inwardly at liturgical fussiness and the ju-jitsu antics of some servers. It seemed some distance from the simple meal of fellowship in the Upper Room instituted by Christ. He remembered an incident at Liverpool Parish Church when he had carelessly placed a maniple (a liturgical vestment) on the wrong arm. One lady said to him afterwards: 'Father — you quite spoiled my mass by having the maniple on the wrong arm'. He notes 'I have never forgotten that — for it so reveals the dangerous obsession with non-essentials which can infect our worship — that the Lord's own service for its proper celebration depends upon a piece of coloured brocade being placed on one arm rather than the other.'

Whatever he had to endure, he was quite determined to embrace all traditions to the full and to be bishop to everyone in the parishes. In November 1974 he wrote in the *Diocesan News*:

'I testify to my enduring conviction that the greatest glory of the Church of England is the parochial system. There is not one corner of England that is not in some parish; there is not one soul who cannot claim the ministration of an Anglican priest. How glorious an opportunity, privilege and responsibility this is. There are many who hold that the parochial system has had its day, but I testify to my own gratitude for it and my own faith in it as something given by God.

'Basically, what is a parish? In its simplest terms, it is an area marked on a map, its boundaries determined by law. In that area, the incumbent has responsibility for the cure of souls for everyone, except those who contract out because they belong to another Christian body. The incumbent is there to care for them in sickness and in health, at the beginning of their lives and at the end of their lives. He is THEIR man and they HIS people, whether they are Christians or not.'

Treacy's claims for the parish and parochial clergymen knew no bounds. In an article in *The Times* (14 December 1974) he stated:

'No body of men is contributing more to the stability and moral foundations of the nation than the parochial clergy. ... It is the man on the beat who matters. The parson going about his work day by day in his parish is the man on whom the Church depends. ... thousands of parochial clergy carry on quietly, saying their prayers, visiting the sick, burying the dead, consoling the bereaved, absolving the penitents, comforting the troubled, raising the money to keep their parishes going, meeting increased demands for the church outside their parishes. Preparing young couples for marriage, teaching in their church schools, writing their parish magazines, preparing their sermons; sometimes stoking the church boiler, cutting the church-yard grass, acting as vergers, and dealing with the multitude of casuals who knock on the vicarage door.'

It is little wonder that he could hammer home the truth that the strength of the Church is in its parishes. He added, 'In the midst of all this, they must sustain that life of the spirit which is the authentication of their ministry'.

We have seen how Treacy vigorously attacked those theologians and radical reformers of machinery who disturbed or hindered, as he saw it, the work of the parochial clergy. When *The Remaking of Christian Doctrine* by Maurice Wiles (Regius Professor of Divinity at Oxford) was published in 1974 he rushed in where cautious men feared to tread. His critics would have said where 'wiser' men feared to tread. Writing as 'nobbut but a working Bishop in an industrial Diocese' in his *Diocesan News* for October 1974, he accused the Regius Professor of cutting the ground from under the feet of faithful clergy and laity by claiming:

'There are serious doubts about the theological and historical evidence for the divinity of Jesus Christ. He argues that the Doctrine of the unique Incarnation of God in Jesus Christ is not required for the whole pattern of Christian belief to be true, or, indeed, for our having good grounds for believing it to be true.

'Are we ordinary Christians who accept the faith of the Creeds, a set of misguided fools? Have we been deceiving ourselves all our lives?

'From millions of Christians the answer will be a resounding "No". In this faith we live, and sustained by this faith, we shall die. We adduce the truth of our experience. In faith, we have accepted it, and in practice we have found it to be true.'

The Regius Professor of Divinity at the other place, Cambridge, Geoffrey Lampe:

'Regretted very much that as a bishop Eric Treacy allowed himself to write or speak in public about theological controversies without seeking advice from those who could have explained to him what the real questions at issue were, and why they were important and deserved serious discussion. Here, I think, it was his loyalty to the C of E and its traditions as he understood them, and also his pastoral concern, misdirected into a desire to prevent what he saw as ordinary commonsense folk from being upset, and to reassure them if he thought they had been, which made him loose off in an impetuous and unthinking way against theologians, whom he didn't understand. I don't think he really wanted to put himself in that position of being a spokesman for the ignorant and prejudiced. After one of his outbursts in print I thought it my duty to write to him and persuade him to invite Prof Maurice Wiles, the object of his attack, to come and discuss his ideas with Wakefield clergy. He was very willing to arrange this, and the visit took place. I think it did some good at the time, but Eric was not temperamentally suited to the business of trying patiently to understand people who, from his own point of view, were sabotaging the real task of evangelism and pastoral care.'

Maurice Wiles indeed visited Wakefield for a day and met a number of clergy, including Treacy who was engagingly charming, admitting that whilst disagreeing with some of the Professor's statements he thought he might have been hasty in condemning him. Maurice Wiles makes an interesting observation on Treacy's theological position on which he was asked by me to comment. 'What struck me on that occasion [the Wakefield visit] was a lack of subtlety of mind. He appeared to be a man with a few firm but basic convictions which gave shape to a very practical faith, but who had neither the inclination nor the kind of mind that could readily combine that position with questioning or modifying the accepted form of those convictions in the sort of way that modern scholarship seems to call for. But all that is based on very little acquaintance.'

Treacy never learned this kind of lesson. When a book of essays, *The Myth of God Incarnate*, was published he fired a salvo from retirement which landed in *Church Times* (5 August 1977). He admitted that he had not read the book, only about it, but it did not stop him from flailing the message of the contributors to the book of essays. It was a message which hurt him as he believed it would hurt his Lord and the Church. He adopted his usual approach of a guise within a guise. 'I write as a simple chap, a bit weak in theology; but there are millions like me, and thank goodness, rather fewer who seem to enjoy theological disputation.' He was stating an obvious fact. He was speaking for the mass of ordinary churchgoers and his reception was the greater, his communicating thrust the deeper because in truth he was ordinary. There was no other bishop quite like him. People were not only grateful for his words but also helped by them. Many ordinary people are thoughtful people too and his 'fan' mail came from many such quarters. Bishop George Clarkson wrote to him at the time of *The Remaking of Christian Doctrine* controversy: 'You know me as one who is apt to stint praise — but I can't help telling you how deeply moved and grateful I am for your *Diocesan News*. It is high time for the plain speaking you use about our basic beliefs and I pray that under Donald [Coggan of Canterbury] and Stuart [Blanch of York] we may get much more of it. Our folk are worried and bewildered by what seems to them to be a frightened uncertainty in the minds of our leaders that they may be charged with unfashionableness. So more power to your elbow.' It was enough that Treacy was continually putting fresh heart into clergy and laity who increasingly thanked God for him.

It is easy to see why Treacy gave such support to his parochial clergy. Even so, the steady drift of clergy into specialist ministries, whole-time teaching and the like did not by-pass the Wakefield Diocese although there was no question of extending specialist ministries in the Diocese. Some clergy who left the parochial ministry saying they could better exercise their ministry outside the institutional framework of the Church irritated Treacy. His suspicion was that many were leaving the parochial ministry for less respectable reasons than those to which they would admit. There were those who had found it far tougher than they thought it would be, and the diminished standing of the clergyman in the community had demanded a spiritual depth and energetic response that they were not able to give. The clerical collar was something to be discarded and the streets of the parish were exchanged for school corridors and the Burnham Scale. He admitted being bitter about some of the defectors — for that is how he regarded them — and wrote 'I am tired of these folk who produce impressive reasons for deserting the front line'.

If the front line was the parish there was no greater event in it than the Institution of a new incumbent. Here he was at his happiest best. The Service and the 'do' afterwards were inseparable.

'When I heard that he had died, I wept. I find it hard still to believe that he will never come into a room with his lovely smile — or was it a mischievous grin? — and that I shall never feel his hand on my shoulder again. He was a Prince among men, and showed you what a priceless thing it is to be a priest.' So writes David Young (now Rector of Patrington in the Diocese of York), just one of the many priests whom Treacy Instituted to take charge of a parish. When he spoke the words 'Receive the cure of souls which is both thine and mine' they knew he meant it, for he knew and loved his men and his and their parishes. It had been so from the time that he was Archdeacon of Halifax. Sidney Righton recalls his induction into Linthwaite in November 1950 when Treacy had been Archdeacon for only a short time. 'It was a very windy night. As we moved over from the Vicarage to the Church he said "You'll know you are Vicar here when you have been wrapped round that steeple a few times in the winter gales." How right he was! I was once solemnly walking in front of the coffin in a funeral procession, and was lifted bodily in my heavy cape over a "table" tombstone beside the Church porch and deposited five yards away — so strong was the wind. He knew the circumstances of his parishes intimately.'

Some clergy never failed to be surprised, occasionally alarmed, at how much he knew about their parishes and their problems. He was a welcome visitor to parochial meetings although his presence usually indicated a problem. After a visit to one parish which was in a sad way financially he noted:

'So sad that its chief source of income is a bingo session every Monday evening. The Vicar clearly thinks that there is no future for the parish, and the church should be declared redundant. He is suffering from an overdose of William Temple College Sociology! Equally clearly, the parish think they have a future and vigorously resist any suggestion that they are redundant. My sympathies are with the parish. But it is difficult to tell the Vicar to get cracking in the presence of his parishioners. One tough Yorkshireman took a colossal swipe at the Vicar, accusing him of laziness and not visiting his flock. When I told him that I had not come to listen to public attacks on the incumbent, he stumped out of the meeting muttering darkly to himself — this showing that Yorkshiremen can give it, but can't take it.'

Treacy looked for 'normality' in would-be priests. He became an advocate of the whole business of the selection of candidates for ordination returning to the bishop. As he wrote in *Church Times* (2 June 1977): 'I believe this to be a solemn and sacred responsibility, and one which the bishop should, in normal circumstances retain to himself. It is not something which, for administrative convenience, should be delegated to a central body as is the case at present.' He wanted selection conferences at diocesan level and thought men could be trained in a better way than being immersed in theological colleges. His views were provocative but he was not the person to organise a definite movement by recruiting like-minded bishops (and there were some) to obtain what he desired.

Donald Aldred, formerly of the Wakefield Diocese and now Vicar of Burley in Wharfedale in neighbouring Bradford Diocese, remembers:

'My first real meeting with Eric Treacy was one Saturday evening when he gave me an appointment at his Vicarage in Halifax because my Vicar had told him I wanted to be ordained. I remember the weekend appointment because the "working long hours" image of Eric Treacy was coming across to me, although I had at first thought it unusual that an appointment which I had expected to take place in the day was fixed for an evening. I remember feeling very much at ease quickly with him — he had this gift I always thought — and he had just asked me why I wanted to be ordained when his 'phone in the hall rang. Quickly, he said something like "Now you've got a minute or two to think about your answer before you have to tell me", and when he returned and I said "I find it hard to put it into words" he said "Most of us do, so I suppose those two minutes have been an agony for you deciding what to say to me". I remember the interview concluding with him saying he thought I had a vocation and would write to the Bishop of Wakefield [Roger Wilson] informing him accordingly. He added "this means you should be sent to a CACTM selection course because this Bishop usually accepts my recommendations which is a bit different than when I was Rector of Keighley and used to advise Bishop Blunt of Bradford. He seemed to be a law to himself inasmuch as the ones I recommended he would sometimes have nothing to do with, whereas the ones I suggested turning down he'd often go straight ahead and ordain!"'

Many correspondents have remarked that Treacy had a 'nose' for a good man. Like everyone he had his blind spots but even then he usually managed accurately to predict the future for a man. After interviewing one candidate he noted:

'Why is that I am so put off by young men who effect side-whiskers? Does this untidy growth of hair denote virility? Is it thought to be attractive to the other sex? Surely, it must indicate some degree of vanity. This young man had a carefully groomed growth of hair down the side of his face and enormous self-confidence. I found it difficult to get a word in. I was not impressed by him. I could see him in a few years' time as a typical little altar priest laying down the law to the congregation. Nevertheless, when he goes to a Selection Conference, I am pretty sure that they will recommend him for training. I would give a lot to meet an ordination candidate who was a normal, healthy and not-too-intense young man. It is long since I did.'

Fortunately Treacy was later to meet and hand-pick many such men during his Wakefield episcopate.

For Treacy pastoral care meant loving. The loving was sustained by his prayers for his clergy. He brought imagination and foresight as well as humility to his prayer desk. Above all he was possessed of that instinct which enabled him to be there when he was needed. For any bishop there is a time for anger and a time for gentleness, a time to see and a time not to see, a time to speak and a time to keep silent, a time to break and a time to mend. Despite an overfull diary he was ruthless in shedding anything that prevented him from ministering this care. He so mastered time that he always had time for his clergy, the men on their beats. An unexpected knock on the door of a vicarage would bring Treacy just when he was needed. He listened, considered and then bishop and incumbent would pray. He had the capacity to be wounded by what wounded them.

So busy — yet always available. What greater hurt could any bishop suffer than to be told by a priest in a difficult time that he had not troubled him because he thought he would be too busy to listen to him? It could never have happened to Treacy. As the Bishop of Carlisle [David Halsey] said at Treacy's funeral service, 'Some said he should have left more to others. Whether that is true or not, one thing is certain, that even if the names of his clergy were not always properly entered on the card index, they were inscribed on his heart and in his prayers together with the man's wife and family. Eric was a big man in every sense of the word, with a heart that never exhausted its capacity for love, and living, and caring and serving.'

Many was the time when he would get back to Bishop's Lodge late at night after an evening service or function to find a pile of telephone messages. Instinct told him which could wait and which needed immediate attention however late the hour. A telephone call would be made and without further ado he was off again to see one of his clergy, returning in the early hours of the morning. The people of the Diocese may have guessed but they did not see the frequently and utterly emotionally drained and physically exhausted Treacy asleep in his car on returning to Bishop's Lodge, too tired to get out of it.

The impact and effect of Treacy on his clergy are best considered briefly by taking one or two examples from an avalanche of reflections. One clergyman writes: 'During a period of considerable strain within parish life here, the Bishop appeared unannounced one afternoon, sat himself down in the arm chair and said "Well, how are you? You're looking tired". I would expect someone had advised him about our situation and I greatly appreciated his prayerful interest out of the blue. This was the first time in eleven years' ministry in three dioceses that any bishop had shown such pastoral concern.'

Sometimes an overworked priest — and Treacy knew which of his men were working as he worked — did not so much need counsel on taking life more slowly but a practical solution administered by the episcopal boot. Two days after meeting one of his exhausted clergy at a meeting, that priest received a letter: 'Here is the £100 I promised you for a holiday. Please get away as soon as you can for a rest, and ring me up as soon as you get back, so that we can meet for a talk. I hope that you are feeling a bit better now. You coped splendidly on Saturday evening at our ecumenical "do".' On another occasion Treacy stood over a priest and his wife whilst they packed their belongings for a much needed break at his expense.

Treacy's pastoral concern for his clergy showed itself from the Halifax period onwards. Bishop Forbes Horan (former Bishop Suffragan) was vicar of Huddersfield when Treacy was at Halifax and remembers him as:

'A man who really *did* care for people. He never spared himself if he could be of help to someone going through a "bad" time.

'I remember how constantly I used to look out of my study window and see Eric coming up the path and at once my troubles seemed to lighten. "Ah! Eric will know the answer to this one!" And he always did, for he seemed to be able to grasp the important part of the problem and his advice was always practical and often amusing.

'How can one describe this to someone who didn't know him? I don't know, but what I do know is that he constantly made me feel less of a failure than I probably was and certainly more able to cope.'

Not all clergy, unlike lay people, found him easy of approach. Canon Frank White observes:

'One aspect of Eric Treacy's ministry which should not be overlooked was that some of his clergy were afraid of him. This is not a matter of opinion, nor is it a generalisation; I have in mind several men whose confidences I enjoyed. Eric was physically a formidable figure, large in frame and sometimes florid in countenance with a very direct manner of speech (sometimes extremely direct!) all of which seemed to some of the quieter brethren to be forbidding and overwhelming. They therefore tended to shrink away from him. Another result was that such men did not care to make the first approach when they needed his help. It is not surprising that he himself had great difficulty in understanding the situation even when one or two friends pointed it out. Not unnaturally he knew of the loving heart and immense goodwill which motivated all his dealings and he found it hard to understand that they were cloaked from some of those whom he most wished to help. Yet it was so.'

This can be explained only by understanding Treacy's mingled character. To say he could be prelatical is to risk censure from his dearest admirers. But it was there in the respect and dignity of the Office of Bishop. One former priest of the Diocese, Maurice Turner, who admired Treacy, explains it in this way:

'He was one of the dying race of Prince-Bishops. He could be autocratic and self-confident and swift of decision and action. He could give you a fishy-look if you seemed to oppose him. But he was a passionate champion and protector of the parish system. Eric could humble his clergy but he also fought for them. He had been a parish priest himself and so supported his under-shepherds. This, in a decade when Episcopacy and Incumbency were undergoing traumatic change following Synodical Government, Morley Report etc. Eric is the epitome of the changes — an erosion of traditional roles.
    'Eric was "ancient and modern" — a traditionalist but also astonishingly daring and contemporary. He knew what his clergy were going through. He could be fiercely "jealous" of his Episcopal status and authority ... He could treat you like one in warmth of friendship and understanding and ability to listen, but also make you feel very small at times. He was clearly aware of faults and motivations in himself as well as others and frequently showed humility in that awareness.'

'For me there will only be one bishop' says one of his clergy who has served a number. Such words have been repeated in countless ways in the contributions which I have received. They loved their bishop: their father-in-God loved them. A letter Treacy received in retirement expressed sentiments shared by many: 'You have been such a wonderful pastor, Eric, the sort of pastor any decent priest longs to be but seldom succeeds in being, as you have done.'
    There were other aspects of Treacy's episcopal ministry which drained his spiritual, mental and physical energy and must have hastened the heart attacks which clouded his last years. He was taken through many a vale of misery which he had to use for a well.

21
Compassion Unlimited

A priest — and a bishop is still a priest — is like other men. A priest is not as other men! Both statements are true. How could it be otherwise? He is one who hates sin but loves sinners, who can see what a man might be rather than what he is. This was the way that Jesus dealt with His disciples. It is the way of the priest. Before he can see beyond the bland or troubled exteriors of other people he should see himself as he really is, as Christ sees him. Priests who know others but not themselves are using their priesthood as an escape or as a means of self assurance. For Treacy the priesthood was the servant of the person and not the person the servant of the priesthood.

When a man is chosen to be a bishop it is, or should be, as much for what he is as for what he has done. The verdict of history shows that high office can have a dual effect upon its holder. It may enable or disable. It is never an unmixed blessing. The person should not decrease as the entry in Crockford increases.

The combination of vulnerability and confidence in Treacy made him the most human of bishops. Canon T. S. Wetherall comments: 'The most striking thing about him was his transparent honesty about his own opinions and feelings. I felt I knew where I was with him, and would always trust him to have nothing up his sleeve — unlike many bishops for whom secretiveness is an occupational hazard since they hear so many confidences.' But his straight-forwardness in revealing his mind — and his weaknesses, for he never tried to escape responsibility for past blunders — could be itself a mask. He once told a group of Keighley Young Conservatives, 'Frankness is not only right — but it is good tactics.'

Words Treacy used at the funeral of one of his clergy, taken from a memorial stone in a Macclesfield church yard, fit him completely and perhaps lead us towards an explanation of the enigma and tension within him. 'A man of granite with the heart of a child.' Although people who knew him well or who saw him in action at close quarters remember him in quite different ways this combination of qualities surfaces. One priest writes: 'I think he saw himself as an ecclesiastical Montgomery making masterful decisions. But when the decision involved, eg closing down a parish, he had a streak of sentimentality which sometimes stopped him carrying them out.'

'A man of granite with the heart of a child' was evident in his pastoral relationships. His character could be read by looking at his eyes. They were always alive, sometimes challenging but always sympathetic. Those people who knew him over a long period of years were privileged to witness the growth of a soul. His ecclesiastical career was the triumph of sheer character. His character had been shaped by the circumstances of his life. His life was committed to Christ and the service of His Church. *Gravitas* had come. His inner resources seemed greater than before, his spiritual wells deeper. One of his episcopal neighbours was the scholarly John Moorman, Bishop of Ripon 1959-75, who offers a random thought: 'He was humble and a little lacking in self confidence. He would say: "Of course I'm the last person who ought to speak on this subject, but . . ." and then he would say something sensible and useful . . . I always found him shrewd and judicious; and once told him that, if I were in a real difficulty, I would seek his advice before that of any other bishop or archbishop. He was surprised at my saying this, but I meant it.' In fact, Treacy's confidential counsel was increasingly sought by his peers and his superiors.

There were those for whom he was responsible too! More than most bishops of his time Treacy was called upon to 'Hold up the weak, heal the sick, bind up the broken, bring again the outcasts, seek the lost'.

Clergy are no less prone to pressures and problems than lay people. A bishop has to spend a portion of his time rebuking clergy for minor offences or trends such as spending too much time in the pub, foolish but not sinful associations with women in the parish, and laziness in pastoral duty. If such matters are allowed to go by default, they may be the beginning of the downward slide to more serious things. Sometimes a bishop's duty is more painful. Treacy records one example:

'A most difficult interview with one of the clergy. He is a dear, kind chap but totally incapable of making decisions or facing problems. He is priest in charge of a parish which is in a state of collapse. The only thing I can do is to ask him for his resignation from the parish. This, I hate doing, because, in spite of his incompetence, he is such a nice chap. Yet to leave him there, is to do him more damage than he will do to the parish. There is no doubt that once these Yorkshire parishes get their teeth into a man they keep them there. They are not given to making allowances. The one thing that they will not tolerate is weakness — stubbornness they can understand, as they can be bullied by their vicar — but weakness, no.'

There were cases where the incumbent went quietly if not swiftly. There were other 'encumbrances' who 'sat it out' in their freehold, defiant but lonely. Other occasions there were when Treacy could not bring himself to wield the axe or produce a stick or even rebuke harshly. Sometimes cases came before the secular courts.

The Diocese of Wakefield was suffering grievously from what can only be described as an outbreak of *practising* promiscuous homosexuality. Many a priest was saved from prosecution only by Treacy's intervention. On more than one occasion as Bishop of Pontefract he refused to institute a known homosexual priest to a living. There was a good deal of meaning in the words of a senior prelate who wrote to Treacy, on his accession to Wakefield: 'The task ahead of you is not an easy one, but God will give you grace in the bringing of order and sanity of churchmanship and newness of life where it is greatly needed.' Treacy commented ruefully to a friend after a number of court cases, 'Sometimes I think I have inherited a cesspool rather than a diocese.'

An article written in retirement for *Church Times* (4 March 1977) entitled *Pity the odd men out* attracted a good deal of attention. In it he wrote:

'As a diocesan bishop I frequently had to deal with personal problems arising from this issue [homosexuality]. There were some which were disgraceful and inexcusable, which seriously damaged the Body of Christ, and which laid upon me the responsibility of depriving a priest of his orders. There were cases which certainly qualified for the label of corruption.

'I must make my position clear. I have no time for those who flaunt their homosexuality; I have no time for Gay Liberation. My experience is that the Christian with homosexual tendencies is the last person to flaunt them.

'I am concerned about the discrimination which is directed against homosexuals. In so many ways they are made to feel outcasts. The Church to which they belong seeks neither to understand their problem nor to speak in their defence. It manages to make them feel that they constitute a problem it would rather be without. And I do not believe that this would be the way of our Lord in dealing with them.

'I believe that Jesus is as likely to call to the priesthood a man with homosexual tendencies as men who would seek satisfaction in marriage ... Whatever the man's emotional balances he is called to faithful marriage or faithful chastity. A priest with homosexual leanings must no more give way to physical expression of them than an unmarried heterosexual priest should practice fornication.

'Let these few lines of mine persuade people to get this matter in proportion; to rid themselves of prejudice; to recognise that no man chooses to be homosexual; to do all they can to cure the loneliness felt by men who have this cross to bear; and to recognise the tremendous contribution made to the life of the Church down the centuries by those who have been homosexually inclined. I am sure that a study of genius would reveal a very real relationship between homosexuality and genius.

'Personally I would not hesitate to accept a man for ordination who admitted homosexual tendencies. To refuse such a man would be tantamount to saying that this was a situation beyond the redeeming love of God to overcome. If I believed the man's vocation to be genuine, I should hesitate to contradict the calling of God.'

Treacy was probably led to write in this vein because homosexual clergy he knew 'are amongst the finest priests I know. I would even say that they were better priests for being homosexual. It is a curious thing which I don't pretend to understand, but the male homosexual has a tenderness, an imaginative sympathy, that others don't have'.

At a Requiem Eucharist at Wakefield Cathedral on 18 May 1978 the Provost, John Lister, spoke of what he discerned as a change in Treacy: 'He never ceased to learn; perhaps this was why he never ceased to astonish us ... When he was a younger man, he found moral lapses hard to understand; yet during his episcopate clergy involved in sexual troubles found in him true love and compassion; and one priest at least who tried twice to commit suicide came round on each occasion to find him sitting by his bedside.'

Treacy's retirement reflections were more than generous in view of the agonising problems homosexual clergy had given him. Furthermore, he appeared more liberal in his outlook than was in fact the case. He wrote privately: 'There is a real problem about accepting a man who is homosexual as an Ordination Candidate. There is in such a man the possibility of a moral lapse later in his ministry. The nature of his work often places intolerable temptations in his way.

At times of stress and loneliness, there is danger of a lapse with the most serious consequences for the Church.'

For Treacy the most depressing cases were those where priests had perhaps themselves been corrupted as children or youths and, later in life, during a difficult time, committed some homosexual act not with a child but with an adult. Of one such case from his Halifax years Treacy observed: 'He (the accused priest) told me the whole story. It started with some wretch who introduced him to buggery when he was a youngster at school . . . Is any punishment too severe for the sort of man who interferes with youngsters and starts them off on the path of unnatural affection? That wretched man should be standing in the dock, not X. Some blame too attaches to parents who fail to warn their youngsters of this kind of thing.'

On the question of homosexual offences involving the corruption of young boys Treacy inclined 'to the view of Dr Cyril Garbett that such men never change, and that what they have done once, they will do again. Bishops not only have a responsibility for their clergy, but for the whole people of God, and they are not justified in allowing their compassion to put other people at risk.'

Adult homosexual relationships, that were within the law, presented Treacy and his fellow bishops with a greater difficulty. Sharing his thoughts with his fellow bishops he wondered:

'What our attitude should be to such relationships where there is a continuing fidelity between two male friends who have set up house together. I do not think that we have any right to suggest that there is anything sinful about it. People must have companionship and we cannot expect them to live in isolation, but where there is homosexual promiscuity resulting in the frequent change of partners, we are bound to take notice and to make it clear that we cannot tolerate scandal. As indeed we would where there was promiscuity in heterosexual relationships. There has, of course, been a great change in people's attitudes to homosexuals, but the Church cannot take the view that openly homosexual relationships do not matter. They do, and they need to be handled with sympathy, but with firmness. We have to face the fact that in working class areas such relationships are still thought to be scandalous.'

At his consecration a bishop is asked 'to be to the flock of Christ a shepherd, not a wolf' and to 'so minister discipline, that you forget not mercy'.

Treacy must have stood in more witness boxes than any other bishop speaking up for his clergy — and for some lay people too. Whatever he might have said to them in private by way of counsel and admonition, 'on the day' there he was testifying on behalf of his men speaking only of the good they had done. When a priest was convicted and had to leave the parish Treacy always referred to him when instituting his successor, in such terms as 'I wish to say a word of recognition for the ministry that AB exercised here. Let it not be forgotten that he was the means of helping a lot of people to a deeper understanding of the Faith and its practice. We remember him tonight and shall continue to pray that he be given courage for the years ahead.'

Treacy's loving pastoral heart sometimes clouded his judgement. He was too quick to speak for people in the witness box. Police officers began to feel that he was letting them down in certain cases for his was the testimony that could often, but not always, lead to an acquittal in a case which seemed 'open and shut'. After the acquittal of one man Treacy later discovered evidence of the person's obvious guilt and admitted to the police during one of his informal visits to the Academy, 'I was conned'.

Priests in financial difficulties were helped times without number. How he helped them — how he was let down by them! Few cases of this nature came before the Courts, but if and when they did, there was Treacy to help and to reassemble the broken pieces afterwards. Meanwhile if a priest were imprisoned there were his wife and family to consider. The parson's freehold has no advantage when a wife or a widow has to leave the house relatively quickly. When a burden could properly be shared, Treacy involved the Diocesan family. On one occasion he circulated a note to clergy saying 'that if there are any people in your parish who feel moved to help Mrs A., I am prepared to receive their offerings, and to administer them on behalf of Mrs A. and her children'.

Much of this might be described as a bishop going about his normal work. There was a difference, however, in view of the number of problems that caught the attention of the press and made headline news. This added an agonising dimension to Treacy's problems, as he was having to minister in the glare of surrounding publicity.

When in 1974 the Superior of the Community of the Resurrection, Hugh Bishop, resigned his office and was subsequently released from his vows, leaving the Mirfield Fathers after 34 years, Treacy was deeply saddened. Hugh Bishop was widely respected in the Church of England — a colourful figure with a sense of the dramatic. He caused a great deal of distress to many people when he appeared in a BBC television programme *Anno Domini* on 1 December 1974 freely admitting his increasing agnosticism and the need for a close human relationship with someone with whom he could share everything. Hugh Bishop now writes:

'If Eric Treacy was not a great man, he was an exceedingly good man — which I guess is nearer to the Gospel. He was one of the kindest and most generous people I have ever known. He was always unsparing of himself but especially if anyone was in any trouble. I have known of clergy who had got themselves into trouble whom he dealt with with seemingly inexhaustible compassion and patience though never, I think, with sentimentality or weakness.

'I certainly did not share all his opinions — he was unashamedly and consistently, sometimes courageously "square" — but that didn't make the least difference to our relationship or to our attitude to each other. He had much too great a respect for the individual and much too much humility for him ever to dismiss anybody or to presume any sort of infallibility for his own opinions.

'When I asked to be released from the Community and left Mirfield I don't doubt that it was a shock to him and he had no natural sympathy with, or perhaps even understanding of, the reasons which led me to make that request but he certainly never doubted my integrity or faltered in his friendship. Loyalty was, of course, one of his characteristics and he was the most loyal of friends to me. Even when I put him in a very difficult position through ill-judged remarks made off the cuff in a TV programme after I left Mirfield, which I greatly wish now had never been transmitted, he remained unfailingly loyal to me though he must have been under considerable pressure to dissociate himself from me. But there were no complaints and not a flicker of change in his attitude to me. I owe a great debt to him, probably greater than I know.'

In fact the decision to allow the broadcast was only taken after a bishop's wife had seen the programme *before* transmission and thought that, on the whole, it was best to go ahead with it. Treacy knew only too well, from his own experience, that television is a dangerous and tricky business for the cameras do not help one to make careful and balanced statements.

Hugh Bishop was right on all counts. Treacy was pressed to remove Hugh Bishop's licence for the Wakefield Diocese when he left the Community but this he would not do. He may have been hurt by the Hugh Bishop affair but it brought no breach between the two Christians and their friendship continued until the end.

There was one event during Treacy's episcopate which rocked much more than the Diocese and the Church of England. On 5-6 October 1974 an all-night exorcism was performed in the choir vestry of St Thomas' Church, Gawber, near Barnsley. The Vicar, Peter Vincent, and a Methodist Minister, Raymond Smith, their wives and two laymen, Donald James and John Eggins were present. The subject of the exorcism was one Michael Taylor who almost immediately afterwards murdered his wife Christine in a most horrifying way. Her eyes and her tongue were pulled out and death was due to the inhalation of blood from her facial injuries. Michael Taylor claimed that forces beyond him were responsible for his actions and associated the killing with the events of and leading up to the exorcism. There is no doubt that at the time of the murder Michael Taylor was suffering a catathynic crisis, a state of deep hypnotic trance.

At the murder trial at Leeds Crown Court, Harry Ognall QC, quite correctly indulged in an attack on those people connected with the exorcism, and the general tenor of the observations of the trial judge and Mr Ognall were such that they considered the moral responsibility for the death of Christine Taylor lay with those who sought to exorcise evil spirits from Michael Taylor. Accordingly the Wakefield Coroner, Philip Gill, thought it right and proper to open a fresh inquest, which took place from 21 to 23 April 1975. Treacy instructed solicitors to represent Peter and Sally Vincent at the Inquest.

We are not here concerned with any details of this shocking case but with the extravagances of the Charismatic Movement and exorcism, and Treacy's attitude to each. The two are linked. The Barnsley case had its roots in a Charismatic group with which Michael and Christine Taylor had become involved.

The growth of the Charismatic movement within the churches has been sudden and swift. Hitherto, Pentecostalism had existed outside the established churches and was more often an hysterical harangue than a body of believers. However, it caught the minds and hearts of many people in the churches, not least of some priests of the Anglican and Roman Churches and ministers of Nonconformist churches. The outward sign of the movement was joy, even ecstasy in worship and the gift of tongues. It was regarded as a movement of renewal and could not be disregarded in view of the quality and standing of some of its leading adherents. They stressed that Charismatic renewal had a real place within church life and was not in its essence 'separatist'. Such could be taken in at a superficial glance. In reality the Charismatic Movement has been and is in this writer's opinion, divisive, delusory and dangerous. Its fellowship meetings, 'come togethers' or whatever name they trade under, are essentially gatherings where emotion is whipped up and reason is cast aside. In a contrived atmosphere of emotion and excitement the babble of voices is enough to extinguish rather than to release the Spirit: not the silent waiting upon God for the Charismatic, but an artificial forcing of His Spirit.

The reports reaching Treacy of the effect of the Charismatic Movement within his diocese suggested it to be elitist and separatist. Earlier his anxiety about its effect in and upon the parishes had caused him to despatch his Suffragan Bishop of Pontefract, Richard Hare, to one of the renewal meetings, to 'keep an eye on things' and to report back. Testimonies are part of the staple diet of such gatherings. Often the confessional nature of the testimonies is such as to make those associated with the Billy Graham era seem like formal speeches on a particularly dull day at a convention of accountants. Sacramental confession, voluntary and specific, is equally natural and salutary. Charismatic confession in an hypnotically charged atmosphere of 'praising the Lord' does not so much set people free as enslave them. It is difficult to harness their allegiance to the Church and there is little evidence to suggest that they are moved to greater care and compassion in the community. Never mind what the movement affirms, what does it reveal? 'By their fruits ye shall know them'.

Returning to the meeting attended by Richard Hare, a fellow spectator comments: 'At the end the Bishop was asked to say a word. He said "This is not my cup of tea" and mentioned his own worries about the possible divisive influence of the movement — very much the Bishop Treacy line. Within a year Bishop Hare was up to his neck in it.' As indeed he was, much to Treacy's distress, and he is now regarded as its leading episcopal light in the Councils of the Church of England.

It has to be said that Treacy did not understand the Charismatics. Although he had an evangelical faith of enthusiasm and joy it was not effusively emotional and did not rely on frequent and obvious revelations of the Spirit. He always thought it a very great pity that services of healing and laying on of hands, in which he believed, had become entangled with and extended by Charismatics. Nevertheless he held out a pastoral hand to the Charismatics in a blessing and with affection. This was particularly evident at a Swanwick Conference of all his clergy in 1975. Writing to 'my friends in the Charismatic Movement' *(Wakefield Diocesan News* 1975) he concluded:

'1. Remember that you have not a monopoly of the Holy Spirit, and that the Holy Spirit comes to whom He wills and in different ways.

2. Do not ride too lightly to the discipline of the Church to which you owe loyalty. Sometimes discipline may seem to be cramping, but it codifies the corporate mind of generations of Christians.

3. Beware of forcing the Spirit.

4. Remember that there are dangers in the movement. Face them and exercise that care which will enable you to test the spirit.'

One can be attracted by the fervour of a Movement whilst being repelled by its assurance. Many Charismatics are a holy huddle, harmless in their eccentricities that are more noticeable for their spark than their flame. Unfortunately the movement has attracted the morbid and the neurotic, the inadequate and the wild goat — often people in greater need of psychiatric care than the suffocating embrace of the Charismatics. This is recognised by many of its thoughtful adherents such as Richard Hare, who see the dangers as well as the liberating tendencies of the movement. Alas, in too many cases and parishes the Charismatics who claim to have the Baptism of the Spirit are devisive because they are arrogant or appear to be so. Their way is the only way. Arrogance is hardly the true mark of the sinner that repents and is saved.

The ministry of healing and deliverance, of casting out evil spirits from people who have become possessed, is part of the Charismatic ministry. The Diocese of Wakefield must have been surprisingly full of evil spirits and demons, judging from the amount of exorcising that was being carried out all over the Diocese, almost all of it without Treacy's knowledge or consent. Wakefield does not appear to have been unique judging by the revelations in other dioceses following the Barnsley exorcism. It was a scandalous state of affairs. In 1972 a commission convened by the then Bishop of Exeter (Robert Mortimer) and having both Roman Catholic and Anglican members, had made two sensible recommendations for the regulation of exorcisms: no exorcism should take place until the possibility of mental or physical illness had been excluded and 'a thorough investigation had been made of the patient in terms of spiritual values', and that no exorcism should take place without the explicit permission of the bishop. Neither recommendation had been put into general effect.

On 2 April 1975 Treacy released a press statement stating that he had instructed his clergy that all excorcisms should cease, at least until he had the Report of a Diocesan Commission which he had urgently set up to review all aspects of Exorcism: its relationship to the Charismatic Movement; its relation to psychiatric medicine, and the field of mental health. Meanwhile he accepted what his priest, Peter Vincent, had been trying to do in the Barnsley case and though saying he was misguided, did not judge him to have done anything which would justify removing him from or asking him to resign his benefice. It was another case of his overflowing pastoral heart overriding what the episcopal head knew ought to be done.

When the Diocesan Commission reported, Treacy accepted its recommendations — the chief of which was that 'No formal rite or service purporting to deliver a person or place from evil possession or demonic attack is permitted in the Diocese of Wakefield, unless expressly authorised by the Bishop of Wakefield himself, or his Commissary, whose consent must be sought on every individual occasion'. A set prayer preceded by a reading from the Bible and followed by the Lord's Prayer and the Blessing was specified for use in an emergency.

The debate throughout the Church triggered off by the Barnsley case continued for months. That there is place for exorcism within the Christian Church can be shown to be right. That special training should be given to priests to exercise this ministry was as obvious as it had been lacking.

In dealing with the problems which beset him on every side Treacy showed a remarkable robustness. He had the ability to stand shocks and not to be put off balance by the unexpected. His breaking point had to be beyond that of the people he led. His pastoral work was backed by prayer. He saw prayer less as waiting upon God as breaking into the presence of God. Because he did not find praying natural or easy he persevered all the more with prayers. The fruits of perseverance showed. People in sore distress very soon realised that Treacy was not like an oil lamp, self consuming, but like an electric bulb drawing on a source of power outside itself. After all, a priest can only give to others what he has found for himself. And giving to others was what Treacy did until the day he died.

22

Our Bishop

A clergyman was invited to a big dinner by a very well-known person in the business world, who was also a Baptist. 'Who is the main speaker', he asked. 'Our Bishop, of course' was the Baptist's reply.

The doorman and domestic staff of a London club which included many bishops among its members always looked forward to a visit from 'Our Bishop' and, once, when Treacy was ill, asked another Diocesan Bishop how 'Our Bishop' was getting on!

Provost Spafford of Newcastle tells of:

'An old choirman who died after many years' service at his Church in the Wakefield Diocese, and his widow (a Congregationalist) desired to give to the Church a substantial memorial. In the end she provided two new lavatories with all mod-cons in the choir vestry. The day drew near for the dedication of this gift, which we did with all solemnity. Her one wish was the Bishop might do the deed but unhappily he was unable to be there. However, the old lady, who found great difficulty in speaking any sentence on the subject without prolonged tears, telephoned me and begged that as the Bishop could not be at the Service please would I make sure that he was — sob, sob, — the sob, sob, — first — sob, sob — to use them. Needless to say I enjoyed passing on the request.

'The fact that this meant so much to the old lady is illustrative of the way in which he captivated the hearts of so many. She had only met him once briefly and her husband had been there as well. That was enough for her to feel that only he could do the deed rightly. In this case it was an old lady but the Bishop's appeal was to young and old and I think rather more to men than to women. — People found in him a man of God who was also one of them, not perhaps as common a situation as one might like to find.'

'Our Bishop' was also 'our friend' to thousands — yes thousands — of people who had perhaps met him only once and then perhaps fleetingly. Following a visit to a Deaf Institute a deaf child said of Treacy 'He does not make me feel different Mummy'. 'No Bishop had ever visited me *because I'm me*' wrote a lady 'until Bishop Treacy called unexpectedly one day. He did not want anything, he was not filling in time, he came to see me.'

W. G. Gibson, Vicar of Sowerby, refers to the relationship of Bishop and incumbent:

'An "ordinary" relationship that was itself a wonderfully warm one. I have always loved St Peter's Church (a fine Georgian building) and done all I could to help the congregation to maintain it, repair it, clean it, cherish it. Sometimes the Bishop and Mrs Treacy would visit it — just to look at it, and sit in it — to "soak" in its peace, and enjoy its beauty. Their joy — shown on their faces — was all the thanks I ever needed from them . . . I was very ill, at one time, and after an operation in Halifax, was taken to Cookridge Hospital for further treatment. During this period the Bishop visited me, and laid hands upon me with prayer for me. I remember well how remarkable was the fact that I experienced as much sense of spiritual *power* from the Bishop's hands laid upon me — as the sense of physical power produced by receiving the Deep X-Ray Treatment, as one is laid under those high machines. In no way was this sense of power self-induced. I am spiritually experienced enough to realise that often the Sacraments come to us with no kind of emotional or physical experience whatsoever — except obviously — the *taste* of bread and wine, or the *touch* of a person's hand. But in this — there was real power throbbing through all my senses.'

When Treacy walked into a room it glowed. He had presence, it was more than that too. One of his Wakefield clergy, Ken Cove, now Vicar of Ambleside, recalls going to see Treacy when he was offered the parish of Appleby. 'Our concern was having spent all my ministry in industrial areas of the Wakefield Diocese; *would we be happy* as a family in a country area. Eric replied, "My dears, you take it with you". How simple! How true!' It was certainly true of Treacy.

Treacy's sense of fun and vigour as well as sensible forthrightness cheered many an individual and revitalised many a congregation. If the words 'Christian humanity' have a literal meaning then they describe Treacy. He was a good man who went about doing good. Is that not what his Lord had done in Galilee?

He loved a good story and was quick to tell them against himself. Some he did not hear. Trevor Bone, now Vicar of St Edward, Barnsley, but formerly Precentor of Leeds Parish Church, recalls a misprint on their monthly service sheet: 'One Evensong the then Vicar of Leeds (C. B. Sampson) drifted over during the Magnificat, stuck a finger at the sheet and said, or rather growled "Have you seen *that?*" I looked in the direction indicated and saw that the Venerable Eric Treacy had been raised to the *Archbishopric* of Halifax. Sampson added, "He'll dine out on it for the next six months". '

Donald Aldred, recalls a Confirmation at his former parish of Gomersal:

'The pulpit had a door on it which did not close securely — I didn't think to advise Eric of this before he went into the pulpit. It was early on in his sermon when he was making a point about God being outside as well as within us, when in stepping back with his hand on the door it opened and he nearly fell down the three steps — to the obvious amusement of the youngsters in the front pews. But, quick as a flash, he said something or other about his point being proved because "if there's a down there, there must also be an up there" which allowed the kids to laugh and get their amusement out of their system and then settle down and listen to him more intently, which they did.'

Sam Doubtfire, then Vicar of Ripponden, remembers Treacy arriving for a civic service. He was not untypically late and was taken round the back and into the Church via the Vicar's Vestry. 'Once robed he entered through the Vestry door into the Sanctuary just as the organ and choir began the Nunc Dimittis and in a whispered aside he said, "OK, don't rub it in. I can take a hint". '
    Treacy's own brand of humour was that as purveyed by Charlie Chaplin, Harold Lloyd, Buster Keeton, the Marx Brothers or Dad's Army. He enjoyed the uninhibited ridiculousness of the Marx Brothers or the pathos common to all life portrayed so well by Charlie Chaplin, the eternal little man. People who were always just getting away with it, like Harold Lloyd (like Treacy!) amused him as much as those inscrutable people who just went on taking it like Buster Keaton. It was an uncomplicated humour and sense of fun. As he said, 'We don't laugh at a child slipping on orange peel — only at some pompous ass dressed up as a Mayor falling down the Town Hall steps'. He often referred to the 'ghastly humourlessness of politics and politicians' but appreciated maddening but loveable avuncular figures such as Lord Boothby and Quintin Hogg (Lord Hailsham) — 'licensed jesters' he called them.
    Satire he condemned and lewd acts and crude jokes in public he attacked. He and May were special guests of the Stanley Urban District Council at a reception and dinner to mark its demise following local government reorganisation on 18 May 1974. The function was held at the Wakefield Theatre Club. In the cabaret, two comedians, Lambert and Ross, were cheap, crude and lewd. They called it a 'naughty vicar' sketch! The Treacy's walked out and to those who wrote applauding his action he replied: 'It was all very unpleasant, and I am sorry for the members of the Stanley UDC who were in no way responsible for the tone of the entertainment. Suffice to say that the performance had come to the point at which my wife and I felt we could no longer remain in the Theatre. There is a danger of giving approval to things by silent acquiescence, which was something I did not wish to appear to be doing.'
    Although Treacy had the special gift of communicating with all sorts and conditions of people there were some relationships which deeply troubled him. The two chief industries of the Wakefield Diocese are textiles and mining, one to the north the other to the south. As Bishop Suffragan of Pontefract, Treacy had spent much of his time in mining communities. He learned at first hand how and why the spirit of these places was closely communal. Although he could not directly identify himself with the miners he behaved in such a way as to have their

friendship, affection, respect and trust. The miners felt he understood the daily dangers with which they were faced and the longer term health hazards that claimed many of them as victims. Inwardly Treacy felt less at ease with them than they with him.

He was honoured by being invited to preach at the fifty-fifth Miners' Festival Service at Durham Cathedral on 18 July 1964.

On Tuesday evening, 20 March 1973, seven men set out for their night's work with their friends at Lofthouse Colliery, near Wakefield. They descended in the cage. Then it happened! The waters broke through 1,750ft underground, and those men were trapped. There followed six days of unremitting and agonising anxiety during which prodigious efforts were made to reach the miners. A mining community knows all about this. Days when hope almost goes, only to return as some hard new factor is seized upon — days when wives and children sit out their long and tortured vigil.

Coming home after a long day in London and hearing of the tragedy, Treacy went straight to the pithead with May in the early hours of the morning, ministering to the people. It was not easy to do. He referred to a feeling of helplessness when writing in the *Diocesan News* for May 1973: 'Although our motives were to show sympathy, especially to the families of the men who were trapped underground, we felt to be intruders. Not — let me hasten to add — because *they* made us feel intruders — but because we both felt that nothing that we could say or do *from outside* could penetrate the suffering and anxiety which haunted those for whom mining was a way of life, and for whom the pit — with its gaunt buildings — was a place that held them to itself in a relationship of love and hate.'

Maurice Turner was Vicar of nearby Alverthorpe, at the time of the Lofthouse Colliery disaster and writes:

'The Low Laithes [Alverthorpe: $3\frac{1}{2}$ miles from the pit bottom] rescue attempt over the suspected place of entombment was not the main rescue effort and was less focused upon by the Media. Bishop Eric concentrated his concern at the Colliery pithead ... It will ever remain one of my deepest regrets that just some such diffidence in me caused me never to think of inviting him to Low Laithes when we were trudging across fields. The miners, filling in the gaping old working shafts with material on conveyers, running day and night, took rest sitting about with their snap (or what we supplied to them) or sitting on straw bales and improvised wind shields against the chill of the clear nights. I sat with them in front of roaring fires or braziers and drank tea or coffee or soup with them and found myself a Bevin Boy again. If only I could have had Eric with me I could have made the way in for him to get to their hearts as I felt sure that he could. Their rough magical humour (even then not wholly suppressible), their fortitude in adversity and passionate self-giving for mates at risk, would have found a ready affinity with Eric's own brand of humour.'

There was a Memorial Service in Wakefield Cathedral on 6 May for the seven men who lay entombed in that sealed underground chamber at Lofthouse. In his address Treacy led the minds of the mourners away from that tomb to another one which was found empty on Easter morning. His words were simple: 'I believe that we survive after death, that the spirit leaves the body and passes over to another life. I do not pretend to understand this, nor can I explain it — all I can do is to accept it.' Families and friends wrote to thank Treacy for the 'helpful Christian message. We believed what you said'. Again they felt that Treacy understood.

A Memorial was erected directly above where the bodies of six of the seven men were believed to lie — only one body was recovered. It was dedicated by Treacy on 24 November 1974. 'Let this be a place of pilgrimage to which young people will be brought from our schools that they may learn the lesson of duty — which takes men daily to their work, braving danger to give the nation its life.'

During the notorious winter of confrontation of 1973/74 Treacy did not endear himself to the Tory Government by urging Prime Minister Edward Heath to regard and treat the miners as a special case. In a lone letter to the *Daily Mirror*, which prompted some councillors of the Diocese to call him 'Marxist', he praised the miners and made his appeal an emotional one: 'It is on men like these, working in conditions like this, that our industrial prosperity depends. As they say in Yorkshire "Think on't". These are tough men and they will fight, and they will stand together. They do not pay much attention to those who lecture them about inflation and the rest, whose lungs are not clogged with dust, whose limbs are not broken and twisted from accidents in the pit, whose wives and families are not each day haunted by the fear of disaster and sudden death.'

The miners knew they had a gallant supporter and defender in Treacy. This applied not only to men down the pits and on the coal face but also at The National Union of Mineworkers' headquarters. Arthur Scargill, President of the Yorkshire Area of NUM who 'felt privileged to know' Treacy writes:

'I became friendly with Eric Treacy at the time of the Lofthouse Colliery Disaster when he demonstrated great compassion and understanding for those at Lofthouse, and for all those connected with the mining industry.

'I thought that his sermon at the Memorial Service was excellent and drew the comparison with the former coal owners and the National Coal Board with its modern-day approach. He made it clear to the packed congregation in Wakefield Cathedral that the blame lay with those who had exploited the seams of coal in the 1800s; and had also exploited the men who worked in the industry.

'Several times following the Lofthouse tragedy, we had occasion to meet and I always found him stimulating to talk to — a man of considerable knowledge of all aspects of the Yorkshire way of life. He obviously took the trouble to acquaint himself with all the material facts concerning the mining industry so that he could discuss with miners and their leaders from a position of authority.'

Despite the feelings frequently expressed to him by miners and some other industrial workers he still had a feeling of unease, a tension within himself. 'The Church is not really going to come to grips with the industrial situation with its present kind of organisation, nor in the unidentified way that an Incumbent is in relation to the industrial community. Until he is subject to their risks of unemployment, redundancy and the rest of it, they will look upon him as a nice bloke who smokes a pipe and is soulful and will lend a helping hand where he can.

They will not look upon him as one who belongs where they belong.' Nowhere did he put it better than in his tape recorded contribution to *All One Body* (Darton Longman & Tod 1969) when he said:

'As I lay on my stomach at the coalface talking to some of the miners, one of whom was whistling through his lungs as he spoke — he had pneumokoniosis — I thought to myself, "At teatime this afternoon I shall be out of this place, I shall have a bath and I shall probably talk to my friends about my day at the pit. But you will be down here again tomorrow morning, and you will go on coming down here until you are carried out dead. The difference is that I come down here to see you, to give you a cheerful greeting, and I am going out again. How can I minister to you in your situation unless I come down this pit and stay with you every day and get dust in my lungs?"

'This may be dramatising a bit, and I may be underrating, for all I know, the effect that my visit as Bishop of the diocese had on those people. But from my side, I felt that I was a curious intruder going down into a world to which we have condemned a very large number of people in order that we might have our industrial prosperity; and that all my ministry, as I have moved amongst industrial workers, as I chat to them in the streets, as I meet them, they look at me as if to say, "Brother, you don't know half of it", and that is the blockage.'

Treacy was not aware just how much the weight of his arm round a person's shoulders meant — even just his presence. At Lofthouse it is doubtful if words could have been as effective. One miner — not a Christian — refers to Treacy as 'Our Bishop'. That is indicative of a general opinion. That is why the Treacys were invited to go to King Arthur's Castle (NUM Headquarters at Barnsley) shortly before his retirement. There he was presented with a miner's lamp in recognition of his services to the mining community. He was moved. He had served.

The late Methodist minister, W. Walker Lee, refers to the widespread acceptance of Treacy as 'Our Bishop' in words penned shortly before his death:

'There wasn't a trace of prelacy in the bishop. He belonged to the people, gave himself unstintingly to the people, loved the people, lived with the people. Wherever you went in West Yorkshire, and in whatever company you found yourself, Eric Treacy was known and loved — whether that company was Anglican, Free Church, or no church at all. He was in constant demand for speaking engagements to audiences both sacred and secular. To all of them he was "Our Bishop". Whenever any issue of national or local or moral importance arose, both press and TV invariably turned to him for his comments. And this, not because he was outstandingly intellectual but because he lived and worked and ministered among the people.'

W. Walker Lee also refers to Treacy's ecumenism:

'It went very deep indeed. It had everything to do with the mission of the Church to contemporary society. It was not enough for Treacy that the churches should do all they could together in their concern to serve the community, as long as this did not violate any of their separate disciplines. He longed for them to be one in the profoundest sense. He hated the thought of conformity, and he saw a vision of the one great church in which there would be a rich variety of worship and experience and proclamation, but under the one discipline and authority.

'Several times a year he invited the leaders of the various denominations to have breakfast with him at Bishop's Lodge. We always celebrated the Service of Holy Communion together in his private chapel, and then we would spend the morning together in his study considering not only the large issues of our various churches, but giving the most patient thought to this or that situation in his diocese where we could work more closely together. Those were occasions of deep, happy fellowship, which enriched all of us who were privileged to share in them.'

Treacy's outreach had always been wide but never so great as at Wakefield. With it came an ever increasing flow of engagements and the problems of his diary. Treacy made a note:

'My programme is —

6.45am	Rise
7.00am	Breakfast
7.15am-07.45am	Read letters
8.00am-09.00am	Exercise — 4 mile walk
9.00am-09.30am	Chapel
9.30am-11.00am	Letters — dictate
11.00am-12.30pm	Meetings or interviews
12.30pm- 1.30pm	Lunch — plus $\frac{1}{2}$ hour reading
2.00pm- 5.00pm	Visit clergy, meetings or functions
5.00pm- 6.00pm	Sign letters — reading
6.15pm	High tea
6.30pm	Leave for evening engagement — confirmation, Institution, Speech Day, Dinner, or evening committee
10.00pm-11.30pm	Do as I like

'It's a pretty punishing programme but, I guess, not unlike those of other Bishops.

'There are some obvious and regrettable deficiencies in the list; too little time for prayer and reading. I must confess myself trapped in this timetable. I repeatedly try to break out of it, but without success. As day succeeds day, the demands get greater, the interviews increase in number, the telephone rings incessantly, my attempts to delegate achieve less success as so many things need the Bishop's decision. The awful thing is that I can't manage a day off per week, although I am constantly advising the clergy to do this. I do, however, manage occasionally to get two days per month right away from the Diocese.

'Preparation is one of my great difficulties, because I cannot speak "off the cuff". I have to put my address on paper. I take the view that sermons at Institution Services — and elsewhere — are immensely important.'

This timetable was more often extended than not and includes only the barest outline of his activities. It was the timetable of a compulsive worker.

Treacy had originally made it clear that his intention was to retire towards the end of 1975 when he would be 68. However, a note appeared in the *Diocesan News* for August 1974 'At the instigation of the Archbishop of York, and after careful consultation with him, I have decided that it would be right for me to defer my retirement. I would not have agreed to change my plans in this way, were it not that the Archbishop has expressed to me his concern that so many Diocesan Bishops plan to retire in the current year and early next year.'

This advice, if such it can be termed, must have seemed like a gift from on high! Treacy did not want the thought of retirement at the back of his mind, but rather completely out of his mind. But there were those who worried a great deal about his constant outpouring of himself in self-giving and loving. Treacy's besetting sin — and it was a sin — was his inability to relax. It was the habit of a lifetime. He had spasms of self-discipline in this regard but they were spasms!

If May could not apply the brake, then it was clear no member of the Diocesan team could do so. Having vacated Pontefract for Wakefield in 1968 Treacy was fortunate in being able to choose a new Bishop Suffragan of Pontefract and an Archdeacon of Pontefract, for he had decided to separate the two Offices. Gordon Fallows, Principal of Ripon Hall, Oxford, became Bishop of Pontefract. The relationship between Treacy and Gordon Fallows was perfect — a happy combination and the happiest time of Treacy's episcopate. Gordon Fallows was cerebral and he was able to steady Treacy on many an occasion when Treacy's heart was leaping into misguided action. There was a very deep mutual respect between the two men. Gordon Fallows was the epitome of the 'steady man' so much admired by Treacy. He came to Wakefield as an able administrator, a good scholar, a man with a great sense of humour, a leader yet not a dominator, of wide experience including a period as Vicar of Preston and Archdeacon of Lancaster. He was a Liberal Churchman and widely respected as such. They complemented each other; he was steady where Treacy could be rash and he had a theological grasp where Treacy relied on intuitive understanding.

Treacy had not expected to keep him for long and the parting came all too soon in 1971 when the Diocese of Sheffield claimed him as its Bishop. At the time Gordon Fallows wrote to Treacy of his 'three ecstatically happy years' with him: 'As you know Edna and I could have lived out our working days here [Wakefield] with complete joy and satisfaction and fulfilment. Such was our harmony — both diocesan and domestic. You and May were responsible for that blissful contentment we have experienced here.

'Oh, how much I have learned to my profit at your side. And how much I learned to admire — magnanimity, courage, and compassion.'

Naturally Gordon Fallows saw the shadows as well as the sun. In some random reflections he notes:

'I do not think Eric was really gripped by the iniquities in world affairs. He had to have an opinion on them to the point sometimes of being opinionated. But he did not always see the real issues. (This could be a reason why he was not at ease with university audiences.)

'In political matters he was usually left of centre but he had not a liberal mind.

'I think he greatly exaggerated the importance of the House of Lords.

'He was annoying when he made pronouncements on subjects on which he had insufficient knowledge.

'But he was a very considerable person indeed. As I went about the Diocese I used to do so with a shadow on my back. Wherever I went it would be "How's Dr Treacy", "How's Mr Treacy", "How's *the* Bishop". He was genuinely loved.'

On one occasion someone asked Gordon Fallows if he was interested in railways. I think he must have enjoyed replying "Not since I was ten."

He was succeeded at Pontefract by Richard Hare who was Archdeacon of Westmorland and Furness. Treacy's good friend, Ted Henderson, became Archdeacon of Pontefract and C. B. Beverley 'Bev' became Treacy's Personal Assistant as well as Assistant to Albert Nurse, the Diocesan Secretary, whom he succeeded in that office in 1971. In 1972 John Lister, Archdeacon of Halifax, became Provost of Wakefield Cathedral and he was succeeded as Archdeacon by John Alford.

Treacy's relations with his Cathedral Church of All Saints were rather formal. The Catholic worship of the Cathedral was not to Treacy's personal taste. Naturally he did all that was required of him — and more — but there was not a wholehearted warmth of feeling towards the Cathedral, although he provided a new Bishop's throne in memory of his parents. However, it was at the Cathedral that he gave some memorable devotional addresses which showed the Cathedral congregation that their bishop was a spiritual pastor and could draw from deeper spiritual wells than was always obvious to the public. In private, priests and other people seeking counsel knew differently.

Provost Lister remembers Treacy's impatience with the tawdry and second rate. 'There was a famous occasion here one Sunday evening when as preacher at Evensong he did not get into the pulpit until seven-forty. The scorching letter which he wrote to my predecessor (Phil Pare) could have surely set the place alight had it been placed within it!' Treacy's 'staggering' letters were received by many people but when letter writer and recipient next met Treacy acted as if nothing had happened unless the recipient took him to task or challenged him and then he apologised. He could forgive as easily as he expected to be forgiven — sometimes too easily on each side.

The outbursts of exasperation and temper were invariably followed by sackcloth and ashes. It had ever been thus: Mrs Jean Horsfall remembers an 'Open' Church Council Meeting at Halifax. 'The choir had been grumbling over his choice of music and I with the arrogance of youth decided to voice their views. We stood across the floor from one another and argued heatedly. The following morning he rang me up, and apologised for having lost his temper. This made a great impression on me, that a man of his standing should apologise to a 20-year old girl.'

There were some painful confrontations after Treacy had raised expectations in people that had not been fulfilled. It may have been because he had said more than he intended or implied more than he meant. This was true in the matter of at least one senior appointment in the diocese. It is a physical impossibility for two men to get into the same pair of gaiters! It was as painful for the man overlooked as it was embarrassing for the appointed one! These were not unusual defects in one who wanted to run a 'happy ship', yet defects they were.

Consultations with his staff and agreement with them over a course of action did not necessarily, even usually, mean that that would be the course that would be pursued.

Treacy rarely persuaded his first choices as senior colleagues to join him at Wakefield. It is a pity for some strong personalities from outside the Diocese were invited into it, but they said 'No'. With one particular appointment, namely the Suffragan Bishopric of Pontefract in 1968, Treacy was blocked from two other directions — No 10 Downing Street and Lambeth Palace. He was told by the then Archbishops' Secretary for Appointments (W. 'Bill' H. Saumarez Smith) that his choice was not on the highly confidential Lambeth list for preferment. Some extraordinarily unsuitable people were — in Treacy's judgement and he was provided with a list of a dozen whom to consider. 'Only one name really appealed to me, the rest, I thought, were either not cut out to be No 2s, or were not "Bishop stuff" . . . I think I shall be awkward and insist on the man I want. After all, I shall have to work with him, and, surely, I know best the sort of man my own diocese needs.'

Eventually, 'Donald Ebor (Donald Coggan, Archbishop of York) summoned me to his room (at Church House, Westminster) to discuss my letter in which I had asked for the appointment of X as my suffragan. He didn't actually veto it, but he said that he hoped I would not put him in the position of having to say No . . . If I can't have X I shall insist upon the man of my choice from outside the Diocese. Two names that come to me are Gordon Fallows, at present Master (sic) of Ripon Hall, Oxford, and Freddie Temple, nephew of the great William, and now Vicar of St Mary's Portsea'.

When Treacy took himself to see John Hewitt, the Prime Minister's Patronage Secretary:

'He tells me that nothing has changed in the manner of appointing suffragans, and that I could, in spite of the pressures brought upon me, petition the Crown for my own nomination to receive the Royal approval. Obviously, I would hesitate to do this if it meant ignoring the declared view of the Archbishop. After all, there must be some obedience in the Church, especially between Diocesan Bishops and their Primate.

'Hewitt and I went on to discuss other pending appointments, notably that to the vacant canonry at Westminster Abbey, due to the death of Joost de Blank. Y is in line for it, and Hewitt wanted to know if he would be suitable. I certainly supported this. (Biographer's note — Y was not appointed). I find it hard to believe that a nobody like me is consulted about such appointments, but in a world in which nobodies are somebodies, I suppose I must get used to it.

'I am immensely attracted by John Hewitt, who is the best kind of civil servant: a man of great integrity and charm, and the best kind of Anglican layman. So long as the senior Anglican appointments pass through his hands, we need have no fears. He is a sound judge of men, a good listener, and humble in the use of the power that inevitably rests in his hands.'

As we have seen Gordon Fallows was appointed to Pontefract making for a rich and complementary relationship between Diocesan and Suffragan. Freddie Temple became Bishop Suffragan of Malmesbury in the Diocese of Bristol in 1973. X has not become a Bishop!

Basically the Diocese of Wakefield was a 'one man show' under Treacy. He could be inspiring and stimulating to work for but not always as easy to work with as one might suppose. He could be infuriating. He was so much an individualist and a man of impulse that his style of ministry could not but be wholly personal. In this weakness was also his strength for it was a personal ministry and a very human episcopate which led to such an enormous number of people looking to him as 'Our Bishop'.

23
Changing Gear

Treacy's heart kept reminding him of its existence. He had little heeded the periodic warnings which he had received. His robust physique, ruddy and craggy face disguised any illness from which he was suffering. Apart from the hernia operations and periodic attacks of gout (which seem unfair when inflicted on a teetotaller) he had one or two heart spasms.

Spells in hospital seemed but a further opportunity to extend his outreach. As a patient he was the life and soul of the ward once he had recovered from the operation. The droves of visitors calling throughout the day were an embarrassment to the nursing staff but they could not say 'no' to those who wanted to visit one whom they too loved. He was always popular with doctors and nurses.

The hospital chaplain's ministry had been important to him ever since Edge Hill days. After a fortnight in hospital having a fourth hernia operation in 1968 he reflected on the difficulty of maintaining his spiritual exercises. 'I have to confess that except for the reception of the Holy Communion every other day, my devotional life was practically non-existent; except for the shortest prayer of commendation each night. I had hoped that I should be able to say my offices each day, but such was not the case. I found it almost impossible to sustain concentration for long. I was restless and in a good deal of discomfort for much of the time. All I felt that I could do was to lean on God and trust that he would understand. Am I a very feeble Christian, or is it a general experience in sickness? This experience brought home to me how important it is hold up the sick in our prayers — that we do for them that which they are unable to do for themselves.'

Stuart Brand, Hospital Chaplain at Pinderfields General Hospital, Wakefield, has two anecdotes of Treacy as Bishop rather than as patient:

'There was a Confirmation in the Fieldhead Hospital Social Hall in 1974. The hospital had recently been opened and the chaplains had gathered a number of candidates from the hospital patients and prepared them for confirmation. In addition to 18 Anglican candidates there were three Roman Catholics so the service was a joint one between Eric Treacy and the Bishop of Leeds. The two Bishops shared most of the service together and each confirmed their own candidates. It was good to see them join and clap in time with the music for such choruses as "give me joy in my heart, keep me praising" in a very relaxed manner. One of the patients, on arising from his knees after his confirmation, said "I wish you many years of Christian happiness, sir". Another, after the blessing, said (in a loud stage whisper) "Good, now we can go and have a cup of tea!"'

'On one occasion during his sermon in St Faith's Chapel, Stanley Royd Hospital, he paused to look at his notes, and an old lady in the congregation said, in another stage whisper, "Who's that old —— then" to which her companion replied "I don't know, let's be getting out now". For once Bishop Treacy seemed at a loss for words and merely grinned and picked up the thread of his sermon from the point he had left off.'

Treacy's prayer list had always been a lengthy one but inevitably it was longest at Wakefield. The chapel at Bishop's Lodge was not a place of retreat, a kind of atomic-proof shelter, but a launching pad for blasting off into the world. Monday morning began with Holy Communion for the Diocesan staff and the 'family' of Bishop's Lodge: Winnie and George Holmes who looked after Bishop's Lodge and the Treacy's; Mrs Val Douglas, Treacy's Secretary, who writes 'The very simplicity of the service and the surroundings and the group with the common interest made it so memorable; and an occasion of importance to us all.'

Life at Bishop's Lodge was simple and simply lived. Neither he nor May was domesticated in any way. May, the charming hostess, had never learned to cook. Kitchen life was a foreign country to Treacy. In December 1977 when May had to go into hospital for a (successful) replacement hip operation, Treacy wrote to Val Douglas: 'All goes well so far. After a week hanging about at the hospital, she had the operation yesterday morning and rang me up this evening to see if I was having proper meals!... After eight days on my own I am making some interesting discoveries about running a home and I have decided that it's easier running a Diocese!'

Val Douglas adds: 'One of the great disappointments of his life was that they had no children. May had one stillborn child soon after the marriage and no more were possible. By the time I knew them, they were quite philosophical about this — in fact, May had quite decided that it had been meant, in order that she could share his life so completely and give him her undivided support and attention. Nevertheless, he would have made a wonderful father! They were one of the closest married couples that I have known. The first indication that he had entered the house was the shout of "May" echoing round the lodge!'

The whole Diocese had been the family of Eric and May Treacy in a very deep way — emotional, spiritual — and in some ways practical. As Eric and May were inseparable from each other so too the Diocese had been welded to them. Yet physical separation had to come.

The extension of time in Wakefield that Treacy had received, far from helping him to prepare for resignation and retirement, led him even more fully, if that were possible, into the life of his family, the Diocese. He was more, not less, in demand and not only as an 'elder statesman'.

In December 1975, in spirit forlorn, he made some notes:

'As the end of the year approaches, I have to come to terms with the fact of retirement next year. It is something that I dread, but I am told that the more you dread it, the easier it is to take because the reality turns out to be so much better than the anticipation.

'Obviously, after 27 years in the Diocese, it is going to be a terrible wrench in terms of relationships. There are clergy in the Diocese whom I have confirmed, married, ordained, and instituted to their first benefice.

'In the nature of things a man approaching 70 is starting to go off. If he is slowing up, tiring more quickly, his memory grows dim; he is more reluctant to face new ideas because he feels safer with the old ones. But at the same time as these processes are taking place, there comes a growing conviction that these things may happen to other people but that you are the one miraculous exception. So it is wise to fix your date for an honourable discharge, in the hope that when you go people would rather you stayed.

'There are absurdities about the retirement of Anglican Bishops. For some years I have, as Bishop of Wakefield, served on central bodies of the Church, to which my overloaded diary has prevented my giving the attention I would wish. The day I retire as Bishop of Wakefield, I cease to serve on these bodies — and at the precise moment that I could give more time to them, as well as a good deal of experience.

'The same thing is true of the House of Lords. For four years I have found it impossible to attend its proceedings with any degree of regularity. The day I retire from my See, I cease to be a member of the Lords. In a word, just as I might have the time to contribute something to the corporate wisdom of the House of Lords, I lose the opportunity of doing so. Ah well, it is ungracious to complain after a life so full of interest and unmerited privilege.'

In April 1976 the official announcement came that Treacy would retire on 31 October. He had to brace himself for what he knew would be difficult 'farewells'. They were. Crowds flocked to the services which had been arranged at the chief centres of the Diocese — Barnsley, Huddersfield, Halifax (an understandably emotional one) and finally in the Cathedral on 31 October, the eve of All Saints. By this time his feelings were of numbness and dumbness: 'Numb — because for the last few weeks we have moved from one farewell gathering to another, and have received so many tributes of affection that we have difficulty in coping with this continuous stirring of the emotions. Dumb — because I can never properly convey to you what is in my heart. I cannot find the words to express to you my gratitude for your affection, for your prayers, and for your partnership in the Lord's work.'

Before the service he had spoken to one of his close friends words that may not have been very Christian but they must have come from the gushing wells of his heart. 'Wouldn't it be wonderful if, after I have preached my final sermon, I should drop dead.' God does not often grant this kind of desire so the physical move and retirement had to be faced. Treacy made it clear that he would not accept invitations to reappear in the Diocese, a rule which he kept rigorously. There is one thing that made his going a little less painful, namely, the news that his successor was to be Colin James, Bishop Suffragan of Basingstoke, an appointment which pleased him a great deal.

The place of retirement had been fixed years before when he and May had acquired a small house on the lower slopes of Skiddaw called The Ghyll in which many Wakefield Diocesan clergy and laity and other friends had stayed. The Ghyll was situated in a charming little village called Applethwaite just outside Keswick. The house was originally two woodmen's cottages which were made into one by an admirer of William Wordsworth for him to live in. He did not do so because a small local mill led him to fear the prospect of industrialisation. May's two sisters, Katherine and Margaret Shone, also lived in Applethwaite. The Ghyll had been a blessed place of retreat where Treacy had sought and received renewal many times in his episcopate. He loved the Lake District. The hills cast their own spell. He could lose himelf amongst them with a good hard apple and a Mars Bar, the becks and streams providing liquid refreshment. His temperament found satisfaction in the wild, uncertain and untamed places — the tempestuousness of Wastwater, the stormy wastes of the Scafells and the stark flanks of Helvellyn.

The Ghyll was small but there were several acres of land with it. There were the problems common to country dwellers — a constant battle with nettles, with trees that sprang up where they shouldn't and trees that would not grow where they should, with water that capriciously decided to take courses that did not appear on the map, with various rodents which found succulence in the wooden supports of the outhouses. He had to battle with other men's live stock and with vandals who pushed down the dry stone walling, as well as with unauthorised campers who arrived and departed leaving a pig sty behind them.

A place to 'get away from it all' was exactly what Treacy needed in his active ministry. And Applethwaite *was* away from it all. There was no village shop. Provisions had to be obtained from Keswick. The nearest rail transport was from Penrith or Appleby some 18 or 28 miles respectively. Somehow he did not foresee what it would be like for permanent retirement — isolated and inaccessible, not a place where people could 'drop in' whilst passing.

What Treacy needed above all was to *re-tyre*. It was not to be. As an anaesthetic against retirement he embarked upon an impossible range of commitments. He was planning to write no less than five books and a regular series of articles for *Church Times* and was accepting preaching and conference engagements throughout the country. He undertook the active chairmanship of Age Concern, Cumbria, and the presidency of numerous steam railway preservation societies. There was to be a great deal of railway and landscape photographic work. He was desperate to be active in the Carlisle Diocese, but this was not easy to arrange although he was appointed to exercise a particular pastoral ministry towards all the retired clergy in the Diocese. The Bishop of Carlisle circularised the clergy saying 'Many of you, of course, will know him already and will know how fortunate we are to have the help of such a deeply caring, spiritual pastor, ministering to us in the Diocese.'

Treacy was in such demand for special engagements that it was easy to fill his diary — but it was neither what he wanted nor needed. All those who knew him well feared those consequences of his retirement that he himself had dreaded. It did not take long for the expected signs to appear in the voluminous correspondence emanating from The Ghyll. As early as 1 April 1977 he wrote to Donald Aldred, 'Although it is getting on for six months since we retired, we are both feeling terribly deprived. Somebody sent me a tape of the Enthronement service of the new Bishop and it was more than we could take! Nothing against the new Bishop, whom I like tremendously — but it just brought back 1968 with unbearable vividness. I can sum it up by saying that I think that euthanasia is better than retirement.'

Letter after letter was written in this vein and when people went to visit him they could not help but see what the painful reality of retirement meant to him. Writing on 10 February 1978 to Bishop Philip Wheeldon (one-time Bishop Suffragan of Whitby and with the unusual distinction of twice being elected and subsequently serving as Bishop of the same Diocese — Kimberley and Kuruman, 1961-65 and 1968-76) who had retired to live in the Wakefield Diocese, Treacy said:

'I must say that I envy you having appointment as Assistant/Bishop in the Dio of Wakefield — it's a grand diocese which I love beyond words — and Colin must be a wonderful chap to work with . . .

'As Bp to Bp I suppose I can have a bit of a gripe. The parish in which we live contains no less than five retired clergy (including a Bp, an Archdeacon and a couple of Canons), so I am not exactly over-employed. There are 114 Confirmations in this Diocese next year, and I have been given three to do. The Bp of Carlisle is a nice chap and May and I are fond of him and his wife, but I have absolutely no part in the life of the Diocese. I find it all rather depressing as I feel wasted. I suppose that reveals some degree of pride on my part. I was so interested to read in your letter that you had found that retirement demanded a major effort in adjustment. I can't pretend that I have yet completed the process. Don't you find in retirement that everything is so "ad hoc" — that there is no continuing pastoral thread running through everything you do? Enough of this self pity!'

Treacy was fortunate that the Vicar of Crosthwaite, the parish in which he lived, was one of his much loved Wakefield priests, Sam Doubtfire, whom he had made deacon and instituted into his first living. Sam Doubtfire writes of Treacy's concern not to tread on the toes or hog the limelight:

'Certainly when we arrived in the Parish almost together — he was very sensitive to the problems there could be (and were) and never once gave unsolicited advice. He would help when asked — but retirement was hard. There was a particular time when he felt so low that he almost changed his views that clergy should not retire into the area they have ministered in. He hated the idea of slow deterioration, and while he knew why people held back on inviting him to do things — he found it hard to slow down and to accept 'ill health'. In a way his retirement was a bereavement experience because Wakefield and the people there were his family and his heart never really left them. May coped much better — but that is because her temperament is different.'

Treacy knew his condition, but seemed utterly unable to prize himself away from it. In a letter to his oldest and closest friend, Bishop Roger Wilson, on 30 December 1976 he had written:

'Well — as Michael Ramsey would say "Here we are". It's nearly two months since we moved, and we aren't really straight yet. We brought far more furniture than we needed, with the result that we are almost begging visitors to accept gifts of various bits of furniture.

'I cannot pretend that I have reconciled myself — yet, to my retired state. I am being a pain in the neck to poor May with my fits of depression. I really am ashamed of myself as it is horribly obvious that I do not possess the inner resources to meet this situation. It has taken a long time for me to discover the truth about myself. I read in a desultory kind of way; I write lots of letters; I get up, I go to bed. If I oversleep, I suddenly realise that it doesn't matter because no one is waiting for me ... This sounds awful — forgive me, but I feel that I can speak more freely to you than anyone else, apart from May.'

The 'ad hoc' engagements, though numerous and involving a great deal of travel, were no substitute for a particular sphere of work, a responsibility. The base had gone, the roots had been torn up. It was a tragedy he had to bear with May — though not alone for he was in the prayers of a multitude of people as they were in his. There had been a suggestion that he might become an honorary episcopal overlord to army chaplains. How he would have loved that but it would have necessitated living somewhere more accessible to the mainstream of England than The Ghyll. York would have been ideal.

Treacy's nephew, Vivian Bowern, writes:

'It was very clear to me that here was a man who lived for his work. His utilisation of physical and nervous energy was total. Catnaps were essential to allow him some small recharging of his batteries. Yet even in the confines of his family — or perhaps more accurately, of May's family — he always managed to show that real interest and concern which marked his life, alongside the obvious signs of tiredness that went with his pace of work.

'Later as I knew him better, I began to wonder how he could possibly retire; how he could live without his work. There was perhaps a certain inevitability, even a clear design, that his life should end soon after his work.'

On 13 May 1978 Treacy left The Ghyll for Appleby to photograph one of his favourite steam locomotives, No 92220 *Evening Star*, which was hauling the 'Western Border Venturer' returning from Carlisle to Cardiff. David Ward, Passenger Marketing Manager of British Rail, London Midland Region, was on the train and recalls the occasion:

'On arrival at Appleby at about 16.15 a stop was made for the locomotive to take water and for the passengers to take photographs of the locomotive. I alighted and crossed the footbridge to the downside of the station. The footbridge was fairly busy and it was just beginning to rain. I noticed about three yards in front of me Bishop Eric Treacy walking in the same direction and accompanied by another man. On the flight of steps from the footbridge down to the platform Eric Treacy slipped and fell rather heavily on his bottom. The rain on the wooden steps had made the steps rather slippery. Eric Treacy quickly pulled himself up on the handrail and I heard his companion ask if he was all right and Eric Treacy replied to the effect that he had a soft enough bottom. Half way down the platform, I stopped to talk to one of the station staff and did not see Eric Treacy again as he proceeded towards the locomotive.'

Treacy stopped to exchange words with John Bellwood of York regarding a proposed visit to the North Yorkshire Railway to which Treacy was looking forward. Then he collapsed and died shortly afterwards, having suffered a major coronary attack. The doctor called to certify the death contacted Ken Cove, then Vicar of Appleby who, as he recalls, 'was also able to alert Sam Doubtfire and the Bishop of Carlisle. I was able to identify him for the police; some two hours later all was cleared up and I was able to drive his car and possessions over to Mrs Treacy. It may have been some comfort that these acts were done by someone with a great affection for both of them.'

The blow to May can only have been of heart breaking devastation and numbing shock, softened only by the sure knowledge that her 'man of granite with the heart of a child' was truly with his and her Lord.

Tributes tumbled like a waterfall. In a short space of time May received over 1,600 letters coming from the broadest sweep of life but each person rising up to call him blessed.

The funeral and burial was at Crosthwaite on 19 May. To a packed church. Bishop Halsey of Carlisle spoke of the man every person in that church could recognise. 'No one could be with Eric Treacy without being the better for it. One old friend of his said to me earlier this week, "Eric was such a rich personality; he enriched all with whom he came into contact. But he was a rich personality that was prodigal in his sharing, and whoever you were and whatever you had done you would come out of his presence with a new hope; a new determination, ready to fight on or to start again, but always feeling that life was worthwhile and that God cared. And how his people loved him.'

There was a Requiem Eucharist at Wakefield Cathedral as in many Churches throughout the Diocese. Memorial and Thanksgiving services were held at the Parish Churches of Keighley and Halifax and finally a Memorial Service at Wakefield Cathedral on 27 June at which the Archbishop of York (Stuart Blanch) preached.

Something more unusual was pending. On the day of Treacy's death David Ward of British Rail heard the news when the train stopped at Garsdale:

'Subsequently on the train journey back to London, I had time to think of the impact Eric Treacy's life had made on so many people and particularly railwaymen and railway enthusiasts and came to the conclusion that a Memorial Service at Appleby Station with passengers brought to the service by a steam-hauled train might be very appropriate. My thinking was influenced not only by the need to pay tribute to Eric Treacy but also by the fact that he had died enjoying his favourite hobby and at the side of the railway line he loved best. Furthermore, by good fortune the layout of Appleby Station was ideal from the practical point of view of holding a Memorial Service.'

David Ward began to take soundings and found that everyone he spoke to was wondering how they could pay public tribute to Eric Treacy. The idea of a Memorial Service appealed to everyone. May agreed from the outset but expressed the wish that the theme of the day should be Easter not Good Friday.

It was the most ambitious programme involving steam locomotives which had been attempted on British Rail since the withdrawal of steam locomotives for normal traction purposes in 1968. The Memorial Service for the Railway Bishop was fixed for 30 September. There were two trains named, for the day, the 'Lord Bishop' and the 'Bishop Treacy', from London and the West Riding of Yorkshire respectively. Various engines comprised the overall motive power but three Treacy steam specials were involved, BR Class 9, 2-10-0 No 92220 *Evening Star*; LNER A3, 4-6-2, No 4472, *Flying Scotsman*; and SR 'Merchant Navy' 4-6-2 No 35028 *Clan Line*. Thus one thousand people were taken in 24 coaches to Appleby. Motorcoaches and cars also arrived in large numbers. By the time the Memorial Service started well over four thousand people were in the congregation. The weather was mixed and there was a short sharp shower during the service. One notable member of the congregation was heard to remark that Eric Treacy was known to enjoy a little mischief and perhaps this was him having a little bit of fun.

A one minute's silence was started and ended by the whistle of *Evening Star*. Bishop Gordon Fallows gave a short address. There was a lesson, a few prayers and two hymns of praise and triumph sung in a way that showed that death is a junction not a terminus. The person who wrote to British Rail afterwards saying it was 'the finest tribute to any single man I have known in my life' summed up the feelings of all those present.

David Ward, who had not known Treacy personally, had come to feel the magic of his personality during the marvellous and intricate planning that had gone into making the Memorial Service so memorable. Treacy's name had been an Open Sesame for anything he wanted. David Ward's can be the last word of that day:

'The magnificent evening sunset set the seal on the whole day's events. The Settle and Carlisle line passes through some of the wildest country in England and it is exceptional to get good weather. Eric Treacy had described Ribblesdale as his favourite amongst the Dales and we had arranged to stop both the "Lord Bishop" and the "Bishop Treacy" at Ribblehead on their return journeys for a 20-minute stop for scenic purposes. The return journey over Aisgill with the sun setting in the West had been wonderful, but at Ribblehead, quite unlike the normal wild weather experienced at this station, we found an absolute stillness with the contours of the hills standing out clearly against the final setting of the sun. There was a serenity and tranquillity in the atmosphere which those of us familiar with the Settle and Carlisle line had never previously experienced and we felt that the hand of Eric Treacy and providence had a hand in it.'

There is an empty place on the lineside which can never be filled.

Class 86/2 electric locomotive No 86.240 worked the 'Lord Bishop' between Euston and Farington Junction (Preston). This locomotive is one of British Rail's most modern high-power 100mph electric locomotives. Another rare tribute was made when it was decided to name this locomotive *Bishop Eric Treacy*. It is doubtful whether any name could have given wider pleasure than this and the ceremony was carried out by May at Penrith Station on 3 May 1979.

There is to be an annual 'Bishop Treacy Photographic Competition' for young railway photographers. Other visible memorials include a teak seat with brass plaque in Crosthwaite Churchyard, plaques at Keighley and Halifax Parish Churches. There is a plaque on Appleby Station itself commemorating the 'Railway Photographer, Pastor to Railwaymen, Lover of Life and Railways'.

In February 1980 the Wakefield Cathedral Centenary Development Programme was launched, designed to ensure that the Cathedral enters its second century adequately equipped to continue and extend its lively spirit and secular involvement which has characterised its first 100 years. £450,000 is needed and perhaps the major feature is to be the building of a Memorial Hall close by the Cathedral as a tribute to Eric Treacy. It will be known as The Treacy Memorial Hall. This will provide a community centre and a meeting place for the Diocese.

The most abiding monument to Eric Treacy lies elsewhere.

24
Inside the Rock

What is left of Eric Treacy other than the visible memorials that bear his name — a Cathedral Hall and a locomotive — together with a wealth of photographs testifying to the lure, spell and glory of a vanished age of steam?

What else? Eric Treacy has left no permanent mark on the organisational Church. No major reforms, resolutions or reports carry his name. He was ever sceptical of the modern passion for passing resolutions and report breeding which, like gushing taps, empty the cistern of energy that could be more constructively employed. He saw the Church trundling along in spite of the General Synod and its vapourings.

His major speeches and sermons and writings into which he put so much time and energy will be forgotten as a generation of receptive receptacles passes on.

He leaves behind him no profound work of original thought. Theology was not his strong suit and regarded as 'high falutin' when he could not understand it.

Will he be remembered as a Christian leader? He often criticised in others what he could be guilty of himself, namely confusing the making of controversial statements, the ability to make pithy topical remarks, the cultivation of glamour, the banging of drums and the blowing of trumpets with the exercise of leadership. There were times when he almost assumed a demagoguery echoing the baser sentiments of the ubiquitous 'silent majority' if not actually appealing to them. The gift of the gab led to impulsive utterances which at times cosseted those he sought to challenge and irritated those he wanted to protect.

There were occasions when a more philosophical approach to a particular issue would have been more efficacious than a pragmatic one.

Democracy was too much like a corset for regular wear. He preferred autocracy. Benevolent despotism was his natural milieu.

He was in very unfamiliar domains when dealing with such subjects as homosexuals, the Charismatic Movement and exorcism. Perhaps he did not always fully comprehend or see the problem behind the problem. Therefore in ministering to persons in these areas he may not have been dealing with their deepest needs. His compassion knew no bounds but, like his zeal, it was not always influenced or directed by his mind.

There are bishops and priests who evade the truth about themselves within the rounds of devotion or in meditational retreat, finding escape in the aroma of professional piety. Others seek shelter in the pack that produces a 'party' line about issues which can stimulate but may emasculate. Others are in danger of being consumed by never ceasing activity which leaves little time for reflection, personal assessment and rejuvenation.

Eric Treacy did know what was in himself, and those who knew him over a long period of years saw the changes, the growth in spiritual matters and the coming of wisdom and gravitas in a most remarkable way. In his character there was tumult, weakness, enthusiasm, grandeur — and humility. At one moment he stood head and shoulders above others as a man of drive and personality, of spiritual and moral authority, and the next doing or saying something wayward and irresponsible. He hated his weaknesses even though he repeated them. His candour about his own mistakes was attractive compared with the humbug of some public figures, but colleagues felt he sometimes took it to the extreme point of self-indulgence. Nevertheless, whenever he spoke he hoped he would be His Master's Voice. When he searched for the *mot juste* he wanted it for puncturing complacency and not for use as self inflation. He was only too aware when his words obstructed The Word. After one sermon he made a note, 'A lot of platitudes — a sermon of which I am really ashamed'.

If Eric Treacy's failures were manifold, they were not nearly so numerous as his gifts.The impact of his death, no less life, on people draws us to the root of this man whose personality embraced a maze of contradictions yet contained a core of concord. Here we find the answer to 'What else?'.

When Eric Treacy died, one diocesan bishop broke down and wept; another wrote 'Eric really was a superb bishop, one I have tried to copy'; and another, 'We miss his prophetic and fearless utterances more than we can say. I pray that some of his Elijah will descend on a present day Elisha'.

A miner comments 'I'm not a Christian, but I've known a lot of parsons. The only one I could talk to in an ordinary way as man to man was Eric Treacy'. A convicted murderer adds 'If ever a man left a living memorial to what he contributed to his short time in society, it was Eric Treacy; by his example and dedication he turned many, who had lost the path, back to it, replaced hate with kindness and gave abundance of love'. *The Times* obituary notice referred to 'the breadth of his judgement and his integrity. Highly articulate as he was, both as a speaker and on paper, his pronouncements often served to conciliate widely different standpoints . . .'

It may be trite, but it is not less true, to say that he walked with kings, yet never lost the common touch. How numerous are the correspondents who begin their letters with 'I'm only an ordinary person but Bishop Treacy understood . . .' It was the extraordinary ordinariness of Eric Treacy that enabled him to communicate naturally and unaffectedly with so many people to such great effect.

Eric Treacy's rich and abiding legacy is simply himself. That is more important than words or even deeds. He has left indelible marks in the hearts of multitudes. He was the perfect guide up the mountain side of life to the climbers — encouraging and inspiring, but it was their muscles and determination which enabled them to reach the summit. All too often as a bishop his broad shoulders and strong back had to be used to carry someone who had no longer the stamina or the will to carry on. Once at the summit Eric Treacy was able to probe into areas which the person wanted to keep shut, examining motives ever so gently and lovingly, but firmly, revealing self-deception and those things which hampered spiritual or mental progress. He did not pretend to have all the answers, and never tried to give the impression of a sanctity he did not possess. Yet he gave himself and God used him to heal and to rescue. From the mountain top he would clean the spectacles so that the perspective was less cloudy and the pilgrim was ready for the downward trek to face the days ahead — but not alone. 'He helped me back to reality' is the testimony of one young person. For Eric Treacy, Christianity was not a heap of phrases but a way of looking at life and living it out.

There was plenty of rejoicing too. Fun, impishness (some imp!) and laughter were close companions. His laughter was never shallow or cynical. He may have experienced sadness and disappointment, but his faith in Christ enabled him to rejoice and be glad.

The strengths and weaknesses were interlocked too. To see him irritated was a sight. He could detonate when he considered a bang was better than balm. Those who were close to him had access to the brake. A beautiful old but redundant Church had been progressively vandalised. Diocesan Secretary, Bev, was instructed to arrange for a contractor to have the building razed to the ground the next day. The following day, the Bishop asked the Diocesan Secretary if he had carried out instructions. The answer was 'no'. The Bishop was grateful. The Bishop was saved. It was the same Diocesan Secretary who would occasionally ask the meaning of a difficult Sunday Gospel he could not understand. Eric Treacy would sit down and say 'Well, this is what I think it means' and go on to explain in an illuminating and simple way the Christian message of the day. There was the freshness of the early Church about him, as if everything was new and humming with vitality. It was easy to catch what he taught — and catch for keeps!

Eric Treacy was the firm voice of the Church — strong, stable, satisfying, serviceable and sometimes stern. For him the Church was the ark of the faithful, the instrument of evangelism and the servant of society. It was each and all of these together.

In an age in which it was typical to speak of the Church of England in language of semi-cynical disparagement he reacted by singing its praises. Nowhere was this sound heard more than in relation to the Christian pastor among his people, by which in every parish throughout the Diocese Christ and the things of Christ were — or should have been — proclaimed and kept in remembrance. This did not mean that he cushioned the faithful. They were told in blunt language when their effectiveness was minimal — and why! Christ's word was not a flame in their hearts nor His claims a compelling force in their wills. When their prayers were a routine performance, their communions infrequent and uninspired it was because Christ was no intimate of theirs — they could not declare or serve because they had not seen and heard. Some congregations were hotbeds of malice and quarrelling. Eric Treacy had some admonishing words for them — and pastoral guidance too.

To the vast number of people outside the Church he was a challenger and a guide whether they heard or forebore. A thick mist lay over most issues of the times. Whatever the issue, Eric Treacy had a view. Some of his Christian commonsense was prophetic as he spoke to as well as against the spirit of the age. Unbelievers and partial believers remember his words and recall his presence. And if he could not always reach the doubter on the intellectual plane he could get through to their hearts. One thing is certain — he served.

The influence of, and dependence on, May was very great. It was a partnership for and of a lifetime. It was always 'Eric and May' in the parishes and Diocese they served, so that the two seemed inseparable. Here is our bishop — and lo there is May also! Bishop Gordon Fallows recalls a wonderful slip when May said 'When we were ordained' instead of 'married'. Similarly at a vicarage meal — and there cannot be many parsonages in which they did not have their feet under the table — an incumbent remembers May saying something about ' "we ordained some really nice young men at the ordination last week" and Eric turned on her, and with a wink at us "May, when were you made a Bishop? It was I who ordained them" '.There was a lot of amusing banter between Eric and May in public. Her charm saved him on many occasions from dropping unnecessary bricks or avoiding the corns on the feet he trod on! She underscored his views and was even the motivating conviction of some issues, principles and prejudices.

Everyone says they were a 'special' couple — they were. Niece Helen Bowern writes:

'He has been a rock in my life — first, just a secure part of my childhood, later an enlarger of my experience, a never-failing guide and adviser when needed. He combined the roles of uncle and godfather to perfection. In the early days I viewed him with love, but also a little awe: later, when I recognised that even he had human failings too, I loved him all the more. I have learned much about toleration and compassion from him. Though he could be a most intolerant man at times, particularly with the family. As a teenager, staying at Halifax and Dewsbury with them, I learnt much about a truly loving marriage — not by the obvious signs of devotion, but by the fact that Uncle Peter would sometimes speak with apparent harshness to Aunt May and leave their relationship no whit changed.—They were completely inter-dependent, relying totally upon each other; he could not have lived the kind of life he did without her support at every moment. I think even as very young children we realised their especial closeness.'

Helen Bowern refers to Eric Treacy as 'Uncle Peter'. He was called Peter by May, family and close friends. It began as a reaction against 'Eric - Little by Little' but ended as being appropriate, for as Bishop Halsey of Carlisle reminded the congregation at Eric Treacy's funeral:

'There was a rock-like quality in all his life and ministry, and men and women of all walks of life found they could depend on him and indeed talked about him as The Bishop, as if there were only one Bishop and that everybody would understand who it was they meant. Rock-like in faith, in conviction, in honesty, in friendship, in caring. Eric was all that and perhaps it is with Jesus Christ's own words in our minds that we should this afternoon take leave of him and remember him. Eric Treacy, Priest, one time Bishop of Wakefield, Jesus said, "I tell you, you are Peter and on this rock I will build my church and the power of death shall not prevail against it". '

As we have seen in the foregoing pages Eric Treacy, like St Peter, was capable of deep affection. He was impulsive and capable of doing and saying both courageous and outrageous things without counting the cost. He had the intuition of the enthusiast. Analysis and hermeneutical problems were avoided by a non-academic mind, though instinct and intelligence usually took him to the right answer. He was an individualist and liked his own way and could deal summarily with anyone who hindered him — and repented and apologised as rapidly the next day.

He lived and loved with his heart, and so he responded eagerly, enthusiastically, naturally and completely to people and to situations. He was intensely dependent upon the warmth, support and encouragement of personal relationships.

Having penetrating insights into the needs of others, so he saw deep into himself. He was humble and constantly worried about being superficial and shallow. Only at the end of his days did the shadow of the absence of a university degree leave him. He found moral courage difficult as it involves being somewhat cold and deliberate. Preaching on St Peter, Eric Treacy said: 'Again and again — when he thought he had managed to progress in his efforts to be a good follower of Jesus, he would trip himself up and suffer the misery of knowing himself a failure.' But, he added, 'That is one Peter. We meet an entirely different one in the Acts of the Apostles. A man changed — sharing with Paul the burden and leadership of the young Church'. *There* is the similarity. Strength out of weakness, a changed man, a maturer man, a man at the disposal of the Master but still with hesitations and capable of making blunders both great and small. Eric Treacy once said, 'When I was weakest, I found strength; I have been enabled to do things of which I never thought myself capable; in some remarkable way I have been given self-control when I most needed it; again and again — but not always — I have been prevented from making a fool of myself. Often I have found myself given just what I needed for a particular subject.'

This is not the summing up of or a judgement on a life so recently lived on earth. Eric Treacy was a man of love and courage, holding fast to that which was good; who rendered evil to no man; who strengthened the faint hearted; who supported the weak; who helped the afflicted: and who gave honour to all people. He spoke deeply to so very many people and is one of the shining lights adorning the Church which he loved beyond measure. His personal influence and gift of friendship knew no bounds. He practised and he preached a sturdy down-to-earth and up-to-heaven Christianity.

To the man who asked Eric Treacy 'You have enjoyed baiting Yorkshiremen — have you ever caught one?' the answer is 'Yes'. Eric Treacy caught shoals and, like Peter the fisherman, if he caught them for himself he also caught them for Christ.

Index